THE CENTURY PSYCHOLOGY SERIES

Richard M. Elliott, *Editor*
Kenneth MacCorquodale, *Assistant Editor*

Verbal Behavior

BY THE SAME AUTHOR

The Behavior of Organisms

Walden Two

Science and Human Behavior

Schedules of Reinforcement
(with C. B. Ferster)

B. F. SKINNER

Verbal Behavior

. . . .

APPLETON-CENTURY-CROFTS, Inc.
New York

597-1

LIBRARY OF CONGRESS CARD NUMBER:

57-11446

PRINTED IN THE UNITED STATES OF AMERICA

To

JULIE and DEBBIE,

my primary sources

PREFACE

IT HAS TAKEN a long time to write this book. A classification of verbal responses in an early version of Part II was completed in the summer of 1934. A few supporting experiments were then carried out with the Verbal Summator, and statistical analyses were made of several literary works, of data from word-association experiments, and of guessing behavior. All this material was used in courses on Literary and Verbal Behavior at the University of Minnesota in the late thirties, at Harvard University in the summer of 1938, and at the University of Chicago in the summer of 1939. A manuscript of the present scope was to have been completed under a Guggenheim Fellowship in 1941, but the war intervened. The Fellowship was resumed in 1944-45 and a version nearly completed. It was the basis of a course on Verbal Behavior at Columbia University in the summer of 1947, stenographic notes of which were circulated by Dr. Ralph Hefferlein in mimeographed form the following year.

In the fall of 1947 material was extracted from the manuscript for the William James Lectures at Harvard University, several hundred mimeographed copies of which have since been circulated. In preparing these lectures it was found that the manuscript had begun to take on the character of a review of the literature and that the central theme was becoming obscure. In completing the manuscript for publication, therefore, summaries of the literature were deleted. Completion of the final manuscript was postponed in favor of a general book on human behavior (*Science and Human Behavior*) which would provide a ready reference on matters not essentially verbal. The present version is more than twice as long as the James Lectures and contains many changes made to conform with recent progress in the experimental analysis of behavior, human and otherwise. With the exception of the last two chapters, it was written during the spring term of 1955 at Putney, Vermont.

The work has been generously supported by the Society of Fellows of Harvard University (a three-year fellowship), the University of Minnesota (a one-half year sabbatical leave), the Guggenheim Foundation (a one-year fellowship), and Harvard University (the William James Lectureship and a sabbatical leave). To all of these, thanks are due. Unfortunately it is impossible to make an adequate acknowledgement of the generous help received from students and colleagues during these years and from criticisms of earlier versions, published or unpublished. The final manuscript has profited greatly from critical and editorial help by Mrs. Susan R. Meyer and Dr. Dorothy Cohen and from careful preparation by Mrs. Virginia N. MacLaury.

Cambridge, Mass. B. F. Skinner

CONTENTS

Part V: The Production of Verbal Behavior

Verbal Behavior

Part I
A PROGRAM

Chapter 1

. . . .

A Functional Analysis of Verbal Behavior

MEN ACT upon the world, and change it, and are changed in turn by the consequences of their action. Certain processes, which the human organism shares with other species, alter behavior so that it achieves a safer and more useful interchange with a particular environment. When appropriate behavior has been established, its consequences work through similar processes to keep it in force. If by chance the environment changes, old forms of behavior disappear, while new consequences build new forms.

Behavior alters the environment through mechanical action, and its properties or dimensions are often related in a simple way to the effects produced. When a man walks toward an object, he usually finds himself closer to it; if he reaches for it, physical contact is likely to follow; and if he grasps and lifts it, or pushes or pulls it, the object frequently changes position in appropriate directions. All this follows from simple geometrical and mechanical principles.

Much of the time, however, a man acts only indirectly upon the environment from which the ultimate consequences of his behavior emerge. His first effect is upon other men. Instead of going to a drinking fountain, a thirsty man may simply "ask for a glass of water"—that is, may engage in behavior which produces a certain pattern of sounds which in turn induces someone to bring him a glass of water. The sounds themselves are easy to describe in physical terms; but the glass of water reaches the speaker only as the result of a complex series of events including the behavior of a listener. The ultimate consequence, the receipt of water, bears no useful geometrical or mechanical relation to the form of the behavior of "asking for water." Indeed, it is characteristic of such behavior that it is impotent against the physical world. Rarely do we shout down the walls of a Jericho or successfully command the sun to stop or the waves to be still. Names do not break bones. The consequences of such behavior are mediated by a train of events no less physical or inevitable than direct mechanical action, but clearly more difficult to describe.

Behavior which is effective only through the mediation of other persons has so many distinguishing dynamic and topographical properties that a special treatment is justified and, indeed, demanded. Problems raised by this special mode of action are usually assigned to the field of speech or language. Unfortunately, the term "speech" emphasizes vocal behavior and is only awkwardly applied to instances in which the mediating person is affected visually, as in writing a note. "Language" is now satisfactorily remote from its original commitment to vocal behavior, but it has come to refer to the practices of a linguistic community rather than the behavior of any one member. The adjective "linguistic" suffers from the same disadvantage. The term "verbal behavior" has much to recommend it. Its etymological sanction is not too powerful, but it emphasizes the individual speaker and, whether recognized by the user or not, specifies behavior shaped and maintained by mediated consequences. It also has the advantage of being relatively unfamiliar in traditional modes of explanation.

A definition of verbal behavior as behavior reinforced through the mediation of other persons needs, as we shall see, certain refinements. Moreover, it does not say much about the behavior of the listener, even though there would be little verbal behavior to consider if someone had not already acquired special responses to the patterns of energy generated by the speaker. This omission can be justified, for the behavior of the listener in mediating the consequences of the behavior of the speaker is not necessarily verbal in any special sense. It cannot, in fact, be distinguished from behavior in general, and an adequate account of verbal behavior need cover only as much of the behavior of the listener as is needed to explain the behavior of the speaker. The behaviors of speaker and listener taken together compose what may be called a total speech episode. There is nothing in such an episode which is more than the combined behavior of two or more individuals. Nothing "emerges" in the social unit. The speaker can be studied while assuming a listener, and the listener while assuming a speaker. The separate accounts which result exhaust the episode in which both participate.

It would be foolish to underestimate the difficulty of this subject matter, but recent advances in the analysis of behavior permit us to approach it with a certain optimism. New experimental techniques and fresh formulations have revealed a new level of order and precision. The basic processes and relations which give verbal behavior its special characteristics are now fairly well understood. Much of the experimental work responsible for this advance has been carried out on other species, but the results have proved to be surprisingly free of species restrictions. Recent work has shown that the methods can be extended to human behavior without serious modification. Quite apart from the possibility of extrapolating specific experimental findings, the formulation provides a fruitful new approach to human behavior in general, and enables us to deal more effectively with that subdivision called verbal.

The "understanding" of verbal behavior is something more than the use of a consistent vocabulary with which specific instances may be described. It is not to be confused with the confirmation of any set of theoretical principles. The criteria are more demanding than that. The extent to which we understand verbal behavior in a "causal" analysis is to be assessed from the extent to which we can predict the occurrence of specific instances and, eventually, from the extent to which we can produce or control such behavior by altering the conditions under which it occurs. In representing such a goal it is helpful to keep certain specific engineering tasks in mind. How can the teacher establish the specific verbal repertoires which are the principal end-products of education? How can the therapist uncover latent verbal behavior in a therapeutic interview? How can the writer evoke his own verbal behavior in the act of composition? How can the scientist, mathematician, or logician manipulate his verbal behavior in productive thinking? Practical problems of this sort are, of course, endless. To solve them is not the immediate goal of a scientific analysis, but they underline the kinds of processes and relationships which such an analysis must consider.

TRADITIONAL FORMULATIONS

A science of behavior does not arrive at this special field to find it unoccupied. Elaborate systems of terms describing verbal behavior have been developed. The lay vocabulary abounds with them. Classical rhetoric, grammar, logic, scientific methodology, linguistics, literary criticism, speech pathology, semantics, and many other disciplines have contributed technical terms and principles. In general, however, the subject here at issue has not been clearly identified, nor have appropriate methods for studying it been devised. Linguistics, for example, has recorded and analyzed speech sounds and semantic and syntactical practices, but comparisons of different languages and the tracing of historical changes have taken precedence over the study of the individual speaker. Logic, mathematics, and scientific methodology have recognized the limitations which linguistic practices impose on human thought, but have usually remained content with a formal analysis; in any case, they have not developed the techniques necessary for a causal analysis of the behavior of man thinking. Classical rhetoric was responsible for an elaborate system of terms describing the characteristics of literary works of art, applicable as well to everyday speech. It also gave some attention to effects upon the listener. But the early promise of a science of verbal behavior was never fulfilled. Modern literary criticism, except for some use of the technical vocabulary of psychoanalysis, seldom goes beyond the terms of the intelligent layman. An effective frontal attack, a formulation appropriate to all special fields, has never emerged under the auspices of any one of these disciplines.

Perhaps this fact is responsible for the rise of semantics as a general account of verbal behavior. The technical study of meaning was already under way as a peripheral field of linguistics when, in 1923, Ogden and Richards [1] demonstrated the need for a broader science of symbolism. This was to be a general analysis of linguistic processes applicable to any field and under the domination of no special interest. Attempts have been made to carry out the recommendation, but an adequate science of verbal behavior has not been achieved. There are several current brands of semantics, and they represent the same special interests and employ the same special techniques as heretofore. The original method of Ogden and Richards was philosophical, with psychological leanings. Some of the more rigorous systems are frankly logical. In linguistics, semantics continues to be a question of how meanings are expressed and how they change. Some semanticists deal mainly with the verbal machinery of society, particularly propaganda. Others are essentially therapists who hold that many of the troubles of the world are linguistic error. The currency of the term "semantics" shows the need for a science of verbal behavior which will be divorced

[1] Ogden, C. K., and Richards, I. A., *The Meaning of Meaning* (New York, 1923).

from special interests and helpful wherever language is used, but the science itself has not emerged under this aegis.

The final responsibility must rest with the behaviorial sciences, and particularly with psychology. What happens when a man speaks or responds to speech is clearly a question about human behavior and hence a question to be answered with the concepts and techniques of psychology as an experimental science of behavior. At first blush, it may not seem to be a particularly difficult question. Except on the score of simplicity, verbal behavior has many favorable characteristics as an object of study. It is usually easily observed (if it were not, it would be ineffective as verbal behavior); there has never been any shortage of material (men talk and listen a great deal); the facts are substantial (careful observers will generally agree as to what is said in any given instance); and the development of the practical art of writing has provided a ready-made system of notation for reporting verbal behavior which is more convenient and precise than any available in the nonverbal field. What is lacking is a satisfactory causal or functional treatment. Together with other disciplines concerned with verbal behavior, psychology has collected facts and sometimes put them in convenient order, but in this welter of material it has failed to demonstrate the significant relations which are the heart of a scientific account. For reasons which, in retrospect, are not too difficult to discover, it has been led to neglect some of the events needed in a functional or causal analysis. It has done this because the place of such events has been occupied by certain fictional causes which psychology has been slow in disavowing. In examining some of these causes more closely, we may find an explanation of why a science of verbal behavior has been so long delayed.

It has generally been assumed that to explain behavior, or any aspect of it, one must attribute it to events taking place inside the organism. In the field of verbal behavior this practice was once represented by the doctrine of the expression of ideas. An utterance was felt to be explained by setting forth the ideas which it expressed. If the speaker had had a different idea, he would have uttered different words or words in a different arrangement. If his utterance was unusual, it was because of the novelty or originality of his ideas. If it seemed empty, he must have lacked ideas or have been unable to put them into words. If he could not keep silent, it was because of the force of his ideas. If he spoke haltingly, it was because his ideas came slowly or were badly organized. And so on. All properties of verbal behavior seem to be thus accounted for.

Such a practice obviously has the same goal as a causal analysis, but it has by no means the same results. The difficulty is that the ideas for which sounds are said to stand as signs cannot be independently observed. If we ask for evidence of their existence, we are likely to be given a restatement in other words; but a restatement is no closer to the idea than the original utterance. Restatement merely shows that the idea is not identified with a single expression. It is, in fact, often defined as something common to two or more expressions. But we shall not arrive at this "something" even though we express an idea in every conceivable way.

Another common answer is to appeal to images. The idea is said to be what passes through the speaker's mind, what the speaker sees and hears and feels when he is "having" the idea. Explorations of the thought processes underlying verbal behavior have been attempted by asking thinkers to describe experiences of this nature. But although selected examples are sometimes convincing, only a small part of the ideas said to be expressed in words can be identified with the kind of sensory event upon which the notion of image rests. A book on physics is much more than a description of the images in the minds of physicists.

There is obviously something suspicious in the ease with which we discover in a set of ideas precisely those properties needed to account for the behavior which expresses them. We evidently construct the ideas at will from the behavior to be explained. There is, of course, no real explanation. When we say that a remark is confusing because the idea is unclear, we seem to be talking about two levels of observation although there is, in fact, only one. It is the *remark* which is unclear. The practice may have been defensible when inquiries into verbal processes were philosophical rather than scientific, and when a science of ideas could be imagined which would some day put the matter in better order; but it stands in a different light today. It is the function of an explanatory fiction to allay curiosity and to bring inquiry to an end. The doctrine of ideas has had this effect by appearing to assign important problems of verbal behavior to a psychology of ideas. The problems have then seemed to pass beyond the range of the techniques of the student of language, or to have become too obscure to make further study profitable.

Perhaps no one today is deceived by an "idea" as an explanatory fiction. Idioms and expressions which seem to explain verbal behavior in term of ideas are so common in our language that it is impossible to avoid them, but they may be little more than moribund figures of speech. The basic formulation, however, has been preserved. The immediate successor to "idea" was "meaning," and the place of the latter is in danger of being usurped by a newcomer, "information." These terms all have the same effect of discouraging a functional analysis and of supporting, instead, some of the practices first associated with the doctrine of ideas.

One unfortunate consequence is the belief that speech has an independent existence apart from the behavior of the speaker. Words are regarded as tools or instruments, analogous to the tokens, counters, or signal flags sometimes employed for verbal purposes. It is true that verbal behavior usually produces objective entities. The sound-stream of vocal speech, the words on a page, the signals transmitted on a telephone or telegraph wire—these are records left by verbal behavior. As objective facts, they may all be studied, as they have been from time to time in linguistics, communication engineering, literary criticism, and so on. But although the formal properties of the records of utterances are interesting, we must preserve the distinction between an activity and its traces. In particular we must avoid the unnatural formulation of verbal behavior as the "use of words." We have no more reason to say that a man "uses the word *water*" in asking for a drink than to say that he "uses a reach" in taking the offered glass. In the arts, crafts, and sports, especially where instruction is verbal, acts are sometimes named. We say that a tennis player uses a drop stroke, or a swimmer a crawl. No one is likely to be misled when drop strokes or crawls are referred to as things, but words are a different matter. Misunderstanding has been common, and often disastrous.

A complementary practice has been to assign an independent existence to meanings. "Meaning," like "idea," is said to be something expressed or communicated by an utterance. A meaning explains the occurrence of a particular set of words in the sense that if there had been a different meaning to be expressed, a different set of words would have been used. An utterance will be affected according to whether a meaning is clear or vague, and so on. The concept has certain advantages. Where "ideas" (like "feelings" and "desires," which are also said to be expressed by words) must be inside the organism, there is a promising possibility that meanings may be kept outside the skin. In this sense, they are as observable as any part of physics.

But can we identify the meaning of an utterance in an objective way? A fair argument may be made in the case of proper nouns, and some common nouns, verbs, adjectives, and adverbs—roughly the words with respect to which the doctrine of ideas could be supported by the appeal to images. But what about words like *atom* or *gene* or *minus one* or *the spirit of the times* where corresponding nonverbal entities are not easily discovered? And for words like *nevertheless, although,* and *ouch!* it has seemed necessary to look inside the organism for the speaker's intention, attitude, sentiment, or some other psychological condition.

Even the words which seem to fit an externalized semantic framework are not without their problems. It may be true that proper nouns stand in a one-to-one correspondence with things, provided everything has its own proper name, but what about common nouns? What is the meaning of *cat?* Is it some one cat, or the physical totality of all cats, or the class of all cats? Or must we fall back upon the idea of cat? Even in the case of the proper noun, a difficulty remains. Assuming that there is only one man named Doe, is Doe himself the meaning of *Doe?* Certainly *he* is not conveyed or communicated when the word is used.

The existence of meanings becomes even more doubtful when we advance from single words to those collocations which "say something." What is said by a sentence is something more than what the words in it mean. Sentences do not merely refer to trees and skies and rain, they say something about them. This something is sometimes called a "proposition"—a somewhat more respectable precursor of speech but very similar to the "idea" which would have been said to be expressed by the same sentence under the older doctrine. To define a proposition as "something which may be said in any language" does not tell us where propositions are, or of what stuff they are made. Nor is the problem solved by defining a proposition as all the sentences which have the same meaning as some one sentence, since we cannot identify a sentence as a member of this class without knowing its meaning—at which point we find ourselves facing our original problem.

It has been tempting to try to establish the separate existence of words and meanings because a fairly elegant solution of certain problems then becomes available. Theories of meaning usually deal with corresponding arrays of words and things. How do the linguistic entities on one side correspond with the things or events which are their meanings on the other side, and what is the nature of the relation between them called "reference"? Dictionaries seem, at first blush, to support the notion of such arrays. But dictionaries do not give meanings; at best they give words having the same meanings. The semantic scheme, as usually conceived, has interesting properties. Mathematicians, logicians, and information theorists have explored possible modes of correspondence at length. For example, to what extent can the dimensions of the thing communicated be represented in the dimensions of the communicating medium? But it remains to be shown that such constructions bear any close resemblances to the products of genuine linguistic activities.

In any case the practice neglects many important properties of the original behavior, and raises other problems. We cannot successfully supplement a framework of semantic reference by appealing to the "intention of the speaker" until a satisfactory psychological account of intention can be given. If "connotative meaning" is to supplement a deficient denotation, study of the associative process is required. When some meanings are classed as "emotive," another difficult and relatively undeveloped psychological field is invaded. These are all efforts to preserve the logical representation by setting up additional categories for exceptional words. They are a sort of patchwork which succeeds mainly in showing how threadbare the basic notion is. When we attempt to supply the additional material needed in this representation of verbal behavior, we find that our task has been set in awkward if not impossible terms. The observable data have been preempted, and the student of behavior is left with vaguely identified "thought processes."

The impulse to explicate a meaning is easily understood. We ask, "What do you mean?" because the answer is frequently helpful. Clarifications of meaning in this sense have an important place in every sort of intellectual endeavor. For the purposes of effective discourse the method of paraphrase usually suffices; we may not need extraverbal referents. But the explication of verbal behavior should not be allowed to generate a sense of scientific achievement. One has not *accounted for* a remark by paraphrasing "what it means."

We could no doubt define ideas, meanings, and so on, so that they would be scientifically acceptable and even useful in describing verbal behavior. But such an effort to retain traditional terms would be costly. It is the general formulation which is wrong. We seek "causes" of behavior which have an acceptable scientific status and which, with luck, will be susceptible to measurement and manipulation. To say that these are "all that is meant by" ideas or meanings is to misrepresent the traditional *practice*. We must find the functional relations which govern the verbal behavior to be explained; to call such relations "expression" or "communication" is to run the danger of introducing extraneous and misleading properties and events. The only solution is to reject the traditional formulation of verbal behavior in terms of meaning.

A NEW FORMULATION

The direction to be taken in an alternative approach is dictated by the task itself. Our first responsibility is simple *description:* what is the topography of this subdivision of human behavior? Once that question has been answered in at least a preliminary fashion we may advance to the stage called *explanation:* what conditions are relevant to the occurrence of the behavior—what are the variables of which it is a function? Once these have been identified, we can account for the dynamic characteristics of verbal behavior within a framework appropriate to human behavior as a whole. At the same time, of course, we must consider the behavior of the listener. In relating this to the behavior of the speaker, we complete our account of the verbal episode.

But this is only the beginning. Once a repertoire of verbal behavior has been set up, a host of new problems arise from the interaction of its parts. Verbal behavior is usually the effect of *multiple causes*. Separate variables combine to extend their functional control, and new forms of behavior emerge from the recombination of old fragments. All of this has appropriate effects upon the listener, whose behavior then calls for analysis.

Still another set of problems arises from the fact, often pointed out, that a speaker is normally also a listener. He reacts to his own behavior in several important ways. Part of what he says is under the control of other parts of his verbal behavior. We refer to this interaction when we say that the speaker qualifies, orders, or elaborates his behavior at the moment it is produced. The mere emission of responses is an incomplete characterization when behavior is *composed*. As another consequence of the fact that the speaker is also a listener, some of the behavior of listening resembles the behavior of speaking, particularly when the listener "understands" what is said.

The speaker and listener within the same skin engage in activities which are traditionally described as "thinking." The speaker manipulates his behavior; he reviews it, and may reject it or emit it in modified form. The extent to which he does so varies over a wide range, determined in part by the extent to which he serves as his own listener. The skillful speaker learns to tease out weak behavior and to manipulate variables which will generate and strengthen new responses in his repertoire. Such behavior is commonly observed in the verbal practices of literature as well as of science and logic. An analysis of these activities, together with their effects upon the listener, leads us in the end to the role of verbal behavior in the problem of knowledge.

The present book sets forth the principal features of an analysis from this point of view. Part II sketches the topography of verbal behavior in relation to its controlling variables and Part III some of the consequences of the interaction of variables. Part IV describes the manipulation of verbal behavior in the act of composition, while Part V considers the activities involved in editing and in the creative production of behavior which are usually called verbal thinking. No assumption is made of any uniquely verbal characteristic, and the principles and methods employed are adapted to the study of human behavior as a whole. An extensive treatment of human behavior in general from the same point of view may be found elsewhere.[2] The present account is self-contained.

One important feature of the analysis is that it is directed to the behavior of the individual speaker and listener; no appeal is made to statistical concepts based upon data derived from groups. Even with respect to the individual speaker or listener, little use is made of specific experimental results. The basic facts to be analyzed are well known to every educated person and do not need to be substantiated statistically or experimentally at the level of rigor here attempted. No effort has been made to survey the relevant "literature." The emphasis is upon an orderly arrangement of well-known facts, in accordance with a formulation of behavior derived from an experimental analysis of a more rigorous sort. The present extension to verbal behavior is thus an exercise in interpretation rather than a quantitative extrapolation of rigorous experimental results.

[2] Skinner, B. F., *Science and Human Behavior* (New York, 1954).

The lack of quantitative rigor is to some extent offset by an insistence that the conditions appealed to in the analysis be, so far as possible, accessible and manipulable. The formulation is inherently practical and suggests immediate technological applications at almost every step. Although the emphasis is not upon experimental or statistical facts, the book is not theoretical in the usual sense. It makes no appeal to hypothetical explanatory entities. The ultimate aim is the prediction and control of verbal behavior.

Chapter 2

General Problems

VERBAL BEHAVIOR AS A DEPENDENT VARIABLE

OUR SUBJECT matter is verbal behavior, and we must accept this in the crude form in which it is observed. In studying speech, we have to account for a series of complex muscular activities which produce noises. In studying writing or gesturing, we deal with other sorts of muscular responses. It has long been recognized that this is the stuff of which languages are made, but the acknowledgement has usually been qualified in such a way as to destroy the main point. As Jespersen [1] said many years ago, "The only unimpeachable definition of a word is that it is a human habit." Unfortunately, he felt it necessary to add, "an habitual act on the part of one human individual which has, or may have, the effect of evoking some idea in the mind of another individual." Similarly, Bertrand Russell [2] asserts that "just as jumping is one class of movement . . . so the word 'dog' is [another] class," but he adds that words differ from other classes of bodily movements because they have "meaning." In both cases something has been added to an objective description.

It is usually argued that the addition is necessary, even when behavior is not verbal. Any effort to deal with behavior as a movement of the parts of an organism meets at once the objection that it cannot be mere movement which is important but rather what the movement means, either to the behaving organism or to the observer. It is usually asserted that we can *see* meaning or purpose in behavior and should not omit it from our account. But meaning is not a property of behavior as such but of the conditions under which behavior

[1] Jespersen, O., *Language* (New York, 1922).
[2] Russell, B., *Inquiry into Meaning and Truth* (New York, 1940).

occurs. Technically, meanings are to be found among the independent variables in a functional account, rather than as properties of the dependent variable. When someone says that he can see the meaning of a response, he means that he can infer some of the variables of which the response is usually a function. The issue is particularly important in the field of verbal behavior where the concept of meaning enjoys unusual prestige.

In defining verbal behavior as behavior reinforced through the mediation of other persons we do not, and cannot, specify any one form, mode, or medium. Any movement capable of affecting another organism may be verbal. We are likely to single out vocal behavior, not only because it is commonest, but because it has little effect upon the physical environment and hence is almost necessarily verbal. But there are extensive written languages, sign languages, and languages in which the "speaker" stimulates the skin of the "listener." Audible behavior which is not vocal (for example, clapping the hands for a servant, or blowing a bugle) and gestures are verbal, although they may not compose an organized language. The skilled telegraphist behaves verbally by moving his wrist. Some of these forms normally arise only after vocal behavior has been established, but this is not necessarily so. Writing and typing may be either primordially verbal or transcriptions of a prior vocal form. Pointing to words is verbal—as, indeed, is all pointing, since it is effective only when it alters the behavior of someone. The definition also covers manipulations of physical objects which are undertaken because of the effect upon people, as in the use of ceremonial trappings. In the case of any *medium,* the behavior is both verbal and nonverbal at once—nonverbal in the effect upon the medium—verbal in the ultimate effect upon the observer. Ceremonial languages, and the languages of flowers, gems, and so on, are of little interest, because they have small vocabularies and little or no grammar, but they are nevertheless verbal under the terms of the definition. Because vocal verbal behavior is the commonest form, we may deal with it as representative. Where necessary or helpful, parallel problems in other forms may be considered.

Vocal Behavior

Vocal verbal behavior is executed by an extensive musculature—the diaphragm, the vocal cords, the false vocal cords, the epiglottis, the soft palate, the tongue, the cheek, the lips, and the jaw. The most complete record of a single instance of an utterance would be an electrical or mechanical report of the action of all the muscles involved. At the moment this is of theoretical interest only, since nothing like it has ever been made. Fortunately, a science of verbal behavior need not wait. The complex muscular responses of vocal behavior affect the verbal environment by producing audible "speech." This is a much more accessible datum.

The acoustic product of vocal verbal behavior may be recorded phonographically. The record may be converted into visible form and analyzed for greater convenience into pitch-intensity spectra. The acoustic report is less accurate than a report of muscular action because different muscular patterns presumably produce the same sounds, but it is at least feasible. It is also more convenient because it uses fewer terms or dimensions. Probably nothing of importance is lost, because the scientist stands in essentially the same position as the listener and for many purposes may ignore any property of verbal behavior which does not produce a difference in the sound-stream. Even so, an acoustic report tells us more than we usually want to know, except when acoustic details are to be specially emphasized, and it soon becomes awkward.

Another kind of record was made possible by the discovery that speech could be broken into constituent sounds and by the invention of a phonetic alphabet to represent these sounds. (Both of these advances, of course, antedated scientific study.) A sample of verbal behavior can be recorded by placing appropriate symbols in a corresponding order, as is done, however inexactly, in writing with the English alphabet. So far as we are concerned here, such a record simply makes it possible to identify some of the acoustic properties of an utterance. The transcription permits the reader to construct a facsimile of the behavior which will have the same effect upon the verbal community as the original sample. It is a practical and economical record, because an indefinite number of different acoustic events may be represented with a few symbols.

This use of a "phonetic" alphabet makes no commitments about the functional significance of the units identified. We may use English spelling to record bird calls *(to-whit, to-whoo,* or *peewee),* or the noises of inanimate things *(pop* and *boom),* in the sense that in reading such records aloud one constructs a reasonable facsimile of the original songs or noises. But this does not mean that birds and drums speak in English "phonemes." The analytical (rather than transcriptive) function of the phoneme in modern linguistics arises, on the one hand, from an excursion into phonology which will not have to be made here and, on the other, from the study and comparison of the practices of whole verbal communities. The linguist is concerned with such facts as these: (1) in one verbal community the responses *pin* and *bin* have different effects or occur under different conditions, while in another verbal community they have the same effect or occur under the same conditions; (2) in one verbal community the responses *pit* and *bit* have different effects or occur under different circumstances, while in another verbal community they have the same effect or occur under the same circumstances; (3) in that community in which *pin* and *bin* have the same effect, *pit* and *bit* also have the same effect; and in that community in which *pin* and *bin* have different effects, *pit* and *bit* also have different effects. These facts present problems which lie beyond the mere transcription of verbal behavior, because they include references to the conditions of occurrence of verbal behavior or to effects upon a listener. We shall deal with these additional facts in another way here.

A record of an utterance in a phonetic alphabet provides, of course, less information about its properties than an acoustic report, but there should be no objection if we can show that the properties which have been preserved are the effective properties of verbal behavior. This brings us to an important principle in the analysis of behavior. We distinguish between an instance of a response and a class of responses. A single response, as an instance of the activity of an organism, may be described as fully as facilities will permit. But when we are concerned with the prediction of *future* behavior it may be either impossible to predict the great detail of the single instance or, more likely, unimportant to do so. All we want to know is whether or not a response of a given class will occur. By "of a given class" we mean a response showing certain selected properties. We may want to know whether a man will open a door although we do not care how he turns the knob. We do not dismiss the details of turning the knob as unlawful or undetermined; we simply deal with his opening the door without accounting for them. The property of behavior by virtue of which we classify a response as "opening a door" is our principal interest. In the same way, we do not need to know all the details of a vocal response so long as the sound-pattern which it produces achieves a given effect upon a specified verbal community. There are many practical and theoretical reasons for recording and analyzing given instances of vocal behavior in as great detail as possible, but they do not coincide with our interests in the prediction and control of verbal behavior, at least in the present state of the science. The "phoneme" was an early recognition of the principle of the defining property of a response. Unfortunately for our present purposes the extension of the concept to historical and comparative linguistics has obscured its relevance in defining a unit of verbal behavior in the individual speaker.

The problem of the speech-sound becomes somewhat clearer, and perhaps loses some of its importance, when we compare other modes of behavior. If verbal behavior were never vocal, there would be no sciences of phonology and phonetics. Yet most of the problems to be considered in the study of verbal behavior would remain. In a community in which all verbal behavior was written, we should have to identify "speech-marks," and discover their essential geometric properties. If such a language resembled modern script, we should have to study a large number of marks which functioned as, say, the letter *a* in order to identify their common features and to discover what properties could for most purposes be ignored. If such a community spoke only with typewriters, the range of properties would be narrow. The advantage of a narrow range for the reader, as well as the scientist, is suggested by the frequent instruction "Please print." Graphology provides a rudimentary "phonetics" of written verbal behavior; here again the "significances" require other techniques of analysis.

A "direct quotation" is a record of verbal behavior which depends more explicitly upon a knowledge of the conditions under which the behavior occurred. It is often, however, little more than an acoustic or phonetic transcription which permits the reader to reconstruct relevant properties of the original behavior. The spoken report that someone said *It is four o'clock* actually reconstructs an instance of verbal behavior. A written report permits the reader to reconstruct it for himself.

A technique which permits the reconstruction of a datum is unusual. Science does not generally resort to models or mimicry; its descriptions of events do not resemble those events. In the field of nonverbal behavior we usually do not report behavior by imitating it. Yet in speaking a language under study the scientist uses mimicry in lieu of the more usual method of description which bears no point-to-point correspondence with the thing described. (This distinction is discussed further in Chapter 5.) Russell [3] has pointed out that some rare instances of verbal behavior, such as the Coronation Oath or the Lord's Prayer, have proper names. He also mentions the method, due to Gödel, of assigning numbers to words and hence to all possible sentences. The indexing system in a library assigns proper names (identifying numbers) to the large samples of verbal behavior known as books. It is not probable, however, that these foreshadow a descriptive system in which all verbal responses will be given names which bear no greater resemblances to the things named than the resemblances between events and descriptions in science elsewhere.

No matter how tempting it may be to utilize the special possibility of phonetic transcription or direct quotation to reconstruct the behavior being analyzed, it must be emphasized that from the point of view of scientific method an expression such as *It is four o'clock* is the name of a response. It is obviously not the response being studied, because that was made by someone else at some other time. It simply resembles that response in point of form. The conditions responsible for the original response may not share anything in common with the conditions responsible for the response on the part of the describing scientist. This practice, called hypostasis, is an anomaly in scientific method. The field of verbal behavior is distinguished by the fact that the names of the things with which it deals are acoustically similar to the things themselves. As Quine [4] has said, "A quotation is not a description, but a hieroglyph; it designates its object not by describing it in terms of other objects, but by picturing it." Quine is speaking here of the written report of written verbal behavior. In no other science is this possible, because in no other science do names and the things named have similar structures.

A quotation is usually something more than an acoustic or phonetic transcription, hieroglyph, or name. In the first place, it usually, though not inevitably, breaks a fairly continuous sample of behavior into parts. Such breaks need not reflect actual pauses or other properties of the temporal or stress pattern of the behavior. In quoting a speech episode, we separate it not only into speech-sounds, represented by letters, but into larger units called words or sentences, represented by spatial breaks or punctuation. The difference between a phonetic report and a direct quotation is seen in the training needed in the two cases. A small phonetic repertoire will suffice to

3 Russell, B., *Inquiry into Meaning and Truth* (New York, 1940).

4 Quine, W. V., *Mathematical Logic* (New York, 1940), p. 26.

transcribe English speech for purposes of reconstruction. But thousands of different "words" must be learned before direct quotations can effectively be written down. The process includes, of course, "learning to spell" and, in particular, to distinguish between homophones. The ability is generally acquired in the process of learning to write and, once acquired, is often taken for granted. We are likely to overlook the fact that a process of analysis is actually taking place.

We are also likely to overlook the fact that in a direct quotation we are inferring something about the conditions under which a response was emitted, or about characteristic effects on a listener. A fairly good phonetic transcription may be made of a language one does not speak, or, as the stenographer often shows, of a familiar language without otherwise reacting as a listener. But the units of direct quotation specify verbal responses as units under functional control. In making a distinction between *through* and *threw,* or between *Send me two* and *Send me, too* we are specifying either the normal conditions under which the responses are made or their normal effects upon a listener. In the *indirect* quotation greater emphasis is placed upon these additional variables. *He said that he would go* permits only a very rough reconstruction of an actual verbal response; only "go" has survived from the possible original *I will go,* and we cannot even be sure that another response characteristic of the same situation was not actually made. But we know with some certainty what kind of situation it was and what kind of effect the remark could have had.

A Unit of Verbal Behavior

From the muscular or acoustic record of verbal behavior we pass through phonetic transcription to direct and indirect quotation. As we do so, we retain less and less information about the specific instance. This loss of detail can be tolerated if properties essential for prediction continue to be described. At the same time we begin to add inferences or facts about the conditions under which the response was made. In undertaking to predict or control verbal behavior, we must, of course, take such additional variables into account, but their status must be clarified. Traditional units of verbal behavior never make a sharp distinction between observed and inferred. Consider, for example, the concept of "word." As used by the layman and by many linguists, a word may be nothing more than an utterance ("I want a word with you" or "The last word"), or a conventional subdivision of an utterance ("What would be two or three words in English is often only one in German"), or a supposed or real objective counter or token ("to choose a word" or "to string words together"), or something common to two or more modes of behavior ("a word may be either spoken or written"). With less justification we even speak of the same word in two languages ("French and English use the same word for 'accord' "), or in two historical stages of the same language, or in two cognate forms (" 'adamant' is the same word as 'diamond' "). Sometimes "word" seems to mean merely a standard lexical design ("the word 'fast' ").

What is needed for present purposes—and what the traditional "word" occasionally approximates—is a unit of behavior composed of a response of identifiable form functionally related to one or more independent variables. In traditional terms we might say that we need a unit of behavior defined in terms of both "form and meaning." The analysis of nonverbal behavior has clarified the nature of such a unit under laboratory conditions in which the expediency of the unit may be submitted to rigorous checks. An extrapolation of this concept to the verbal field is central to the analysis represented by the rest of this book. The kinds of behavior in which we are usually interested have, as we have seen, an effect upon the environment which has a return effect upon the organism. Such behavior may be distinguished from activities which are primarily concerned with the internal economy of the organism by calling activities which operate upon the environment "operant behavior." Any unit of such behavior is conveniently called "an operant." For most purposes "operant" is interchangeable with the traditional "response," but the terms permit us to make the distinction between an *instance* of behavior ("So-and-so smoked a cigarette between 2:00 and 2:10 P.M. yesterday") and a *kind* of behavior ("cigarette smoking"). The term "response" is often used for both of these although it does not carry the second meaning easily. The description of an instance of behavior does not require a description of related variables or of a functional relation. The term operant, on the other hand, is concerned with the prediction and control of a *kind* of behavior. Although we observe only instances, we are concerned with laws which specify kinds.

The distinction raises the issue of formalism. A response, as an instance, can be completely described as a *form* of behavior. An operant specifies at least one relation to a variable—the effect which the behavior characteristically, though perhaps not inevitably, has upon the environment—and is therefore not a purely formal unit. A formal specification cannot be avoided, since a response can be said to be an instance of an operant only through objective identification. But identification is not enough. As an instance of a verbal operant, the response must occur as a function of a certain variable. In this way we may distinguish between the operant *fast* in which the controlling variable is shared by the operant *speedy* and the operant *fast* in which the controlling variable is similar to that in the operant *fixed*.

A long-standing problem in the analysis of verbal behavior is the size of the unit. Standard linguistic units are of various sizes. Below the level of the word lie roots and affixes or, more rigorously, the small "meaningful" units called morphemes. Above the word come phrases, idioms, clauses, sentences, and so on. Any one of these may have functional unity as a verbal operant. A bit of behavior as small as a single speech-sound, or even a pitch or stress pattern, may be under independent control of a manipulable variable (we shall see evidence of such "atomic" verbal operants later). On the other hand, a large segment of behavior—perhaps a phrase like *vast majority* or *when all is said and done* or *the truth, the whole truth, and nothing but the truth* or a whole sentence such as *Haste makes waste*—may be shown to vary under a similarly unitary functional control. Although parts of these larger operants have the same form as parts of other operants or even of whole units, there may be no functional interaction. If this seems at odds with traditional linguistic analysis, it must be remembered that the verbal operant is exclusively a unit of behavior in the individual speaker. The functional unity of a large operant and the extent to which the presence of that operant in the repertoire of the speaker may affect operants of similar form must be decided by a study of the behavior of that speaker. In the practices characteristic of a verbal community, it may not be possible to establish the functional unity of a similar large sample of behavior.

We observe that a speaker possesses a *verbal repertoire* in the sense that responses of various forms appear in his behavior from time to time in relation to identifiable conditions. A repertoire, as a collection of verbal operants, describes the *potential* behavior of a speaker. To ask where a verbal operant is when a response is not in the course of being emitted is like asking where one's knee-jerk is when the physician is not tapping the patellar tendon. A repertoire of verbal behavior is a convenient construct. The distinction between "verbal operant" and "word" is matched by that between "verbal repertoire" and "vocabulary." A person is said to possess a vocabulary of so many thousands of words if these words are observed in his verbal behavior during a period of time. But a vocabulary is usually regarded as a warehouse of inanimate tools from which the speaker makes appropriate selections as he speaks. We are concerned here not only with the fact that certain specific forms of verbal behavior are observed but that they are observed under specific circumstances. These controlling circumstances add a dynamic character to "repertoire" which is lacking in "vocabulary."

Probability of Response

Some parts of a verbal repertoire are more likely to occur than others. This likelihood is an extremely important, though difficult, conception. Our basic datum is not the occurrence of a given response as such, but the probability that it will occur at a given time. Every verbal operant may be conceived of as having under specified circumstances an assignable probability of emission—conveniently called its "strength." We base the notion of strength upon several kinds of evidence.

Emission of Response

If a response is emitted at all, the operant is probably strong. Emission is a better sign of strength, however, if the circumstances are unusual. In one type of verbal slip, for example, the response which intrudes upon or distorts behavior (see Chapter 11) is not appropriate to the immediate situation and therefore appears to be especially strong. A response which appears under inappropriate, difficult, or ambiguous circumstances but is not a slip is probably strong for the same reason. The scientist who continues to talk shop during a thrilling football game or in a noisy subway and the steamrolling conversationalist who will brook no interruption give evidence of especially strong repertoires. Other forms of verbal behavior—for example, writing—present evidence of the same sort.

Among the unusual circumstances which give evidence of strength we may include inadequate verbal stimuli; from the fact that one sees his name in unclear or briefly exposed printed material or hears his name in a noisy conversation in a room we infer the strength of his name in his own repertoire.

ENERGY-LEVEL

Emission of a response is an all-or-none measure. It enables us to infer strength only in terms of the adequacy of the conditions under which emission occurs. A second sort of evidence suggests that strength lies along a continuum from zero to a very high value. A response may be executed with a certain energy, which is not to be confused with "strength" as a synonym for "probability." Energy seems to vary with probability, and is frequently accepted as a measure of strength.[5] An energetic and prolonged *NO!* is not only a strong response, it suggests a strong *tendency* to respond which would not easily be overcome by competing forces. On the other hand, a timid brief *No* is accepted as an instance of a weak operant from which we infer some inadequacy in the independent variables. Relative energy permits a similar inference. From the response *a RED kite* we conclude that the redness was of special importance to the speaker, while from *a red KITE* we infer the special effectiveness of the kite itself as a variable. Under certain circumstances, a change in energy level may take place rapidly, as in the case of Mr. Winkle in the *Pickwick Papers,* who, just before falling into an alcoholic sleep, cried,

> "Let's—have—'nother—bottle," commencing in a very loud key, and ending in a very faint one.

Other properties of verbal behavior vary with the energy level. At low levels the part of the response which produces "voicing" drops out to leave the familiar whisper. At the other end of the continuum other topographical properties are affected. Probably because of the mechanism of the speech apparatus, the pitch level of a response tends to vary with the energy. Other things being equal, the louder the response the higher the pitch. Pitch level may therefore sometimes be taken as an indicator of strength. In the behavior of young children the low and scarcely audible "proper remark" upon a social occasion and high-pitched playground shouting suggest the range of possible values. Other forms of verbal behavior generally have a more limited range. In written verbal behavior some indication of strength may be found in the size of letters, pressure of the pen, underlining, and so on. Some allowance for comparable characteristics is made in the de-

[5] It is possible that energy and probability co-vary only after the energy of the response has been differentially reinforced (see *Science and Human Behavior,* p. 95).

sign of type. These are now mainly conventional devices, but they retain some trace of an original variation with operant strength.

Speed

Another property of emitted verbal behavior is the speed with which successive parts of a sample follow one another or the speed with which a response appears after the occasion for it has arisen. In general we accept the implication that strong verbal behavior is rapid and that hesitant speech indicates little strength. A ready answer is one which the speaker is "strongly inclined to make"; a delay in answering leads us to suspect that something is possibly amiss in the controlling circumstances. The weakness may be due to competitive behavior. A man deeply engrossed in a book may respond to a call or a question with delays of the order of several seconds. In young children, when verbal behavior is weak because it is still in the process of being acquired, delays of the order of minutes are sometimes observed. A child thirteen months old had acquired the response *Light.* Upon one occasion he was shown a light and asked, "What is it? What is that?" He made no response for at least a full minute, and the attempt to get him to respond was given up. He had turned to play with a toy when the response came out clearly. In pathological behavior delays may be still greater. An early report of an example is due to Head,[6] who asked one of his aphasic patients to count. The patient did not reply *until ten minutes had passed,* when he suddenly began *One, two, three, four,* . . . . . We sometimes infer the strength of the verbal behavior of a correspondent from the speed with which a letter is answered, and traces of speed in handwriting supply similar evidence. The frantic gesture exemplifies speed of responding in still another mode of verbal behavior.

Repetition

A third possible indication of relative strength is the immediate repetition of a response. Instead of saying *NO!* with great energy one may say *No! No! No!* A sort of wholesale repetition is implied in *A thousand times no!* Energy and repetition may be combined. Occasionally it is possible to observe a decline in strength as successive responses drop off in energy, pitch, and speed: *NO!* NO! *No! no.* Repetition is apparently responsible for a class of expressions which imply special emphasis—for example, *Come, come, come* and *Now, now.* Ex-

6 Head, Henry, *Aphasia* (New York, 1926).

pressions such as *again and again, round and round,* and *miles and miles* are complicated by an additional principle but probably also show the effect of strength. *A very, very sad mistake* serves in place of *A VERY sad mistake.* Repetition may be diluted by intervening behavior. In the response *No, it's not. Not at all. It's not a question of what I think* the exceptional strength of the form *not* is evident in its repetition.

Limitations on Evidence of Strength

It is easy to overestimate the significance of these indicators. If two or more properties of behavior indicate the same thing, they must vary together; but energy, speed, and repetitiveness do not always satisfy this test. We classify people according to the general strength of their verbal behavior in a way which suggests that our measures are closely associated. For example, the garrulous person (when he *is* garrulous) talks loudly, rapidly, and repeats himself, while the taciturn man speaks slowly, quietly, and seldom repeats. But in single instances these measures are altered through other circumstances, and the exceptions must be explained. For example, a poorly memorized answer may be delayed because of its weakness, but during the delay the aversive character of the situation increases, and when the response is finally emitted the energy level may be high. The apparent discrepancy between delay and force of response requires a special account.

Another complication is that our measures—energy level, speed of response, and even repetition—enter into the construction of different *forms* of response. In English this presents no great difficulty. Absolute levels of pitch and intensity are not "distinctive," nor are relative pitch levels important. Changes in pitch, however, distinguish different types of utterance. Energy of response cannot be taken as an inevitable indicator of strength so long as it serves to make *DE-sert* a different response from de-*SERT*. The prolonging of a sound does not necessarily mean strength when it serves as "quantity," nor is reduplication always a useful instance of repetition of form.

Energy, speed, and repetitiveness are all affected by special conditions of reinforcement. We speak more energetically to the deaf and more slowly to anyone who has difficulty in following us; and we repeat in both cases. Repetition may be needed against a noisy background (*Hear ye! Hear ye!*). To someone at a distance we raise the energy and pitch of our voice and prolong each sound when possible. A quick loud response is more likely to get results in a competitive situation, for example, in reciting in a classroom. We can allow for special conditions of this sort in evaluating any given measure only by inferring operant strength, not from the fact that one speaks loudly, but from the fact that he speaks at an energy level above that which would ordinarily prevail *under the same circumstances.* There is some consolation in the fact that changes in strength due to these special conditions usually exaggerate "natural" strength. They may lead us to mistake the relative importance of an indicator but not its direction or sign.

Unfortunately other kinds of consequences oppose normal evidences of strength. Extreme values of any of these properties interfere with the effect upon the listener. The verbal community, as a collection of listeners, forces speech toward a standard level of speed, energy, and repetitiveness. If a child speaks loudly, he is told not to shout. If he mumbles, he is told to speak up. If he hesitates, he is told to hurry. If his words come tumbling out, he is told to be deliberate. To repeat oneself is bad form, and the double negative, which is merely the innocent result of a strong *No,* is called ungrammatical and illogical.

But if the indicators are somewhat obscured by these conflicting interests, evidence of strength still survives. We still make practical inferences about a speaker's behavior from his energy, speed, and repetitiveness. A complete levelling to a monotone is not achieved and is in fact also opposed by the community. In some kinds of verbal behavior—for example, in reading aloud—the controlling variable generates behavior at a fairly constant level of strength. Except for unfamiliar or poorly learned responses, a text ordinarily does not strengthen one response above another. But a series of responses of uniform energy and speed is not effective upon the listener. The reader is therefore encouraged to introduce spurious signs of strength. He reads *as if* his behavior were determined, not by a text, but by an assortment of variables similar to those in "real" speech. Now it is significant that he does this by modulating pitch, energy, and speed. From these indicators of strength the listener infers a plausible set of determining conditions. The reader has shown good "interpretation."

We also supply indicators for other reasons. If we are shown a prized work of art and exclaim *Beautiful!*, the speed and energy of the response will not be lost on the owner. We may accentuate the effect by using repetition: *Beautiful, beautiful, simply beautiful!* This is so fully understood by everyone that it becomes part of a culture to simulate characteristics of strength whether appropriate independent variables are present or not—whether the picture is an occasion upon which such verbal behavior would naturally be strong. This would scarcely be the case if the significance of our indicators had been entirely obscured by other considerations.

Over-all Frequency

A third type of evidence is the over-all frequency with which a response appears in a large sample of verbal behavior. For example, the number of times a speaker emits *I, me, my,* and *mine* is sometimes taken to indicate the strength of his behavior with respect to himself as a controlling variable—his "egocentricity" or "conceit." Other responses have been used to indicate other themes. With such a measure it can be shown that a writer's interests change from year to year—that he becomes more or less preoccupied with sex, death, or any other subject. The practice recognizes the general notion of a varying probability of response and the relevance of an over-all frequency in measuring it, but such interpretations depend upon certain assumptions which are not always justified.

Word counts are often attempts to develop a purely formal analysis of the dependent variable alone. Verbal behavior is studied without regard to the circumstances under which it is emitted. But although it may be useful to know that a response of a given form is frequently emitted, it is also important to know the prevailing conditions. Since our unit of analysis is not purely formal, we cannot be sure that all instances of a response are instances of the same operant. Nor can we be sure that frequency is not primarily attributable to the frequency of occurrence of controlling variables. In the case of egocentricity, the speaker himself is always present and his changing inclination to talk about that subject may be significant; but a response such as *snow* presumably varies with the seasons. A change in frequency may not reflect a changing tendency to "talk about snow when snow is present" but merely certain changing circumstances. Even the frequency of responses such as *I, me, my,* and *mine* may vary as a function of the listener to whom the verbal behavior is addressed. Unless we know that such a listener remains present or absent, a change in frequency cannot be used to infer a change in an underlying tendency to emit such forms.

Although over-all frequencies are interesting and often satisfactory data, they depart from our program of dealing with the individual speaker upon a given occasion. The data are more often relevant to studies of characteristic practices of a given verbal community, and hence to the commoner preoccupations of linguistics. Nevertheless, use may sometimes be made of such data in inferring characteristic processes in the individual speaker.

Probability and the Single Instance

Although the English language contains many expressions which suggest that the concept of probability of response is a familiar and useful one, certain problems remain to be solved in using it in the analysis of behavior. Under laboratory conditions probability of response is easily studied in an individual organism as frequency of responding. Under these conditions simple changes in frequency can be shown to be precise functions of specific variables, and such studies supply some of the most reliable facts about behavior now available. But we need to move on from the study of frequencies to a consideration of the probability of a single event. The problem is by no means peculiar to the field of behavior. It is a basic one wherever the data of a science are probabilistic, and this means the physical sciences in general. Although the data upon which both the layman and the scientist base their concepts of probability are in the form of frequencies, both want to talk about the probability of a *single forthcoming event*. In later chapters in this book we shall want to consider the way in which several variables, combining at a given time, contribute strength to a given response. In doing so we may appear to be going well beyond a frequency interpretation of probability, yet our evidence for the contribution of each variable is based upon observations of frequencies alone.

INDEPENDENT VARIABLES AND RELATED PROCESSES

The probability that a verbal response of given form will occur at a given time is the basic datum to be predicted and controlled. It is the "dependent variable" in a functional analysis. The conditions and events to which we turn in order to achieve prediction or control —the "independent variables"—must now be considered.

Conditioning and Extinction

Any operant, verbal or otherwise, acquires strength and continues to be maintained in strength when responses are frequently followed by the event called "reinforcement." The process of "operant conditioning" is most conspicuous when verbal behavior is first acquired. The parent sets up a repertoire of responses in the child by reinforcing many instances of a response. Obviously, a response must appear at least once before it is strengthened by reinforcement. It does not follow, however, that all the complex forms of adult behavior are in the child's unconditioned vocal repertoire. The parent need not wait for the emergence of the final form. Responses of great intricacy can be constructed in the behavior of an organism through a procedure illustrated by the following demonstration experiment. We undertake to condition a pigeon to pace the floor of its cage in the pattern of a figure-8. Let us assume that the pigeon is hungry and that we can present food quickly and conveniently as a reinforcer. We need not wait until a figure-8 emerges in its entirety in order to reinforce the behavior. We begin by reinforcing any behavior which is part of the final pattern. In case the pigeon remains relatively immobile, we may have to begin by reinforcing any slight movement. The bird will soon become active, though as yet in no particular pattern. We then withhold reinforcement until the bird begins turning in one specific direction, let us say clockwise. The slightest movement in this direction is immediately reinforced. Later, reinforcement is withheld until an extensive movement is made. Complete circular movements soon appear. This is half the desired result. The operant is then partially extinguished as reinforcements are withheld until the bird turns in a counterclockwise direction. It may be necessary to reinforce an occasional clockwise movement. Eventually the bird makes complete turns in both directions. The two parts of the pattern are now available but not yet in the required order. It is now possible to wait for a single figure-8 pattern before reinforcing. Under suitable conditions, the final relatively complex performance can be achieved in a short period of time.

In teaching the young child to talk, the formal specifications upon which reinforcement is contingent are at first greatly relaxed. Any response which vaguely resembles the standard behavior of the community is reinforced. When these begin to appear frequently, a closer approximation is insisted upon. In this manner very complex verbal forms may be reached. (We shall see in Chapter 4 that there are other ways of evoking a complex response in order to reinforce it. The present method of "progressive approximation" is usually relevant only in the early stages of setting up a verbal repertoire.)

If the contingencies of reinforcement are for any reason ever relaxed, the properties of the verbal response undergo a change in the other direction. The degeneration of the forms of military commands is an example. Consider a sergeant with a new squad to be conditioned to follow his commands. The sergeant begins with a verbal response borrowed from the larger verbal community, for example, the response *March!* At first this may need to be clearly enunciated, but the squad soon executes the appropriate response regardless of many specifications of the command, partly because other aspects of the situation begin to control the behavior. The form of the response then characteristically degenerates, and may eventually reach the stage of a mere forceful expulsion of air with some voicing but little or no shaping. It is only because the appropriate behavior of the squad survives the deterioration in the behavior of the sergeant that the final form is effective. The squad, as a group of listeners, has been progressively reconditioned. A new squad, however, may bring back the more specific form of response in the behavior of the sergeant.

Reinforcing consequences continue to be important after verbal behavior has been acquired. Their principal function is then to maintain the response in strength. How often the speaker will emit a response depends, other things being equal, upon the over-all frequency of reinforcement in a given verbal community. If reinforcements cease altogether through some change of circumstance, an operant grows weak and may effectively disappear in "extinction."

Operant reinforcement, then, is simply a way of controlling the probability of occurrence of a certain class of verbal responses. If we wish to make a response of given form highly probable, we arrange for the effective reinforcement of many instances. If we wish to eliminate it from a verbal repertoire, we arrange that reinforcement shall no longer follow. Any information regarding the relative frequency of reinforcement characteristic of a given verbal community is obviously valuable in predicting such behavior.

Stimulus Control

A child acquires verbal behavior when relatively unpatterned vocalizations, selectively reinforced, gradually assume forms which produce appropriate consequences in a given verbal community. In formulating this process we do not need to mention stimuli occurring prior to the behavior to be reinforced. It is difficult, if not impossible, to discover stimuli which evoke specific vocal responses in the young child. There is no stimulus which makes a child say *b* or *ă* or *ē,* as one may make him salivate by placing a lemon drop in his mouth or make his pupils contract by shining a light into his eyes. The raw responses from which verbal behavior is constructed are not "elicited." In order to reinforce a given response we simply wait until it occurs.

Prior stimuli are, however, important in the control of verbal behavior. They are important because they enter into a three-term contingency of reinforcement which may be stated in this way: in the presence of a given stimulus, a given response is characteristically followed by a given reinforcement. Such a contingency is a property of the environment. When it prevails, the organism not only acquires the response which achieves reinforcement, it becomes more likely to emit that response in the presence of the prior stimulus. The process through which this comes about, called "stimulus discrimination," has been extensively studied in nonverbal behavior. Numerous examples will be described in later chapters.

Motivation and Emotion

Although reinforcement provides for the control of a response, we do not use reinforcement as such when we later exercise control. By reinforcing with candy we strengthen the response *Candy!* but the response will be emitted only when the child is, as we say, hungry for candy. Subsequently we control the response, not by further reinforcement, but by depriving or satiating the child with candy. Nonverbal responses are controlled in the same way. Whether a door is opened with a "twist-and-push" or with an *Out!,* we make the response more or less likely by altering the deprivation associated with the reinforcement of getting through the door. If the response has been reinforced in several different ways, we may control it by changing, not the deprivation, but the impending reinforcement. We increase the probability that a man will cross a room by placing a currently reinforcing object on the other side. By removing such an object or, better still, placing it near the man, we reduce the probability of his crossing the room.

When an operant is acquired it becomes a member of a group of responses which vary together with the relevant deprivation. A man gets a drink of water in many ways—by reaching for a glass of water, by opening a faucet, by pouring water from a pitcher, and so on. The verbal operant *Water!* becomes a member of this group when it is reinforced with water. The probabilities of all operants so reinforced vary together. Responses in all classes are made more likely to occur when we deprive the man of water or cause him to lose water—for example, by inducing violent exercise, by feeding him salt which must be excreted, or by raising the temperature of his surroundings so that he sweats. On the other hand, we make all such responses less likely to occur by causing the man to drink large amounts of water.

Such operations are said by the layman to create or allay a "state of thirst." Such a concept is only as valid or useful in prediction and control as the observations upon which it rests. The important events are the operations which are said to change the state of thirst. In predicting and controlling the verbal response *Water!* we do not change thirst directly; we engage in certain operations which are said to change it. It is simpler to omit any reference to a "drive" and say that the probability of the response *Water!* can be changed through these operations.

Suppose, however, that in addition to drinking water our speaker has also used water to extinguish fires. Until we have tested the point, we cannot be sure that a response acquired when he has been reinforced with water while thirsty will be emitted when the wastebasket catches fire. If there is any functional connection, it must be found in certain events common to drinking water and extinguishing a fire. If the response *Water!* has been reinforced with the visual stimulation supplied by water prior to water in the mouth, and if this stimulation plays a role in controlling the behavior of extinguishing a fire, then the response acquired only under water deprivation may occur in the case of a conflagration. The group of operations which affect the strength of *Water!* suggests, in common parlance, some general "need for water" rather than "thirst." But we should have to examine all behavior in which water plays an essential role in order to define this need. We may say that we increase the strength of any response which has been reinforced with water, including the verbal response *Water!,* by strengthening any behavior which "requires water for its execution." (In more technical terms, the latter would be described as any behavior under the control of water as a discriminative stimulus.)

Aversive Control

There are other types of consequences which alter the strength of a verbal response. Behavior may be reinforced by the reduction of aversive stimulation. When an aversive stimulus itself is reduced, we call the behavior *escape*. When some condition which characteristically precedes an aversive stimulus is reduced, we speak of *avoidance*. Thus, if the verbal response *Stop it!* is reinforced when it brings about the cessation of physical injury, the response is an example of escape. But *Don't touch me!* may be reinforced when it brings about the cessation of the threat of such injury—of events which have previously been followed by such injury and which are therefore conditioned aversive stimuli—and the behavior is then called avoidance. When a speaker has had a history of such reinforcement, we control his verbal behavior by creating appropriate circumstances. We make him say *Stop it!* by pummeling him, or *Don't touch me!* by threatening to do so.

A complete account of the verbal behavior of the individual speaker would lead us to survey other variables in the fields of motivation and emotion, but the processes here are seldom, if ever, uniquely related to verbal behavior. Some relevant points are discussed in Chapter 8.

THE LISTENER AND THE TOTAL VERBAL EPISODE

Our definition of verbal behavior applies only to the speaker, but the listener cannot be omitted from our account. The traditional conception of verbal behavior discussed in Chapter 1 has generally implied that certain basic linguistic processes were common to both speaker and listener. Common processes are suggested when language is said to arouse in the mind of the listener "ideas present in the mind of the speaker," or when communication is regarded as successful only if an expression has "the same meaning for both speaker and listener." Theories of meaning are usually applied to both speaker and listener as if the meaning process were the same for both.

Much of the behavior of the listener has no resemblance to the behavior of the speaker and is not verbal according to our definition.[7] But the listener (and the reader as well) is reacting to verbal stimuli —the end-products of the behavior here analyzed—and we are naturally interested in the fate of such stimuli. On the one hand they evoke responses of glands and smooth muscles, mediated by the autonomic nervous system, especially emotional reactions. These exemplify classical conditioned reflexes. On the other hand verbal stimuli control much of the complex skeletal behavior with which the individual operates upon his environment. The relevant processes in both these broad areas will be taken up as needed in what follows. In neither case do the verbal stimuli differ in any particular from other kinds of stimulation. The behavior of a man as listener is not to be distinguished from other forms of his behavior.

Our interest in the listener is not, however, merely an interest in what happens to the verbal stimuli created by the speaker. In a complete account of a speech episode we need to show that the behavior of the listener does in fact provide the conditions we have assumed in explaining the behavior of the speaker. We need separate but interlocking accounts of the behaviors of both speaker and listener if our explanation of verbal behavior is to be complete. In explaining the behavior of the speaker we assume a listener who will reinforce his behavior in certain ways. In accounting for the behavior of the listener we assume a speaker whose behavior bears a certain relation to environmental conditions. The interchanges between them must explain all the conditions thus assumed. The account of the whole episode is then complete.

[7] We shall see later that in many important instances the listener is also behaving at the same time as a speaker.

Part II
CONTROLLING VARIABLES

Chapter 3

. . . .

The Mand

In a given verbal community, certain responses are characteristically followed by certain consequences. *Wait!* is followed by someone's waiting and *Sh-h!* by silence. Much of the verbal behavior of young children is of this sort. *Candy!* is characteristically followed by the receipt of candy and *Out!* by the opening of a door. These effects are not inevitable, but we can usually find one consequence of each response which is commoner than any other. There are nonverbal parallels. *Out!*, as we have seen, has the same ultimate effect as turning a knob and pushing against a door. Both forms of behavior become part of the repertoire of the organism through operant conditioning. When a response is characteristically reinforced in a given way, its likelihood of appearing in the behavior of the speaker is a function of the deprivation associated with that reinforcement. The response *Candy!* will be more likely to occur after a period of candy deprivation, and least likely after candy satiation. The response *Quiet!* is reinforced through the reduction of an aversive condition, and we can increase the probability of its occurrence by creating such a condition—that is, by making a noise.

It will be convenient to have a name for the type of verbal operant in which a response of given form is characteristically followed by a given consequense in a verbal community. The basic relationship has been recognized in syntactic and grammatical analyses (expressions such as the "imperative mood" and "commands and entreaties" suggest themselves), but no traditional term can safely be used here. The term "mand" has a certain mnemonic value derived from "command," "demand," "countermand," and so on, and is conveniently brief. A "mand," then, may be defined as a verbal operant in which the response is reinforced by a characteristic consequence and is therefore under the functional control of relevant conditions of deprivation or aversive stimulation. Adjectival and verbal uses of the term are self-explanatory. In particular, and in contrast with other types of verbal operants to be discussed later, the response has no specified relation to a prior stimulus.

A mand is characterized by the unique relationship between the form of the response and the reinforcement characteristically received in a given verbal community. It is sometimes convenient to refer to this relation by saying that a mand "specifies" its reinforcement. *Listen!, Look!, Run!, Stop!,* and *Say yes!* specify the behavior of a listener; but when a hungry diner calls *Bread!,* or *More soup!,* he is specifying the ultimate reinforcement. Frequently both the behavior of the listener and the ultimate reinforcement are specified. The mand *Pass the salt!* specifies an action *(pass)* and an ultimate reinforcement *(the salt).*

A mand is a type of verbal operant singled out by its controlling variables. It is not a formal unit of analysis. No response can be said to be a mand from its form alone. As a general rule, in order to identify any type of verbal operant we need to know the kind of variables of which the response is a function. In a given verbal community, however, certain formal properties may be so closely associated with specific kinds of variables that the latter may often be safely inferred. In the present case, we may say that some responses, simply because of formal properties, are very probably mands.

The pattern of response which characteristically achieves the given reinforcement depends, of course, upon the "language"—that is, upon the reinforcing practices of the verbal community (see Appendix). But we have to explain not only the relationships between patterns of response and reinforcements, but the maintenance of the behavior of the *listener.* When we come to consider other types of verbal operants, we shall find that the behavior functions mainly for the benefit of the listener, and in that case his behavior is not difficult to explain. The mand, however, works primarily for the benefit of the speaker; why should the listener perform the necessary mediation of reinforcement?

What needs to be explained, in other words, is the total speech episode. This can be done by listing all relevant events in the behavior of both speaker and listener in their proper temporal order. The deprivation or aversive stimulation responsible for the strength of each must be specified, and the reinforcing contingencies must explain the origin and continued maintenance of the behavior. Several interchanges between the two organisms frequently occur.

Figure 1 represents an episode in which one person asks another for bread. The problem of motivation is disposed of by assuming a hungry speaker and a listener already predisposed to reinforce him with bread. The first physical interchange takes place when the mere presence of the listener provides the occasion (S^D)[1] for the speaker's mand *Bread, please!* The speaker does not ordinarily emit the response when no one is present, but when a listener appears, the probability of response is increased (Chapter 7). The visual and other stimulation supplied by the listener is indicated by the first ↑ in the diagram. The speaker's response (*Bread, please*) produces a verbal stimulus for the listener. The interchange here (the first ↓↓) is in the form of auditory stimulation which supplies the occasion (S^{DV}) for the nonverbal response of passing the bread. Though we have assumed a listener predisposed to give bread to the speaker, the behavior does not appear indiscriminately. The speaker's mand *(Bread, please)* establishes an occasion upon which the listener can, so to speak, successfully give bread. The interchange of the bread is indicated by the second ↑. The effect upon the speaker is to reinforce the mand by the presentation of bread, and this completes the account so far as the speaker is concerned. It is characteristic of many cultures, however, that the successful reinforcement of a mand is followed by another verbal response, designed to assure similar behavior of the listener in the future. In the diagram, this is indicated by the verbal response *Thank you.* This response is under the control of the stimulation provided by the preceding parts of the episode indicated in the diagram as the second S^D. The auditory stimulation (the second ↓↓) supplies a reinforcing stimulus for the listener, which accounts to some extent for the behavior of passing the bread. This verbal stimulus may also contribute to the occasion for a verbal response on the part of the listener *(You're welcome)* which, when heard by the speaker, reinforces the response *Thank you.* These last two interchanges are not an integral part of the speech episode containing a mand; they supplement our assumptions respecting the motivation of the two individuals. (The effect of a verbal response in serving as a reinforcement is further discussed in Chapter 6.)

[1] S = stimulus, R = response. The superscript V identifies verbal terms. S^D is technically a *discriminative* stimulus, i.e., not an eliciting stimulus.

Kinds of Mands

The mand represented in Figure 1, in which the listener is independently motivated to reinforce the speaker, is commonly called a *request*. The response serves merely to indicate that the speaker will accept what the listener is already disposed to give. It is, to repeat, an occasion for successful giving. Often, however, the speaker's response, in addition to specifying a reinforcement, may need to establish an aversive situation from which the listener can escape only by providing the appropriate mediation. When the listener's behavior is

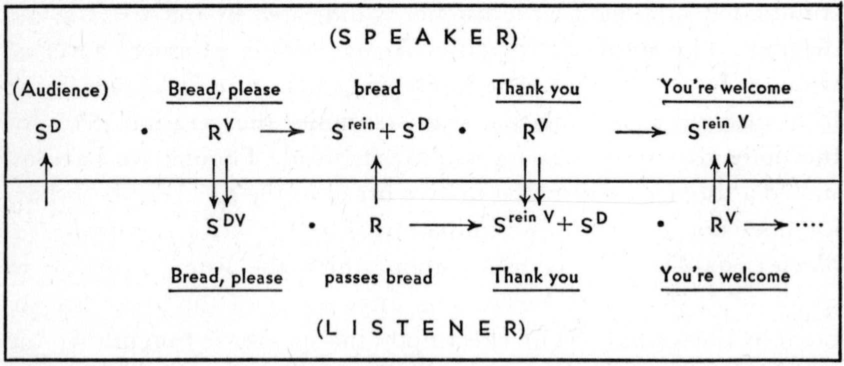

Figure 1

thus reinforced by reducing a threat, the speaker's response is called a *command*. *Hands up!* not only specifies a form of action, it constitutes a threat from which the victim can escape only by holding up his hands. The threat may be carried by a characteristic intonation or may be made explicit, as in *Your money or your life!*, where the first two words specify the reinforcement and the last two the aversive consequences with which the listener is threatened. Military commands are obeyed because of a sort of standing threat.

A paradigm showing the interaction of speaker and listener in a command is shown in Figure 2. Here again the first interchange is from listener to speaker. The presence of the listener constitutes the occasion for verbal behavior (S^D) and also in this instance an aversive stimulus (S^{av}) from which the speaker's response will bring escape. Let us say that the listener is in the speaker's way. The response *Step aside!* specifies an action on the part of the listener and its intonation constitutes a threat. Heard by the listener (at ↓↓), these evoke the appropriate response of stepping aside which, in clearing the way for the speaker, reinforces his mand. The reinforcement is also the occasion for a change in his behavior, possibly quite conspicuous, by virtue of which the threat is withdrawn. This change reinforces the listener for stepping aside (at ↓).

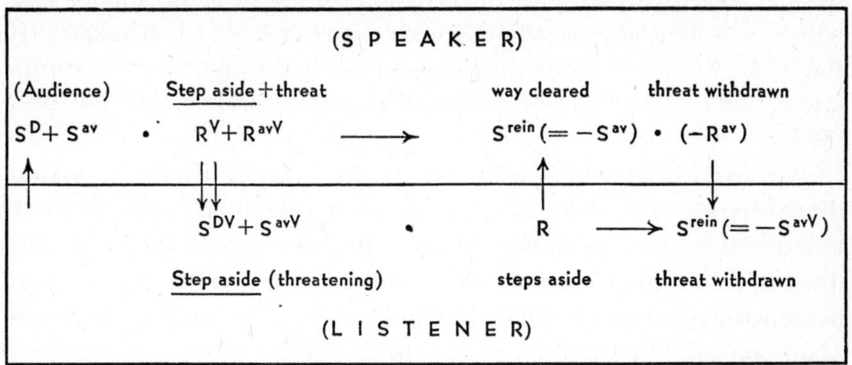

FIGURE 2

There are other ways in which the speaker may alter the probability that the listener will respond in an appropriate fashion. A mand which promotes reinforcement by generating an emotional disposition is commonly called a *prayer* or *entreaty*. A *question* is a mand which specifies verbal action, and the behavior of the listener permits us to classify it as a request, a command, or a prayer, as the case may be. In Figure 3 we assume that the listener not only provides an audience for the speaker but creates a situation in which the

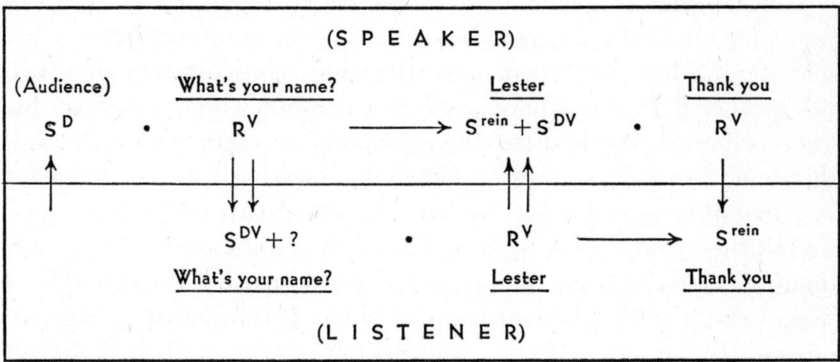

FIGURE 3

speaker will be reinforced by being told the listener's name. The speaker's mand *What's your name?* becomes (at the first ↓↓) a verbal stimulus for the listener who replies either because of a standing tendency to respond to the speaker or an implied threat in the speaker's response, or because the speaker has emotionally predisposed him to reply. His reply at ↑↑ completes the paradigm for the speaker, but it also serves as the occasion for the response *Thank you,* which completes the paradigm for the listener if that is necessary. If the speaker has controlled the listener mainly through aversive stimulation, *Thank you* may be replaced by some visible relaxation of a threat.

(An analysis of this sort seems to do violence to the temporal dimensions of behavior. All of the events represented in one of these paradigms might take place in two or three seconds. The events described, however, *can* occur within a brief period, and we can demonstrate the reality of such a linkage by interrupting the chain at any point. The function of the interlocking paradigm is to check the completeness of our account of verbal behavior. Have the behaviors of both speaker and listener been fully accounted for? Have we identified appropriate states of deprivation or aversive stimulation in all cases? Have we correctly represented the actual physical interchange between the two organisms? In this account of the speech episode, it should be noted that nothing is appealed to beyond the separate behaviors of speaker and listener. By assuming the conditions supplied by a listener, we analyze the behavior of a speaker, and vice versa. By putting the two cases together we construct the total episode and show how it naturally arises and completes itself.)

Several other classes of mands may be distinguished in terms of the behavior of the listener. In mediating the reinforcement of the speaker, the listener will occasionally enjoy consequences in which the speaker does not otherwise participate but which are nevertheless reinforcing. When these consist of positive reinforcement, we call the mand *advice (Go west!).* When by carrying out the behavior specified by the speaker the listener escapes from aversive stimulation, we call the mand a *warning (Look out!).* When the listener is already inclined to act in a given way but is restrained by, for example, a threat, the mand which cancels the threat is commonly called *permission (Go ahead!).* When gratuitous reinforcement of the behavior of the listener is extended by the speaker, the mand is called an *offer (Take one free!).* When the speaker characteristically goes on to emit other behavior which may serve as reinforcement for the listener, the mand is a *call*—either a call to attention or the "vocative" call-by-name.

Classifying the behavior of the speaker in terms of the characteristics of the mediating behavior of the listener may be distinguished from the traditional practice of defining requests, commands, prayers, advice, warnings, permission, offers, and calls in terms of "the intention" of the speaker. In general, intention may be reduced to contingencies of reinforcement. In the present case the conspicuous differences lie in the behavior of the listener and the conditions which control it. But these result in different contingencies of reinforcement for the speaker, which yield different dynamic properties, different interrelationships among responses, different intonations, and so on.

Since verbal behavior in the form of the mand operates primarily for the benefit of the speaker, repeated mands are likely to move the listener to revolt. It is customary to soften or conceal the mand character. The response *Water!* is not so likely to be successful as *I'm thirsty,* the form of which is characteristic of a type of verbal operant to be described in Chapter 5, or *May I have some water?,* which appears to specify only the less burdensome act of saying *Yes.* (The pretense is exposed if the listener simply says *Yes.*) *Would you mind getting me a drink?* also specifies merely a verbal response *(No, not at all),* but the implied mand may be effective because of the suggested deference to the inclination of the listener. Explicit deference appears in tags such as *if you don't mind, if you please,* or simply *please.* When emphasized, these may convert a mere request into the stronger entreaty.

The inclination of the listener to respond may be heightened by flattery or praise, as in *Get me a drink, my good fellow.* The Lord's Prayer is a mixture of mands and praise following this pattern. The praise may be made conditional upon the execution of the reinforcement, as in *Be a good fellow and get me a drink,* which may be translated *Only if you get me a drink will I call you a good fellow.* Gratitude may be withheld until the listener responds, as in *I'll thank you to get me a drink.* Open bargaining is sometimes resorted to, as in *Give me a drink and I'll tell you all about it.* The abundance of such supplementary techniques merely emphasizes the precariousness of the reinforcement of the mand.

Any response used in conjunction with different mands specifying different reinforcements comes under the control of different deprivations and acquires certain general properties. *Please* is the best known example. It is strengthened by almost any state of deprivation, and is often emitted without further specification of the behavior of the reinforcer. Mands of lesser generality include the emphatic forms

So!, *Now!*, *Now, then!*, and *Here!* where the common consequence is the response of the listener in paying attention. Since the listener's subsequent behavior may be relevant to many states of deprivation, these responses come under a rather broad control. Generalized mands reinforced by the attention of the listener are often used in conjunction with other types of verbal behavior to be considered later.

The mand relation is clearest when it is in exclusive control of a response, but it is also effective in combination with other kinds of variables. A hungry man may show a high frequency of responses which, if they were mands, would be said to specify food, even though they appear under circumstances which more clearly suggest other types of verbal operants to be described below. Such "multiple causation" of a single response is treated in Chapter 9.

Dynamic Properties of the Mand

The energy level of the mand may vary from very faint to very loud, and the speed with which it is emitted when the occasion arises may vary from very fast to very slow. If the pattern is of substantial length, it may be executed slowly or rapidly. If the reinforcement is not immediately forthcoming, the response may be emitted only once or may be repeated. These properties vary as the result of many conditions in the past and present history of the speaker. Particularly relevant are level of deprivation and intensity of aversive stimulation and the extent to which a given listener or someone like him has reinforced similar responses in the past (or has refused to do so). Such conditions have a relatively greater effect upon the mand than upon the other types of verbal behavior to be discussed in later chapters. The wide range of dynamic properties which result makes the mand a very expressive type of operant.

The probability and intensity of the listener's behavior may also vary over a wide range. If the listener is not already predisposed to act, the probability of his mediating a reinforcement may depend upon the effectiveness of the aversive stimulation supplied by the speaker. Some listeners are accustomed to taking orders—they have felt the unconditioned aversive consequences of not doing so—and respond appropriately to simple mands. Others are more likely to react to softened forms. The intonation, loudness, or other indication that the speaker will supply aversive consequences has an appropriate effect. A hesitant or weak request or command is least likely to be reinforced. A loud and threatening response is likely to be reinforced subject only to the relative strength of listener and speaker. It is to be noted that mands are characteristic of most hypnotic instructions, and the extent to which the subject co-operates or obliges the hypnotist will depend upon the kinds of variables here being considered. These variables enter into what is called the authority or prestige of the speaker.

The net result of a long history of responding to mands is a general tendency no longer easily traced to any form of deprivation or aversive stimulation. The listener obliges and may not even be aware (see Chapter 5) that he is doing so. A classroom experiment designed by F. S. Keller illustrates this point. The instructor says, "Before *summing up* these influences, there is an *additional* one that should be mentioned. I can illustrate this best with an example." At this point he turns to the blackboard and writes

$$\frac{5}{4}$$

DO IT ON PAPER

The instructor then continues, "What you did was the result of the 'set' or 'attitude' that you had at the moment you were presented with this stimulus situation. Examples of this are *multiple* and you could supply them from your own experience by the hour. Usually no one is aware of the *times* when they occur in everyday life, but our generalization is the *product* of laboratory experimentation and can readily be checked." He then puts on the board

$$\frac{4}{3}$$

DO IT ON PAPER

When the number of those who multiplied in the first instance is compared with the number who multiplied in the second, there is almost always more multiplying in the second case. The underlined words, which of course are not emphasized in the instructions, exert some control over the listener's behavior.

Traditional Treatment

In the traditional treatment of verbal behavior, the "meaning" of a mand is presumably the reinforcement which characteristically follows it. The meaning of *Candy!* is the kind of object frequently produced by that response. But "what is communicated" would appear to be "the speaker's need for candy," which refers to the controlling state of deprivation. The concept of the mand, or of the verbal operant in general, explicitly recognizes both contingency of reinforcement and deprivation or aversive stimulation and is free to deal with these variables in appropriate fashion without trying to identify a relation of reference or a process of communication.

Apart from these questions of semantics, the formulation carries some of the burden of grammar and syntax in dealing with the dynamic properties of verbal behavior. The mand obviously suggests the *imperative* mood, but *interrogatives* are also mands, as are most *interjections* and *vocatives,* and some *subjunctives* and *optatives.* The traditional classifications suffer from a mixture of levels of analysis. In particular they show the influence of formal descriptive systems in which sentences are classified with little or no reference to the behavior of the speaker. It is here that the shortcomings of grammar and syntax in a causal analysis are most obvious. Appropriate techniques are lacking. As Epictetus said, "When you are to write to your friend, grammar will tell you how to write; but whether you are to write to your friend at all, grammar will not tell you." The use of the mand as a unit of analysis does not mean that the work of linguistic analysis can be avoided, but it simplifies our task by isolating the behavior of the individual speaker as an object of study and by making appropriate techniques available.

In choosing between descriptive systems on the basis of simplicity and effectiveness, the greater familiarity of the classical approach should not be put into the balance. Consider, for example, the following quotation:

> In many countries it has been observed that very early a child uses a long *m* (without a vowel) as a sign that it wants something, but we can hardly be right in supposing that the sound is originally meant by children in this sense. They do not use it consciously until they see that grown-up people, on hearing the sound, come up and find out what the child wants.[2]

Although this passage may be said to make an intelligible point in connection with an episode which is intelligibly reported, much is left to be done. It is not the most advantageous account *for all concerned,* for the psychological terms it contains raise many problems.

[2] Jesperson, O., *Language* (New York, 1922), p. 157.

How would the point be made in the present terms? The expression "uses a long *m* as a sign that it wants something" becomes "emits the sound *m* in a given state of deprivation or aversive stimulation." The expression "the sound is not originally meant in this sense" becomes "the relation between the sound and the state of deprivation or aversive stimulation is innate, or at least of some earlier origin, and the response is not verbal according to our definition." "They do not use it consciously . . ." becomes "It is not conditioned as a verbal response. . . ." And ". . . until they see that grown-up people, on hearing the sound, come up and find out what the child wants" becomes ". . . until the emission of the sound leads listeners to supply reinforcements appropriate to a particular deprivation." The whole passage might be translated:

> It has been observed that very early a child emits the sound *m* in certain states of deprivation or aversive stimulation, but we can hardly be right in calling the response verbal at this stage. It is conditioned as a verbal operant only when people, upon hearing the sound, come up and supply appropriate reinforcement.

The distinction between learned and unlearned response is much easier to make in terms of a history of reinforcement than in terms of meaning and conscious use. An important example is crying. Vocal behavior of this sort is clearly an unconditioned response in the newborn infant. For some time it is a function of various states of deprivation and aversive stimulation. But when crying is characteristically followed by parental attentions which are reinforcing, it may become verbal according to our definition. It has become a different behavioral unit because it is now under the control of different variables. It has also probably acquired different properties, for parents are likely to react differently to different intonations or intensities of crying.

The simplicity of such a translation is very different from the simplicity of the original account. The translation is simple because its terms can be defined with respect to experimental operations and because it is consistent with other statements about verbal and nonverbal behavior. The original account is simple because it is familiar and appropriate for casual discourse. It is the difference between the systematic simplicity of science and the ready comprehensibility of the layman's account. Newton's *Principia* was not simple to the man in the street, but in one sense it was simpler than everything which the man in the street had to say about the same subject.

THE EXTENDED MAND

A mand assumes a given form because of contingencies of reinforcement maintained by the listener or by the verbal community as a whole. The stimulating conditions which prevail when such a response is emitted and reinforced do not enter into the definition of the unit. When a mand is reinforced by a reduction in unconditioned or conditioned aversive stimuli, stimuli occurring prior to the response must, of course, be taken into account, but these serve a different function from the stimuli being considered here. Stimuli affecting the speaker prior to the emission of verbal behavior are often important and are never wholly irrelevant, as we shall see in the following chapters. The probability of emission of a response is greatest when the stimulating conditions closely resemble those which have previously prevailed before reinforcement. But past and present circumstances need not be identical; indeed, any aspect or feature of the present situation which resembles the situation at the time of reinforcement may be supposed to make some contribution to the probability of response.

An example of extended stimulus control is seen when people mand the behavior of dolls, small babies, and untrained animals. These "listeners" cannot possibly reinforce the behavior in characteristic fashion. Nevertheless, they have enough in common with listeners who have previously provided reinforcement to control the response, at least when it shows appreciable strength. The fact that reinforcement is unlikely or impossible may affect the dynamic properties. The response may be weak, or emitted in a whimsical fashion, or accompanied by suitable comment (Chapter 12). On the other hand, such behavior often occurs when its "irrational" aspects are not seen by the speaker. We acquire and retain the response *Stop!* because many listeners stop whatever they are doing when we emit it, but as a result we may say *Stop!* to a car with faulty brakes or to a cue ball which threatens to drop into a pocket of the pool table.

The same process leads in the extreme case to the emission of mands in the absence of any listener whatsoever. The lone man dying of thirst gasps *Water!* An unattended king calls *A horse, a horse, my kingdom for a horse!* These responses are "unreasonable" in the sense that they can have no possible effect upon the momentary environment, but the underlying process is lawful. Through a process of stimulus induction situations which are similar to earlier situations come to control the behavior, and in the extreme case a very strong response is emitted when no comparable stimulus can be detected.

There are many familiar nonverbal instances of stimulus induction. It may be true that one cannot open a door without a door or eat a meal without a meal, but in a state of great strength parts of even the most practical behavior occur in the absence of the stimulation required for proper execution. A baseball player who has dropped the ball at a crucial moment may pantomime the correct throw with an empty hand. A thirsty person may "pretend" to drink from an empty glass. Many gestures appear to have originated as "irrational" extension of practical responses. The traffic officer extends his hand, palm outward, toward an oncoming car, as if to bring the car to a stop by physical means. The gesture functions as a verbal response, but it exemplifies the extension of a practical response through stimulus induction to a situation in which normal reinforcement is impossible. Verbal behavior may more easily break free from stimulus control, because by its very nature it does not require environmental support—that is, no stimuli need be present to direct it or to form important links in chaining responses.

Superstitious Mands

There are mands which cannot be explained by arguing that responses of the same form have been reinforced under similar circumstances. The dice player exclaims *Come seven!*, for example, even though he has not asked for and got sevens anywhere. Accidental reinforcement of the response appears to be the explanation. The experimental study of nonverbal behavior has shown that merely intermittent reinforcement, such as that provided by chance throws of seven, is sufficient to maintain a response in strength. The player may readily admit that there is no mechanical connection between his response and the behavior of the dice, but he retains the response in some strength and continues to utter it, either whimsically or seriously under sufficient stress, because of its occasional "consequences." Mands which specify the behavior of inanimate objects often receive some reinforcement in this sense. The response *Blow, blow, thou winter wind,* for example, is usually uttered when the wind is already blowing, and the correlation between behavior and effect, though spurious, may work a change in operant strength.

Other "unreasonable" mands owe their strength to collateral effects not strictly specified in the form of the response. Many responses mand emotional behavior even though, because of the special ways in which such behavior is conditioned, true emotional responses on the part of the listener cannot be carried out to order. The mand *O dry your tears* has no effect upon lacrimal secretion. We cannot write a paradigm similar to that of Figure 1 in which the mand has the form *Weep, please!* because we cannot complete the account of the listener. A verbal response may be part of a larger pattern, however, which produces tears in the sensitive listener or reader for other reasons. Intonation and other properties are important in eliciting emotional behavior, and an emotional speaker will supplement his responses with very generous sound effects. We do not say *Cheer up!* in a dull tone, for we cannot leave the effect upon the listener to the mand alone. Properly pronounced, however, such a response may have an effect. The general process is not characteristic of the mand, and the same result is frequently (and probably more easily) obtained without the mand form.

The Magical Mand

There are mands which cannot be accounted for by showing that they have ever had the effect specified or any similar effect upon similar occasions. The speaker appears to create new mands on the analogy of old ones. Having effectively manded bread and butter, he goes on to mand the jam, even though he has never obtained jam before in this way. The poet exclaims *Milton, thou shouldst be living in this hour!*, although he has never successfully addressed Milton before nor brought anyone to life with a similar response. The special relation between response and consequence exemplified by the mand establishes a general pattern of control over the environment. In moments of sufficient stress, the speaker simply describes the reinforcement appropriate to a given state of deprivation or aversive stimulation. The response must, of course, already be part of his verbal repertoire as some other type of verbal operant (Chapters 4 and 5).

This sort of extended operant may be called a magical mand. It does not exhaust the field of verbal magic, but it is the commonest example. Flushed with our success under favorable reinforcing circumstances, we set out to change the world without benefit of listener. Unable to imagine how the universe could have been created out of nothing, we conjecture that it was done with a verbal response. It was only necessary to say, with sufficient authority, *Let there be light!*

The form *Let* is taken from situations in which it has been effective *(Let me go, Let him have it),* but we do not specify the listener who will make this instance effective.

Wishing frequently takes the mand form and must be classified as a magical mand if the consequences specified have never actually occurred as the result of similar verbal behavior. The speaker may specify some reinforcing state of affairs either for himself *(O to be in England, now that April's there!*) or for others (*Happy birthday!*). In *cursing,* the mand specifies punishing circumstances. The curse is more clearly a mand when it enjoins the listener to arrange his own punishment; *Oh, go jump in the lake!* is somewhat more explicit as to the modus operandi than *Bad luck to you!*

The form *may* is associated with mands in many ways. *You may go* is permission (as contrasted with *You can go)* and, as we have seen, permission is a type of mand. *May I go?* is a mand for verbal action which is to have the form of permission. In *I may (possibly) go* or *Maybe I'll go, may* is an example of a kind of verbal behavior (to be discussed in Chapter 12) which is close to the mand. In *May you always be happy* or *May you suffer the torments of Job* the form is a sort of generalized mand (*cf. Please*). In the expanded form *I wish that* (or *My wish is that*) *you may always be happy,* the *may* keeps the same "optative" function. *Would* is another common generalized mand (*Would God I were a tender apple blossom*). *O* serves something of the same function (*cf.* Browning's wish to be in England in April), but also serves to point up the mand character of vocatives (*O Captain, my Captain!*) and questions (*O what can ail thee, knight-at-arms*). When the accompanying response is not in the form of a mand (*O, Brignall banks are wild and fair*), *O* may be regarded as manding the attention of the listener or reader. This is evidently its function in such an example as *O, what a beautiful morning!*, in which case it functions very much like the more specific mand *Look,* noted below.

The Mand in Literature

As several of these examples suggest, certain forms of literary behavior are rich in mands. Some of these are vocatives (*Reader, I married him*), some mand verbal behavior (*Call me Ishmael*), and some mand the attention of the reader (*Listen, my children, and you shall hear . . .*). Because of the tenuous relation between writer and reader, many of these are necessarily magical. Lyric poems in particular are rich in literary mands. Of the first lines of English lyric poems in a number of anthologies about 40 per cent were found to be of a form most characteristic of mands. Fifteen per cent of these specify the behavior of the reader: he is to pay attention, with both eyes and ears. The poet is affected here by the reinforcements which are responsible for the vulgar forms *Look, See,* and *Listen*—forms which mainly call attention to the speaker (*Listen, have you seen George?, Look, can you give me some help?* or *See here, what are you up to?*). *See* is also used to mand attention to something being described (*There he stood, see, and I said to him . . .*). The poetic variant of *See* is *Behold.* The poet mands the listener to see someone sitting upon a grassy green and to hark, not only to his words, but to the lark. He also mands him to speak up (*Tell me, where is fancy bred?*), to be quiet (*Oh, never say that I was false of heart*), and to co-operate in various practical affairs related to the poet's deprivations: *Come, let us kiss, Come live with me and be my love, Take, O take those lips away,* or *Drink to me only with thine eyes.* These are not always *magical* mands—though an appropriate reinforcement would possibly come as a surprise—but other examples seem to be necessarily so (*Go and catch a falling star*). When the reader is manded to alter or control his emotions (*Then hate me when thou wilt, Weep with me, Love me no more*), these specifications cannot be followed to the letter, as we have seen, but collateral results may not be inappropriate.

In another 15 per cent of the first lines, the poet begins by addressing someone or something besides the reader. Crimson roses are asked to speak, spotted snakes with double tongues are asked to vanish, and Ulysses, worthy Greek, is asked to appear. The remaining 10 per cent of probable mands are plain statements of wishes (*A book of verses underneath the bough . . .*) or statements prefixed with *Let, May, O,* or *Would.*

The richness of these examples from literature exemplifies a general principle which will be confirmed again in later chapters. "Poetic license" is not an empty term. Literature is the product of a special verbal practice which brings out behavior which would otherwise remain latent in the repertoires of most speakers (see Chapter 16). Among other things the tradition and practice of lyric poetry encourage the emission of behavior under the control of strong deprivations—in other words, responses in the form of mands. Evidently the lyric poet needs many things and needs them badly. He needs a reader and a reader's attention and participation. After that he needs to have someone or something brought to him or taken away. Verbal behavior strengthened as the result of these various deprivations is emitted, in spite of its manifest ineffectiveness or weakness, because of the poetic practice. The lyric form warrants or permits "unreasonable" behavior, and in so doing it supplies the student of verbal behavior with especially useful material.

Chapter 4

Verbal Behavior under the Control of Verbal Stimuli

THE SPECIFIC RELATION between response and reinforcement which defines a mand does not, as we have seen, involve a specific prior stimulus. Prior stimuli are not, however, irrelevant. An example of a controlling stimulus has already been cited. Verbal behavior is reinforced only through the mediation of another person, but it does not require the participation of such a person for its *execution*. When it is emitted in the absence of a listener, it generally goes unreinforced. After repeated reinforcement in the presence, and extinction in the absence, of a listener, the speaker eventually speaks only in the presence of a listener. Practically all verbal behavior is thus controlled by an audience, as we shall see in detail in Chapter 7.

The mand may come under a narrower stimulus control if a given response is reinforced only upon a special occasion. A child who has acquired the mand *Candy!* may emit the response regardless of external circumstances and will do so if its deprivation is great. The response is more likely to appear, however, in the presence of anyone who has previously reinforced with candy, and it is still more likely to appear in the presence of such a person if he is conspicuously holding candy. We can demonstrate three levels of probability of response resulting from three relative frequencies of reinforcement. When no listener is present, the likelihood of reinforcement is low and the response is not likely to be emitted. When a listener appears, the probability of reinforcement is increased and the probability that a response will be made also rises. If the listener then takes candy from his pocket, a further increase in the probability of reinforcement is followed by a further increase in the probability that the child will say *Candy!* But where the appearance of a person as a listener at the second stage increases the probability of many forms of verbal behavior (as will be noted again in Chapter 7), the appearance of the candy at the third stage has a special effect upon the response *Candy!* alone.

When the response appears under these circumstances, the child is not "naming" or "describing" candy. Such terms are more appropriately used to describe responses showing no relation to a specific reinforcement (see Chapter 5). In a very large part of verbal behavior a given form of response does not yield a specific reinforcement and hence is relatively independent of any special state of deprivation or aversive stimulation. Instead, the control is exercised by prior stimuli. We shall see later that the usefulness of verbal behavior to the group as a whole depends largely on this condition. Without considering specific advantages at this point, we may turn directly to the technique employed to bring a verbal response under stimulus control.

A step in the direction of destroying the relation with a particular state of deprivation is taken by reinforcing a single form of response in ways appropriate to many different states. If we have reinforced a selected response with food when the organism is hungry, we may also reinforce it with water when the organism is thirsty. We may then increase the strength of the response by depriving the organism of either food or water. This process could be continued until we had exhausted all reinforcements associated with forms or modes of deprivation or with release from all sorts of aversive conditions. The response would then exist in some strength except when the organism was completely satiated and free of aversive stimulation.

The effect of this procedure in releasing a response from a specific controlling condition is usually achieved in another way. Instead of using a great variety of reinforcements, each of which is relevant to a given state of deprivation or aversive stimulation, a contingency is arranged between a verbal response and a *generalized conditioned reinforcer*. Any event which characteristically precedes many different reinforcers can be used as a reinforcer to bring behavior under the control of all appropriate conditions of deprivation and aversive stimulation. A response which is characteristically followed by such a generalized conditioned reinforcer has dynamic properties similar to those which it would have acquired if it had been severally followed by all the specific reinforcers at issue.

A common generalized conditioned reinforcer is "approval." It is often difficult to specify its physical dimensions. It may be little more than a nod or a smile on the part of someone who characteristically supplies a variety of reinforcements. Sometimes, as we shall see in Chapter 6, it has a verbal form: *Right!* or *Good!* Because these "signs of approval" frequently precede specific reinforcements appropriate to many states of deprivation, the behavior they reinforce is likely to be in strength much of the time.

In destroying the specificity of the control exercised over a given form of response by a given condition of deprivation or aversive stimulation, we appear to leave the form of the response undetermined. Previously we could produce the response *Water!* by depriving the organism of water and the response *Food!* by depriving the organism of food. But what is to take the place of deprivation in controlling a response which has achieved a generalized reinforcement? The answer, of course, is some current stimulus. In destroying the specificity of one relation, we make it possible to set up another. We may use our generalized reinforcer to strengthen response *a* in the presence of stimulus *a,* response *b* in the presence of stimulus *b,* and so on. Whether the speaker emits response *a* or response *b* is no longer a question of deprivation but of the stimulus present. It is this controlling relation in verbal behavior which proves to be of great importance for the functioning of the group.

Another common generalized reinforcement is escape from or avoidance of aversive stimulation. One man may stimulate another aversively in many ways— by beating him, restraining him, or depriving him of positive reinforcers, not to mention many sorts of "verbal damage." This stimulation can be used to strengthen behavior, verbal or otherwise, because its cessation is reinforcing. Conditioned aversive stimuli (stimuli which frequently precede or accompany aversive stimulation) are also reinforcing when their withdrawal is contingent upon behavior.

The withdrawal of aversive stimulation may be generalized in much the same way as approval. We have already appealed to such control in explaining why the listener reinforces a mand which specifies or implies a threat and specifies the behavior on the part of the listener which will reduce it. The threat implied by the mand *A glass of water!* is reduced by giving the speaker a glass of water. The principle explains the behavior of the speaker as well. Release from the threat implied in *Say 'I don't mean it'* is achieved by saying

I don't mean it. Violence is not necessarily implied for there are mild forms of aversive stimulation. A question contains a mild generalized threat in the sense that, if we do not answer, censure will follow. The slight threat which arises during any pause in a conversation is dispelled by executing almost any form of verbal behavior.

The control of verbal behavior exercised by a threat is most effective from the point of view of the welfare of the group when there is no surviving specific connection between a response and the type of aversive stimulation from which it brings release. The speaker who speaks aimlessly from an excessive "desire to please" (as the effect of excessive approval) resembles the speaker who compulsively "searches for something to say" under generalized aversive stimulation. The form of the behavior is trivially determined (see Chapter 8).

In analyzing the stimulus control of verbal behavior, it is convenient to distinguish between instances in which the controlling stimuli are themselves verbal and those in which they are not. The present chapter is confined to responses under the control of audible or written verbal stimuli supplied by another person or by the speaker himself. A further distinction may be made in terms of the resemblances between forms of stimulus and response. The three principal categories to be discussed are echoic, textual, and intraverbal behavior.

We are concerned here only with the effect of verbal stimuli in evoking verbal responses. There are, of course, other effects. The listener reacts to verbal stimuli in a variety of ways, some of which will be analyzed in this and the following chapters. A summary account will be given in Chapter 6.

ECHOIC BEHAVIOR

In the simplest case in which verbal behavior is under the control of verbal stimuli, the response generates a sound-pattern similar to that of the stimulus. For example, upon hearing the sound *Beaver,* the speaker says *Beaver.* Evidence of a tendency to engage in such "echoic" behavior comes from many sources. Mands of the general form *Say 'X'* characteristically produce responses in the listener showing a point-to-point correspondence between the sound of the stimulus and the sound of the response. But echoic behavior commonly appears in the absence of an explicit mand. In the standard "word association" experiment a stimulus word is presented and the subject is asked to report the first word he finds himself saying in response to it. It is necessary to instruct the subject not to repeat the stimulus word; even so, a fragmentary echoic behavior appears in what are called "clang associations"—responses which are alliterative or rhyming or otherwise similar to the stimulus word. A fragmentary self-echoic behavior (see below) may be shown in reduplicative forms like *helter-skelter, razzle-dazzle,* and *willy-nilly*. Pathological echoic behavior is seen in "echolalia," in which a bit of speech heard by the patient is repeated possibly many times. Echoic behavior is most commonly observed in combination with other types of control (see Chapter 9). In a conversation, for example, a slightly atypical response is often picked up and passed from speaker to speaker. The two halves of a dialogue will generally have more words in common than two monologues on the same subject. If one speaker says *incredible* instead of *unbelievable,* the other speaker will in general, and because of the present relation, say *incredible.*

A fragmentary echoic behavior is evident when one speaker adopts the accent or mannerisms of another in the course of a sustained conversation. If one member of a group whispers, perhaps only because of laryngitis, other members tend to do so. In Tolstoy's *War and Peace* a woman imitates her dying father, trying "to speak more by signs as he spoke, as though she too had a difficulty in articulating."

The Reinforcement of Echoic Behavior

An echoic repertoire is established in the child through "educational" reinforcement because it is useful to parents, teachers, and others. It makes possible a short-circuiting of the process of progressive approximation, since it can be used to evoke new units of response upon which other types of reinforcement may then be made contingent. The educational reinforcement is usually supplied with the aid of mands of the type *Say 'X'* where the listener, becoming a speaker, is reinforced if his response yields the sound pattern *'X.'* The procedure continues to be used in formal education to permit the teacher to set up new forms of behavior or to bring a response under new forms of stimulus control, as, for example, in naming objects (see Chapter 5). In all these cases we explain the behavior of the reinforcing listener by pointing to an improvement in the possibility of controlling the speaker whom he reinforces. It is essential, however, that specific reinforcement be entered in the paradigm. In Figure 4, for example, we find the first interchange taking place from listener to speaker as the listener constitutes an audience and mands a response by saying *Say 'Beaver.'* To the speaker this functions as the verbal stimulus in the echoic operant *Beaver*. When heard by the listener (at ↓↓) the speaker's response then reinforces the mand *Say 'Beaver.'* We assume that the listener is operating under circumstances in which it is reinforcing to hear the speaker say X. Perhaps he can then take further steps having reinforcing consequences, or, as a parent, he is reinforced as his child acquires a verbal repertoire. In any case, he acts to release the threat in his mand *Say 'Beaver'* and thus supplies the reinforcement for the speaker's echoic response.

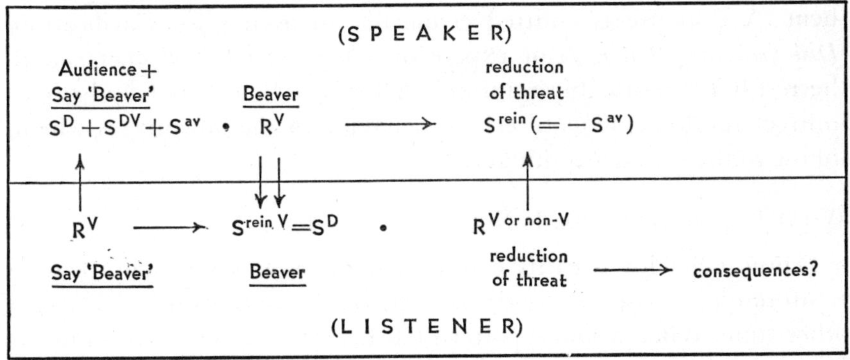

FIGURE 4

Echoic behavior continues to receive reinforcement even when the listener is no longer explicitly "educating" the speaker. For example, one is occasionally reinforced for repeating something to a third person, where the third person, as listener, supplies reinforcement for reasons to be discussed in Chapter 5. There are also many indirect sources of echoic reinforcement. For example, we are reinforced for echoing verbal forms emitted by others in a conversation because these forms are more likely to be effective parts of their repertoires. Echoic responses are useful and reinforced when they serve as fill-ins. In answer to the question *What will happen to the international situation during the next few weeks?* the student may begin *During the next few weeks, the international situation . . .*, which may be purely echoic but, especially if the situation demands speed, self-reinforcing if it provides a breathing space for the composition of the rest of the sentence.

Echoic behavior is reinforced when it continues to reinstate the stimulus and to permit the speaker to react to it in other ways. If we have been given complicated directions to be followed, it may be advantageous to repeat them echoically. Told to move to the right, we may respond more accurately if we first respond verbally: *to the right.* There are standard situations in which the repetition of instructions is specifically reinforced. The chef in a cafeteria repeats the order given him by the counter clerk, as the engineer on a ship repeats the order given him by an officer on the bridge. By confirming the order received, the echoic response brings the behavior of the clerk or the officer on the bridge to an end (see Chapter 8), and this may be reinforcing to the chef and the engineer. Moreover, they presumably carry out orders more effectively for having repeated them. A response is emitted echoically in asking for clarification (*Did you say 'Beaver'?*) or expansion (*Beaver? What beaver?*), and the result is presumably reinforcing. In Part V we shall find other indirect reinforcements of echoic behavior in the advantages which follow to the speaker as thinker.

What Echoic Behavior Is Not

Echoic behavior is easily confused with responses which are self-reinforcing because they resemble the speech of others heard at some other time. When a sound pattern has been associated with reinforcing events, it becomes a conditioned reinforcer. If someone repeatedly reinforces behavior with the verbal stimulus *Right!,* we must not exclude the possibility of the speaker's reinforcing himself in the same way. The young child alone in the nursery may automatically reinforce his own exploratory vocal behavior when he produces sounds which he has heard in the speech of others. The self-reinforcing property may be merely an intonation or some other idiosyncrasy of a given speaker or of speakers in general. A child whose mother often entertained at bridge imitated quite accurately the unintelligible noise of a room full of people talking volubly. The adult acquires intonational patterns which are automatically reinforcing because they are characteristic of, say, a person of prestige. Specific verbal forms arise from the same process. The small child often acquires verbal behavior in the form of commendation used by others to reinforce him: *Tommy is a good boy,* just as the adult may boast of his own ability "in order to hear himself praised." The process is important in the automatic shaping up of standard forms of response. This is not echoic behavior, however, because a verbal stimulus of corresponding form does not immediately precede it.

A distinction must also be drawn between echoic behavior and the *later* reproduction of overheard speech. The answer to the question *What did so-and-so say to you yesterday?* is not echoic behavior. Like the answer to the question *What was so-and-so wearing when you saw him yesterday?* it is an example of a type of verbal operant to be described later. There may be a formal correspondence between the stimulus heard yesterday and today's response (a correspondence which has, indeed, far-reaching consequences), but it does not make the behavior echoic. A special temporal relation is lacking. An echoic repertoire may, of course, enter into the mediation of such behavior.

Also to be distinguished from echoic behavior is the later reproduction of speech as a result of the "instruction" to be discussed in Chapter 14, where the speaker emits responses acquired from the verbal behavior of others which bear a formal correspondence to such behavior but which are now under the control of other stimuli, verbal or otherwise.

Echoic behavior does not depend upon or demonstrate any instinct or faculty of imitation. The formal similarity of stimulus and response need not make the response more likely to occur or supply any help in its execution. The fact is, there *is* no similarity between a pattern of sounds and the muscular responses which produce a similar pattern. At best we can say that the self-stimulation resulting from an echoic response resembles the stimulus. The resemblance may play a role in reinforcing the response, even in the echoic relation, but it has no effect in evoking the response. A parrot does not echo a verbal stimulus because the stimulus sets up a train of events which naturally lead to a set of muscular activities producing the same sounds; the parrot's distinguishing capacity is to be reinforced when it makes sounds which resemble those it has heard. What is "instinctive" in the parrot, if anything, is the capacity for being thus reinforced. Echoic behavior, like all verbal behavior, is shaped and maintained by certain contingencies of reinforcement. The formal similarity between stimulus and response is part of these contingencies and can be explained only by pointing to the significance of the similarity to the reinforcing community.

That a verbal stimulus has no tendency to generate a response with the same sound-pattern is all too clear when we examine the long process through which echoic operants are acquired. Early echoic behavior in young children is often very wide of the mark; the parent must reinforce very imperfect matches to keep the behavior in strength at all. We might say that the child "has no way of knowing how to execute a particular response for the first time"; strictly speaking, we should say that the response is not yet a function of any variable available to the parent. Nothing in the pattern to be echoed will help until some overlapping echoic behavior occurs. "Trying to make the right sound," like trying to find one's hat, consists of emitting as many different responses as possible until the right one appears.

Theobald, in Samuel Butler's *Way of All Flesh,* used the wrong technique:

> [Ernest was] very late in being able to sound a hard "c" or "k," and, instead of saying "Come," he said "Tum. . . ."
>
> "Ernest," said Theobald . . . , "don't you think it would be very nice if you were to say 'come' like other people, instead of 'tum'?"
>
> "I do say tum," replied Ernest . . .
>
> Theobald noticed the fact that he was being contradicted in a moment . . .
>
> "No, Ernest, you don't," he said, "you say nothing of the kind, you say 'tum,' not 'come.' Now say 'come' after me, as I do."
>
> "Tum," said Ernest. . . .
>
> ". . . Now, Ernest, I will give you one more chance, and if you don't say 'come,' I shall know that you are self-willed and naughty."
>
> . . . The child saw well what was coming, was frightened, and, of course, said 'tum' once more.
>
> "Very well, Ernest," said his father, catching him angrily by the shoulder. "I have done my best to save you, but if you will have it so, you will," and he lugged the little wretch, crying by anticipation, out of the room.

When some echoic behavior has been acquired, the acquisition of a new unit is simplified. Exploratory behavior may be narrowed. In acquiring an echoic repertoire the skillful speaker increases the chances that he will correctly echo new material by learning not to respond as he has already responded ineffectively, just as he learns not to look where he has already looked for his hat. Partially echoic responses will be made to a novel stimulus as the result of earlier similar contingencies. The process of approximation will proceed more rapidly if the speaker can approach a given sound step by step, hitting upon a partially corresponding pattern which is then repeated and distorted through explicitly acquired modulations. When such devices are lacking, even the experienced phoneticist has only to continue to respond until a successful echoic response appears.

The process of "finding" a sound is pointed up by the well-known fact that the young child emits many speech sounds which he will later find difficult to execute in learning a second language. This is not because enunciation has become more difficult, or because the speech apparatus has somehow been warped. The development of a large echoic repertoire appropriate to a given language makes it harder to echo verbal stimuli which do not belong in the language. When the occasion for a new echoic response arises (as when someone says *Say 'th'* to a French-speaking person), a standard but inaccurate form will appear—probably something like *z*, which is the closest echoic pattern in the mother tongue. The strength of such behavior in the adult speaker causes it to replace exploratory responses which approximate the stimulus pattern more closely and which would have been more readily available in the young child. The same principle is evident at another level in folk-etymologies. The American farmer who calls the Reine Claude plum *Rain Cloud* is echoing a large verbal pattern with the response from his repertoire which most closely approximates it. If such a response is available, it takes precedence over a new form composed of smaller echoic units —a form incidentally which is likely to have less reinforcing effects upon the speaker himself.

The Smallest Echoic Operant

What is the smallest unit of verbal behavior? The smallest acoustic or geometric unit available in describing speech or writing as physical events is not at issue here. The question concerns the smallest response under the functional control of a single variable. Echoic behavior offers special advantages in approaching this question, because the formal correspondence between stimulus and response-product can be demonstrated at the level of "speech-sounds" or acoustic properties.

In a correctly echoed response, the formal correspondence is usually good. The initial consonant of the stimulus resembles the initial consonant in the sounds produced by the response, and so on. But this does not mean that there is necessarily a functional connection between each pair of such properties or features. The operant may have a larger pattern. The chemist will repeat *diaminodiphenylmethane* correctly and with ease, where an equally intelligent man with no experience in chemistry may need to try many times before producing a successful response. This does not mean that the chemist has any special ability to string together long series of separate sounds. His everyday experience has built up larger echoic units. These may be as large as *diamino* and *diphenylmethane,* or merely *di, amino, phenyl,* and *methane.* Perhaps the affixed *-yl* and *-ane* have some functional unity. The layman has none of these units available. Like the native speaker of French who first tries to echo the sound *th,* he will probably emit only roughly similar units from his established repertoire. *Diamino* might yield *dynamo,* for example. On the other hand, the chemist finds that his special repertoire is of little help in echoing complex patterns in other technical vocabularies.

The first echoic operants acquired by a child tend to be fairly large integral patterns, and they are of little help in permitting him to echo novel patterns. A unit repertoire at the level of separable "speech-sounds" develops later and often quite slowly. Small echoic responses may be reinforced by parents and others for the express purpose of building such a repertoire. The child is taught to repeat small sound-patterns such as *ä, sp,* and so on. Such a basic echoic repertoire may be acquired at the same time as other forms of verbal behavior or even larger echoic units. The child may emit responses as large as syllables, words, or even sentences as unitary echoic operants. For help in echoing a novel stimulus, however, he falls back upon the single-sound repertoire.

This minimal echoic repertoire is optimal for evoking a response in order to set up other kinds of stimulus control. Suppose we wish to teach a child to name the alligator at the zoo. As we shall see in Chapter 5, we want to do this by reinforcing the response *alligator* in the presence of the alligator. But we cannot wait until such a response appears spontaneously, and the method of progressive shaping may take too much time. If we can evoke the response as an assemblage of small echoic units never before arranged in this order, the behavior can be suitably reinforced, and the alligator as a stimulus will acquire some control over the response. Somewhat similar contingencies arise without deliberate educational arrangement in everyday discourse. We pick up a large part of our verbal repertoire by echoing the behavior of others under circumstances which eventually control the behavior non-echoically. The advantage gained possibly supplies another example of indirect reinforcement of echoic behavior persisting into adult life.

An educational program which emphasizes minimal correspondences between verbal stimulus and verbal response is not necessary in developing a basic echoic repertoire. Minimal echoic operants seem to become functional as a matter of course when larger correspondences have been set up. Having acquired a dozen complex echoic responses all of which begin with the sound *b,* the child may correctly echo a thirteenth pattern which begins with *b* to the extent of beginning the larger response with *b* also. When this happens, we must recognize the functional independence of an echoic operant as small as *b*. Even a fairly large repertoire of echoic operants does not mean, however, that a full set of units at the level of speech-sounds will develop. Intelligent people stumble in echoing unfamiliar words or names, even though they contain no new speech-sounds, and there are evidently great individual differences in the tendency to do so.

What is the size of the minimal unit reached in this process? When an echoic repertoire is established bit by bit, as in educational reinforcement, units of correspondence are specifically reinforced as such, but the final product of a repertoire of large operants, or even of small educational operants, is not clear. (It is not a question of the dimensions needed to represent speech for purposes of scientific recording, for these may never be functional in the behavioral process.) The speech-sound (or the linguist's "phoneme") is not necessarily the smallest unit. The skilled mimic has what we may call a "fine-grained" repertoire which permits him to echo novel sound-patterns accurately. It also permits him to imitate intonations, accents, and vocal mannerisms, as well as sounds which are not verbal at all, such as the noises produced by birds, animals, and machines.

The degree of accuracy insisted upon by a given reinforcing community is important. In general, the speaker does no more than is demanded of him. In a verbal community which does not insist on a precise correspondence, an echoic repertoire may remain slack and will be less successfully applied to novel patterns. Sometimes an echoic repertoire includes stable relations between stimuli and responses which do not exactly match—for example, the lisper may "match" *s* with *th* and continue to do so with the acquiescence of the reinforcing community.

The possibility of a minimal repertoire explains the apparent ease with which most speakers engage in echoic behavior. It might be said that the echoic stimulus "tells the speaker more explicitly what to say" than do the objects or properties of objects which are "named" in another type of verbal operant (Chapter 5). If we can *echo* the names of playing cards more rapidly and for a longer period of time without fatigue than we can *name* the cards themselves, this is presumably because of the advantages of the minimal echoic repertoire. The special effects of a minimal repertoire have no doubt encouraged belief in a faculty or process of imitation, in which the formal similarity of stimulus and response is thought to have some functional significance, but the advantage of echoic behavior can be explained in other ways.

Other types of verbal operants also give rise to minimal repertoires, but we shall find that nowhere else is it possible to reduce the functional correspondences between stimuli and responses to such small units or to so small a number of units. Echoic behavior is therefore exceptional in the extent to which novel occasions may give rise to accurate responses. It is also exceptional in the extent to which the reinforcement of such behavior contributes to the general strengthening of the basic repertoire, and hence to the strengthening of all echoic operants. An advantage similar to that of the echoic repertoire may be detected in onomatopoetic verbal behavior, as we shall see in Chapter 5.

The question of the *largest* echoic unit is not easily answered. We cannot echo an indefinitely protracted verbal stimulus, partly because the early portions become too remote in time, partly because different portions interfere with each other, and partly because other kinds of responses (especially the intraverbal responses discussed below) intervene. A clear-cut case is the repetition of a series of digits. The length of the verbal stimulus which can be successfully echoed varies with many conditions—such as motivation or fatigue—and is sharply reduced in some cases of aphasia.

Self-Echoic Behavior

Since a speaker usually hears himself and thus stimulates himself verbally, he can also echo himself. Such behavior is potentially self-reinforcing if it strengthens stimulation used in the control of one's own verbal behavior. It appears in pathological form in "palilalia"—a condition in which the individual first responds either by echoing the verbal behavior of someone else or for some other reason and continues by echoing himself. An early report [1] described a man who was accustomed to reading aloud the captions at a silent moving picture and who began to repeat them again and again. When his wife became annoyed and exclaimed "For God's sake, Bob, shut up!" he

[1] Critchley, MacDonald, *J. Neurol. and Psychopath.*, 8 (1927), 23.

replied, "I can't shut up, I can't shut up, I can't shut up . . .," eventually trailing off into an inaudible mumble. The phrase which continues to "run through one's head" (the French *ritournelle*) is possibly a normal manifestation of the same effect.

It is difficult to demonstrate a purely echoic relation if the variables responsible for the first instance of a response may continue to operate in producing the second. Repetition may be nothing more than evidence of excessive strength. Psychotic "verbal perseveration" or "verbigeration" showing a repetition of form may be self-echoic, or it may be merely the "unedited" effect of other types of variables. In analyzing the multiple causation of normal speech, however, it will be useful to appeal to the possibility of self-echoism. In all kinds of self-echoic behavior we have to consider the possibility that the verbal stimulus may be covert.

TEXTUAL BEHAVIOR

A familiar type of verbal stimulus which controls verbal behavior is a text. Like the echoic stimulus it is the product of earlier verbal behavior which is not at issue here. When a child learns to read, many verbal operants are set up in which specific responses come under the control of visual (or, as in Braille, tactual) stimuli. Because the stimuli are in one modality (visual or tactual) and the patterns produced by the response in another (auditory), the correspondence of form which makes possible the fine grain of the minimal repertoire of echoic behavior is lacking. The problem of a minimal repertoire remains, however. A text may be in the form of pictures (in so far as the response consists simply of emitting an appropriate vocal form for each picture), formalized pictographs, hieroglyphs, characters, or the letters or symbols of a phonetic alphabet (regardless of the accuracy or consistency with which the alphabet records vocal speech). The minimal textual repertoire will depend upon the nature of the text.

A speaker under the control of a text is, of course, a reader. His behavior in response to such verbal stimuli may show many interesting characteristics to be described in Chapters 5 and 6. We are concerned here only with his vocal behavior as it is controlled by the written or printed stimulus. Since the term "reading" usually refers to many processes at the same time, the narrower term "textual behavior" will be used here. In the textual operant, then, a vocal response is under the control of a nonauditory verbal stimulus.[2]

Textual behavior, like echoic behavior, is first usually reinforced for explicitly "educational" reasons. Interested persons supply generalized conditioned reinforcers for vocal responses which stand in certain required relations to the marks on a page. If a child responds *cat* in the presence of the marks *CAT* and not otherwise, he receives approval; if he responds *dog* in the presence of the marks *DOG* and not otherwise, he also receives approval, and so on. Why the family, the community, and educational agencies arrange such reinforcements is to be explained in terms of the ultimate advantages gained from having an additional literate member of the group. In an explicit formulation, however, actual reinforcing events must be specified.

Textual behavior receives noneducational reinforcement when a man is paid to read in a public performance, in assisting the blind, and so on. The collateral effects of reading already mentioned, and to be discussed in Chapters 5 and 6, provide automatic reinforcement. Indeed, textual behavior is so strongly reinforced that one is likely to find oneself reading not only letters, books, and newspapers, but unimportant labels on packages, subway advertisements, and billboards. Automatic consequences are used to motivate the beginning reader when a textbook is designed to be "interesting." Such reinforcement is not, however, contingent upon accuracy of response in the manner needed to shape skillful behavior.

A primitive but clear-cut demonstration of the modus operandi of automatic reinforcement is provided by the beginning reader who must hear himself pronounce a word—perhaps several times—before reacting to it with behavior which he has already acquired as a listener. In silent reading self-stimulation from textual behavior is reduced to such a scale that it can no longer be observed by others, but in responding to difficult new material (e.g., complex instructions) the textual behavior of even the expert reader may assume conspicuous proportions as he begins to strengthen self-stimulation by reading aloud. An audible feed-back is relatively more important in reading music. Many performers or singers never learn to read silently and may find it necessary in spotting a musical text to play a few bars on an instrument or at least to whistle or sing it aloud. Comparable

[2] Reading is not an ability or a capacity but a tendency. When we say that a person is "*able* to read," we mean that he *will* behave in certain ways under suitable circumstances involving a verbal nonauditory stimulus.

silent activities supply inadequate stimulation for an identifying response.

Textual behavior may be reinforced because it helps in the acquisition of other types of verbal operants. Just as echoic behavior enables the teacher to evoke a response in order to reinforce it with respect to other types of stimuli, so a text evokes verbal behavior under conditions which lead to other types of control. An illustrated dictionary, by evoking textual responses in the presence of pictures, builds a repertoire with which pictures, or the things pictured, are later named or described. A nonillustrated dictionary has a similar function in building the "intraverbal" repertoires discussed later in this chapter. (The importance of the verbal repertoires generated by texts—or of the place of textual responses in the acquisition of verbal behavior—is shown by the ubiquitous *text*book and the presence of bookstores and libraries in educational institutions.)

No innate tendency to read, on the analogy of a supposed tendency to imitate a stimulus echoically, has been seriously proposed. Nevertheless textual and echoic repertoires have similar dynamic properties. The verbal stimuli exert the same kind of control over both kinds of responses, and the reinforcing contingencies which establish the two sorts of behavior are similar. A text, like a bit of heard speech, is simply the occasion upon which a particular response is reinforced by a verbal community. Two important differences, however, follow from the fact that the product of a textual response is not similar to the stimulus.

The size of the smallest functional unit of textual behavior has long been a practical question in education. Is it best to teach a child to read by single letters or sounds, or by syllables, words, or larger units? Regardless of how he is taught, the skillful reader eventually possesses textual operants of many different sizes. He may read a phrase of several words as a single unit, or he may read a word sound by sound. A basic repertoire at approximately the level of the single letter or speech sound may develop slowly when only larger units are reinforced, but as in echoic behavior it nevertheless appears without special guidance. There is a limit, however, to the process. If the text is phonetic, the development of a minimal repertoire comes to a forced stop at the phonetic level. The small-grained repertoire of mimicry approached in echoic behavior depends upon a similarity of dimensions of stimulus and response which is lacking by definition in textual behavior. If a text is not phonetic, no such limit is imposed.

The distinction is illustrated by the singer who sings by ear and reads music at sight. An echoic repertoire is developed by every skillful singer; any melodic pattern lying within his pitch range may be accurately duplicated, and the grain of the minimal repertoire with which this is done may become smaller and smaller almost without limit. Eventually the dimensions of the stimulus consist of a continuous range of frequencies to which the dimensions of the response correspond more or less precisely. In sight-reading from a printed text, however, the dimensional systems are different. The response continues to be representable as a point on a continuous range of frequencies, but the text now consists of a geometric arrangement of discrete points. The good sight-reader with absolute pitch may satisfy very strict reinforcing contingencies; a given note on a staff is the occasion upon which a tone of a given pitch is reinforced. But there is no reason why such a text need be punctate; quarter tones have been employed and there is theoretically no reason why finer subdivisions are not feasible. The points of the scale then fuse into a line, any position on which corresponds to a position on the pitch-continuum of the response (compare the notation for "*glissando*"). This is still not echoic behavior, because the stimulus is visual and the response auditory, but the grain of such a repertoire could be as fine as that of the echoic case in which the singer reproduces a heard tone. Since this condition prevails only for a text capable of being represented in one or at most a very few dimensions, it is of little importance in the analysis of verbal behavior in general.

A second difference between textual and echoic behavior also follows from the difference in formal similarity between stimulus and response-product. In echoic behavior, the correspondence upon which reinforcement is based may serve as an automatic conditioned reinforcer. The speaker who is also an accomplished listener "knows when he has correctly echoed a response" and is reinforced thereby. Such reinforcement brings the form of the response closer and closer to the form of the stimulus, the limit being the most precise correspondence possible either with respect to the vocal capacity of the speaker or his capacity to judge similarity. (Any interference with either the echoic stimulus or the stimulation generated by the echoic response may mean a defective topography—as seen in the verbal behavior of the deaf-mute.) The automatic reinforcement of reading an "interesting" text, however, has merely the effect of increasing the probability of occurrence of such behavior; it does not differentially reinforce correct forms at the phonetic level.

Some self-correction is possible in larger samples of textual behavior. One may respond first with a garbled syllable, word, or phrase and then change to a correct form which "sounds right" or "makes sense." This depends upon the prior conditioning of the response of the listener, and a response usually "sounds right" or "makes sense" only if it is of substantial size. A comparison of stimulus and response-product cannot shape the behavior of the reader below the level of, perhaps, the syllable rather than the speech sound of echoic behavior. Mispronunciation, even above the level of the syllable, is a familiar characteristic of textual behavior, and for this reason it is often easy to spot a repertoire of verbal behavior which is basically, or at least originally, textual.

Self-Textual Behavior

Reading a text which one has written oneself is so common that its importance may be missed. We frequently create a text ("make a note") to control our own behavior at a later date. For example, we remind ourselves to *do* something or help ourselves to *say* something, as in lecturing or recalling a passage we have read. There is a special advantage, as we shall see in Part V, in going over notes in "thinking about a problem" or in "clarifying one's thoughts." The relatively permanent nature of a text, as compared with the echoic stimulus, makes self-textual behavior ordinarily more important than self-echoic, and the former demonstrates in a more obvious fashion the occasional advantages of the latter mentioned in the preceding chapter.

TRANSCRIPTION

The only verbal behavior so far considered has been vocal. The speaker creates an auditory pattern which is reinforced when it affects the listener as an auditory stimulus. A response which creates a visual stimulus having a similar effect is also verbal according to our definition. Since verbal behavior may consist of writing rather than speaking, other correspondences between the dimensions of stimulus and response need to be considered.

Writing, unlike speaking, requires support from the external environment. It occurs only in a "medium." We must deal separately with at least three stages: (1) obtaining the necessary instruments or materials, (2) making marks of differentiated form, and (3) transmitting these marks to the reader. Stage 2 is most important in the present analysis, but if Stage 1 cannot occur because, for example, materials are not at hand or responses at that stage are too weak, no response will be emitted at Stage 2 in spite of possibly great strength. Written behavior is an advantageous form to consider in discussing composition and editing. In vocal behavior there is sometimes a distinction between the mere emission of a response and emission in such a manner that it affects a listener (Chapter 15) but this is much less obvious than the distinction between Stages 2 and 3 above.

When both stimulus and response are written, they may be in similar dimensional systems, and all the characteristics of echoic behavior follow, except that they now are expressed in visual rather than auditory terms. The automatic shaping of response resulting from a comparison with a stimulus of similar dimensions was the goal of the copybook as a device for teaching handwriting. The minimal repertoire may be fine-grained; just as echoic behavior approaches mimicry, so what we may call copying approaches drawing. Indeed, copying a manuscript in an unfamiliar alphabet is identical with copying a set of pictures. Drawing, like vocal mimicry, requires an extraordinarily complex repertoire. It is as difficult to draw well as to mimic well, and there are great individual differences in the ability to do so.

Copying a text in a *familiar* alphabet differs from drawing in the size of the "echoic" unit. The skilled copyist possesses a small number of standard responses (the ways in which he produces the letters of the alphabet) which are under the control of a series of stimuli (the letters in the text). Ultimate reinforcement depends upon a correspondence between response unit and stimulus unit, but, just as echoic behavior may resemble the pattern echoed very loosely (differing in pitch, speed, intonation, and other properties), so the repertoire with which one copies a text may produce visual forms differing within fairly wide limits from the visual stimulus. In copying from print to script, or from upper to lower case, geometrical similarities between stimulus and response may be trivial or even lacking. There is then no self-corrective effect: such kinds of writing from copy cannot approach the unit repertoire of drawing.

A written response may also be controlled by a vocal stimulus, as in taking dictation. The commoner response units of the English alphabet permit a longhand transcription. The minimal repertoire of the amanuensis or stenographer shows a highly efficient correspondence between the visual properties of the pattern produced by the response and the auditory properties of the stimulus. The unit of correspondence may be fairly large, as in the word-sign or as small as, say, a characteristic which represents the presence or absence of voicing. These correspondences are wholly conventional, and no claim has been made for an innate mechanism similar to imitation, even though the behavior of the skilled stenographer may become as "natural" as the echoic behavior of the skilled mimic.

Transcription—either in the copying of written material or in taking dictation—receives many special educational and economic reinforcements and continues to be sustained by other consequences in everyday life. We see such repertoires at work whenever people transcribe verbal behavior for any purpose whatsoever. The relations thus established are effective, though not so obvious, when a response of transcription intrudes upon other written behavior. For example, in writing a letter when someone is talking, we may transcribe an overheard word even though it has no relation to the variables responsible for the rest of the letter. Similarly, in writing while reading, we may copy a word to produce a similar distortion of the behavior in progress (see Chapter 11).

Other forms of verbal behavior (for example, gesturing) may show correspondences between response and stimulus which raise similar problems of the minimal unit repertoire.

INTRAVERBAL BEHAVIOR

In echoic behavior and in writing from copy there is a formal correspondence between stimulus and response-product. In textual behavior and in taking dictation there is a point-to-point correspondence between different dimensional systems. But some verbal responses show no point-to-point correspondence with the verbal stimuli which evoke them. Such is the case when the response *four* is made to the verbal stimulus *two plus two,* or *to the flag* to *I pledge allegiance,* or *Paris* to *the capital of France,* or *ten sixty-six* to *William the Conqueror.* We may call behavior controlled by such stimuli *intraverbal.* Since formal correspondences are not at issue, we may consider both vocal and written stimuli and vocal and written responses in all four combinations at the same time.

Many intraverbal responses are relatively trivial. Social formulae often show this sort of control, for example. *How are you?* may be merely a stimulus for *Fine, thank you* where the response is purely intraverbal. The response *please* is often little more than an intraverbal appendage to a mand. "Small talk" is largely intraverbal, and serious conversation is not always clearly anything else. More important examples are found in the determination of grammatical and syntactical sequences (Chapter 13). *Why?* is often the stimulus for a response beginning *Because. . . ,* no matter what else may follow. When a long poem is recited, we can often account for the greater part of it only by supposing that one part controls another in the intraverbal manner. If we interrupt the speaker, the control may be lost; but a running start will restore it by recreating the proper verbal stimulus. The alphabet is acquired as a series of intraverbal responses, as are also counting, adding, multiplying, and reproducing mathematical tables in general. Most of the "facts" of history are acquired and retained as intraverbal responses. So are many of the facts of science, though responses are here also frequently under another kind of control to be discussed in the following chapter. A question is frequently the stimulus for an extended answer which has no other important controlling variable. The completion items on an objective examination stimulate intraverbal responses in much the same fashion. Many apparent metaphors and literary allusions often have only an intraverbal origin. In such expressions as *He was fit as a fiddle* or *He was pleased as Punch,* we need not look for the process involved in true metaphor (Chapter 5) but may seek an explanation for the responses *fiddle* and *Punch* in the intraverbal history of the speaker. Fowler's "Irrelevant Allusions" [3] may be explained in the same way. In the response *The moral, as Alice would say . . . ,* the stimulus word *moral* invokes the intraverbal response *as Alice would say.* (The fact that a literary allusion may supply color or prestige is related to another variable to be considered in Chapter 6.)

Chaining

Any one link in a chain of intraverbal responses is not under the exclusive control of the preceding link. We see this when a chain (such as saying the alphabet, giving the value of *e* to twenty places, or reciting a poem) has been interrupted and cannot be reinstated by the last emitted link. A running start picks up more remote controlling stimuli and may be effective. On the other hand

[3] Fowler, H. W., *Modern English Usage* (London, 1930).

"haplological" errors show the occasional power of a single link. These occur when two links are identical; the speaker reaches the first and continues with the responses which follow the second. (Haplography—a similar sort of mistake in copying a text—is, as we should expect, much commoner than the intraverbal sort. The complex behavior of the copyist—looking from original text to copy, and back again for "the same word"—is relatively unaffected by more remote stimuli.)

Many important characteristics of chained verbal responses, or of intraverbals in general, are clarified by a comparison of musical behavior. In playing from memory, the haplological anticipatory jump to a concluding phrase, the reverse haplology of being unable to find the concluding phrase because an earlier linkage keeps recurring, and the "running start" frequently needed to begin playing *in medias res* are all obvious parallels. Music also provides evidence of the importance of self-stimulation in "intraverbal" chains. The singer who cannot produce notes at the proper pitch may "loose the melody" in either sight-reading or singing by ear or from notes.

Common examples of intraverbal chaining are described by the term "literary borrowing." All verbal behavior is, of course, borrowed in the sense of being acquired from other people. Much of it begins as echoic or textual behavior, but it does not continue as such when the echoic or textual stimulus is no longer present. A "borrowed" collocation of words in a literary passage is usually traced to intraverbal connections acquired at the time of the original contact with the source. Proof of borrowing is a matter of demonstrating that parallel passages cannot be plausibly explained in any other way. Intraverbal sequences are deliberately acquired because of their usefulness to the writer in following R. L. Stevenson's principle of the "sedulous ape" or in encouraging the multiple literary sources of Chapter 9.

"Word Association"

One effect of this extensive conditioning of intraverbal operants is the train of responses generated in "free association"—or, as we say in the case of a train very different from our own, a "flight of ideas." One verbal response supplies the stimulus for another in a long series. The net effect is revealed in the classical word-association experiment. Here the subject is simply asked to respond verbally to a verbal stimulus, or to report aloud any responses he may "think of"—that is, find himself making silently. Echoic and textual responses are commonly produced but are either prevented by instruction or excluded from the results. Such an experiment, repeated on many subjects or on one subject many times, produces a fair sample of the responses under the control of a standard stimulus in a given verbal community. The diagnostic use of individual responses will be considered in Chapter 10. We are interested here in the intraverbal relation itself.

The reinforcements which establish intraverbal operants are often quite obvious and specific. The contingencies are the same as in echoic and textual behavior: a verbal stimulus is the occasion upon which a particular verbal response characteristically receives some sort of generalized reinforcement. In classroom recitation, the right answer is the response which is reinforced upon the verbal occasion created by the question. It is therefore more likely to be emitted when the question is asked again. In reciting a poem or in giving a long account of an historical episode, each segment (we need not specify the beginning and end exactly) is the occasion upon which a particular succeeding segment is reinforced as correct.

The intraverbal relations in any adult repertoire are the result of hundreds of thousands of reinforcements under a great variety of inconsistent and often conflicting contingencies. Many different responses are brought under the control of a given stimulus word, and many different stimulus words are placed in control of a single response. For example, educational reinforcement sets up many different intraverbal operants involving the cardinal numbers. *Four* is part of the occasion for *five* in learning to count, for *six* in learning to count by twos, for *one* in learning the value of π, and so on. On the other hand, many different verbal stimuli come to control the response *four*, e.g., *one, two, three*. . . or *two times two make*. . . . Many different connections between verbal responses and verbal stimuli are established when different passages are memorized and different "facts" acquired. The word-association experiment shows the results. Occasionally one intraverbal operant may predominate, but in general the response which will be made to a verbal stimulus when no other condition is specified can be predicted only in a statistical sense from the observed frequencies in word-association tests.

It was once thought that the types of association in intraverbal responses represented types of thought processes. C. G. Jung, in his famous *Studies in Word Association*, used a complex system of classification from which "psychical relationships" were to be reconstructed. Nearly fifty subclasses were distinguished. If the verbal stimulus *sea* yielded *lake,* it was Subordination; if *cat* yielded *animal,* it was Supraordination; if *pain* yielded *tears,* it was Causal Dependence; and so on. But such a logical classification has little, if any, connection with the conditions of reinforcement responsible for intraverbal behavior. We may assume, on the contrary, that, aside from intraverbal sequences specifically acquired, a verbal stimulus will be an occasion for the reinforcement of a verbal response of different form when, for any reason, the two forms frequently occur together. A common reason is that the nonverbal circumstances under which they are emitted occur together.

We may speak of the tendency to occur together as "contiguous usage." In the usual word-association experiment, the clang associations are, as we have seen, either echoic, textual, or transcriptive operants. The remaining intraverbal operants appear to be explained by contiguous usage. There are times when it is well to have certain operants in readiness. We appealed to this principle in pointing to possible reinforcements for echoing the speech of others in a conversation. Contiguous usage describes another case: when talking about *lakes,* it is advantageous to have the form *sea* available. In accounting for a specific intraverbal operant it is necessary to substitute an actual reinforcing event for an "advantage." In general, however, it is enough to show that the form *sea* is likely to occur in the context of *lake; animal* in the context of *cat; tears* in the context of *pain;* and so on. If logical or causal connections have any relevance, it is in describing the conditions which produce these contextual properties of the physical world. Certain exceptions, in which frequency of response does not follow frequent contiguous usage, may be traced to specific reinforcements, especially where responses have a limited currency or where the history of the speaker is unusual.

The responses given to a list of stimulus words naturally depend on the verbal history of the speaker. Groups of speakers may show group differences. It is not surprising that male and female college students tend to give different responses to such a stimulus word as *ring,*[4] while medical students differ from students of law in their responses to such a stimulus word as *administer.*[5]

The nature of the stimulus control in intraverbal behavior is

[4] Goodenough, F. L. *Science, 104* (1946), 451-456.
[5] Foley, J. P., Jr., and Macmillan, Z. L., *J. Exp. Psychol., 33* (1943), 299-309.

shown by responses to verbal stimuli containing more than one word. The stimulus *red* in the usual word-association experiment may yield *green, blue, color,* or any one of many other responses, for there are many different circumstances under which it appears as part of the occasion for the reinforcement of such responses. Similarly, the stimulus word *white* will yield *black, snow,* and so on. But in an American verbal community, in the absence of other specific determiners, the compound verbal stimulus *red, white...* will yield *blue* in preference to any other. The compound stimulus is a much more specific occasion than either part taken separately, and it is an occasion upon which the response *blue* is characteristically made and reinforced. In the same way, such an expression as *That has nothing to do with the...* will produce *case,* or one or two other forms to the exclusion of all others,[6] although these words, taken separately, would produce a great variety of responses. The more complex the stimulus pattern, the more specific the verbal occasion, and the stronger the control exerted over a single response.

Just as one may echo oneself or read the verbal stimuli which one has produced, so one may respond intraverbally to self-generated stimuli, as many of the examples cited above suggest. The behavior which generates the stimuli may be covert.

The Intraverbal Unit

The number of intraverbal relations in the repertoire of an adult speaker probably greatly exceeds the number of different forms of response in that repertoire, since a given form may have many functional connections. The total is further increased by the fact that units of different size overlap. Some intraverbal operants are composed of, or share parts with, others. Such an operant may be as small as a single speech-sound, as in reciting the alphabet or using certain grammatical tags, or it may be composed of many words, as in reciting a poem or "borrowing" an expression. When we come to consider the multiple causation of verbal behavior, we shall find it possible and often profitable to appeal to an intraverbal unit consisting simply of a stress pattern. (Only through intraverbal behavior of this sort can one presumably learn to speak in iambic pentameter or to compose limericks with ease.)

Except for specific intraverbal linkages in limited areas of knowledge, there is no minimal repertoire similar to that which approaches

[6] Carroll, J. B. *Psychometrika, 6* (1941), 297-307.

mimicry in echoic behavior or permits the skilled reader to pronounce a new word in a text. A novel verbal stimulus may evoke intraverbal responses because of resemblances to other stimuli, but there is no reason why such behavior should be consistent or show any functional unity of small parts. In studying intraverbal responses to novel stimuli, Thorndike [7] did not find any consistent tendencies to respond in a standard fashion. This was true even for stimuli taken from an international language which used such tendencies for mnemonic purposes.

Translation

A special case of intraverbal behavior is translation. The modus operandi is usually conspicuous in the beginning language student, who first acquires a series of intraverbal operants in which the stimuli are in one language and the responses in another. The "languages" many be of any of the sorts considered in Chapter 7. A parent may translate the "little" language of his children to a stranger, as the scientist translates professional jargon to the layman. Simple paraphrase is in this sense translation. As in intraverbal behavior in general, either stimulus or response may be written or spoken without altering the basic process.

In the commonest case, the stimuli are in the new language, the responses in the old. Faced with a passage in the new language, the translator emits (let us say aloud) appropriate intraverbal responses. If these fall into something like a familiar pattern, he may then react in any or all of the ways appropriate to a listener (see particularly Chapters 5 and 6). Such self-stimulation is reminiscent of the early stages of reading. It provides for the self-correction of units somewhat above the level of the single speech-sound. Eventually the translator improves upon this crude procedure by developing more efficient intraverbal operants, mainly of larger patterns, and by acquiring normal listening or reading behavior under the control of the new language without the aid of translation.

When the translation is from the old to the new language, the translator may not react to his own behavior as a listener at all. He composes a sentence in the new language only as a series of intraverbal responses. It may or may not be effective in an appropriate verbal community. If the speaker is not yet a listener in that community, there will be no automatic correction of his behavior.

[7] Thorndike, E. L., *Studies in the Psychology of Languages* (New York, 1938).

When two languages are independently acquired, there may be few intraverbal connections between them. A skillful bilinguist may not, as a matter of fact, be able to give a ready translation when this is *first* required of him. His skill in this respect improves in such a way as to suggest that he is acquiring a set of intraverbal operants. If he becomes a language teacher, for example, he may acquire a whole battery of intraverbal stereotypes which have no useful place in his behavior as a bilinguist when he is not teaching.

The bilingual speaker may function as a sort of translator in other ways. By responding to a single set of circumstances in two languages, he provides the listener with a possible bridge from one to the other. It is more difficult to say what happens when such a person listens to a passage in one language and restates it in another. The case is often offered as showing the need for some such concept as "idea" or "proposition," since something common to two or more languages appears to account for their interchangeability. But to say that a translator gets the meaning from one response and puts it into another is not to *explain* his behavior. To say that he emits behavior in one language which is controlled by the variables which he infers to have been responsible for a response in another language is also elliptical. He may react to a response in one language in some of the ways characteristic of a listener and then describe his own reaction in the other language, but this should not yield a strict translation. His response as a listener may, however, operate to confirm a translation achieved in other ways. He tries out a translation, comparing the effects of the two versions upon himself and changing the translation until the effects are roughly the same. But this does not account for the behavior which he thus compares.

DYNAMIC PROPERTIES OF VERBAL BEHAVIOR UNDER THE CONTROL OF VERBAL STIMULI

When the verbal stimuli in control of echoic, textual, and intraverbal behavior are reasonably clear and strong and the repertoires well established, there is not likely to be much variation in speed or energy of response. Reading aloud is likely to be monotonous just because one part of a text does not differ greatly from another in the extent of its control. This is also true of echoic stimuli when the speaker is enjoined to "repeat after me." The intraverbal recitation of a poem is often a monotonous affair, where the only variation comes from differences in the extent to which the behavior has been conditioned.

This dynamic uniformity follows, not only from the uniformity of stimuli, but from the use of a generalized reinforcer, which works to rule out variations in motivational variables. In many cases uniformity is specifically reinforced. In transcription, for example, a steady level of strength may be most efficient in producing usable copy, just as mere vocal communication may profit from the same properties. Under other circumstances, however, vocal behavior gains if it shows some dynamic variety. This is especially true when it is important to the listener that the behavior reflect the circumstances under which it was originally emitted—that is, when the variables affecting the original writer are permitted to have some effect upon the behavior of the vocal reader and hence upon the ultimate listener. This would be commoner if a text represented the dynamic properties of speech more accurately. In repeating what one has just heard as echoic behavior the dynamic variety of the stimulus may be communicated, particularly if the echoic repertoire approaches that of mimicry, and intraverbal behavior in response to vocal stimuli may have similar dynamic characteristics. But when the stimulus is a text —whether the behavior is textual or intraverbal—the dynamic properties of the original speech are lost—except, for example, when a word is underlined for emphasis. Under such circumstances the good reader or the trained reciter or actor will, as we noted in Chapter 2, introduce a variety of speeds, intonations, and energy levels which are not controlled by the intraverbal stimulus but are added to the behavior because of collateral reinforcing contingencies of the sort to be discussed in Chapter 6. Although the behavior may still be merely textual or intraverbal, it has some of the variety of verbal operants under other types of controlling relations. As Evelina said of Garrick "...I could scarcely believe he had studied a written part, for every word seemed to be uttered from the impulse of the moment." [8]

THE "MEANING" OF VERBAL RESPONSES MADE TO VERBAL STIMULI

Echoic, textual, and intraverbal behavior are sometimes dismissed as "spurious language." They are not important to the theorist of

[8] Burney, Fanny, *Evelina* (Everyman Edition), p. 22.

meaning because the correspondences between responses and controlling variables do not raise important problems of reference. The only relevant semantic relation appears to be between the response and the *source* of the verbal stimulus in the behavior of the speaker who originally produced it, and this is only distantly related to the behavior of the current speaker. We shall return to the problem of reference again in the next chapter.

In accounting for verbal behavior as a whole, effective functional relations must not be overlooked because of a preoccupation with meaning. Echoic and intraverbal operants and, in literate people, textual operants as well are usually an important part of verbal behavior. The contribution of such responses is particularly important when we come to examine how variables combine in sustained speech, and how the effect of the speaker's own behavior leads him to compose and edit what he says and to manipulate it in verbal thinking.

Chapter 5

The Tact

In all verbal behavior under stimulus control there are three important events to be taken into account: a stimulus, a response, and a reinforcement. These are contingent upon each other, as we have seen, in the following way: the stimulus, acting prior to the emission of the response, sets the occasion upon which the response is likely to be reinforced. Under this contingency, through a process of operant discrimination, the stimulus becomes the occasion upon which the response is likely to be emitted.

In echoic, textual, and intraverbal operants the prior stimulus is verbal. There are two important types of controlling stimuli which are usually nonverbal. One of these has already been mentioned: an *audience* characteristically controls a large group of responses through a process to be discussed in detail in Chapter 7. The other is nothing less than the whole of the physical environment—the world of things and events which a speaker is said to "talk about." Verbal behavior under the control of such stimuli is so important that it is often dealt with exclusively in the study of language and in theories of meaning.

The three-term contingency in this type of operant is exemplified when, in the presence of a doll, a child frequently achieves some sort of generalized reinforcement by saying *doll;* or when a teleost fish, or picture thereof, is the occasion upon which the student of zoology is reinforced when he says *teleost fish.* There is no suitable term for this type of operant. "Sign," "symbol," and more technical terms from logic and semantics commit us to special schemes of reference and stress the verbal response itself rather than the controlling relationship. The invented term "tact" will be used here. The term carries a mnemonic suggestion of behavior which "makes contact with" the physical world. A tact may be defined as a verbal operant in which a response of given form is evoked (or at least strengthened) by a particular object or event or property of an object or event. We account for the strength by showing that in the presence of the object or event a response of that form is characteristically reinforced in a given verbal community.

It may be tempting to say that in a tact the response "refers to," "mentions," "announces," "talks about," "names," "denotes," or "describes" its stimulus. But the essential relation between response and controlling stimulus is precisely the same as in echoic, textual, and intraverbal behavior. We are not likely to say that the intraverbal stimulus is "referred to" by all the responses it evokes, or that an echoic or textual response "mentions" or "describes" its controlling variable. The only useful functional relation is expressed in the statement that the presence of a given stimulus raises the probability of occurrence of a given form of response. This is also the essence of the tact.

As a matter of fact, we should not apply any of the traditional terms to some instances of the present type. One may be conditioned to say *How d'you do?* under appropriate circumstances. As a question, this resembles a mand, but it is often nothing more than a unitary response characteristically reinforced upon an appropriate occasion. *Thank you* is often nothing more than a response appropriate to a class of occasions on which one has been given something. In a special case a response which is characteristically emitted by someone else begins as an echoic response but is eventually controlled by a non-verbal stimulus. In stepping into an elevator, for example, we may have some tendency to emit the appropriate *Going up!* even though we have never been employed as an operator. In the proper mood we may emit the response, as we say, "whimsically." We are not announcing the presence of, or indicating a condition of, the elevator; we are simply emitting behavior commonly heard and repeated under the circumstances. The same formula explains a familiar verbal slip in which one greets another person with one's own name. The sources of this are obvious in the case of the young speaker; a child of two regularly greeted his father with *Hi, Bobby!* which was his father's characteristic way of greeting him.

It serves no useful purpose, and may be misleading, to call a tact an "announcement," "declaration," or "proposition," or to say that it "states," "asserts," or "denotes" something, or that it "makes known" or "communicates" a condition of the stimulus. If these terms have any scientific meaning at all, beyond a paraphrase of the present relation, they refer to certain additional processes to be considered in Part IV. We shall see, for example, that the tact is more likely to be "asserted" than any other type of operant but, taken by itself, is not for that reason an assertion.

The Controlling Relation

The tact emerges as the most important of verbal operants because of the unique control exerted by the prior stimulus. This control is established by the reinforcing community for reasons to be noted in a moment. It contrasts sharply with the controlling relations in the mand, where the most efficient results are obtained by breaking down any connection with prior stimuli, thus leaving deprivation or aversive stimulation in control of the response. Either explicitly or as the effect of common contingencies, a response is reinforced in a single way under many different stimulating circumstances. The response then comes to "specify" its characteristic consequences regardless of the condition under which it occurs. In the tact, however, (as well as in echoic, textual, and intraverbal behavior) we weaken the relation to any specific deprivation or aversive stimulation and set up a unique relation to a discriminative stimulus. We do this by reinforcing the response as consistently as possible in the presence of one stimulus with many different reinforcers or with a generalized reinforcer. The resulting control is through the stimulus. A given response "specifies" a given stimulus property. This is the "reference" of semantic theory. Roughly speaking, the mand permits the listener to infer something about the condition of the speaker regardless of external circumstances, while the tact permits him to infer something about the circumstances regardless of the condition of the speaker. These "inferences" need to be more sharply represented by analyzing the reinforcing practices of the community which maintain mands and tacts in strength.

A tact which is established with a completely generalized reinforcement might be called "pure" or "objective." Whether the response is emitted at all may depend upon other variables; but whenever it is emitted, its form is determined solely by a specific feature of the stimulating environment. A truly generalized reinforcement is, however, rare (see in particular Chapter 6), and pure objectivity in this sense is probably never achieved. Verbal behavior in which the reinforcement is thoroughly generalized, and the control of which therefore rests almost exclusively with the environment, is developed by the methods of science. The reinforcing practices of the scientific community thoroughly suppress the special interests of the speaker. This is not necessarily a sign of superior ethics in scientists; it is merely an evolved practice which has proved to be particularly valuable. It is responsible for much of the power of the scientific method (Chapter 18).

Reinforcement of the Tact

A child is taught the names of objects, colors, and so on when some generalized reinforcement (for example, the approval carried by the verbal stimulus *Right!*) is made contingent upon a response which bears an appropriate relation to a current stimulus. A typical series of events is suggested in the paradigm in Figure 5. Here we assume that

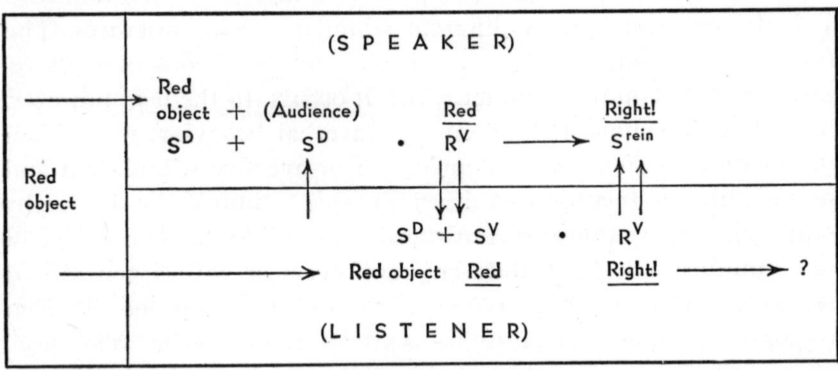

Figure 5

a red object stimulates both speaker and listener. The object together with the presence of the listener as an audience, and possibly an appropriate mand for verbal action emitted by the listener (for example, *What color is that?*) is the occasion upon which the verbal response *Red* on the part of the speaker receives the reinforcement *Right!* It does this because the response becomes a verbal stimulus which properly corresponds to the stimulation from the red object to provide the occasion upon which the listener says *Right!*

The ultimate reinforcement of the listener in Figure 5 requires an additional explanation. This is "educational" reinforcement; that is, it is reinforcement supplied primarily because it establishes and maintains a particular form of behavior in the speaker. The tact as a verbal operant is mainly useful to the listener, for reasons which we shall examine in a moment; but an adequate explanation of the paradigm in Figure 5 will require the listing of specific reinforcing events below the horizontal line. Some of these are supplied by the culture; for example, the praise a parent receives for a talented child supplies conditioned reinforcement for any behavior on the part of the parent which increases the verbal repertoire of the child. In educational institutions such reinforcements are particularly provided for, again by the verbal community, through economic reinforcement. The teacher is paid to reinforce the child appropriately.

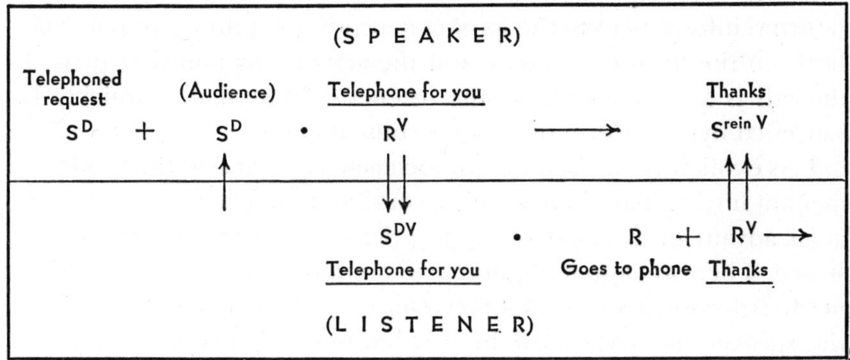

FIGURE 6

We come a little closer to the ultimate explanation of behavior in the form of the tact when we examine a case in which the stimulus which the tact specifies is not directly accessible to the listener. Under these circumstances the behavior of the speaker may be reinforcing to the listener by constituting the occasion for behavior which could otherwise not occur. In the paradigm of Figure 6 it is assumed that the speaker is in contact with a state of affairs not known to the listener; he has answered the phone and learned that the call is for the listener. The telephoned request plus the listener as an audience is a standard occasion upon which the speaker responds *Telephone for you*. This becomes an important verbal stimulus for the listener who then goes to the phone and is reinforced for doing so for extraneous reasons. He guarantees the strength of similar behavior on the part of the speaker in the future by emitting the verbal response *Thanks!* as an appropriate reinforcer.

In very general terms we may say that behavior in the form of the tact works for the benefit of the listener by extending his contact with the environment, and such behavior is set up in the verbal community for this reason. But a general statement does not specify the particular events which will account for any given instance. In educational reinforcement the contingencies between responses and appropriate stimuli are rather sharply maintained. The principal effect is in determining the form or topography of behavior (in "shaping up" responses) and in sharpening the stimulus control. When the speaker's behavior reinforces the listener for merely incidental reasons, the somewhat similar contingencies may be deficient. *Thanks!* is a less discriminating reinforcement than *Right!* The correspondence between the speaker's *Telephone for you* and the actual request voiced on the telephone cannot differ too widely because the listener's return reinforcement to the speaker depends upon the correspondence between the form of response and the actual telephoned request. If the call is for someone else, the listener's *Thanks!* may quickly be cancelled by some form of aversive consequence.

Less explicit reinforcements of the tact correspond to the reinforcement of intraverbal responses from contiguous usage. In general there is an advantage if responses appropriate to a current situation are strong. There are also many automatic reinforcements from the effect of the behavior upon the speaker himself. An environment to which the speaker has responded in this fashion may exert a more discriminative control over other behavior, verbal or nonverbal. For example, by correctly classifying an object the speaker may react more appropriately to it. The sources of ultimate reinforcement from this effect will be clear when we examine in detail the effect of verbal behavior upon the speaker himself.

The Listener's Response to a Tact

Theories of meaning usually consider the behaviors of both speaker and listener at the same time. The practice is encouraged by the notion of the "use of words," which appears to free the word from the behavior of speaker or listener so that it may stand in some relation of reference to an object. The listener's response to a tact is obviously influenced by the correspondence between form of response and controlling stimulus, but the place of this correspondence in the speaker's behavior has seldom been analyzed. The substitution of one stimulus for another in the conditioned reflex has suggested a biological basis for the notion of reference. Thus J. B. Watson argued that "words function in the matter of calling out responses exactly as did the objects for which the words serve as substitutes." [1] He cites Swift's story of a man who carried a bag of objects which he could

[1] Watson, J. B., *Behaviorism* (New York, 1924), p. 233.

display instead of speaking in words. "Soon the human has a verbal substitute within himself theoretically for every object in the world. Thereafter he carries the world around with him by means of this organization." But it is, of course, a rather useless world. He cannot eat *sandwich* or pull a nail with *claw hammer.* This is a superficial analysis which is much too close to the traditional notion of words "standing for" things.

The same objection may be urged against Bertrand Russell's interpretation of the behavior of the listener in his *Inquiry into Meaning and Truth:*

> Suppose you are with a man who suddenly says "fox" because he sees a fox, and suppose that, though you hear him, you do not see the fox. What actually happens to you as a result of your understanding the word "fox"? You look about you, but this you would have done if he had said "wolf" or "zebra." You may have an image of a fox. But what, from the observer's standpoint, shows your understanding of the word is that you behave (within limits) as you would have done if you had seen the fox. Generally, when you hear an object-word which you understand, your behavior is, up to a point, that which the object itself would have caused. This may occur without any "mental" intermediary, by the ordinary rules of conditioned reflexes, since the word has become associated with the object.[2]

But we do not behave toward the word "fox" as we behave toward foxes, except in a limited case. If we are afraid of foxes, the verbal stimulus *fox,* which we have heard in the presence of real foxes, will evoke an emotional reaction; if we are hunting, it may create the condition we call excitement or delight. Possibly the behavior of "seeing a fox" can be fitted into the same formula, as we shall see later. But the verbal stimulus *fox* does not, because of simple conditioning, lead to any practical behavior appropriate to foxes. It may, as Russell says, lead us to look around, as the stimulus *wolf* or *zebra* would have done, but we do not look around when we see a fox, we look at the fox. Only when the concepts of stimulus and response are used very loosely can the principle of conditioning serve as a biological prototype of symbolization.

The practical behavior of the listener with respect to the verbal stimulus produced by a tact follows the same three-term relation which has already been used in analyzing the behavior of the speaker. We may suppose that in the history of the particular listener described

[2] Russell, B., *Inquiry into Meaning and Truth* (New York, 1940), p. 82.

by Russell the stimulus *fox* has been an occasion upon which looking around has been followed by seeing a fox. We may also suppose that the listener has some current "interest in seeing foxes"—that behavior which depends upon a seen fox for its execution is strong, and that the stimulus supplied by a fox is therefore reinforcing. The heard stimulus *fox* is the occasion upon which turning and looking about is frequently followed by the reinforcement of seeing a fox. Technically, the behavior of turning and looking is a discriminated operant, rather than a conditioned reflex. The difference is important. The verbal stimulus *fox* is not a substitute for a fox but an occasion upon which certain responses have been, and probably will be, reinforced by seeing a fox. The behavior which is controlled by the fox itself—looking toward or riding after—cannot be evoked by the verbal stimulus, and there is therefore no possibility of a substitution of stimuli as an analog of a sign or symbol.

Consider another example. When a cook tacts a given state of affairs with the simple announcement *Dinner!*, she creates a verbal occasion upon which one may successfully sit down to the table. But the listener does not sit down to, or eat, the verbal stimulus. The kind of response which can be made to both the dinner and the verbal stimulus *Dinner!* is exemplified by the salivary response conditioned according to the Pavlovian formula. The practical behavior of the listener (the consequences of which are ultimately responsible for the development of the verbal response in the first place) must be formulated as a discriminated operant involving three terms, no two of which provide a parallel for the notion of a symbol.

The relative frequency with which the listener engages in effective action in responding to behavior in the form of the tact will depend upon the extent and accuracy of the stimulus control in the behavior of the speaker. Some of the factors which may interfere with a close correspondence between response and stimulus will be discussed in Chapter 6. Frequency of effective action accounts in turn for what we may call the listener's "belief"—the probability that he will take effective action with respect to a particular verbal stimulus. In general this will vary between speakers (to reflect the listener's judgment of the speaker's accuracy, honesty, and so on) and between responses (depending upon the plausibility of the response in connection with the rest of a given situation).

Whether a listener takes effective action will also depend upon whether the response has been a tact or is merely echoic, textual, or intraverbal. But we have seen that the type of verbal operant is not indicated by the form of a response alone. Under some circumstances behavior characteristically has the form of the tact, but there are many circumstances under which the particular type must be indicated by collateral responses if the listener is to act appropriately. We shall discuss responses which have this function in Part IV.

It was possible to classify mands in terms of the different reasons why the listener reinforces; in the same way we may account for the fact that a response in a tact differs from the same response in an echoic, textual, or intraverbal operant. The tact *chair* has an advantage over these other types because it appears to "say something" about the object which evokes the response. The tact appears to contribute more "information" than echoic, textual, or intraverbal behavior. It supplies a link between the behavior of the listener and a relevant state of affairs. But the linkage is merely longer when the speaker's behavior is controlled by the verbal behavior of someone else. All shades of difference between verbal operants reflect different sets of variables in the behavior of both speaker and listener. The component behavioral processes are the same wherever they occur.

The Stimulus Control of the Tact

All verbal behavior is controlled by prior stimulation arising from an audience, as we shall see in Chapter 7, but an audience when present reinforces verbal responses differentially depending upon the form of response or the occasion or both. Echoic and textual behavior are by no means always approved or otherwise reinforced. The speaker's behavior is therefore under the control of additional properties of the occasion. The listener may mark the occasion as propitious with such verbal stimuli as *What did he say?* or *What does that say?* These are mands for verbal action which indicate dispositions to reinforce echoic and textual behavior respectively. A given occasion also may or may not be propitious for behavior in the form of a tact. A given object does not remain the inevitable occasion for the reinforcement of an appropriate response, and the probability of response therefore comes to vary with the occasion. The listener may help by saying *What is that?* or by manding behavior in the form of a tact in other ways. Another property may be the novelty of the occasion. Familiar objects lose their control because the community eventually withholds reinforcement except under special conditions. Only objects which are unusual in some respect, or which occur in unusual surroundings, are important to the listener and hence provide the occasion for reinforcing the speaker. A pool table at the bottom of a swimming pool, a fire hydrant in the parlor, or a seal in the bedroom are more likely to evoke tacts than the same objects under commonplace conditions. Obviously what is novel for the speaker may not be so for the listener, so that the rule is not uniformly applicable.

Generalized reinforcement makes the tact relatively independent of the momentary condition of the speaker, and in this respect the tact resembles echoic, textual, and intraverbal behavior. There is a difference, however, in the stimulus control. Behavior which is "descriptive of the environment" is less likely to be dynamically "flat." The tact does not need to be dressed up to be "expressive." It is usually emitted with modulations of intensity and speed reflecting not only the presence or absence of stimuli controlling a specific form of response but other relevant conditions of both occasion and speaker. The "interpretation" of the skilled reader or actor gives to textual or intraverbal behavior the dynamic character of the tact. This character is due in part to certain special consequences, to be analyzed in Chapter 6, which oppose the leveling effect of a generalized reinforcer. More important, however, is the lack of the point-to-point correspondence between response and controlling stimulus seen in echoic and textual behavior.

All stimuli, verbal or otherwise, vary in intensity and clarity of pattern, and the control they exert is affected accordingly. Above a certain level, however, echoic and textual stimuli have fairly prescribed effects. If we undertake to get someone to say *violin,* for example, we may resort to a verbal stimulus plus a mand for echoic behavior: *Say 'Violin.'* The dimensional correspondences in echoic behavior determine the response with great precision. We could also use a textual stimulus with an appropriate mand, *Read this: VIOLIN,* where another sort of point-to-point correspondence would restrict the response almost as narrowly. The same order of specificity may be achieved by saying *Tell me what this is* and designating a violin, since the reinforcing contingencies are almost as specific as in echoic or textual behavior in spite of the fact that there is no point-to-point correspondence between the violin and the response *violin.* But this specificity does not hold for all possible stimuli as we shall discover in a further examination of stimulus control.

THE EXTENDED TACT

If a chair, acting as a stimulus, simply made the response *chair* probable, and if a cribbage board, acting as a stimulus, simply made the response *cribbage board* probable, we could deal with the "semantics" of verbal behavior merely by supplying an inventory of tacts. But a verbal repertoire is not like a passenger list on a ship or plane, in which one name corresponds to one person with no one omitted or named twice. Stimulus control is by no means so precise. If a response is reinforced upon a given occasion or class of occasions, any feature of that occasion or common to that class appears to gain some measure of control. A novel stimulus possessing one such feature may evoke a response. There are several ways in which a novel stimulus may resemble a stimulus previously present when a response was reinforced, and hence there are several types of what we may call "extended tacts."

Generic Extension

The property which makes a novel stimulus effective may be the property upon which reinforcements supplied by the community are contingent. This "generic extension" is illustrated when a speaker calls a new kind of chair a chair. The property responsible for the extension of the response from one instance to another is the property which determines the reinforcing practice of the community. Since it is also the important property for the listener upon a novel occasion, the extended response is acceptable and useful.

If the extended response is itself reinforced, as is likely, the stimulus is henceforth no longer wholly novel, and a second instance need not exemplify generic extension. The stimulus class has been enlarged, however, and further extension facilitated. In this manner we eventually come to respond *chair* to a very large number of objects. To discover the "essence" of chair, we should have to examine the actual contingencies of reinforcement in a given community. In generic extension, in contrast with other kinds of extension to be noted shortly, the defining properties tend to be practical. The stimulus control of *chair* is dictated ultimately by the use which the reinforcing community makes of chairs. For the same reason the controlling stimuli tend to be "objects." In characterizing a given stimulus we are most likely to refer to objects rather than to properties (to chair rather than green), not because objects are more readily or immediately or substantially "perceived," but because of the practical considerations involved in the growth of a stimulus class.

Responses to single properties may show generic extension, however. The extended response is accepted by the community and reinforced to establish a still larger stimulus class. When we say *The race is to the swift,* we designate the important practical property of those who win races. When an extension of this sort is reinforced by the verbal community, the tact becomes a standard operant under the control of a single property. No further process of extension is involved when the response is later emitted in the presence of a novel stimulus possessing this property. Since the control exerted by a novel stimulus is due to properties shared with the original stimulus, the response still exemplifies our fundamental three-term relation of stimulus, response, and reinforcement. Only a single property of the stimulus is specified, however, in accounting for later responses. This formulation is much simpler than traditional explanations of the same data, which appeal to various processes of generalization, equivalence, or analogical thinking, by virtue of which the speaker is able to *transfer* a response to a new stimulus. We do not need to say that the speaker "discovers a similarity and expresses it by transferring a response." The response simply occurs because of the similarity.

As we shall see later, generic extension takes place even though the speaker is not able to respond to the similarity in any other way—when he is not "aware," as we say, of the similarity.

Metaphorical Extension

A second type of extension takes place because of the control exercised by properties of the stimulus which, though present at reinforcement, do not enter into the contingency respected by the verbal community. This is the familiar process of metaphor. Traditional accounts, from Aristotle on, have generally assumed that, like generic extension, metaphor is a special achievement requiring a special faculty of analogical thinking. But the basic process is again adequately represented by our three-term relation; the only difference between metaphorical and generic extension is in the kind of property which gains control of the response.

An example of metaphorical extension is provided by the child who, upon drinking soda water for the first time, reported that it tasted "like my foot's asleep." The response *My foot's asleep* had previously been conditioned under circumstances which involved two conspicuous stimulus conditions—the partial immobility of the foot and a certain pinpoint stimulation. The property which the community used in reinforcing the response was the immobility, but the pinpoint stimulation was also important to the child. Similar stimulation, produced by tasting soda water, evoked the response. In this example, the pinpoint stimulation was private, a condition which raises several difficult problems in the analysis of behavior, as we shall see later, but which is useful here in permitting us to distinguish between the property which served the community as the basis of reinforcement and the property responsible for the extension of the response to a novel stimulus. The community could not have used pinpoint stimulation alone to set up such a response.

A metaphorical tact in which both properties are public may be analyzed in the same way. When for the first time a speaker calls someone a mouse, we account for the response by noting certain properties —smallness, timidity, silent movement, and so on—which are common to the kind of situation in which the response is characteristically reinforced and to the particular situation in which the response is now emitted. Since these are not the properties used by zoologists or by the lay community as the usual basis for reinforcing a response, we call the extension metaphorical. (In dealing with metaphor, we are here interested only in the appearance of the extended tact. In *Juliet is [like] the sun* we must explain the appearance of the response *sun* when no sun is actually present. We do so by noting that Juliet and the sun have common properties, at least in their effect upon the speaker. Sometimes the property responsible for the extension is also directly tacted, when the problem of identifying it is automatically solved. In *The child is bright as a dollar* we account for *dollar* by noting something possessed in common by dollars and the child in question. This something is precisely the stimulus property responsible for *bright*. The speaker has identified the property responsible for his extension of the response. In these expressions the responses *like* and *as* are of another sort, to be discussed in Chapter 12.)

When a metaphorical response is effective and duly reinforced, it ceases to be primarily a metaphor. A man is seldom called a mouse in an extended tact. *Mouse* has become a standard form in the reinforcing community in which small size, timidity, and other properties play an acknowledged role. The response *leg* evoked by the leg of a table probably only rarely represents metaphorical extension. We cannot be sure that a response is or is not an example of metaphorical extension, however, unless we know the history of the speaker. *Bright as a dollar* is probably more often than not a standard response, functioning as a single verbal unit. In ordinary usage it is little more than a polysyllabic synonym for *bright*. Its metaphorical origin may be of little current significance. We can claim metaphorical extension only if we know that *dollar* has been independently established as a response to a collocation of properties including brightness and that no intraverbal linkage has been established by earlier contiguous occurrences of *bright* and *dollar*. Such an expression as *dull as ditch water* is a more convincing example because *ditch water* is no longer commonly conditioned under circumstances in which the property of dullness could acquire control.

Sometimes a comparison of practices in different verbal communities will throw some light on the importance of metaphorical extension. Any response which is peculiar to a given community is presumably not the result of *current* metaphorical extension, even though it may appear to be a metaphor. The hole in a needle is not called *eye* in every language. Such a metaphorical extension may occur in any language, but it has not always done so often enough to be reinforced and established as a standard term. The frequent appearance of the response in English must therefore be attributed largely to current reinforcement of the whole expression in connection with needles, rather than to metaphorical extension.

Traces of a functional extension may survive in an otherwise dead metaphor. We shall see in Chapter 9 that a verbal response often acquires strength from more than one variable. It is possible that the idiomatic operant *eye of a needle* is stronger because the response *eye* is also reinforced when made to the somewhat similar geometric pattern of the animal eye. Because of this auxiliary source of strength, the response should be more readily acquired when a needle is first seen, should be more readily made upon any given occasion, and should in the long run hold its own against competing synonyms and hence survive in the language.

When an extended metaphor is reinforced and thus stabilized as a nonextended tact, it has the effect of isolating a new stimulus property or group of properties possibly not hitherto identified in the language. If we first acquire the response *leg* in connection with animals and extend it to the legs of tables and chairs on the basis of geometrical and functional similarities, the properties common to all these cases acquire control of the response and are subsequently respected by the community. The purely physiological and anatomical properties of the original stimulus become unimportant. When we have extended the response *wing* from parts of birds and insects to stage scenery, airplanes, buildings, and armies, the response is controlled by a subtle geometrical property common to all of these. The role which the process of metaphorical extension plays in isolating this property will be discussed in a later section of this chapter.

The distinction between generic and metaphorical extension is between a contingent and an adventitious property of the stimulus. Generic extension respects the original reinforcing practice, which persists unchanged in the verbal community even though the range of effective stimuli may be extended as more and more instances with new collateral properties are reinforced. The total number of stimulus properties respected by the language is not increased. In metaphor, however, new properties of nature are constantly being brought into control of verbal behavior. These become stabilized as standard tacts, subject in turn to further generic or metaphorical extension.

The metaphorical expressions of a given speaker or writer reflect the kinds of stimuli which most often control his behavior. This fact is commonly used in inferring conditions about the life of a writer either when such facts are not otherwise known or in order to establish authorship. Caroline Spurgeon's "imagery" [3] is metaphor according to the present definition. The argument may be restated as follows: when a situation simply evokes unextended tacts, the behavior tells us something about the situation but very little about the speaker, but metaphorical responses have been acquired *under other circumstances,* about which inferences may therefore be made.

The same principle may be applied to the metaphorical behavior of a verbal community. Consider, for example, all the metaphorical responses which have served in place of, or as a supplement to, the response *bright.* These extensions have presumably been emitted upon occasions marked by bright objects. But they must first have been conditioned to bright stimuli of other sorts. We ought, therefore, to be able to make a list of the commonest bright objects simply by going through the heading *bright* in a dictionary of metaphors. In one such dictionary [4] about fifty similes beginning *bright as* were found to continue with terms referring to heavenly phenomena,

[3] Spurgeon, C., *Shakespeare's Imagery* (New York, 1935).

[4] Wilstach's *Dictionary of Similes.* The figures are not to be taken as showing frequency of usage, since only one instance of each metaphor is ordinarily listed.

particularly the sun and stars. Sixteen others referred to light reflected from water in some form. Five referred to artificial sources, such as beacons or lamps, and seven to reflecting surfaces. Nine referred to objects of art. The flora and fauna of brightness included humming birds, diadems, glowworms, peacocks, lilies of the vale, poppies, and a new-blown rose.

As in the magical mand, many of these responses would never have been emitted except under the special encouragement of the literary community, which again provides sensitive examples of verbal behavior. There is another reason, however, why weak responses appear in metaphor. In analyzing a response extended metaphorically on the basis of brightness, we assume that the writer was faced with a bright object and was inclined to say something about it. We may also assume that he either could not say *bright,* possibly because of the kinds of variables to be discussed in Chapter 15, or had already said it without getting a fully satisfactory effect. Under such circumstances behavior has a sort of blanket strength in which weakly-determined responses are emitted and in which, therefore, the tenuous property responsible for metaphorical extension may be effective.

The form of metaphor called a simile provides another sort of pressure toward emitting weak responses. If, instead of saying *It was bright,* the poet begins *It was as bright . . . ,* he finds himself trapped. The *as . . .* may have been nothing more than a response to the intensity of the stimulus, similar to *very,* but it commits the poet to completing a figure of speech. The commitment is often fulfilled with very weak forms of response.

It is not only the poet who traps himself in this way. Instead of saying *He was very stupid,* a speaker may begin *He was as stupid as. . . .* If no common property of stimuli produces a metaphorical extension, the completion must be left to an intraverbal response—for example, a dead metaphor. If this fails, and if intraverbal responses are not available, or are taboo or otherwise objectionable, a stock form may be resorted to: *He was as stupid as you could well imagine,* or *. . . as I don't know what.*

An expression having the standard form of metaphor is sometimes clearly the completion of a metaphorical frame with intraverbal or other material. In *Bright as night is dark,* we must suppose that the present situation strengthened *bright* and that *bright* in turn strengthened *night* and *dark.* These are not metaphorical extensions but intraverbal responses which fill out a standard syntactical framework. (See Chapter 14.)

Sometimes a genuine extension seems to occur when no similarity between stimuli expressible in the terms of physical science can be demonstrated. There are several possible explanations. Two stimuli may have a common effect upon the responding organism, which mediates the extension of the response. In the example *Juliet is the sun,* it is possible that a physical similarity could not be plausibly established. Only to Romeo did Juliet glow with the light of dawn. The metaphorical extension might have been mediated by, say, an emotional response which both the sun and Juliet evoked in him. Similarly, when the color scarlet is described as like *the blare of a trumpet,* it is not necessary to search for common properties in visual and auditory stimuli. Both scarlet and a trumpet-blare have some common effect (perhaps as an unusual or alarming stimulus, or a stimulus commonly associated with pageantry) which may mediate the extension of the response. The common effect need not be itself metaphorical.

The properties of things or events which underlie metaphorical extension are a matter for empirical study. In what way are the links in a chain similar to the series of episodes in a "chain of events"? Where is a man when he is "on top of the world" or when he has "suffered a moral fall"? How do we "shut our eyes to the truth"? Answers to questions of this sort would reveal effective properties of the environment which are important for the study, not only of verbal behavior, but of human behavior in general. Metaphor, thus defined, is close to the Freudian "symbol." The properties or conditions by virtue of which something may serve as a symbol for something else are precisely the properties or conditions responsible for metaphorical extension.

Verbal behavior would be much less effective if metaphorical extension were not possible. Even when a nonextended tact is available, the metaphor may have an advantage. It may be more familiar, and it may affect the listener in other ways, particularly in arousing emotional responses. Although "one picture is worth more than ten thousand words" for certain purposes, it is not easy to picture certain properties of objects, and these are often just the properties dealt with successfully through metaphorical extension. It might be possible in certain kinds of symbols or in surrealistic art to suggest or show that Juliet is the sun to Romeo, but the trick is more easily turned in the verbal medium. The extended tact frees the properties of objects one from the other, and thus makes possible a recombination which is not restricted by the exigencies of the physical world.

Metaphorical extension is most useful when no other response is available.[5] In a novel situation to which no generic term can be extended, the only effective behavior may be metaphorical. The widespread use of metaphor in literature demonstrates this advantage. Literature is prescientific in the sense that it talks about things or events before science steps in—and is less inclined to talk about them afterward. It builds its vocabularies, not through explicit definition or generic extension, but through metaphor.

Nowhere is this better illustrated than in the field of psychology itself. Human behavior is an extremely difficult subject matter. The methods of science have come to be applied to it very late in the history of science, and the account is still far from complete. But it is the field in which literature is most competent, secure, and effective. A Dostoyevsky, a Jane Austen, a Stendahl, a Melville, a Tolstoy, a Proust, or a Joyce seem to show a grasp of human behavior which is beyond the methods of science. Insofar as literature simply describes human behavior in narrative form, it cannot be said to show understanding at all; but the writer often seems to "say something" about human behavior, to interpret and analyze it. A person is not only described as taking part in various episodes, he is *characterized.* This is a significant expression, for it suggests where metaphor, as a prescientific vocabulary, finds its place. Among other techniques in literature, personality is described and analyzed with certain typologies. In early literary forms, animals tend to be used as such a classificatory scheme. Professor Wells [6] has compiled a useful list of these theriotypes. A man may be an ass, an owl, a snake, or a rat. The comparable adjectives—stupid, wise, treacherous, or mean—lack the full effect of the metaphorical extension in the theriotype.

The familiar animals are, of course, rather quickly exhausted, but literature builds its own terms. The writer can deal effectively with,

[5] Unfortunately, metaphor is also often useful when there is nothing to say. John Horne Tooke pointed this out: ". . . though Similes appear with most beauty and propriety in works of imagination, they are frequently found most useful to the authors of philosophical treatises: and have often helped them out in many a dead lift, by giving them an appearance of saying something, when indeed they had nothing to say. For Similes are in truth the bladders upon which they float; and the Grammarian sinks at once if he attempts to swim without them." (*The Diversions of Purley,* p. 59, edition of 1857.)

[6] Wells, F. L., "Excursion among Spiders," *Sewanee Review,* 1937, *V,* 75-90.

as Thomas Carew [7] put it, "those heroic virtues for which antiquity/ Hath left no name but patterns only,/Such as Hercules, Achilles, Theseus." When we say that a man performs a Herculean task, we do not say simply that the task required great strength or was undertaken industriously or was possibly odious; we say all this and more in a single word. Fable, myth, allegory—in short, literature in general—create their own vocabularies by connecting verbal forms with descriptions of particular events or occasions from which they may then be metaphorically extended. A complex interpersonal relation may be succinctly described as "crying 'Wolf,'" while a complex emotional adjustment may be summed up as "sour grapes." It would take a long sentence, or more likely a paragraph or even a chapter, to deal with either of these in nonmetaphorical fashion. When the literary expression is reinforced in its own right, it becomes useful in straight description. This takes the metaphorical force out of the heroic virtue and gives us no clue as to what is happening when the term is used metaphorically. It leads, however, to a more and more complex and effective nonmetaphorical terminology descriptive of human personality. The scientific effectiveness of such a vocabulary will derive from the actual contingencies of reinforcement in the scientific community, not from its metaphorical origins. Any survival of the latter would interfere with scientific use.

The difference between the generic and the metaphorical tact is one of the great differences between science and literature. Scientific verbal behavior is set up and maintained because of certain practical consequences. Nothing beyond a generic extension will eventually serve, as we shall see in Chapter 18. In literature there are no similar practical consequences and metaphorical extensions therefore prevail. No one will deny that they are effective; but the advantage we gain by reading Dostoyevsky or Joyce, in coming to share their "knowledge" or "understanding" of human nature, is very different from the advantage gained from scientific study.

Metonymical Extension

Metaphor, as here defined, includes similes and several minor variations distinguished in classical rhetoric. A separate category is advisable for what we may call metonymy, using the word to include several other classical figures, including "synecdoche." Here an extension of a tact occurs when a stimulus acquires control over the

[7] Carew, T., "Pretensions of Poverty," *Poems, Songs, and Sonnets* (London, 1670).

response because it frequently *accompanies* the stimulus upon which reinforcement is normally contingent. Thus, we say *The White House denied the rumor,* although it was the President who spoke, or *You haven't touched your dinner,* when the important fact was that the dinner was not *eaten.* We account for such behavior by noting that the President and the White House, and touching and eating, frequently occur together.

An effort has been made to explain metonymy in terms of logical relations among stimuli. Various types have been defined accordingly. The relation may be that of person to office (antonomasia), of part to whole (synecdoche), and so on. But these relations, like those appealed to in the classical analysis of word association, merely explain why the stimuli occur together in nature. Any two contiguous stimuli will show this effect regardless of why they are contiguous.

Metonymical extension does not freely occur in both directions. We do not describe the refurbishing of the White House by saying that the President received a new coat of paint. This lack of symmetry is easily explained by the way in which metonymical extension differs from generic and most metaphorical extension. Generic extension is based upon a property entering into the reinforcing contingency. The extended response has, therefore, an appropriate effect upon the listener, who responds effectively to the state of affairs described. In metaphor, this result cannot be guaranteed because the property responsible for the extension may not be equally important to the listener or as effective upon his behavior. He may therefore be surprised to hear the response made to the novel stimulus or, if he is not in contact with the stimulus, the action he takes with respect to it may cause trouble. Nevertheless, the property responsible for metaphorical extension usually has some functional significance. Metonymical extension, however, may be the result of a purely accidental association of stimuli, and the metonymical tact is therefore likely to confuse the listener and to fail to prepare him for effective action. Only those extensions are effective which do not lead to conflicting results. We may say *A fleet of twenty sail,* in the familiar textbook example of "part for whole," because the listener will undoubtedly suppose that the rest of each ship is also present, but we cannot say that the ships were flapping idly in the breeze without producing collateral effects which are best avoided.

There is actually very little spontaneous metonymy. Most examples in everyday speech and in literature, like most apparent metaphors, are responses which have been independently reinforced and thus established as functional units. Metonymical extension may explain the origin of these expressions in the verbal environment, but it is not needed to account for instances in the behavior of the individual speaker. One reason for the rareness of true metonymy is that the controlling and contingent properties are so loosely associated that the response is generally of little value when a standard response is lacking. Closely associated properties quickly produce standard controlling relations. Thus it has often been pointed out that *orange* and *violet,* now used as terms for color, must have been extended from an earlier application to objects. Since the association of objects and colors is very close, the metonymical extensions must have been relatively effective when they first occurred, but for this very reason the responses quickly become standard forms controlled by color alone.

The process involved in metonymical extension commonly leads to behavior which is far removed from the examples of classical rhetoric and is commonly thought not to require a special designation. Let us say that a child is accustomed to seeing an orange on the breakfast table. When on a given morning the orange is missing, the child quickly says *orange.* Let us suppose that we can show that this is not a mand: for example, suppose we can show that an orange will not be taken and eaten when offered. Then, since there is no orange acting as a stimulus, why is the response made? As A. P. Weiss [8] pointed out in discussing this case, we do not need to say that the child "perceives the absence of the orange." The response is evoked by the breakfast table with all its familiar features and by other stimuli appropriate to the time of day. Oranges have frequently accompanied these stimuli, and the response *orange* has been reinforced in their presence. A similar metonymical extension might occur in the other direction. As a result of the same history, an orange, seen for the first time under other circumstances, might evoke the response *breakfast.*

(A more sophisticated speaker will say more than *orange* or *breakfast* under such circumstances. Faced with the breakfast table without an orange, he may say *No orange?* or faced with an orange in the absence of a breakfast table, he may say *That orange reminds me of breakfast.* The responses *no* and *reminds me* are examples of another

[8] Weiss, A. P., *A Theoretical Basis of Human Behavior* (Columbus, Ohio, 1929).

kind of verbal behavior to be discussed in Chapter 12. In both instances something more than a mere metonymical extension has occurred. The response has been strengthened according to this principle, and the speaker has described that fact or commented upon it through additional verbal behavior.)

Solecistic Extension of the Tact

A still more tenuous extension of the tact is so useless and confusing to the listener that it is described with such pejorative terms as malaprop, solecism, or catachresis. The property which gains control of the response is only distantly related to the defining property upon which standard reinforcements are contingent or is similar to that property for irrelevant reasons. This is not to say that some malaprops are not effective or go unreinforced. We may not be seriously disturbed when someone says *dilemma* although a situation is merely difficult, or *feasible* when action is merely possible, and we shall probably not collide with Mrs. Malaprop [9] when she graciously exclaims *You go first and I'll precede you.* A dilemma is not very different from a difficulty, and *precede,* although the opposite of *follow,* nevertheless resembles it in describing a situation involving the order in which people leave a room. Even so, such examples are troublesome to the listener and in many cases may be dangerous. Most verbal communities not only fail to respond effectively to such extensions but provide some sort of punishment for them.

Solecistic extension is not far from metonymy. When a student under the pressure of an examination writes: *The fatigue of a synapse is* mutual with *the refractory phase* and later corrects this to *similar to,* it is not difficult to find common circumstances under which these responses are satisfactorily interchanged. For example, feelings which are mutual are also similar. The term *mutual* is sometimes reinforced in the presence of things possessing the property of similarity and is later evoked by that property alone.

As in metaphor and metonymy, solecistic extension is commonest when no other response is available. Also, as in metaphor and metonymy, some erroneous responses are reinforced by the verbal community and acquire a functional, if not a social, status comparable with that of correct responses. Original mistakes are perhaps almost as rare as original metaphors.

[9] Sheridan, R. B., *The Rivals* (1773).

Nomination

A tact is frequently extended when a person or thing is given a name. A new-born child, a newly-invented machine, a newly-discovered flower, a newly-founded town—these are novel occasions for which standard tacts are lacking. Before what we may call "nomination" takes place, the only available responses are the common nouns and adjectives evoked by miscellaneous properties which the new object shares with previous objects for which tacts have already been acquired. *The-new-baby-at-our-house* is a sort of proper name in the sense that it fairly closely identifies a particular object, but it may not identify this object on other occasions or when spoken by other people, and may not continue to do so as the object changes. A proper name—that is, a name which is characteristically reinforced only in the presence of a particular person or thing or in some relation to such a particular person or thing—is obviously more effective. But where do such names arise? What verbal process is responsible for the first attribution of a name to a new person or object?

Some accepted "proper names" are simply surviving sets of tacts: *The Little Church around the Corner, A Treatise on Probability,* or *Ode to Beauty.* Frequently the property of serial position is used: *Beethoven's Eighth Symphony* is a proper name arising from the designation of a serial order, as is the child's name *Tertius.* New stars are generally named with numbers in the order of their discovery. *New England* specifies a temporal relation, *North Conway* a geographical one.

Most names, however, exemplify the extension of a tact relation. Children are usually given names which the parents have already acquired with respect to other persons—friends, relatives, or admired figures in literature or history. This is expressed by saying that the child is named "after" someone or is a "namesake." Frequently this is an example of generic or metaphorical extension. A baby named for someone whom he actually physically resembles clearly exemplifies metaphor. More often the basis for the extension is some common emotional or other reaction engendered in the parents. If the name is first suggested by someone else, the same common properties make it relatively easy for the parents to apply the name to the child and hence to accept the suggestion. That something of this sort is involved in nomination is clear from the negative case. Names which are clearly not evoked in any measure by a child may be rejected in spite of some reason for using them. Names which have already been acquired in connection with people who arouse incompatible emotional reactions are avoided; parents may resist a name which is borne by an acquaintance who is violently disliked even though it may be a family name.

There are undoubtedly many other processes at work in the naming of children, including cultural factors. It is not an example of the extension of a tact if the only effect of a chosen name is to add prestige or character or to increase the prospects of a child in the world. Such a name is given, just as later a particular haircut or type of dress may be adopted, because of a resemblance which exists, not before naming, but afterwards. The name is, in a sense, a decoration. We say that a child is named Patience or Prudence "after" an abstract virtue. The new-born child is not conspicuously patient or prudent, but to some extent it seems to acquire such an admirable character as soon as named.

"Nicknames" often show a greater freedom, suggesting poetic license, and are thus good examples of the process of nomination. Whimsical names for children such as *Nuisance, Little Accident,* or *Sunshine* and the dubbing of a restaurant *The Greasy Spoon* reveal the basic process.

Proper names appear to be more easily forgotten than other forms of verbal behavior. This may be illusory, for the absence of a proper name from a repertoire can be extremely conspicuous. In describing an object or person with a set of tacts, there are usually many alternative forms if a given response fails, and the speaker himself may not be able to report that the response was missing from his behavior at the time. The very uniqueness of the proper name, however, exposes the process of forgetting. On the other hand, there is good reason to expect that proper names will be more easily forgotten. Insofar as they are strictly "proper"—that is, insofar as they show no extension from other stimuli—they are used and reinforced in a limited situation and a limited number of times. Common names, on the other hand, are appropriate to a much wider range of situations and, as we shall see in a moment, are reducible in part to a minimal repertoire by virtue of which a given operant may derive strength from other operants having something in common with it. If by any chance a proper name shows metaphorical extension it gains a mnemonic advantage. A favorite device of the "memory expert" is to convert a proper name to a description of the person named, no matter how fanciful or implausible the description may be.

The mnemonic value which is gained when a name shows metaphorical extension has a counterpart which works in the other direction. In Morality Plays and allegories, characters are frequently named for the traits they personify or the standard roles they play. Restoration drama followed the same practice, as to some extent did novelists of the nineteenth century, such as Dickens and Trollope. But in naming a character in such a way as to describe his behavior or condition, the author is not interested in making sure that the reader will not forget the name. He is interested in pointing up the personality or role. Trollope's *Mr. Quiverful* is an indigent clergyman with a large family. This condition is to some extent brought to the attention of the reader whenever the proper name is used. The same author's *Mr. Crawley,* on the other hand, is characterized by an excessive humility, or in Hamlet's phrase, as "crawling between Heaven and earth." By giving him the name of Crawley, Trollope characterizes him repeatedly throughout the book.

Guessing

Is it possible to emit a response which would be classified as a tact in the absence of any relevant stimulus whatsoever? Certainly pressure may be exerted to evoke responses resembling tacts. A man can be forced under aversive stimulation to "give the name" of a total stranger—that is, to emit some name in the presence of the stranger. The student may be advised on an examination: "If you don't know, guess." But if the form of the resulting response is not controlled by the stimulus in any way, it cannot be a tact. The tact is a relation, not merely a response, and in the absence of a controlling stimulus no relation can be established.

Traces of control may often be demonstrated when the speaker appears to be guessing. The current situation may have some resemblance to past situations. The student is actually being advised to let such slight resemblances operate in his favor, even though the situation would not otherwise be important enough to evoke a response. Spotting the composer of an unfamiliar piece of music often appears to be guessing, but one may be affected by properties of music which control the name of the composer in some measure even though they are subtle and cannot be identified by the spotter. If we can show that the name guessed has any functional relation with the music being heard, there is evidence of some relation appropriate to a tact.

In the standard guessing situation of tossing a coin and asking "Heads or tails?," the final position of the coin does not control the guesser's response, and the response is therefore not a tact. This does not mean, of course, that the response is undetermined. The question "Heads or tails?" may produce a statistically different first call from the question "Tails or heads?," suggesting echoic or intraverbal influences. If the speaker is asked to guess the outcome of a series of tosses, his behavior will be controlled by his earlier guesses plus a type of behavior similar to that discussed in Part V. Previous experiences in the guessing situation set up tendencies either to repeat or to refuse to repeat earlier calls. In the population at large, therefore, certain fairly standard sequences of "chance" calls are observed.[10]

Dynamics of the Extended Tact

We have seen that the strength of a tact may vary with the clarity or unusualness of the stimulus and with momentary motivational conditions of the speaker, particularly as these are related to special behaviors of the listener (see Chapter 6). The extended tact is subject to another source of variability. When the extension occurs for the first time (and the process is only then of special interest), the probability of the response will depend upon the resemblance between new and old situations. Generic extension, following a property inevitably associated with reinforcement, is likely to be strong. Only in unusual instances is the tendency to respond qualified, and the speaker may comment upon such a weakness with an additional response, such as *sort of* (see Chapter 12). A very unusual chair is not likely to be called a chair, or if it is, it may be qualified as *a sort of chair*. Metaphorical extensions are based upon properties much less closely associated with reinforcement and are likely to be weak, this weakness being described by the speaker himself through the use of such expressions as *like* or *as*. Metaphors are commonest, as we have seen, under the special conditions of "license" in the literary community.

True metonymical and solecistic extensions are rare and are likely to occur only under pressure for "speech at any price" (see Chapter 8). True nomination also shows a very low probability of response in most instances, as is indicated by the characteristic long deliberation

[10] Skinner, B. F., "The Processes Involved in the Repeated Guessing of Alternatives," *J. exp. Psychol.*, 30 (1942), 495-503.

involved in the naming of, not only a new child, but a new device or a work of art. Guessing is the extreme case of a minimal stimulus control and almost always requires strong variables beyond those of the stimulating situation.

ABSTRACTION

Any property of a stimulus present when a verbal response is reinforced acquires some degree of control over that response, and this control continues to be exerted when the property appears in other combinations. If this process of extension were unchecked, chaos would result, since every stimulus shares properties with many other stimuli and should therefore control a great variety of responses. Some extended control is, as we have just seen, permissible and even useful, but a free extension of the tact cannot be tolerated, particularly in practical and scientific matters.

The verbal community deals with this problem by resorting to another behavioral process which sharpens stimulus control and opposes the process of extension. It reinforces responses in the presence of a chosen stimulus property and fails to reinforce, or perhaps even punishes, responses evoked by unspecified properties. As a result, the response tends to be made only in the presence of the chosen property. Suppose, for example, that the community repeatedly reinforces a verbal response in the presence of a small red pyramid. Provided there is no interference from other behavior, the response will henceforth be evoked with varying degrees of probability by any red stimulus, any small stimulus, and any pyramidal stimulus. It is unlikely, however, that the community will also reinforce the response whenever it is made to any one of these fragmentary properties of the stimulus occurring in other combinations. If the response is to be of practical use, it must be pinned down to perhaps one property—let us say shape. The community refrains from reinforcing responses emitted in the presence of red or small objects which are not pyramidal. It continues to reinforce the response, however, whenever any pyramid is present regardless of color, size, or other property. The resulting verbal operant would traditionally be called "the name of the shape of a pyramid" and classified as *abstract*.

If metaphor is often taken to be, not the natural result of stimulus induction, but an achievement attributed to some special faculty or power of the gifted speaker, even more extensive claims are made for a faculty of abstraction. Nevertheless, the process is easily demonstrated in animals other than man. The formula is surprisingly simple when we recall how complicated classical treatments of the subject have been. Pavlov studied the process in his conditioned-reflex experiments. He found that the salivary response of his dog could be brought under the control of a single property of a stimulus, or a given combination of properties, if responses to other properties or combination of properties were not reinforced. As we shall see in the next chapter, the process demonstrated in Pavlov's experiment is seen more often in the behavior of listeners than speakers, but a close parallel of the abstract tact may be set up in lower organisms.[11] A pigeon, for example, which has been reinforced for pecking at a small red triangle projected on a translucent screen will peck at forms having other sizes, colors, or shapes, though at lower rates. But it can quickly be brought to respond preferentially to any one of these properties by reinforcing only when that property is present regardless of other properties.

Textbook examples of abstraction are usually relevant to "intellectual" operations in which the environment is analyzed in practical ways. The examples tend to emphasize fairly simple dimensions of nature, but the process is equally well exemplified where the abstracted property of stimuli cannot be isolated by any other method of analysis. The student who is learning to "spot" the composer of unfamiliar music or to name the artist or school of an unfamiliar picture is subjected to the same contingencies of differential reinforcement. Responses such as *Mozart* or *Dutch* are brought under the control of extremely subtle properties of stimuli when they are reinforced with "right" or punished with "wrong" by the community. But it may be very difficult, if not impossible, to undertake a description of these properties in terms comparable to the mathematical description of a pyramid.

The procedure through which an abstract tact is set up does not *create* the control exerted by the stimulus; it simply sharpens and intensifies it. The property specified by the restricted contingency is

[11] Our definition of verbal behavior, incidentally, includes the behavior of experimental animals where reinforcements are supplied by an experimenter or by an apparatus designed to establish contingencies which resemble those maintained by the normal listener. The animal and the experimenter comprise a small but genuine verbal community. This may offend our sense of the proprieties, but there is consolation in the fact that such a relation as that represented by the abstract tact is susceptible to laboratory study.

the same kind of property, and exerts the same kind of control, as in metaphorical extension. Moreover, the process of abstraction is probably never complete. Metaphorical extensions are not always eliminated, for the opportunity to extinguish all extended responses may never arise. A verbal response is probably never wholly restricted to a specific set of properties, although in the optimal case a single property or a specific collection of properties may for practical purposes be in exclusive control.

Abstraction is a peculiarly verbal process because a nonverbal environment cannot provide the necessary restricted contingency. A single property may control a nonverbal response, but it cannot control *only* one such response unless it is the sole and inevitable accompaniment of another set of properties. Let us suppose that in a given orchard only red apples are edible. This condition means that only when an apple is red will the behavior of picking and eating it be reinforced by certain gustatory stimulation. As a result, the behavior comes to be evoked only by red apples. Also as a result of this, there is some tendency to seize and eat other red objects, provided that they do not differ too markedly from the shape and size of apples. Thus, a shiny new red rubber ball may look "good enough to eat" and may even evoke whimsical eating behavior. But in general we do not tend to eat red books, hats, and so on, simply because we eat only red apples. If there is any such tendency, extinction is bound to occur. Consequently, the single response controlled by the redness of apples does not remain under the control of the property of redness regardless of the other circumstances under which that property occurs.

A verbal response, however, can come under the exclusive control of red because the necessary contingency does not require a practical consequence common to all instances of red. Even though the verbal community is eventually concerned with practical matters, it can maintain the unique contingency required for an abstraction when the practical consequences vary from instance to instance. The listener may be concerned with the redness of a stimulus for many different reasons, and he will behave in response to the speaker's *red* in different ways upon different occasions, but all that he requires of the speaker is that the response *red* be correlated with a red stimulus in each case. The generalized reinforcement provided by the community may rest on a single condition.

The special achievement of the abstract tact in dividing the world into very small parts has nourished the belief that abstraction is always or particularly concerned with single properties, in contrast to the collections of properties called objects or things. It is said, for example, that the referents of abstract terms cannot "stand alone," as objects seem to do, and that this is, in fact, why we have abstraction. But a tact may involve the control of a particular stimulus-*object* in precisely the same way. A response controlled by a single dimension of a stimulus may have special properties, but they are not the special properties of abstraction. When the stimulus is an object, a sort of nonverbal "abstraction" is sometimes possible because a single practical response can be made to a large number of instances. For example, we may classify a large number of objects as chairs by behaving nonverbally with respect to them—by sitting on them. This is a chair-identifying response which, when made in the presence of chairs, receives a practical, nonverbal reinforcement appropriate to the classification. The verbal response *chair* may come under the control of more subtle properties—for example, it may be pinned down to the shape of chairs regardless of their size. But there is no exclusive process of stimulus classification or control. When the response *chair* is restricted to a given stimulus-class by the verbal environment, the process of abstraction follows the same course as in such a response as *red*.

We usually mention objects first in giving an account of the physical world, and languages apparently tend to develop object-terms first. It is easy to account for this by pointing to practical consequences. The slow emergence of words related to single properties—for example, the names of colors—can often be traced in the history of a language. On the other hand, in a logical or epistemological analysis, it is usually more convenient to suppose that the world is built of single-propertied bricks. William James' "blooming, buzzing confusion" suggests chaotic sensory materials rather than a miscellaneous collection of objects. Recently, however, objects have received the benefit of a better sense of protocol. Sensations, or the attributes of sensations, now frequently appear as abstractions rather than as primary sense-data, and objects find a solid foothold at Carnap's [12] zero level of description. But all tacts are pinned down, if they are pinned down at all, *via* the same process. The verbal response *chair* is as abstract as *red*. It is not controlled by any single stimulus. Most of the properties of a single chair which evoke a response on any

[12] Carnap, Rudolph, *Logical Syntax of Language* (New York, 1937).

given occasion—the size, color, material, mode of construction, and so on—are irrelevant. Extension of the response *chair* to other stimuli on the basis of such properties has been curtailed through extinction. Perhaps more extinction is needed to restrict a property-term such as *red* than an object-term such as *chair,* but that depends on the particular case. The response *insect,* although it is controlled by a class of objects, will probably need more differential reinforcement in a given verbal environment than the response *red.* In verbal responses controlled by single properties of stimuli there is less chance of metaphorical spread and therefore less chance that the listener will make an ineffective response.

A predilection for *things* sometimes leads to absurd consequences in the search for defining properties. We try to assemble a set of properties in order to compose a thing. Professor I. A. Richards considers a particularly good example in his *Principles of Literary Criticism.*[13] The quotation is from G. W. Mackail's *Lectures on Poetry.*

> Poetry, like life, is one thing.... Essentially a continuous substance or energy, poetry is historically a connected movement, a series of successive integrated manifestations. Each poet, from Homer or the predecessors of Homer to our own day, has been, to some degree and at some point, the voice of the movement and energy of poetry; in him, poetry has for the moment become visible, audible, incarnate; and his extant poems are the record left of that partial and transitory incarnation.... The progress of poetry, with its vast power and exalted function, is immortal.

The central theme of this passage is apparently the present point. What is the referent of the abstract tact *poetry*? Professor Mackail appears to be arguing that it is something that is never quite present in any one stimulus presentation yet characteristic of a long succession of stimuli. But since *poetry* is a noun, he concludes that poetry must be a thing. A single property is too evanescent. And so word is piled upon word to prove that poetry is both substantial (*substance, energy, movement, power, visible, audible*) and enduring (*continuous, successive, integrated, immortal*).[14] We might try to substantialize the referent of *pyramidal* in the same way:

> Pyramidality, like life, is one thing.... Essentially a continuous substance or energy, pyramidality is historically a connected movement, a series of successive integrated manifestations. Each builder of pyramids,

[13] Richards, I. A., *Principles of Literary Criticism* (New York, 1934), p. 19.

[14] These responses are examples of the impure tact of Chapter 6. The function in this case is to reduce the speaker's anxiety lest poetry escape description altogether.

> from Cheops or the predecessors of Cheops to our own day, has been, to some degree and at some point, the voice of the movement and energy of pyramidality; in him, pyramidality has for the moment become visible, audible, incarnate; and the extant pyramids are the record left of that partial and transitory incarnation. . . . The progress of pyramidality, with its vast power and exalted function, is immortal.

Absurd as this may seem, it is not an unfair example of the reification of entities to correspond with abstract terms. The practice is by no means confined to literary criticism. Compare, for example, the following passage from Philip Jourdain's *The Nature of Mathematics:* [15]

> . . . one word—"mathematics"—is used both for our knowledge of a certain kind and the thing, if such a thing there be, about which this knowledge is. I have distinguished . . . between "Mathematics," a collection of truths of which we know something, and "mathematics," our knowledge of Mathematics. Thus, we may speak of "Euclid's mathematics," of "Newton's mathematics," and truly say that mathematics has developed and therefore had history; but Mathematics is eternal and unchanging, and therefore has no history—it does not belong, even in part, to Euclid or Newton or anybody else, but is something which is discovered, in the course of time by human minds.

(The characteristics which are attributed to people through the use of theriotypes were substantialized by Victor Hugo in *Les Misérables* [Livre Cinquième, V] in this way:

> . . . chacun des individus de l'espèce humaine correspond à quelqu'une des espèces de la création animale; . . . depuis l'huître jusqu'à l'aigle, depuis le porc jusqu'au tigre, tous les animaux sont dans l'homme et . . . chacun d'eux est dans un homme. Quelquefois même plusieurs d'entre eux à la fois.

Many of the traits, abilities, and faculties accepted at one time or another as legitimate concepts in psychology have had an equally lowly origin.)

The referents of abstractions—the properties of stimuli which control abstract tacts—can be discovered only by certain methods of empirical investigation. What do *pyramidality, poetry, chair, red,* or *foxy* really "mean"? If we try to answer this by discovering what they "mean to us," we are behaving empirically, although under a certain handicap. It is easier to discover what they "mean" to someone else. There are many technical problems to be solved before this can be

[15] Reprinted in J. R. Newman, *The World of Mathematics* (New York, 1956), p. 67.

done on a satisfactory scale, but the basic formula is simple: manipulate stimuli and, through the presence or absence of the response, identify the effective controlling properties. Laboratory experiments in concept formation follow this pattern by setting up and testing for the presence of abstract tacts in an artificial verbal community. The same procedures could be used in an empirical survey of abstraction generated by verbal environments outside the laboratory.

The Importance of Abstraction

A proper noun is a tact in which the response is under the control of a specific person or thing. A common noun is a tact in which the response is under the control of a property defining a class of persons or things. A "proper tact" may suffer metaphorical extension (as in *A Daniel come to judgment*); but when it does so, it has obviously come under the control of a subset of properties—in this case, the impartiality of judicial wisdom shown by Daniel—and is therefore functioning as a common tact. A well-established common tact is necessarily an abstraction; it is under the control of a subset of properties which may be present upon a given occasion but probably never exclusively compose such an occasion.

A repertoire of common tacts has many advantages. It is sometimes economical to respond to a total stimulus presentation with a proper name, but an abstract repertoire makes it possible to select and identify only those properties of the presentation which are important to the listener. Such a repertoire also has the great advantage of being available in a novel situation when a proper name is lacking. A series of common tacts which have been conditioned separately with respect to single properties or clusters of properties supply an essentially new and unique response. *The man in the gray coat feeding the swans* may upon a given occasion designate a particular person as specifically as his proper name. But we cannot use the proper name unless we have acquired it with respect to this person. We may nevertheless compose an acceptable substitute by stringing together a series of common responses in this fashion.

The Dynamics of Abstract Tacts

To evoke a response which is under the control of a single property of an object it is necessary not only to present the object but to "specify the property to be reacted to." Thus, to get the response *red,* one must present a red object as well as a verbal occasion on which color responses are especially reinforced—for example, by saying *Tell me what color this is*. In the absence of a special occasion which designates a particular class of tacts, a given nonverbal stimulus does not narrowly control a single response. The stimulus which does is relatively complex.

The strength of an abstract tact reflects its history of reinforcement. Many instances of the response may have been reinforced, but many more may have gone unreinforced or may have been punished, and the strength of the response may be modified accordingly. In general, the ratio of unreinforced to reinforced responses represents what we may call the degree of abstraction. These degrees are often ordered in the form of subordinate classes. If we are looking in the window of a furniture store and are asked *What are you looking at?*, the easiest answer would perhaps be a general gesture of pointing and the vocal response *That*. Pressed with a further question *That what?*, we could almost as easily answer *That thing*. Further demands might lead to a succession of responses: *That piece of furniture, That chair, That armchair, That Swedish-modern armchair* and finally *That Swedish-modern armchair in light maple*. The last is a verbal response reinforced only on rare occasions and under stimulus control which is the result of an exacting contingency of reinforcement. It is therefore a more "difficult" response to make or, in other words, is less likely to be made. The logical classification, as in the case of intraverbal responses and metaphorical tacts, is not directly responsible for relative strength; rather, it is a description of environmental states of affairs which are in turn responsible for relative strengths. In the particular environment of a given individual, of course, some highly abstract terms may be strong and some general terms fairly weak.

THE PROBLEM OF REFERENCE

Semantic theory is often confined to the relation between response and stimulus which prevails in the verbal operant called the tact. Words, parts of words, or groups of words on the one hand and things, parts of things, or groups of things on the other stand in a relation to each other called "reference," "denotation," or "designation." The relation may be as empty as a logical convention or it may provide for the "intention" of the speaker. But how a word "stands for" a thing or "means" what the speaker intends to say or "communicates" some condition of a thing to a listener has never been satisfactorily established. The notion of the verbal operant brings such relations within the scope of the methods of natural science. How a stimulus or some property of a stimulus acquires control over a given form of response is now fairly well understood. The form of a response is shaped by the contingencies prevailing in a verbal community. A given form is brought under stimulus control through the differential reinforcement of our three-term contingency. The result is simply the probability that the speaker will emit a response of a given form in the presence of a stimulus having specified properties under certain broad conditions of deprivation or aversive stimulation. *So far as the speaker is concerned,* this *is* the relation of reference or meaning. There would be little point in using this formula to redefine concepts such as sign, signal, or symbol or a relation such as reference, or entities communicated in a speech episode such as ideas, meanings, or information. These traditional terms carry many irrelevant connotations, arising from their use in describing the relations between the speaker's response and the behavior of the listener and the contingencies of reinforcement imposed by a verbal community.

Even within the verbal behavior of the speaker there are other types of verbal operants suggesting paradigms where other distinctions may be made. Each type of operant has unique properties which resist any effort to arrive at a single comprehensive formula. This is a simple fact about the behavior of speakers and listeners. The subject is extremely complex and cannot be treated satisfactorily by simplified concepts. Even within the narrow relation represented by the tact the traditional notion of meaning is not adequately represented, since over and above a relation of reference we have to consider that of assertion (see Chapter 12) and the question of whether a verbal response is precise, true, and so on (see Parts IV and V). Presumably we could describe the behavior of logician or linguist as he says that a word "stands for" or "means" something or that a proposition is true or false, and in this or some other way we could set up alternative definitions, but the definitions would probably not be useful in an analysis of verbal behavior. We are interested in finding terms, not to take traditional places, but to deal with a traditional subject matter.

In studying the properties of the world of things or events which are responded to verbally we must lift ourselves by our own bootstraps; many properties of nature can be identified and dealt with only through verbal practices. Nevertheless the problem of stimulus control in the tact can be meaningfully examined. If the world could be divided into many separate things or events and if we could set up a separate form of verbal response for each, the problem would be relatively simple. But the world is not so easily analyzed, or at least has not been so analyzed by those whose verbal behavior we must study. In any large verbal repertoire we find a confusing mixture of relations between forms of response and forms of stimuli. The problem is to find the basic units of "correspondence."

We are prepared for this subject by our consideration of other types of verbal behavior. Echoic behavior in particular supplies a good model. The speaker acquires echoic operants of many sizes. He tends to repeat words, phrases, or even sentences. Eventually his behavior shows small echoic units approximately the size of the speech sound, either as the result of direct educational reinforcement or as by-products of the acquisition of larger units. Only because of this minimal repertoire is he able to echo verbal patterns heard for the first time. Textual behavior shows a somewhat similar minimal repertoire. The child may be taught to read by single sounds, words, phrases, or sentences. Regardless of the size of the unit most often reinforced, a minimal repertoire is developed with which he is able to read unfamiliar words. A comparable minimal repertoire was found to be lacking in intraverbal behavior. When many different responses are reinforced under the control of a single stimulus, and when the same response may be reinforced under the control of many stimuli, the speaker acquires little beyond the miscellaneous intraverbal tendencies shown in word-association experiments.

The tact resembles intraverbal behavior in lacking the point-to-point correspondence seen in echoic and textual behavior, but the reinforcing contingencies are nevertheless more consistent than in intraverbal behavior. There is evidently some sort of minimal repertoire. As initially acquired, a tact may be of almost any size. Such an expression as *A needle in a haystack* may be controlled as a unit by a particular type of situation. This is even true of larger responses which appear to involve assertion. A single property of a situation may evoke the response *Haste makes waste*; the speaker has not necessarily *composed* a sentence in the sense of Chapter 14 and is not actually making an assertion. He simply emits a response appropriate to the situation. But much smaller units eventually arise and our task is to discover how far the process goes. What are the smallest identifiable units of response under the control of the separable properties of (usually) nonverbal stimuli?

Our analysis of echoic and textual behavior prepares us for this task by reminding us of the necessity of surveying a response upon many occasions. The minimal units of echoic and textual behavior seldom appear by themselves as whole responses. Nevertheless their functional unity can still be demonstrated. The same rule holds for the tact. It is often supposed that the referent of a response can be identified upon every occasion when the response is made. Where the stimulus appears to be an object, the object is taken as the referent of the response; yet there is always an element of abstraction. We cannot point to a single chair which is the referent of the response *chair.*

The properties of a stimulus which are relevant in evoking a response, either in the individual speaker or according to the practices of a given community, can be discovered only by considering a series of occasions upon which the properties are systematically varied and the presence or absence of the response noted. We cannot solve this problem by giving the relevant property a sort of object-status as a "concept" or "abstraction"—by saying that the response *red* refers to the "concept of red" or to the "redness" of something. We never reinforce a response when a "concept" is present; what is present is a particular stimulus. The referent of an abstract tact, if this term has any meaning at all, is the property or set of properties upon which reinforcement has been contingent and which therefore control the response. We might say that the referent is the *class* of stimuli defined by such a property or properties, but there is little reason to prefer classes to properties. The property correlated with reinforcement must be specified, in physical terms, if we are to remain within the framework of an empirical science.

Whether a response can "stand alone" is not of course a matter of the orthographic practices of a language, for these do not clearly reflect the functional relations involved. The distinction between analytic and synthetic or agglutinated languages, when it is not a distinction of orthography, is mainly concerned with the second-order behavior to be discussed in Part IV. Some verbal behavior cannot stand alone because it is emitted only when other behavior of the speaker forms part of the occasion (see Parts IV and V). Grammatical tags are good examples; for example, there is no occasion upon which the only response of the speaker will be *-ly.* (In the rare exception in which a speaker says *-ly* as a contribution to the verbal behavior of someone else—for example, as a correction—it is clear that he is speaking as if he were adding the tag to his own response.) The other minimal operants described above may present similar problems. Since femininity never stands alone in the absence of something which may be feminine, the feminine ending never occurs alone in speech. The independent functional effectiveness of the minimal unit of response is most easily detected when behavior is the result of multiple causation.

In any pair of tacts we note that the stimuli may be the same, similar, or different and that the responses may be the same, similar, or different. The nine resulting possibilities are shown in Figure 7. Verbal behavior is likely to be most efficient when the conditions rep-

		STIMULUS		
		Same	Similar	Different
RESPONSE	Same	(1) Ideal	(2) Metaphor, Abstraction	(3) Homonymy
	Similar	(4)	(5)	(6) Partial Homonymy
	Different	(7) Synonomy	(8) Partial Synonomy	(9) Ideal

FIGURE 7

resented in Cells 1 and 9 prevail. It has been said that an ideal language would always "express the same thing by the same means and similar things by similar means." Presumably it would also express different things by different means. This is an impossible goal because verbal behavior varies in far fewer dimensions than the world which it must describe. Moreover, the processes responsible for verbal behavior are by no means exclusively concerned with establishing an ideal language. Two well-known violations appear in Cells 3 and 7. In homonymy, the same response is made to quite different stimuli (for example, *fast* is evoked by both speedy and securely-fixed stationary objects). In synonymy, the same stimulus leads to quite different responses (for example, the same event may evoke both *fast* and *speedy*). Where homonymy may lead to inappropriate responses by the listener, synonymy interferes with efficient discourse by exhausting available verbal forms and requiring a more extensive verbal history on the part of the listener. Partial homonymy, in Cell 6, is a necessary consequence of the fact that verbal behavior cannot be modified in as many dimensions as the physical environment; in any large vocabulary responses must resemble each other in some respects "for no good reason." Partial synonymy, in Cell 8, in which a common property of two or more stimuli control different responses is, if not inevitable, at least a very probable result of the incidental and often chaotic conditions under which verbal behavior arises.

The remaining three cells are of special interest here. All varieties of generic and metaphorical extension are represented in Cell 2, where the same form of response is made to similar stimuli. The abstract tact also occurs here. Under such conditions, we have convincing evidence of the functional effectiveness of some part of a total stimulus presentation—of the part or property responsible for the similarity of the stimuli. The remaining Cells, 4 and 5, offer equally convincing evidence of the functional effectiveness of some fraction of a total response. When similar responses are evoked by similar stimuli, in Cell 5, the common element by virtue of which the responses are similar appears to be independently controlled by the common element by virtue of which the stimuli are similar.

The most familiar examples of functional units are traditionally called words. In learning to speak the child acquires tacts of various sizes: words (*doll*), phrases (*on the table*), and sentences (*Kitty's going to sleep*). These larger units are not composed by the speaker in the sense of Chapter 14; they are unitary responses under the control of particular stimuli. (Many complex responses retain some functional unity even in the adult speaker, as we have seen. Standard sentences like *How are you?* and clichés like *vast majority* may not depend upon the separate control of their parts by separate features of the situation.)

From such behavior there eventually emerges a basic repertoire of smaller functional units also at the level of the word. The child who has acquired the responses *I have a doll* and *I have a kitten* upon separate occasions may show some functional unity in the expression *I have a . . .* which is later combined with novel responses under novel circumstances—for example, when the child says for the first time, and without separate conditioning, *I have a drum*. The process may go further. From responses such as *I have a* . . . and *I want a* . . . , a smaller unit response *I* emerges. Small functional units may, of course, be separately learned, particularly through the educational reinforcement supplied by those who teach children to speak, but they also appear to emerge as by-products of the acquisition of larger responses containing identical elements, very much as in echoic and textual behavior. Just as a speaker who possesses well-developed echoic behavior may imitate new complex sound-patterns heard for the first time, so the individual who possesses a well-developed minimal repertoire of tacts may "describe" a new complex situation when seen for the first time.

The relation between a property of a response and a controlling property of a stimulus can be demonstrated only by comparing many instances of the verbal behavior of a single individual. Such a relation need not be obvious to the speaker. It may not be identified with any reaction of a listener or with the reinforcing practices of the verbal community.

Functional units below the level of the word have, of course, been recognized. Some of these have been called "morphemes." The term is usually defined in part by referring to reinforcing practices of the community as a whole with some reference to the recorded history of the language. It would probably only confuse the issue to adopt this term for the unit of verbal behavior here under analysis although it clearly represents a similar analytical process. An example of a verbal operant often smaller than a word is a "root." Although we may be interested in tracing a root in the history of a language, it is functionally significant in the behavior of the contemporary speaker as a minimal unit of response correlated with an identifiable element of a stimulus. If the speaker emits the response *destroy* upon one occasion and the response *destructible* upon another, and if, as is likely, we can identify a common element in the two occasions, then we have evidence for the functional unity of the operant *destr*. . . . That comparable forms are to be found in other languages or that the history of this root may be traced through earlier forms of the same language are interesting related facts, which may explain why the contemporary verbal community establishes operants showing such similarities. But these facts add nothing to the demonstration of the functional unity of the minimal unit in the behavior of this speaker.

Other familiar units below the level of the word are the affixes used for inflectional, syntactical, or other purposes (see Chapter 13).

These have their own histories, too, but they are functional units in the behavior of the speaker only insofar as they correspond with particular features of a stimulating situation. The evidence is clearest when a speaker composes new forms of response with respect to new situations. Having developed a functional suffix *-ed* with respect to that subtle property of stimuli which we speak of as action-in-the-past, the suffix may be added for the first time to a word which has hitherto described action only in the present. The process is conspicuous when the speaker composes a form which is not established by the practices of a particular community. *He singed* is obviously *composed* from separate elements, because the community reinforces the form *He sang*. *He walked* may also have been composed, but since the form is also separately reinforced, the evidence is not so clear. One kind of minimal unit is under control of the subtle properties of stimuli which we distinguish with different "parts of speech"—for example, the speaker may compose adverbs by adding *-ly* to adjectives. Suffixes such as *-ness* or *-hood* are usually readily manipulable as separate elements in composing new terms appropriate to "states of being."

Some apparent minimal units have no respectable genealogy, and they have tended to be neglected by those concerned with historical and comparative data. Many examples have long been familiar, however. An initial *sp* is characteristic of many words in English having to do with emanation from the mouth (*spit, speak, spew*), or from some other point (*sputter, sprinkle, spray*), or with radiation from a point (*spoke, spire, spur*). It would appear, therefore, that the response *sp* has functional unity under the control of a particular geometric pattern common to many stimuli. This does not mean that the form originated in the act of spitting or speaking, or that it necessarily borrows any current strength from behavioral similarities with such acts, or that we should expect to find similar forms in other languages—although an Indo-European root is obviously related. The basic fact is that a stimulus involving emanation or radiation from a point commonly evokes the response *sp*. The response only rarely occurs alone—and even then only in inchoate behavior under stress, in which a novel pattern showing radiation from a point might lead the speaker to stammer *sp* without completing a standard verbal form.

The linguist may acknowledge the functional unity of a verbal unit *sp* but object to classifying it as a morpheme, not only for historical or comparative reasons but because, if we remove the *sp* from the examples given in the preceding paragraph, we are generally left with useless fragments of behavior. But this is important only if we suppose that words are put together from separable parts. Nothing in our analysis of the tact as a unit of verbal behavior compels this belief. What we mean by such a statement is that, although the response *spit* shows a similarity with *speak* and *spew* which may be traced to a common stimulus element with respect to the initial *sp*, it shows no common functional relation to other forms ending in *-it* (*hit, sit, bit,* and so on). These fragments are not meaningless in the sense of being entirely uncontrolled; they appear for good reasons but they may not possess a reason in common. (Often some traces of a similar element may be found. For example, many words having to do with noises generated vocally contain the terminal unit *-each* —e.g., *screech, preach, teach*. It is not entirely fanciful, therefore, to argue that the response *speech* is a combination of *sp* and *eech*. Since the form is established in a given speaker much too early to be clearly a neologism, it is difficult to prove the point.) [16]

Although we may demonstrate a functional unit of verbal behavior in which a response of given form is controlled by a given stimulus, it does not follow that every instance of a response having that form represents the same operant, nor that every instance of a response evoked by that property has that form. It does not follow, for example, that every instance of *sp* is an instance of the unit just described or that every case of radiation will evoke a response containing *sp*. (And it does not follow, of course, that the functional unity of a minimal operant in the behavior of a speaker corresponds to the practices of any community. A child of six took the terminal *-nese,* in *Chinese* and *Japanese,* to refer to the shape of the eyes.)

The smallest units of verbal behavior which function as minimal tacts are not necessarily the separable speech-sounds of echoic or textual behavior. Although the "phoneme" depends upon usage and is not merely a formal unit of analysis—in other words, it depends upon the controlling relations in verbal behavior—it does not represent a unit of response under the control of a property of stimuli.

[16] All the problems of reference arising from the contingencies of reinforcement imposed by a verbal community have their parallels in other types of verbal responses. An example of a "minimal mand" comparable to the *sp-* just discussed is the initial sound *hw-* (usually written *wh-*) occurring in many English interrogatives. It may be argued that it has an independent function as a mand for verbal action, that it may appear alone in moments of stress, that it may appear in neologistic formations, and that it may be necessary to recognize it in explaining some instances of the multiple causation of verbal behavior.

Phonemes are usually defined in terms of the reinforcing practices of a community, but they can also be defined with respect to the behavior of the individual speaker after it has been shaped up by such a community. Having identified a response *bit* under the control of a particular class of stimuli, we notice that although it may vary in many phonetic or acoustic properties, it never begins with the sound indicated in *pit*. Meanwhile we may have established a separate response class involving the form *pit* and found that although it may vary in many properties it never goes so far afield as to sound like *bit*. Although initial *p* and initial *b* are not separately under the control of single stimulus properties, they are always under the control of different properties.

The minimal units in the behavior of an individual speaker could be identified only by an exhaustive study carried out over so short a period of time that the behavior could be regarded as essentially unchanged. The list of units revealed would be very long and by no means as easily expressed as echoic and textual repertoires. The properties of nature which come to control verbal behavior are more numerous and complex than those covered in the accounts provided by physics, because verbal behavior is controlled by many temporary, incidental, and trivial characteristics which are ignored in a scientific analysis. The number of identifiable units of response is not limited by the available forms, moreover, because there is no limit to the size of unit. As the need for more units grows, larger responses are constructed. But even though we can give no satisfactory empirical account of a single repertoire, we can understand the nature of such a repertoire and the possible functional unity of small units of speech. Without some such conception, we could not readily analyze the multiple causation of verbal behavior (Chapter 9), the distortions in form arising from multiple causation (Chapter 11), or the process of composition, in which novel verbal responses are created upon novel occasions.

Reference in an Ideal Language

Under the conditions of an ideal language, the word for *house,* for example, would be composed of elements referring to color, style, material, size, position, and so on. Only in that way could similar houses be referred to by similar means. The words for two houses alike except for color would be alike except for the element referring to color. If no element in the word referred to color, this part of the conditions of an ideal language could not be fulfilled. Every word in such a language would be a proper noun, referring to a single thing or event. Anyone who spoke the language could immediately invent the word for a new situation by putting together the basic responses separately related to its elements. Just as it is tautological to say *Octavia is a female* because the ending of the subject, *-a,* also indicates the sex described by the predicate, so in our ideal language any such assertion would be tautological—or, indeed, simply repetitious. Abstract responses would merely be incomplete responses.

Such a language is manifestly impossible. Even if we could extend the size of verbal units without limit, the shortage of dimensions would force us at some point to introduce nonfunctional similarities among verbal forms and thus to violate the basic rule. For example, the serial order in a long descriptive phrase is usually not itself representative of anything in the situation described. Nevertheless, the increasing separability and manipulability of response elements in a minimal unit repertoire is a step toward ideal conditions.

An ideal language is approached in another way when stimuli and responses have similar dimensions. This is not an essential requirement, since a point-to-point correspondence could exist between different dimensional systems, but to the extent that responses resemble stimuli, responses related to similar stimuli will themselves be similar. Models have this property. We report a state of affairs most completely by reconstructing it—by building an exact duplicate. Such behavior is verbal according to our definition, since a model is built and used because of its effect upon "listeners." It is not quite so impracticable as it may seem, because the model need not always be constructed. The salesman's sample case is part of a verbal repertoire. Pictures are incomplete or superficial models, which correspond to the "thing being talked about" in many more details than phonetic responses. Both the sample case and the illustrated catalogue satisfy the requirement that similar things be expressed by similar means.

Pointing to an object is a variation on model-building. A man may say, *I never go out without carrying my* . . . and finish by displaying an automatic drawn from his belt. The act of display is verbal according to our definition and is equivalent to the verbal response *automatic,* though much more complete as a description. When we point to the cake we wish to buy in a pastry shop instead of describing it, we are also acting verbally. We use the cake in making the response; its correspondence with the "thing described" is, of course, perfect. Whether a cake can be the name of itself, or a gun refer to itself, depends upon how we define "name" and "refer." (Whether we are to include pointing to objects as a system of tacts will depend upon how much of the verbal field we want the term to cover. It raises no important linguistic problem because, as in the case of model-building in general, the repertoire is easily described.)

Model-building has a special status in the field of verbal behavior. We "report" many instances of behavior, human or otherwise, by imitating or re-enacting them. We make very little progress toward a scientific analysis in so doing, since such a "report" is as unanalyzed and as unwieldy as the original datum. The skillful mimic may, however, find the practice useful in casual discussion. It is seldom employed in the scientific study of nonverbal behavior, but it is standard practice in the verbal field. Echoic behavior, however imperfect, is part of the repertoire of all educated men and is customarily used in reporting verbal behavior. As we saw in Chapter 2, in describing a verbal response in vocal direct quotation we model it. When we report it with a phonetic notation (for example, when we write out the quotation in English spelling), we enable the trained reader to model it for himself.

A quotation is a special form of tact which uses the minimal repertoire of echoic behavior. Whether we are to call it echoic or a tact is unimportant. The classifications are based upon contingencies of reinforcement which in this case are the same. Echoic behavior is worth a separate treatment for several reasons, but the kind of reinforcement it receives is often identical with that of the tact. When we respond to a verbal object—say, the heard speech of another person—by emitting echoic responses and thus building a model for it, we tact that object in the only sense in which any object is ever tacted.

A kind of rudimentary model-building is exemplified when a verbal response resembles a *nonverbal* stimulus. In vocal behavior such a relation is called onomatopoeia; in written behavior it is exemplified by the pictograph or hieroglyph. Just as quoting a verbal response is a form of behavior which constructs a model of the object described, so the onomatopoetic response provides a rough acoustic model of a nonverbal but audible "object." Writing out a pictograph or hieroglyph is a form of verbal behavior which constructs a rough visual model of a nonverbal visual object. A conventional set of pictographs is a limiting minimal repertoire similar to echoic behavior at the level of the phoneme. Just as an extension of the echoic repertoire approaches vocal mimicry, so an extension of the pictograph approaches representational art.

There are many kinds and degrees of similarity in onomatopoeia. *Bow-wow* is close to mimicry; *splash* and *bang* are less so. What are sometimes called analogically imitative responses show a more tenuous resemblance, because the similarity is between different modes of stimuli. If the responses *smooth, thin,* and *crag* are similar to smooth, thin, and crag-like things, it is by virtue not of the audible products of speech so much as of the behavior which produces these sounds. Some properties of nonauditory stimuli can be imitated by properties of responses which are not necessarily auditory. For example, *stupendous, sesquipedalian, tiny,* and *bit* report certain nonauditory properties of objects in point of size. Reduplicative responses may resemble stimuli in point of number. *Higgledy-piggledy* suggests a resemblance of what we might almost call character. All such responses are a kind of model-building, in which the builder confines himself to the phonetic bricks of a given language. He makes the best picture he can, without dropping below the level of the speech sound. The pictograph is similarly constrained; it is not a picture precisely because of the limitation of a conventional minimal repertoire.

The role of onomatopoeia in the origin of language has been frequently discussed. Onomatopoetic forms could arise if a previously established echoic repertoire were extended to audible but nonverbal stimuli. It is also possible that onomatopoeia could arise independently of such a prior repertoire, in line with traditional explanations of the origin of language, if vocal behavior were effective upon a listener because it resembled an auditory pattern to which the listener had already been conditioned. Questions of origin are here largely irrelevant. Current contributions from an onomatopoetic relation are less speculative and cannot, indeed, be ignored. Given two otherwise synonymous responses under the control of an auditory stimulus, a response which shows some formal resemblance should have additional strength. Other things being equal, it should prevail in the behavior of the speaker and, therefore, be more likely to survive in the language. Contributions of strength from an onomatopoetic relation need to be considered in dealing with the multiple causation of verbal behavior (Chapter 9).

We cannot go very far toward solving the problem of an ideal language by constructing verbal responses which resemble their controlling stimuli. We cannot echo or imitate blue things or heavy things or truculent things with blue, heavy, or truculent responses. The alternative is to allow one or at most a few properties of each stimulus to acquire control of a separate form of response. No effort is made to respond to all properties of a given stimulus. The most precise result is achieved by the process of abstraction, but the independent mobility of responses in metaphorical extension is also valuable.

The considerable difference between a given state of affairs and the verbal behavior which it comes to control means that, to a listener, verbal behavior lacks the richness, complexity, and detail of "direct experience." The extent to which this is true depends upon the properties selected for reinforcement by a verbal community. The scientist makes one set of responses to a given state of affairs because of the reinforcing contingencies established by the scientific verbal community. The poet emits an entirely different set of responses to the same state of affairs because they are effective in other ways on other kinds of listeners or readers. Which behavior most closely matches the actual situation is a question not so much of fact, accuracy, or comprehensiveness as of the interests and practices of verbal communities.

We may summarize this analysis of the traditional problem of reference by noting the relevance of certain traditional terms. The fact that a verbal response conditioned in the presence of a given stimulus is found to show some strength in the presence of another stimulus showing some of the properties of the first is often called Generalization. In both psychological and logical analyses a special activity on the part of the speaker is often assumed. But Generalization, like Metaphor, is merely a characteristic of stimulus control. The more precise control established by the community in Abstraction has sometimes caused this term to be applied to (1) the history of reinforcement producing the desired result, (2) the resulting response, and (3) the controlling property of stimuli. The term Concept Formation, taken over originally from logic and epistemology, has been applied to essentially the same process. Here Formation carries the sense of (1) but Concept continues to show (2) and (3). On the continuum extending from proper names to minimal abstract tacts, terms at the latter end have often been called Universals. In general, as we proceed along this continuum away from the proper name, the referent grows more difficult to identify. How we represent the ultimate controlling relation is often a matter of taste. In the present analysis we have spoken of defining properties and of classes of stimuli, and in casual discourse we can name these controlling concepts with suffixes such as "red*ness*," "pyramidal*ity*," and so on. In a more sophisticated sense, we may speak of properties common to many instances as concepts, abstractions, universals, notions, and so on, so long as we keep the actual process of demonstration in mind. This is also the point at which the term "idea" might be revived for use through an operational definition.

The "Referents" in Other Types of Verbal Operant

In a behavioral formulation of semantic relations we are under no compulsion to account for all verbal behavior with a single formula. The tact is obviously an important type of verbal response, particularly in its special effect upon the listener. We do not therefore conclude, however, that it is the only genuine kind of verbal behavior or that it establishes a pattern according to which all verbal behavior must be explained. We may avoid fruitless efforts to discover the referents of terms like *which, but, please,* or a sneeze. Echoic and textual operants, because of their point-to-point correspondence with verbal stimuli generated by the behavior of others, may look like tacts, but in dealing with the echoic or textual speaker the original referents may not be relevant. When we repeat or read a passage of verbal behavior, we are not necessarily "referring to anything" in the special sense of the tact. We have seen that the mand also requires a different formulation. Traditionally, this has been explained by arguing that the speaker acquires a word in its meaningful relation to a thing and then *uses* the word to ask for something. This is not only an inaccurate account of the acquisition of many mands, but there are many examples which cannot be so explained. We need not try to identify the "referents" of *Sh!* or *Please!* or *Wake up!* in such a correspondence framework.

Intraverbal behavior has given the greatest difficulty in traditional semantic theory. Since this lacks the point-to-point correspondence with verbal stimuli seen in echoic or textual behavior, it is more likely to be accepted as a response to a nonverbal state of affairs following the pattern of the tact. What are essentially relations between words and words come to be treated as relations between words and things. When we say that the word *Caesar* refers to Caesar, dead though he has been these two thousand years, we are clearly not talking about the behavior of a contemporary speaker. A response of this form is almost certainly intraverbal, if it is not textual or echoic. A process of educational reinforcement has brought it under the control of various sets of *verbal* circumstances. Theoretically we should be able to trace these circumstances back to an instant in which a response was made to Caesar as a man. The study of history assumes valid chains of this sort, and a predilection for primary sources is essentially the avoidance of unduly long, and hence probably faulty, chains. But the verbal behavior of the modern historian is still mostly intraverbal. If we exclude pictures, statues, impersonations, and so on, *Caesar* cannot be a tact in the behavior of a contemporary speaker. Just as word-associations and metaphor are often explained in terms of logical relations (and the psychical processes which they are supposed to represent) so the semantic relation is used to explain the ultimate source of the pattern of the historian's behavior. But it does not explain his current behavior. In the behavior of a speaker in the twentieth century, *Caesar crossed the Rubicon* is a response, not to a specifiable physical event, but to a set of verbal stimuli.

A great deal of scientific, mathematical, and logical discourse is also intraverbal and hence not adequately represented by the semantics of the tact. We do not need to be able to say what an expression midway in the course of a mathematcial calculation "stands for." The expression is accounted for as verbal behavior by tracing its antecedents. Few if any of these may concern the sort of variable involved in a tact. (It is tempting to compare this distinction with that between analytic and synthetic statements, but although all analytic statements may be intraverbal—and hence have no "referents" in terms of the present relation—all synthetic sentences are not necessarily tacts.) Another type of verbal response which cannot be represented by a semantic framework derived from the tact relation is exemplified by such responses as *is, perhaps, not, except,* and *verily,* which are concerned with the manipulation and qualification of other verbal behavior. These have been a heavy burden for traditional schemes of reference but an adequate provision may be made for them elsewhere in an analysis of verbal behavior (Part IV).

VERBAL BEHAVIOR UNDER THE CONTROL OF PRIVATE STIMULI [17]

In the paradigm for the tact in Figure 5 both speaker and listener are represented as in contact with a common object, to which the speaker's response refers. Some verbal behavior, however, is under the control of stimuli to which the speaker alone is able to react. The response *My tooth aches* is controlled by a state of affairs with which no one but the speaker can establish a certain kind of connection. A small but important part of the universe is enclosed within the skin of each individual and, so far as we know, is uniquely accessible to him. It does not follow that this private world is made of any different stuff—that it is in any way unlike the world outside the skin or inside another's skin. Responses to private stimuli do not appear to differ from responses to public events. Nevertheless, the privacy of such stimuli raises two problems.

A first difficulty is encountered in the analysis of behavior in general: the investigator cannot readily point to the stimuli to which he must appeal in predicting and controlling behavior. Possibly this problem will eventually be solved by improved physiological techniques which will make the private event public. In the verbal field, for example, if we could say precisely what events within the organism control the response *I am depressed,* and especially if we could produce these events at will, we could achieve the degree of prediction and control characteristic of verbal responses to external stimuli. But though this would be an important advance, and would no doubt be reassuring as to the physical nature of private events, the problem of privacy cannot be fully solved by instrumental invasion of the organism. No matter how clearly these internal events may be exposed in the laboratory, the fact remains that in the normal verbal episode they are quite private. We have still to answer a broader question, of which the scientific question may be regarded as a special case.

In setting up the type of verbal operant called the tact, the verbal community characteristically reinforces a given response in the presence of a given stimulus. This can be done only if the stimulus acts upon both speaker and reinforcing community. A private stimulus

[17] Some of the points in the present section were first discussed in an article entitled "The Operational Analysis of Psychological Terms," in the *Psychological Review,* 1945, 52, pp. 270-277. A more extensive discussion in reference to a general science of human behavior, appears in *Science and Human Behavior,* particularly in Chapter XVII, "Private Events in a Natural Science."

cannot satisfy these conditions. How, then, does the verbal community establish the contingencies of reinforcement which produce verbal responses to private stimuli? How, for example, is the response *toothache* appropriately reinforced if the reinforcing community has no contact with the tooth? There is no question that responses to private stimuli are established, but how are they set up, what is their relation to controlling stimuli, and what, if any, are their distinguishing characteristics?

There are at least four ways in which a reinforcing community with no access to a private stimulus may generate verbal behavior with respect to it.

(1) A common *public accompaniment* of the private stimulus which eventually controls the response may be used. Let us consider, for example, how a blind man might learn the names of a trayful of objects. The stimulation which eventually enters into control is tactual: the man explores the objects with his fingertips. At the same time he acquires verbal responses echoically from the teacher. The necessary contingency between a given response and the appropriate object is established by the teacher, who identifies by sight the object which the man is touching. The total contingency of reinforcement thus depends upon the blind man's response in the presence of tactual stimuli and the effect of this response upon the reinforcing teacher, who identifies the stimuli by sight. This is a perfectly satisfactory verbal system, which could establish very precise tacts, but only because there is a close correlation between the visual and tactual stimuli generated by objects.

Responses to private stimuli are often reinforced in the same way. One teaches a child to say *That hurts* in accordance with the usage of the community by making reinforcement contingent upon certain public accompaniments of painful stimuli (a smart blow, damage to tissue, and so on).

(2) A commoner practice is to use some *collateral response* to the private stimulus. It is possible that a dentist might be able to identify some condition of a diseased tooth which is so closely correlated with the private stimulation from such a tooth that the response *toothache* could be established according to the pattern of (1) above, but the response is usually established in the young speaker on the basis of other responses which he is seen to make to the private stimulus. The community reinforces as correct the response *My tooth aches* when it observes such collateral behavior as holding the hand to the jaw,

executing certain facial expressions, or groaning in certain temporal patterns.

As a special case of this principle, responses to complex private stimuli are often established on the basis of verbal behavior already conditioned with respect to some of the elements of a complex stimulus. Roughly speaking, a man may describe some inner condition with the verbal repertoire appropriate to its several features and, on the basis of this information, the community may then reinforce an appropriate response to the whole state of affairs. The greater part of a private repertoire (from *heartburn* to *Weltschmerz*) is generally acquired in this way. Since the procedure assumes that elemental responses to private events are already available, the practice does not suggest a solution to the general problem.

(3) A third possibility is that the community may not need to appeal to private stimuli at all; it may reinforce a response in connection with a public stimulus, only to have the response transferred to a private event by virtue of common properties, as in metaphorical and metonymical extension. It has often been pointed out that most of the vocabulary of emotion is metaphorical in nature. When we describe internal states as "agitated," "depressed," or "ebullient," certain geometrical, temporal, and intensive properties have produced a metaphorical extension of responses.

Not all metaphorical expressions evoked by private stimuli exemplify this principle. Although *a sharp pain* or *a burning sensation* may illustrate metaphorical extension arising from a similarity between the stimulation supplied by sharp or burning objects and certain private stimuli, another explanation is possible. The metaphorical step may have occurred *before* the response receded to the private world. In that case we should have no reason to look for a private stimulus having similar properties. If the response *sharp* is first acquired in connection with certain objects with identifiable physical properties not related to their effect upon the human organism—for example, if a needle is called sharp if it shows a certain geometrical pattern in profile or easily penetrates paper or cloth, or if a knife is called sharp if it readily cuts wood, then the extension of the response to a certain type of painful stimulus generated by pricking or cutting is metonymical. Certain stimuli are frequently associated with objects having certain geometrical properties, and the response is therefore transferred from one to the other. *That is sharp* becomes synonymous with *That hurts,* where it was originally synonymous only with *That has a fine point* or *...a thin edge.* Although the community never has access to more than the geometrical shape of the point or edge or the effects of these upon the surface of the speaker, the response *That is sharp* in the sense of *That hurts* is presumably effective and may continue to receive reinforcement. To the speaker, the associated private stimuli are more important than the geometrical properties of the object which produced them, and hence they predominate in controlling the response. When the response is later evoked by private stimuli not accompanied by or produced by a sharp physical object (as when a patient reports that he has a sharp pain in his side), we cannot assume that the state of affairs in his side necessarily has any of the geometrical properties of the original sharp object. It need only share some of the properties of the stimuli produced by sharp objects. We do not need to show that a sharp pain and a sharp object have anything in common; and if they have not, the extension of the response to the private event does not exemplify the present principle. In expressions like *ebullient* or *dampened spirits,* however, we must search for possible similarities between public and private events to explain the metaphorical extension. Something within the skin must "bubble up" or "grow limp or cold" in some sense.

(4) When a response is descriptive of the speaker's own behavior, there is a fourth possible way in which a private stimulus may acquire control. The original contingency may be based upon the externally observable behavior of the organism, even though this stimulates the speaker and the community in different ways. If the behavior is now reduced in magnitude or scale, a point will be reached at which the private stimuli survive although the public stimuli vanish. In other words, behavior may be executed so weakly or so incompletely that it fails to be seen by another person, although it is still strong enough to stimulate the behaver himself. In such a case, the response is eventually made to a private stimulus which is *similar except in magnitude* to private stimuli otherwise accompanied by public manifestations useful to the community. This is possibly only a special case of the first principle above, but it should be noted that when the object described is behavior itself, a reduction in magnitude may affect public and private manifestations differently.

Although these four practices are in a sense ways in which the verbal community circumvents the inaccessibility of private stimuli in setting up verbal behavior under their control, no one of them guarantees the precision of control seen in responses to external manipulable stimuli. In (1) the connection between public and private stimuli need not be invariable, and the collateral responses in (2) may be made to other stimuli. Even in the careful practices of the psychological laboratory, it is doubtful whether terms descriptive of, for example, emotional states are under precisely the same stimulus control from speaker to speaker. The metaphorical extension of (3) may follow unexpected properties, and there is no way in which the stimulus control may be pinned down through the auxiliary processes of abstraction. If the private stimulation which accompanies macroscopic and microscopic behavior in (4) is unchanged except for magnitude, we may expect a greater validity, but the practice is applicable only when the object described is the behavior of the speaker.

The contingencies which establish verbal behavior under the control of private stimuli are therefore defective. The result has been described elsewhere as follows:

> Everyone mistrusts verbal responses which describe private events. Variables are often operating which tend to weaken the stimulus control of such descriptions, and the reinforcing community is usually powerless to prevent the resulting distortion. The individual who excuses himself from an unpleasant task by pleading a headache cannot be successfully challenged, even though the existence of the private event is doubtful. There is no effective answer to the student who insists, after being corrected, that that was what he "meant to say," but the existence of this private event is not accepted with any confidence.
>
> The individual himself also suffers from these limitations. The environment, whether public or private, appears to remain undistinguished until the organism is forced to make a distinction. Anyone who has suddenly been required to make fine color discriminations will usually agree that he now "sees" colors which he had not previously "seen." It is hard to believe that we should not distinguish between the primary colors unless there were some reason for doing so, but we are conditioned to do this so early in our history that our experience is probably not a safe guide. Experiments in which organisms are raised in darkness tend to confirm the view that discriminative behavior waits upon the contingencies which force discriminations. Now, self-observation is also the product of discriminative contingencies, and if a discrimination cannot be forced by the community, it may never arise. Strangely enough, it is the community which teaches the individual to "know himself."

Some contingencies involving inner stimulation do not, of course, have to be arranged by a reinforcing community. In throwing a ball we time a sequence of responses by the stimulation which our own

> movements generate. Here the reinforcing contingencies are determined by the mechanical and geometrical exigencies of throwing a ball, and since a reinforcing community is not involved, the question of accessibility to the behaving individual does not arise. But "knowledge"... is particularly identified with the verbal behavior which arises from social reinforcement. Conceptual and abstract behavior are apparently impossible without such reinforcement. The kind of self-knowledge represented by discriminative verbal behavior—the knowledge which is "expressed" when we talk about our own behavior—is strictly limited by the contingencies which the verbal community can arrange. The deficiencies which generate public *mistrust* lead, in the case of the individual himself, to simple *ignorance*.[18]

A characteristic result of these defective contingencies is that such responses are often controlled by a mixture of stimuli the nature of which is not clear either to the community or listener or to the speaker himself. Even in what appear to be objective descriptions of public events, private stimuli may make a contribution. The techniques of science and of the special contingencies which force abstraction are corrective measures; but elsewhere, particularly in metaphorical extension, private stimuli are often involved. Such a response as *I am hungry* may be reinforced in several ways. The community may reinforce because it knows the history of ingestion of the speaker, as in (1), or has observed collateral behavior probably associated with such a history—for example, the speaker readily eats when offered food or responds with alacrity to the dinner bell—as in (2), or because the speaker has engaged in other verbal behavior describing his tendency to eat or the probability that he will eat, as in (4). The speaker may react to all these himself, as well as to the powerful private stimulation of hunger pangs. A given instance of his response *I am hungry* may therefore be translated as *I have not eaten for a long time* (1), *The smell of food makes my mouth water* (2), *I am ravenous* (3), *I could eat a horse* (4), and *I have hunger pangs.* (The response *I was hungrier than I thought* shows control exercised by public stimuli generated by the ingestion of an unexpectedly large amount of food where earlier private counterparts or accompaniments were ineffective.) While all of these may be synonymous with *I am hungry,* they are not synonymous with each other. For technical purposes the response might be brought under the control of only one of these states of affairs in a particular speaker, but a special set

[18] *Science and Human Behavior* (New York, 1954), p. 260.

of contingencies opposed to those of the community as a whole would be required.

Many expressions which appear to describe the properties of things must be interpreted as at least partly under the control of private stimuli. *Familiar* is a good example. A familiar place is not distinguished by any physical property. It is familiar only to someone who has seen it or something like it before. Any place becomes familiar when frequently seen. The response *His face is familiar* cannot be formulated in the same way as *His face is red.* The condition responsible for *familiar* is not in the stimulus but in the history of the speaker. Having acquired the response with respect to this property, the speaker may emit it in the presence of other objects frequently seen. Having acquired the term with respect to visual stimuli previously seen, he may emit it in the presence of tunes previously heard, tastes previously tasted, and so on. Only by supposing that the individual is reacting to certain features of his own behavior having to do with the effect of repeated stimuli can we account for the full scope of the response.

Beautiful requires a similar explanation. Many attempts have been made, of course, to show that beautiful objects possess certain distinguishing objective features. If we could regard these attempts as successful or potentially successful, there would be no problem here, since the objective properties would explain the extended control of the response *beautiful* just as other properties explain the response *pyramidal.* But if "beauty is in the eye of the beholder," we must appeal to a common effect of such stimuli. If *beautiful* is first acquired with respect to pictures and is then spontaneously emitted for the first time in the presence of music, and if this cannot be attributed to such common physical properties as "unity" or "symmetry," a private stimulus must be involved. The case differs from that of *familiar* by appearing to beg the question. It is not difficult to trace the history of the private stimulus in the case of *familiar,* even though we cannot easily establish its properties. But it appears to be necessary to take it as already in existence in the case of *beautiful.* Those objects which we come to call beautiful only through learning do not raise the present problem,[19] but objects or events which are instantly responded to as beautiful require the additional assumption of a common private event. We might construct a crude parallel by reinforcing ingestive or sexual behavior in the presence of a given visual stimulus and

[19] As an example, compare Stendhal's analysis of the beautiful mistress in *De L'Amour.*

then independently in the presence of a given auditory stimulus. A verbal response now established in connection with one of these stimuli should be evoked by the other by virtue of the common effect in strengthening ingestive or sexual behavior.

In other kinds of responses the participation of private stimuli is more obvious. In the so-called "pathetic fallacy" an object or event is said to be described with terms appropriate to the "state of mind" of the speaker: the sullen man speaks of the sullen sea. The psychoanalytic principle of projection includes examples of verbal behavior describing the behavior of others: the man who is angry frequently calls others angry, the man who is afraid tends to call others afraid, and so on. But although in some cases the speaker may be mixing and confusing private and public events, all responses of this sort do not necessarily prove a private contribution. The public origin of subjective terms must not be forgotten. What appears to be an example of the pathetic fallacy or of projection may exemplify only the reversal of the process by which a response was confined to private events in the first place. Consider, for example, the response *afraid*. We acquire this under circumstances in which public events are available to the reinforcing community, although private accompaniments which may be more important to us eventually control the response. The community may base its reinforcements upon generally fearful stimuli, as in (1) above, or such concomitant responses as sweating, cowering, retreating, or jumping at slight noises, as in (2). Although the concomitant private events may predominate, they never acquire exclusive control of the behavior. In describing the behavior of others with the same terms, we continue to make use of the public manifestations. If we observe that an animal cowers or retreats when someone approaches, we call it afraid, not because we read into the animal our own private accompaniments of fear but because the public characteristics of fearful behavior are clearly represented. We may also call inanimate objects afraid without "projecting" anything. Thus, a child watching several Mexican jumping-beans on a table saw one bean move toward another just before the second bean moved in the opposite direction. The child said *That bean's afraid*. While jumping-beans are not entirely inanimate, the actual events were a coincidence which could be duplicated mechanically—for example, by Michotte's apparatus for the study of the perception of causality.[20] The timing of the two jumps and their

[20] Michotte, A., *La Perception de la Causalité* (Louvain, 1946).

relative directions were enough to evoke the response *afraid*. It does not follow that the boy attributed subjective feelings to the bean.

An example of an unnecessary appeal to private events is discussed by I. J. Lee,[21] who borrows the example from Gregory Wilbur. A three-year-old boy riding in a car over hilly country exclaimed *Hill!* at each change of speed or direction. An especially sudden descent led to the response *Strong hill!* This was described by saying that the boy projected his own strength into the hill. But *strong* is a response acquired early in the normal repertoire under the control of certain intensive aspects of stimuli—tastes, odors, and the pressures, pullings, and pushings of strong persons. In order to prove projection in this case, it would be necessary to show that the response had previously been controlled only by instances involving the child's own strength. The response *Big hill!* which might equally well have been evoked under the same circumstances would not suggest projection.

The extensive verbal behavior usually called animism may have little to do with private stimuli. It may represent a stage in the growth of a verbal environment in which responses describing certain aspects of behavior are extended freely to both animate and inanimate objects. Waves, trees, clouds, and men are all called "angry" when in violent and possibly disorganized motion. When, in a special case, the response is evoked by the speaker's own behavior, certain private stimuli may also be present, but they need play no part in other instances of the response. If we fear the anger of waves or trees, it is not because we project our feelings and contend that they are angry at us, but because all things in violent motion are dangerous. Eventually the verbal environment may force a more useful discrimination in which responses of this sort are narrowly restricted to certain characteristics of the behavior of organisms rather than of things in general, but the control is probably never exclusive. It is only when a man describes trees in a wind as angry because he himself is also angry that we need to appeal to another principle, and this principle may be nothing more than the multiple causation of Chapter 9.

Verbal Responses to the Speaker's Own Behavior

Behavior generally stimulates the behaver. Only because it does so can coordinated behavior, in which one response is in part controlled by another, be executed. Verbal behavior exemplifies the

21 Lee, I. J., *Language Habits in Human Affairs* (New York, 1941).

co-ordination which requires self-stimulation. The speaker may be his own listener—for example, when intraverbal responses generate "free association"—and automatic self-stimulation from verbal behavior is crucial in the analysis of syntactical and other processes involved in composition and thinking (Parts IV and V). We are concerned here with self-tacts—with verbal behavior controlled by other behavior of the speaker, past, present, or future. The stimuli may or may not be private.

Self-descriptive verbal behavior is of interest for many reasons. Only through the acquisition of such behavior does the speaker become "aware" of what he is doing or saying, and why. A man's report of his own behavior is widely used in the social sciences, from cultural anthropology to psychophysics, and the reliability of the informant or subject is a crucial issue. So is the nature of the data obtained. What are the actual *facts* in these sciences? A survey of opinions or attitudes, with a questionnaire or interview, may tell us what a man says he tends to do, but is the tendency or the statement of the tendency the actual datum? In psychophysics, this is the problem of the status of the "verbal report."

Responses to current behavior. The response *I am opening the window* is controlled by stimulation generated in part by the speaker's behavior. The speaker sees the window, the changes in the window, and part of himself engaging in the activity described. There is no problem in explaining how or why reinforcement is provided by the verbal environment. *What are you doing?* is often a practical question, and the answer is useful to the listener. Responses to overt verbal behavior (*I am speaking English*) often have similar consequences.

Although the reinforcing community uses the conspicuous manifestations of behavior, the speaker acquires the response in connection with a wealth of additional self-stimulation. The latter may assume practically complete control—for example, when the speaker describes his own behavior blindfolded. In that case the speaker and the community react to different, though closely associated, stimuli, as in the example of the blind man.

Perhaps the most difficult of all such responses to account for are those which describe "subjective" behavior. The response *red* in the presence of a red stimulus is fairly easily set up and easily understood. Both speaker and community have access to the stimulus, and the contingencies may be made quite precise. The greater part of the science of psychophysics rests upon this solid footing. In the response

I see red, however, *I see* describes an activity of the speaker. The community can impart that response when it has evidence that the individual is responding discriminatively to a given stimulus, but the private stimuli which take over the future control of the response are not necessarily thereby determined. When the individual says *I see red,* he is presumably reacting to events (possibly available only to him) which are similar to, or have accompanied, events present when the community has observed him to make a discriminative response to red stimuli. Such behavior becomes crucial when there is no longer an external red stimulus. The traditional philosophical and psychological explanation has been that the response *red* is never controlled by the external red object but by a private event. When the private event is immediately generated by a red stimulus, it is called the sensation of red; when it occurs for other reasons, or "by itself," it is called an image of red. The difficulties encountered in this mode of explanation have been discussed elsewhere.[22] The status of the private events in seeing is not a problem exclusively concerned with verbal behavior. Two points, however, may be made here.

(1) In explaining how responses may be brought under the control of private stimuli, we have not discovered any process which would permit the narrowing of the control to necessarily private stimuli. We cannot, for example, use the techniques of establishing an abstraction to base a response upon some stimulus *defined by its privacy.* Since sensations and images are by definition private, we are unable to establish a parallel and must explain the behavior in some other way.

(2) The contingencies which force a man to respond to private events with the kind of behavior called knowing (see Chapter 19) often appear to be exclusively verbal. Although automatically generated stimuli enter into the control of co-ordinated behavior in many ways, they are not "seen" or "known"—that is, they are not responded to with behavior which identifies them in the manner of the tact—except through contingencies arranged by the verbal community. As we have noted, it is social reinforcement which leads the individual to know himself. It is only through the gradual growth of a verbal community that the individual becomes "conscious." He comes to see himself only as others see him, or at least only as others insist that he see himself.

[22] *Science and Human Behavior,* Chapter 17.

Responses to covert behavior. Operant behavior tends to be executed in the easiest possible way. In order to condition energetic behavior, it is necessary to reinforce energetic instances differentially. As soon as such reinforcement is withdrawn, behavior declines in energy and continues to do so as long as reinforcements are still achieved. In the case of automatic self-reinforcement, the behavior may become so reduced in magnitude that it is no longer visible to others. Only with the aid of instruments to amplify movements or changes concomitant with movement are we able to detect the existence of such "covert" behavior in others. Verbal behavior is especially likely to drop below the overt level, because it can continue to receive reinforcement by being useful to the speaker in many ways.

The stimuli generated by covert behavior are relatively subtle and easily overlooked. As Ryle has pointed out,[23] men learned to read silently only during the Middle Ages. Prior to that time, a text served to evoke *overt* verbal behavior, to which the reader then reacted in any of the ways characteristic of a listener. Reading silently was possibly discovered late because the stimulation generated is relatively insignificant compared with that from reading aloud. What contingencies eventually led to the suppression of vocal behavior, so that it became silent, we shall probably now never be able to determine. Reading aloud is annoying to others, especially if they are doing the same thing, and punishment may have forced silent reading. But this could not occur and continue to be reinforced until the reader was able to respond to the stimulation arising from covert reading and thus to achieve continuous automatic reinforcement.

Greater ease of execution is only one reason why behavior becomes covert. Another kind of consequence of verbal behavior, to be discussed in the following chapter, is commonly called punishment. An important distinction between overt and covert behavior is that only the former is in many instances punished. There are automatic punishing effects which apply to covert behavior as well, but the organism soon learns to avoid the punishments mediated by others by behaving only at the covert level, as in talking to oneself and day-dreaming.

So long as covert behavior continues to stimulate the individual,

[23] Ryle, Gilbert, *The Concept of Mind* (London, 1949). It would be more accurate to say that what was learned so late was that silent reading could be almost as effective as reading aloud. There are classical references to silent reading. For example, Suetonius (*The Lives of the Caesars,* Book II) says that Augustus would administer a mild reprimand by handing the guilty a pair of tablets which they were to read silently (*taciti—legerent*) on the spot.

as it must do if it is to reinforce him, it may control other behavior. When the latter is verbal and in the form of tacts, we say that the speaker is "describing" his own covert behavior. The verbal community establishes many such responses—often in response to such a question as *What are you thinking about?* (This meaning of "think" will be discussed again in Chapter 19.)

It has already been pointed out that verbal behavior under control of the covert behavior of the speaker may have been acquired when the behavior was overt. The covert behavior evokes the same response as the overt behavior because it is essentially the same stimulus except for magnitude. Some of the stimulation associated with the covert response may, however, simply be a common accompaniment rather than part of the overt. It is not the stimulus used by the community and may not be the stimulus controlling the speaker's description of his own behavior, but it may acquire control of that description in a form of *metonymical* extension.

Responses to past behavior. We cannot plausibly explain the response *I opened the window yesterday* by pointing to the stimuli generated by the actual event. These lie in the past history of the speaker and cannot be the "referent" of the remark in the sense of the controlling variable in a functional analysis. It does not explain such behavior to say that the act is described "from memory."

Responding to one's own past behavior is only a special case of responding to past events in general. What is the time limit on the stimuli controlling tacts? Show a child a watch and say *What is that?* and the response *Watch* is fairly easily explained. Show him a watch, cover it up for one second, and say *What was that?*, and we can reasonably apply the same formula. But it is scarcely plausible when the response is delayed by ten seconds, ten minutes, ten hours, or ten days. Indeed, we will not get the response *Watch* under such circumstances from a young child. The ability to respond verbally "to past events" is acquired, and acquired under explicit reinforcing contingencies arranged by the verbal community for just this purpose.

Reports of events in one's past are never very accurate or complete. Much depends upon the current stimuli which bring such responses about. In evoking a response "to a past event" we usually supply additional information: *What did I show you yesterday when you were sitting over there? I held it in my hand like this.* These additional current stimuli may be said to identify the event to be described or distinguish it from all other events which happened "yesterday," but this does not describe their actual function. Their effect is in part due to the process of instruction to be described in Chapter 14. They evoke responses which, in conjunction with the current stimulation of the question, may evoke the response *Watch.* Such events constitute a very unreliable controlling force. The fact is that this is a much less effective way of evoking the response than the use of a watch as a current stimulus.

In spite of the fact that a great deal of time has gone into the study of the act of recall in the psychological laboratory, no adequate analysis of how a child learns to recall has been undertaken. What happened yesterday is important for the effect which it has on the behavior of the child today. If a child learned to ride a bicycle yesterday, he will ride one more skillfully today. In this sense all the past history of the child is represented in his current conduct. But when the child says *There was an elephant at the zoo,* he appears to be reacting to his past history rather than merely profiting from it. This is a verbal achievement brought about by a community which continually asks the child such questions as *Was there an elephant at the zoo?* The answer must be understood as a response to current stimuli, including events within the speaker himself generated by the question, in combination with a history of earlier conditioning. The neglect of this process is all the more shocking when it is recalled that most procedures in education presuppose it.

Among the events which a man is eventually able to describe after a lapse of time, particularly in response to questions, is his own behavior. Much of this behavior is, of course, verbal. He is able to recall with reasonable accuracy not only what he *did* yesterday but what he *said.* Moreover, he is generally able to describe earlier covert behavior: *I was on the point of telling him what I thought of him.*

Responses to potential behavior. Covert behavior is sometimes merely weak behavior. We may merely "think" *That is an iguana* rather than "say" it, either because the response is poorly conditioned (we aren't sure what an iguana is), the stimulus is unclear or atypical (we cannot see the beast clearly among the leaves), or because the present audience is not typical of the sort which reinforces responses of this kind (we aren't sure our listener cares). Sometimes covert behavior is thought of as simply incomplete or inchoate behavior. The response has not yet reached the point at which it will become overt. This is more likely to be the case with respect to the longer "composed" responses to be described in Chapter 14. Covert behavior may also be strong behavior which cannot be overtly emitted because the proper circumstances are lacking. When we are strongly inclined to go skiing, although there is no snow, we say *I would like to go skiing.* It is not very convincing to argue that such a response is merely a description of covert skiing or covert behavior preliminary to skiing.

Sometimes such a response is based upon executed behavior associated with skiing—getting out one's skis, fussing with harness, and so on. Sometimes it may be a description of variables of which the speaker's own skiing behavior is a function. There remains the possibility that it is a description of private events which are concomitants or precursors of covert behavior. The response may be the equivalent of *This is the way I am just before I go skiing,* or *This is the way I am as I go skiing when there is snow.* The behavior apparently described or referred to need not in that case be actually occurring.

Responses to future behavior. I shall go skiing tomorrow is not, of course, literally a response to future behavior. No matter how we may interpret past events, as in the examples given above, it is clear that future events have no place in a causal analysis. Some instances of this sort may be classed as responses to covert behavior (the speaker observes himself engaging in behavior which will become overt, given the opportunity) or to the concomitant conditions described in references to "potential behavior." Other instances may fall into the following additional classes.

Responses to the variables controlling behavior. We can often, though not inevitably, describe the variables of which our behavior is a function. *I am opening the window because the room is too warm* specifies the aversive condition leading to the action described. Responses to variables which control verbal behavior are discussed in Chapters 12 and 13. Apparent descriptions of future behavior can be explained in the same way if we assume that a response such as *I shall go skiing tomorrow* is actually equivalent to the statement *Current conditions, involving the weather, my schedules, and arrangements I have made with my friends, comprise a set of circumstances of the sort under which I characteristically go skiing.*

Responses to variables often appear as statements of "purpose" or "meaning," as we have already seen. *I am looking for my glasses* appears to include a response to the object of the speaker's behavior, but how can an object with which the speaker is not yet in contact control a verbal response? Such behavior must be regarded as equivalent to *When I have behaved in this way in the past, I have found my glasses and have then stopped behaving in this way,* or *Circumstances have arisen in which I am inclined to emit any behavior which in the past has led to the discovery of my glasses; such behavior includes the behavior of looking in which I am now engaged.* It is not some purposive character of the behavior itself which the individual thus tacts, but the variables in control of the behavior. Similarly, responses to controlling variables often include the forms *ought* or *should.* Some instances of *I ought to go* may be translated *Under these circumstances I generally go, If I go I shall be handsomely reinforced,* or *If I go I shall be released from the threat of censure for not going.*

Responses to the level of probability of behavior. We commonly evaluate the probability of our own behavior with appropriate responses: *I certainly will go, I probably will go,* and so on. We may add an estimate of probability to our descriptions of past behavior. (*Certainly, I opened the window*), of current behavior (*I am opening this window, I hope—it appears to be stuck*), or of potential future behavior (*I think I shall open the window*). Responses of the same sort are frequently added to those larger units of behavior called sentences, the composition of which we shall examine in Chapter 14. Such statements may be regarded as descriptions of characteristics of behavior in progress or of the variables controlling behavior. *The chances are I will go skiing* may be regarded as an evaluation of any of the behaviors listed above or of a current set of variables. In the latter case another observer with the same knowledge might make a similar prediction (*I'll bet you will go skiing*) without knowing about the covert behavior.

This is not an exhaustive treatment of verbal responses which describe the behavior of the speaker. The field is almost unexplored —possibly because in almost every case such behavior is controlled in part by private stimuli. Some of the most curious facts concern instances in which such behavior is impossible: the individual *cannot* describe his own behavior, past, present, or future, or the variables of which it is a function.[24] What is needed is an analysis of the techniques through which the verbal community establishes verbal behavior based upon such events. As we shall see, this is crucial for the production of larger samples of verbal behavior and especially

[24] See Chapter 18 in *Science and Human Behavior,* and Chapter 16 below.

for what is called verbal thinking. A study of these practices might make it possible to develop a better "memory for past events," better techniques of observation for future use, better techniques of recall, and a better manipulation of one's own behavior in problem-solving and productive thinking. It might also yield therapeutic advantages which the layman would describe as an increase in the awareness of, or understanding of, oneself.

Until we have this better understanding of the variables which control responses descriptive of the behavior of the speaker, we can at least accept the fact that such responses are established in most verbal communities, that they are useful as a source of data in the social sciences, and in particular that they may be used in interpreting a substantial part of the field of verbal behavior.

Chapter 6

. . . .

Special Conditions Affecting Stimulus Control

GENERALIZED REINFORCEMENT is the key to successful practical and scientific discourse. It brings the speaker's behavior most narrowly under the control of the current environment and permits the listener to react to that behavior most successfully in lieu of direct contact with the environment. When the correspondence with a stimulating situation is sharply maintained, when the listener's inferences regarding the objective situation are most reliable, we call the response "objective," "valid," "true," or "correct."

Stimulus control, however, is never perfect. Verbal behavior is probably never completely independent of the condition of a particular speaker. Changes may occur in the deprivations which underlie generalized reinforcement. The speaker's alertness may vary between extreme excitability and sleep. He may be affected by emotional variables which are otherwise quite irrelevant to his verbal behavior. In addition to these momentary conditions, the stimulus control may be distorted by certain special consequences which are supplied by a particular listener or by listeners in general under particular circumstances. When the controlling relation is thus warped or distorted, we call the response "subjective," "prejudiced," "biased," or "wishful." We shall be most concerned here with the effect of such consequences in distorting the tact, but echoic, textual, and intraverbal behavior characteristically receive generalized reinforcement and may suffer in the same way. Many of the examples to be considered here could, in fact, be regarded as intraverbal.

SPECIAL MEASURES OF GENERALIZED REINFORCEMENT

The amount of reinforcement accorded the verbal behavior of a particular speaker varies from community to community and from occasion to occasion. A child reared in a family which reinforces generously is likely to possess such behavior in great strength and will talk upon almost any occasion. A child reared in the absence of such reinforcement may be relatively silent or taciturn. The difference may lead a listener who is unfamiliar with the history of reinforcement of a particular speaker to take inappropriate action. He may overestimate the importance of a given situation in responding to a voluble, well-reinforced speaker and may underestimate its importance from the "strong, silent" behavior of a taciturn man. When verbal behavior is reinforced for quantity (compare the legendary weighing of scientific or scholarly papers), the importance of the subject matter or the contribution may also be incorrectly estimated. A curious instance of the reinforcement of quantity was reported by Lecky.[1]

> A monk who had led a vicious life was saved, it is said, from hell, because it was found that his sins, though very numerous, were just outnumbered by the letters of a ponderous and devout book he had written. . . . The escape was a narrow one, for there was only one letter against which no sin could be adduced—a remarkable instance of the advantages of a diffuse style.

The generalized reinforcement accorded the speaker may vary with subject-matter or form of response. Special measures of reinforcement "tell the speaker what is worth talking about." In the extreme case verbal behavior appropriate to a single subject-matter may predominate. The professional writer is subject to strong special reinforcements of this sort. The tendency to rewrite a successful book has often been pointed out. Similarly, an anecdote or joke which has been particularly successful is likely to be told again, perhaps only covertly to the speaker himself as he goes to sleep that night. Again, the histories of speakers will differ in this respect, and the listener must "know his speaker" if he is to take appropriate action.

Generalized reinforcement may be deliberately used to strengthen particular forms or themes in the verbal behavior of a subject, as

[1] Lecky, W. E. H., *History of European Morals,* ii (London, 1869), p. 205.

in Greenspoon's [2] experiment. In a situation designed to resemble an interview or an experiment on verbal habits, the experimenter shapes up the behavior of his subject simply by giving some slight "sign of approval" contingent upon a selected property of behavior. For example, the experimenter smiles or nods whenever a plural noun is emitted. The relative frequency of plural nouns then increases. A speaker can be induced to emphasize particular subject matters with the same technique, but here the approval may act as a discriminative stimulus rather than a reinforcement. If a new acquaintance reinforces some kinds of verbal behavior and not others, the speaker may soon confine himself to kinds reinforced because of earlier discriminations. This is a more plausible explanation when a single nod or smile has the effect at issue. It is no explanation if an earlier discrimination is unlikely, as in the case of plural forms. Moreover, a smile or nod could not serve as a discriminative stimulus to release behavior within a certain category if earlier differential reinforcement of the category had not been effective.

The Distorted Tact

Special measures of generalized reinforcement are most obviously effective when they lead to an actual distortion of stimulus control. In a minor case, the speaker simply "stretches the facts." He overestimates the size of a fish he has caught or minimizes the danger of attack by an enemy. A special measure of generalized reinforcement has led him to misread a point on a scale of measurement.

Stimulus control is not only "stretched" but "invented." A response which has received a special measure of reinforcement is emitted in the absence of the circumstances under which it is characteristically reinforced. We see this in the behavior of children: a response which has been enthusiastically received on one occasion is repeated on a different and inappropriate occasion. In a still greater distortion, a response is emitted under circumstances which normally control an incompatible response. We call the response a lie.

The distortion due to differential generalized reinforcement may be traced in the behavior of the troubadour or in the history of the art of fiction. The troubadour begins, let us say, by recounting actual heroic exploits. Certain parts of his account receive special approval

[2] Greenspoon, J., *Amer. J. Psychol., 68* (1955), 409-416. See also Mandler, George and Kaplan, W. K., *Science, 124* (1956), 582-583.

because they interest or flatter his listeners. A first effect is that these parts survive in future tellings. Under the same differential reinforcement he begins to stretch his report; he exaggerates the size of the battle and the heroism of the participants (hyperbole). Finally, he breaks away from stimulus control altogether, "describing" scenes he has never observed or "reporting" stories he has never heard. As a creative artist, his behavior is now controlled entirely by the contingencies of reinforcement (some of which, of course, he himself may supply as his own listener).

When the distortion arising from a special measure of generalized reinforcement leads the listener to react ineffectively to the behavior of the speaker, the social system composed of speaker and listener may deteriorate. The listener may withhold reinforcement altogether or actually punish the speaker. The system is stable only when the correspondence with controlling stimuli is of no practical importance to the listener, as is the case in literature. The behavior of the literary artist continues to be reinforced because the listener or reader, who ultimately reinforces the speaker or writer, does not react in a practical way. So long as the reader distinguishes between fiction and nonfiction (and the writer usually arranges this through devices to be discussed later), he is not exploited by the distortion of verbal behavior. Impressionable people who send gifts to their favorite comic strip characters are exceptions. The art of fiction has emerged from certain changes in the reinforcing practices of verbal communities. Certain standard forms of verbal behavior, identified as such, evoke only nonpractical behavior in the reader. The writer need not respect standard stimulating circumstances, and his behavior may therefore be freely modified by special reinforcing effects (see Chapter 16).

Release from aversive stimulation as a form of generalized reinforcement is often used in special measure to produce verbal behavior having given properties. A confession is often obtained when aversive stimulation, or conditioned aversive stimulation in the form of a threat, is imposed until a given response has been made. The objection to this procedure (for example, in enlightened legal or governmental design) is precisely that it tends to distort stimulus control: release is usually contingent upon a response regardless of its correspondence with "the facts." The speaker may exaggerate a confession, invent one, or confess only part of an actual defection to obtain release.

NONGENERALIZED REINFORCEMENTS

The stimulus control of the tact may be disturbed by consequences which are more important to the speaker than the generalized reinforcement usually accorded his behavior. These may be classified in terms of the effect upon the listener.

Special Reinforcement from the Operant Behavior of the Listener

Verbal behavior would be pointless if the listener did nothing more than reinforce the speaker for emitting it. The verbal community maintains the behavior of the speaker with generalized reinforcement, but a given listener often takes specific action with respect to what is said. If the listener's behavior is reinforcing for the speaker in his current state of deprivation or aversive stimulation, the speaker's behavior will be affected. Its relation to a controlling stimulus may or may not be modified. Consider, for example, the complex tact *I am hungry*. This is emitted under the control of relevant (usually private) stimuli. The speaker may receive nothing more than a generalized reinforcement—for example, if he is participating in a physiological experiment. But the response may have another effect upon a sympathetic listener who then offers him food. Insofar as the operant is subsequently strong because of reinforcement with food, it will be controlled by the same variables as, say, *Give me something to eat*. When a housewife says *Dinner is ready,* not because of the generalized reinforcement characteristic of the tact, but mainly because her listeners will then come to the table, the response is functionally very close to the mand *Come to dinner!* To the listener who is not hungry or who does not respond by coming to dinner (for example, when the speaker is a chef and the listener the owner of a restaurant), *Dinner is ready!* is characteristically reinforced only when it corresponds to a particular state of affairs. It is then a "pure" tact. A common result is a mixture of controlling relations characteristic of both tact and mand. We might speak of this as an "impure tact."

The action which a listener takes with respect to a verbal response is often more important to the speaker than generalized reinforcement. The behavior of the alert, mature speaker is usually closely related to particular effects. Generalized reinforcement is most obvious and most useful in the original conditioning of verbal behavior.

In some measure, the verbal community continues with such reinforcement into the mature life of the speaker, but upon any particular occasion the speaker is most concerned with "letting the listener know about something"—that is, the strength of his behavior is determined mainly by the behavior which the listener will exhibit with respect to a given state of affairs. In the long run, a great variety of special effects upon special listeners may have the same result as a sustained generalized reinforcement, and the control exerted by the current stimulating situation may be maintained. But the special effect is more likely to bring behavior under the control of special variables.

One form of behavior which has the effect of "letting the listener know," in the sense of leading him to take specific action, is commonly called "announcing." The speaker may announce the presence of a fox in a copse or of Lady X in a drawing room and release appropriate action in each case. Announcement differs from description mainly because the form of the action which the listener is to take is already determined. An announcement "calls the attention of the listener" to a stimulus which then has its own effect. Tacts of this sort are sometimes preceded by mands which specify the action which will bring a given stimulus into control. The announcement of the presence of an important person may be preceded by the mand *Behold!* (*Behold the Lord High Executioner!*). Further action on the part of the listener is taken to the Lord High Executioner himself rather than to a further description by the speaker. Similarly, in *See the balloon, Smell that bacon,* or *Listen to the rain on the roof,* tacts in the form of announcements are preceded by injunctions to engage in the necessary sensory activity which will bring the listener into contact with the stimulus itself.

The term "communication" also suggests that the speaker is controlled by a stimulating situation and is especially reinforced by the action which the listener takes with respect to it. The term does not apply to the mand or to echoic, textual, or intraverbal behavior and is not too easily applied to the tact which results from generalized reinforcement. We shall see in Part III that there are also instances in which both speaker and listener are, so to speak, in possession of the same facts, and hence in which nothing is communicated.

Special behavior on the part of the listener, like a special measure of generalized reinforcement, may distort the stimulus control exerted by a point on a continuous scale. A clock face with the hands at a quarter to two generally yields the response *A quarter to two,* but it may not do so when the behavior of the listener will be more reinforcing if the speaker emits a different response. If the speaker is urging the listener to hurry, for example, he will say *It's nearly two o'clock*—a response which, under generalized reinforcement alone, would be evoked by a different setting of the hands. If the speaker is urging the listener to act more deliberately, however, he may respond to the same stimulus with *It's only a little after half past one.* (Juliet distorted another kind of clock when she detained Romeo by insisting *It is the nightingale and not the lark.*)

When special consequences produce a complete break with the stimulus, we say that the response is invented or "made up." Let us suppose that a small child has lost a penny, that he emits the response *I lost my penny,* and that, as a result, a listener gives him a penny. This special action strengthens the response, possibly to such an extent that it will be emitted again when no penny has been lost. Special behavior on the part of the listener which has never been of any importance to the speaker may become so and generate similar behavior. For example, we may say *Dinner is ready!* in order to interrupt a conversation which has taken a dangerous turn, or to play a joke. Aesop's boy who cried *Wolf!* supplies the classical stereotype. In each of these cases the same behavior on the part of the listener might have been achieved with a mand (*Give me a penny!*, *Leave the room!*, or *Come running!*). The distorted tact is temporarily more effective because it plays upon a greater tendency on the part of the listener to respond appropriately. The usefulness of the distorted tact is only temporary, however, because the social system composed of speaker and listener rapidly deteriorates. The community stops giving the child a penny and may even punish him for lying; the practical joker is ostracized; and the boy finds himself helpless when a wolf at last appears.

Aversive consequences often have a more immediate effect than reinforcement based upon states of deprivation. The stimulus control of a tact is especially likely to be distorted when the response is emitted in avoiding or escaping from aversive consequences. A suborned witness behaves verbally with respect to reinforcing contingencies established by the suborner; the state of affairs which would otherwise be in control may have little bearing upon his behavior.

Special Reinforcement from the Listener's Emotional Behavior

Among the important special effects of verbal behavior are the emotional reactions of the listener. The listener who laughs is disposed to act in ways which are positively reinforcing—for example, he may pay the speaker in the role of entertainer or do him a favor. The salesman tells funny stories to his prospect and is reinforced by the laughter which follows. The speaker bears good news with alacrity and repeats it frequently because of the disposition toward reinforcement engendered in his listener. At other times he may be reinforced by injuring his listener: he may bear or repeat bad news, or criticize or blame the listener, because of the resulting obvious discomfiture. He may be reinforced for describing a gruesome accident by the horror which he engenders in his listener, or for describing an obscene event because the listener blushes or becomes sexually excited. Sarcasm is called sarcasm just because it is biting. The scientist may publish an experimental result a little more quickly if it upsets the theory of a rival. All of this is likely to occur under circumstances in which any injury inflicted upon the listener can be shown to be reinforcing. (Why such an event is reinforcing lies beyond the field of verbal behavior itself.)

Emotional responses of the listener cannot, as we have seen, explain the reinforcement of a mand—neither emotional *reflexes,* such as laughing or crying, nor emotional *dispositions,* such as those in which the individual is moved to attack, to run away from, to injure, or to "be nice to" someone fit the paradigm of Figure 2 on page 39. As we have seen, mands which appear to specify such effects (*Be gay!, O, weep for Adonais!, O hate me when thou wilt!*) are magical and must be explained in special ways. The most reliable method of generating an emotion is to present an appropriate stimulus. In order to get someone to laugh we may tickle him, surprise him in a pleasant way, or act in a laughable manner. The effect is possibly unconditioned—that is, it may not depend upon his prior history. But when we get someone to laugh by telling a funny story, we use stimuli conditioned according to the classical Pavlovian pattern. If a verbal stimulus frequently accompanies some state of affairs which is the unconditioned or previously conditioned stimulus for an emotional reaction, the verbal stimulus eventually evokes this reaction.[3] Thus, if one is afraid of snakes, and if the verbal stimulus *snake* has some-

[3] *Science and Human Behavior,* Chapter 4.

times accompanied real snakes, the verbal stimulus alone may evoke an emotional reaction.

The emotional reaction is usually a by-product of some other verbal function. The verbal environment does not establish the response *snake* primarily to evoke such a reaction on the part of the listener. The pairing of stimuli which ultimately generates the response arises from contingencies related to more practical behavior. The speaker may acquire the response *dead* under the control of a biological state of affairs having practical or theoretical importance. The generic characteristic shared by a dead tree, a dead animal, and a dead man could be fairly precisely defined. But dead objects are frequently associated with stimuli evoking powerful emotional responses, even though these play no part in the contingencies established by the verbal environment for that form of response.

The emotional reaction being evoked by a stimulus may demonstrate the metaphorical or metonymical extension of Chapter 5. In a well-known experiment, Diven [4] recorded changes in the resistance of the skin of the hand produced by the reflex secretion of sweat which is often a conspicuous feature of an emotional reaction. Diven used a list of words as verbal stimuli, and his subjects received an electric shock whenever certain words occurred. If a shock followed the stimulus word *barn,* the word eventually produced an emotional response, and this was extended to other rural words.

Conditioned emotional responses to parts of a literary work often contribute an effect which is to some extent independent of the "prose meaning" of the work. It has even been argued that the prose meaning is useful primarily in maintaining the behavior of the reader or listener so that emotional responses to the separate parts of the work may take place. In T. S. Eliot's *Gerontion,* for example, expressions like "dry month," "hot gates," "decayed house," "windy spaces," "dry brain," "dry season" have an over-all effect which is independent of their order or of any syntactical arrangement in the poem. The adjectives "modify" much more than the nouns which follow them. A mere list of words has something of the same effect, though it will probably not induce the reader to continue to read. The possibility that poetry may be effective in an emotional way, though otherwise nonsense, has often been recognized. Thus A. E. Housman writes: [5]

[4] Diven, Kenneth, *J. of Psychol.*, *3* (1937), 291-308.

[5] Housman, A. E., *The Name and Nature of Poetry* (Cambridge, 1945).

Even Shakespeare, who had so much to say, would sometimes pour out his loveliest poetry in saying nothing.

Take, O take those lips away
That so sweetly were forsworn,
And those eyes, the break of day,
Lights that do mislead the morn.
But my kisses bring again, bring again,
Seals of love, but sealed in vain, sealed in vain.

That is nonsense; but it is ravishing poetry.

This is the kind of meaning which survives the scrambling of literary texts. An early example was prepared by Lord Chesterfield for his son. The passage:

Life consider cheat a when 't'is all I
Hope the fool'd deceit men yet with favor
Repay will tomorrow trust on think and
Falser former day tomorrow's than the
Worse lies blest be shall when and we says it
Hope new some possess'd cuts off with we what.

has something of the flavor or character of the original.[6] It suggests the same period in English literature and even something of its subject in spite of the scrambling. Terms like *cheat, fool, deceit, falser,* and *worse* have an effect apart from any prose meaning. As Joseph Conrad, in describing an example in *Lord Jim,* says, ". . . the power of sentences has nothing to do with their sense or the logic of their construction."

Partly because of the nature of emotional reactions and partly because they do not explicitly enter into reinforcing contingencies, the listener may not be able to identify the stimulus or the property of the stimulus which generates such an effect. In listening to sustained speech or reading a sustained text, ill-defined emotional reactions may arise and disappear without leading to comment or analysis. The following quotation from a notebook supplies an example:

While working at my desk I noticed a sustained mood of mild annoyance, but I could not at once detect the cause. I eventually discovered that I had written the word *Lacking* in such a way that the *L* suggested

[6] When I consider life, 't'is all a cheat
Yet fool'd with hope men favor the deceit
Trust on and think tomorrow will repay.
Tomorrow's falser than the former day.
Worse lies it says, and when we shall be blest
With some new hope, cuts off what we possess'd.

Chesterfield, P.D.S., *Letters of the Earl of Chesterfield* (London, 1774).

> an *H* and the *a* an *o*. The word closely resembled the proper name *Hocking,* which I was at that time familiar with mainly in connection with a book to which I had reacted quite negatively.

The emotional response was evoked by the visual verbal stimulus in spite of the fact that a corresponding textual response (*Hocking*) was not made at the same time and could not, in fact, be made until a special search for stimuli was undertaken.

It is the exceptional environment which sets up self-descriptive behavior with respect to such events. Marcel Proust [7] was the introspective product of such an environment and has recorded at length his search for the precise stimuli generating emotional reactions and the earlier history which gave them their power. The reader of Proust is, as a result, more likely to note passing responses and to make some effort to explain them. It is generally the case, however, that the response occurs before the appropriate stimulus can be identified, and certainly without recognition on the part of the listener or reader of the earlier history responsible for it. The emotional reactions aroused by proper names are involved in "Freudian" forgetting and serve as a special consequence working for or against the process of nomination when a name is given to a new object or person. In testing whether we "like" a name or whether it is appropriate under such circumstances, we are presumably testing conditioned responses of the present sort. Such responses are taken into account in giving names to products or actors and actresses in order to encourage public support or patronage.

Since the emotional response of the listener may be executed without external support, and since it does not have practical consequences which may be related to the physical circumstances of the speaker, we do not say that such reactions of the listener are "right" or "wrong." We shall see in a moment that these terms often function to reinforce or punish behavior, verbal or otherwise; but emotional reactions cannot be modified by operant reinforcement. Insofar as the *speaker* has been conditioned by the emotional effects he has achieved, we may point to a functional connection between his behavior and the emotional behavior of the listener. But such reactions may occur regardless of the sources of the behavior of the speaker, and may even be generated by wholly accidental productions of verbal stimuli.

[7] Proust, M., *A la Recherche du Temps Perdu* (Paris, 1914).

Emotional stimuli not only elicit responses, they establish dispositions to behave which comprise a more practical part of the field of emotion.[8] The result is a change in probability that the organism will behave in a given way, and this change may or may not be accompanied by the glandular and smooth muscle responses classically regarded as the emotion. Important cases are dispositions to react favorably or unfavorably toward the speaker or some other person. Verbal stimuli may generate not only the emotional reflex pattern of anger, but anger as a predisposition to attack someone. Verbal stimuli do not originally have such an effect; the effect is acquired according to the classical conditioning paradigm.

It has often been pointed out that concrete terms usually have greater emotional effects than abstract. The difference is that the concrete term, in the sense of a response under the control of a particular stimulus, is more likely to coincide with emotionally effective stimuli. The abstract term, being controlled by a property of a large class of events, is not likely to be affected by any other event frequently correlated with that property. For the same reason, the concrete term is likely to generate "conditioned seeing"—that is, to evoke "images." [9] The abstract term controlled by a property common to a large number of instances is not likely to be associated with a stimulus appropriate to a single act of seeing.

Emotional responses do not involve precise timing. They tend to be slow and long-lasting. The effect of a verbal stimulus in generating emotional behavior is relatively independent of time and seldom leads to fatigue.

Emotional reactions are not always controlled by specific differentiated forms of response. One may react emotionally to a verbal stimulus merely because it possesses the property of being verbal. "I hear the sound of words; their sense the air/ Dissolves unjointed ere it reach my ear." [10] Under other circumstances a language may have an emotional effect because it is appropriate to a given verbal community. A man alone in a foreign land may react with profound emotion to any speech in his native tongue. Properties of verbal behavior arising from the emotional or motivational condition of the speaker may also arouse appropriate responses. The glib or serious manner, the careless or precise style, the quarrelsome or soothing

[8] *Science and Human Behavior,* Chapter 10.
[9] *Ibid.,* Chapter 17.
[10] Milton, *Samson Agonistes.*

tone of voice may all have effects in this category, quite independently of the form of the response emitted. The effects can in certain cases be incompatible, as Tolstoy notes in describing a character who spoke with "a querulous and irritated voice, that contrasted with the flattering intention of the words he uttered." [11]

Although special consequences of this sort need not disturb the accuracy of the stimulus control, they are especially likely to do so. The writer of the tear-jerker takes liberties with the facts for the sake of a greater emotional response. Justifiable praise is likely to yield to flattery, blame to calumny. The funny story becomes a travesty, and the account of the accident grows more horrible in the retelling. When the emotional effect upon the listener is the only important consequence, stimulus control may be effectively abandoned, as in literature. Emotional effects upon the reader are an important factor in the production of lyric poems as well as other types of poetry, plays, stories, and novels. In the growth of the literary verbal community, the relevance of practical (operant) behavior is reduced to a minimum. The emotional behavior of the reader or listener is the greater part of what survives.

The Strength of the Listener's Reactions

The effect of a given verbal stimulus will vary with many things. The physical characteristics of the stimulus—whether it is clear and within certain speed limits—are important. So is the past experience of the listener with respect to similar patterns: we listen closely to previously interesting speakers and to certain tones of voice. The advertiser strives for a text which resembles texts which have proved most reinforcing. A single word popping out of a hitherto ignored conversation may convert us at once to avid listeners. Contrariwise, we stop listening to someone who speaks scarcely intelligibly, or dully, or without achieving any clear-cut effect, as we stop reading a book which is badly printed or boring. Too long a discourse or chapter, though interesting enough otherwise, may engender fatigue, from which the reader's behavior will recover during a period of "time out."

With respect to a particular speaker, the behavior of the listener is also a function of what is called "belief." We may define this in terms of strength of response. Our belief that there is cheese in the

[11] Tolstoy, L., *War and Peace* (Modern Library Edition), p. 108.

icebox is a function of, or identical with, our tendency to go to the icebox when we are hungry for cheese, other things being equal. Our belief that there is a substantial table in front of us varies with our tendency to reach for it, place things upon it, and so on. If we have just spent some time in a house of mirrors in an amusement park, our belief in this simple fact may be shaken, just as our belief about the cheese may be quickly dispelled by an empty icebox. Our belief in what someone tells us is similarly a function of, or identical with, our tendency to act upon the verbal stimuli which he provides. If we have always been successful when responding with respect to his verbal behavior, our belief will be strong. If a given response is strictly under the control of stimuli with little or no metaphorical extension and no impurity in the tact relation, and if the speaker clearly indicates these conditions (see Chapter 12), we will react in maximal strength. In this sense we "take his word for it" implicitly. It does not matter whether or not he is a specialist. We believe that the expert will tell us *all* about it, but the nonexpert is equally well believed if the above specifications hold, for he will simply stop talking when he does not know what he is talking about.

Various devices used professionally to increase the belief of a listener (for example, by salesmen or therapists) can be analyzed in these terms. The therapist may begin with a number of statements which are so obviously true that the listener's behavior is strongly reinforced. Later a strong reaction is obtained to statements which would otherwise have led to little or no response. Hypnosis is not at the moment very well understood, but it seems to exemplify a heightened "belief" in the present sense. The world is for a time reduced to verbal stimuli which are in practically complete control of the hypnotized subject. Behavior characteristic of listeners appears in a dramatically intensified form. The sharply localized reaction to verbal stimuli in hypnosis is similar to absorption in a book. Macaulay claimed in his last illness that an interesting book acted as an analgesic.

To some extent, the same conditions of "belief" govern a simple conditioned reflex. When the cook announces *Dinner!,* the listener may respond in two ways. By salivating or by responding otherwise with gland or smooth muscle, he demonstrates Pavlovian conditioning. By going to the table and sitting down, he demonstrates a discriminated operant which has been reinforced upon past occasions of a similar sort. His belief in the cook, in the sense of the strength of either type of reaction, will be influenced by the properties of the response *Dinner*. If the cook has burned the meat or permitted the soufflé to fall and therefore says *Dinner!* in an unusually faint or hesitant voice, the listener may walk to the table with less alacrity and with a drier mouth.

The listener's reactions can be intensified through certain rhetorical devices. Repeated verbal stimuli usually elicit more powerful conditioned emotional responses (compare Dickens' repetition of *Little Nell was dead*) and are more likely to evoke operant behavior. The emission of more than one response having a given effect acts like straight repetition. The mand *Don't do that any more; that's enough; stop it now* is likely to be more effective than *Stop it* simply because it piles up stimuli having the same effect. The arrangement of several verbal stimuli to generate surprise, contrast, or crescendo or diminuendo effects is also common. Onomatopoetic verbal stimuli supplement the normal response of the listener by offering fragmentary nonverbal stimuli generating the same response. Hieroglyphs and pictographs evoke behavior of the reader not only as verbal stimuli, but as nonverbal pictures. A long verbal response describes a large object more effectively than a brief one. This correspondence between response and thing is carried to a whimsical extreme in *Alice in Wonderland,* when the mouse's tale is printed in the form of a mouse's tail. The listener or reader often reacts to what we may call the character of a verbal response, and this may coincide with the character of the subject matter; pompous behavior may be especially effective in describing pompous events, disorganized expression may be particularly apt in describing a disorganized state of affairs. The rare word is an effective name for the rare bird. What the critic describes as "suiting the sound to the sense" appears to be the effort of the poet to create verbal responses which have something of the character of the thing described.

Other Reinforcing Aspects of the Listener's Behavior

The speech of persons in extreme states of emotion is characteristically altered and may have a special effect upon the listener for this reason. We may weep in response to *O weep for Adonais,* not because we can weep on demand, or because accompanying verbal stimuli are effective as impure tacts, or because the words are read in a grief-stricken tone of voice, but simply because we observe that an otherwise logically-minded person has resorted to a type of response which he would ordinarily avoid, thus suggesting the depth of his despair. In writing

For thine is
For life is
For thine is the

T. S. Eliot suggests weakness, exhaustion, or lack of conviction. Something of the same effect is produced accidentally when one is reading aloud from illegible copy, where the pauses may suggest weakness on the part of the writer rather than the reader.

All such effects upon the listener or reader have return effects upon the speaker or writer and account for various properties of his behavior. Many rhetorical devices, as properties of the behavior of the writer, are to be explained in terms of the differential reinforcement arising from the effect upon the reader.

Listening or reading often requires preliminary behavior, such as picking up a telephone, putting a talking record on a phonograph, going to a lecture, drawing close to someone speaking in a group, picking up a magazine, or buying a book. The reinforcing consequences of these behaviors are usually verbal: we buy a book in order to read it. Ultimately we attend only certain kinds of lectures, pay attention only to certain conversationalists, and buy only certain kinds of books, because only these preliminary behaviors are reinforced.

The function of a poem in evoking a strong emotional response is not to be confused with its function in reinforcing the reader for picking up the poem and reading it. The emotional reaction takes place on the spot, but evidence of the conditioning is delayed until we observe a continuing or increased tendency to read similar poems. Reinforcing the reader in this way may be of the first importance to the practicing author. He constructs a literary work not only to evoke certain responses in the reader but to guarantee a measure of reinforcement for reading. Certain themes, although powerful, are "poor business," while others, possibly of little literary merit, improve the sale of later books. An appreciable part of verbal behavior cannot be accounted for without taking into account its effects in making the listener pay attention, in making the reader read further, and so on.

Consequences which are designed to increase the frequency of behavior (rather than alter its relation to controlling variables) are the common verbal reinforcers *Good!, Bad!, Right!,* and *Wrong!* When someone executes a response which we wish to preserve or strengthen, we say *Good!* or *Right!,* and we usually try to make this response as immediately contingent upon the behavior as possible. *Yes* has a similar function, well understood by Yes-men. An overly solicitous listener may emit a steady stream of *Yes's, m-m's, uh-huh's,* nods, surprised arching of the brows, and so on. Applause is verbal according to our definition and its use to increase the frequency of occurrence of behavior is seen in its kinship to *Encore, Bis,* etc.[12] Many interjections which have been difficult to classify in grammar are reinforcing or punishing responses. When we say that interjections "show delight or disgust, approval or censure," we overlook the fact that they are made contingent upon the behavior of a speaker and would serve no purpose if they were not. Although a contemporary American may exclaim *Pfui!* when something he himself has undertaken turns out badly, this must be regarded as a magical extension from instances in which the response, contingent upon the behavior of someone else, stands some chance of modifying that behavior in the future. The same is true of exclamations of delight. Although these responses are commonly associated with emotional states and may combine in a form of multiple causation with unconditioned cries, they are ultimately reinforced because they produce changes in the behavior of people (possibly including the speaker himself).

SPECIAL REINFORCEMENT FROM EFFECTS UPON THE SPEAKER HIMSELF

An important fact about verbal behavior is that speaker and listener may reside within the same skin. The speaker hears himself, and the writer reads what he himself has written. Such self-stimulation often evokes further behavior—echoic, textual, or intraverbal—but "talking to oneself" has another function. A man talks to himself, as he talks to another listener or to the verbal community at large, because of the reinforcement he receives. There seems to be no way in which a solitary individual could generate or maintain a verbal

12 An explicit mand for applause is sometimes set up. The master of ceremonies appealing to his audience *Let's give the lady a nice hand* is only echoing the Roman actor's *Nunc plaudite.*

repertoire, but when a community has established verbal behavior through the usual methods and has concurrently conditioned the speaker as a listener, the speaker may talk to himself and will continue to do so in the absence of further reinforcement from the community. There may be an admixture of such self-reinforcement when one is presumably talking or writing to others. The speaker who is particularly under the influence of himself as a listener is sometimes described as egocentric or "loving to hear himself talk."

Automatic reinforcement may shape the speaker's behavior. When, as a listener, a man acquires discriminative responses to verbal forms, he may reinforce himself for standard forms and extinguish deviant behavior. Reinforcing sounds in the child's environment provide for the automatic reinforcement of vocal forms. Such sounds need not be verbal; the child is reinforced automatically when he duplicates the sounds of airplanes, streetcars, automobiles, vacuum cleaners, birds, dogs, cats, and so on. But among the sounds which become important are the verbal responses of his parents and others. The child can then reinforce himself automatically for the execution of vocal patterns which are later to become part of his verbal behavior. At this stage the child resembles a parrot, which is also automatically reinforced when its vocal productions match something heard in the environment. A similar effect may lead to a special manner of speaking or to particular forms of response characteristic of the behavior of others. The effect is often called identification, but we have no need to appeal to a special process here. The listener usually finds certain speakers particularly reinforcing, either because what is said is reinforcing, or because the speakers are reinforcing in other ways. Parents, favorite employers, persons of prestige, and close friends are examples. Since, for one reason or another, it is often reinforcing to hear such people speak, it is automatically reinforcing to speak *as they speak*—with a particular intonation, mannerism, or favorite vocabulary. Terms characteristic of the adult repertoire are likely to be used by children with special frequency when first acquired. This is not echoic behavior, because the borrowed response is not emitted in the proper temporal relation to the verbal stimulus. The borrowing occurs because of the automatic self-reinforcement generated by the speaker as a result of his earlier conditioning as a listener.

Behavior which acquires its formal properties from self-reinforcement may depart from the standards of the community. The speaker and listener in the same skin may undergo the kind of change which is observed over a much longer period of time in the history of a verbal environment. Responses may lack precision, and modified forms may appear. This is evident in the handwriting with which one keeps a notebook compared with the handwriting with which one writes letters. The notebook is more likely to show idiosyncratic word-signs or abbreviations, not to mention letter-forms. Standard responses may fall under more and more unusual stimulus control. Deviant grammatical forms may go undetected. Ambiguous responses are not ambiguous to *this* listener. The speaker who is primarily affected by his own responses as listener tends to be concerned with favorite topics and terms, with literary allusions carrying prestige-value, with stories which the speaker himself finds amusing or interesting, and so on.

"Artistic" verbal behavior may be compared with that of the musician playing for himself. Other things being equal, he plays music which, as listener, he finds reinforcing. In other words, he "plays what he likes," just as the self-reinforcing speaker "says what he likes." The dice player calls his point before the dice have come to rest; his response may be a magical mand, but it is also a way of hearing good news at the earliest opportunity. The parent who is reinforced when his children are praised, praises them himself. The nostalgic who is reinforced by descriptions of old scenes constructs such descriptions himself. The sexually aroused individual is automatically reinforced by his own discussions of sex. The vain man is reinforced by hearing or seeing his name, and he speaks or writes it frequently himself. Boasting is a way to "hear good things said about oneself." The starving man may talk about food if the net effect is reinforcing. A happy phrase—composed, perhaps, for the first time—may be repeated because of its immediately reinforcing effect. " '. . . and silver is an incorruptible metal that can be trusted to keep its value forever . . . an incorruptible metal,' he repeated, as if the idea had given him a profound pleasure." [13]

We may say that verbal behavior tends to be emitted if it describes a condition which is or would be reinforcing to the speaker. Distortion of stimulus control through such effects is widely tolerated in some verbal communities and sharply suppressed in others. In *A Passage to India,* E. M. Forster has described many instances of wish-

[13] Conrad, Joseph, *Nostromo,* p. 300.

ful verbal behavior acceptable within the speaker's community. Dr. Aziz, in showing his English guest through some rather undistinguished caves, was "pretty sure they should come on some interesting old carvings soon," but only meant he wished there were some carvings. In another instance when asked, "Are you married?," he replied, " 'Yes, indeed, do come and see my wife'—for he felt it more artistic to have his wife alive for a moment," though she had been dead for some time.

THE PUNISHMENT OF VERBAL BEHAVIOR

Verbal behavior may be followed by the kind of consequence called aversive or punishing. We have not yet considered this because punishment does not produce or maintain any type of verbal operant, but it must be included among the special effects which modify behavior already established through positive reinforcement.

Punishment is not to be confused with the use of aversive stimulation in generating avoidance or escape. The same kind of stimuli are used, but in punishment they are made contingent upon a response in the same temporal relation as positive reinforcement. The result is complex, and all its features need not be described here.[14] The assumption that a punishing consequence simply reverses the effect of a reinforcing consequence has not survived experimental analysis. There is no evidence that punishment ultimately reduces a tendency to respond. Its principal effect is to convert the behavior, or the circumstances under which the behavior characteristically occurs, into a conditioned aversive stimulus. Any behavior which reduces such stimulation—such as any behavior which is incompatible with or otherwise displaces punished behavior, either in its incipient or final stages—is automatically reinforced. In punishing one response, then, we automatically provide for the reinforcement of responses which are incompatible with it. The principal result accounts for one of the most important properties of verbal behavior, as we shall see in Chapter 15. Meanwhile we may note simply the effect of punishing consequences upon the strength of related verbal operants.

Verbal behavior is, of course, frequently punished. The community which has hitherto reinforced a response may change its practices. A different community is more likely to punish—possibly with

[14] See *Science and Human Behavior*, Chapter 12.

all the manifestations of "zenoglottophobia." Sometimes the whole repertoire of the speaker is affected, and the incompatible behavior then opposes the effect of generalized reinforcement. Usually, however, punishment is a special effect which alters only part of a repertoire.

When we wish to weaken or eliminate a response, we may use a verbal aversive stimulus such as *Bad!*, *Wrong!*, or *No!* Children are frequently punished for verbal behavior by spanking or the threat of spanking. In some cultures, a symbolic punishment consists of washing out the mouth with soap and water. In ancient times the bearer of bad news was in danger of being killed. Where physical punishments are no longer tolerated, recourse is often had to the withdrawal of conditions associated with positive reinforcement, or the threat of such withdrawal. Privileges are taken away and approval or affection withheld. Some forms of verbal behavior meet with punishment or ridicule, others with criticism. Many effectively punishing events are not explicitly arranged as such, for verbal behavior may be followed by adventitious aversive consequences, including effects generated in the speaker himself as listener.

A curious social punishment is itself verbal: one may punish simply by remaining silent when the occasion demands speech. The awkward silence of social intercourse appears to be a by-product of more specific aversive uses. Verbal behavior normally acquires positively reinforcing properties. A cheery *Good morning!* or even the most casual greeting rules out the possibility of a whole class of aversive actions and may be reinforcing because it does so. We can therefore punish by withholding such responses. We do this in snubbing someone, in refusing to answer, or more subtly in simply *neglecting* to answer a question or to comment upon a remark. Schoolboys are commonly punished by being put "on silence," and a similar disciplinary action in a labor union was recently reported in English papers. Other forms of verbal punishment include cryptic, puzzling, and unclear remarks.

Short of punishing a verbal response directly one may supply a warning stimulus in the presence of which verbal responses are frequently punished. *Tut-tut* may not threaten punishment but it reveals that punishment is impending.

One effect upon verbal behavior, whether direct or indirect, is a reduction in energy level. The punished response is subsequently merely muttered or whispered. It may also become covert or silent, or be "forgotten" in the sense of repressed, as we shall see later. Punished behavior may also be emitted slowly or hesitantly. This is not the slowness of the weak behavior resulting, say, from inadequate conditioning or unclear stimuli, but a minimal speed which avoids the accumulation of aversive effects. Mere hesitancy takes a more acute form in some kinds of stammering. The more violent spasms of the stutterer are possibly due to punishment and the inco-ordination resulting from relative changes in energy level and speed. Over and above characteristics of execution, punishment lowers the relative frequency of a response, partly because responses drop to the covert level and escape observation, and partly because displacing forms take precedence.

The effects of punishment upon verbal behavior seem to show generalization. If one response is punished, the effect is felt upon similar responses or responses under similar circumstances. The government employee who must maintain state or military secrets under the penalty of severe punishment may find his entire verbal repertoire affected. He may become "secretive" in everything he does. The beginning writer may become quite unproductive if too frequently criticized. A child severely punished for verbal behavior may become an hysterical aphasic.

In addition to this general weakening of verbal behavior we need to appeal to punishing consequences to explain certain conditions of strength. For example, we may have to show that an operant is strong because it reduces conditioned aversive stimulation. Punished behavior which is not verbal may be relevant. Thus a "rationalization" is a verbal response which describes other, possibly nonverbal, behavior of the speaker in such a way as to make it least subject to punishment.

We manipulate punishing contingencies for practical purposes in evoking verbal behavior. In getting a criminal to confess, for example, a bribe is a special reinforcing consequence designed to overcome the effects of punishment. Granting "immunity" is a direct reduction of punishing consequences. When immunity cannot be granted, a skillful interrogator may work first for a response which is not itself heavily punishable ("Where did you dispose of the weapon?"), may suggest that the behavior at issue is widespread and condoned, and so on. Religious confession and psychotherapeutic techniques of release sometimes follow similar patterns. Forgiveness is the reduction of a conditioned aversive stimulus or threat *after* a response has been made.

THE READER

The responses of the listener which establish and maintain the behavior of the speaker in all the controlling relations we have been examining are matched by those of the reader who eventually modifies the behavior of the writer. The special consequences with which the present chapter is concerned point up several properties of the behavior of the reader which have no important counterpart in the listener. The reader usually, though not necessarily, begins with the *textual behavior* of Chapter 4; his responses are made under the control of visual stimuli. He may then react to his own textual behavior as a listener. It is not necessary that he do so. In reading aloud to children one may not react beyond the merely textual stage, and in reading aloud in a barely familiar tongue, one may become so preoccupied with pronunciation as to neglect all other functions of reader or self-listener. On the other hand, nontextual responses may predominate. Textual behavior as such may not be evident in the advanced reader, even to the reader himself, though it tends to emerge in conspicuous form when he reads a text to which it is difficult to respond in other ways. The stage at which a textual response is reacted to as a vocal verbal stimulus may be seen in children or in the adult reader who is learning to read material printed in a phonetic alphabet. Both the child and the adult reader emit vocal responses under the control of the text and then respond to the self-generated verbal stimuli. The response made as a self-listener is somewhat delayed and clearly a response to the auditory stimulus alone.

Nontextual responses of the reader may come to be made directly to the printed text, and they may be conditioned in the absence of textual behavior. Thus, children may react appropriately to cards reading *Run, Sit, Clap hands,* and so on, without engaging in vocal behavior. Normally, however, the reader's reactions are first a consequence of textual behavior and then a collateral activity in which textual responses are short-circuited. We react to many signs, such as *SILENCE* in a library or *BARBER* on a shop window, by taking appropriate action without necessarily engaging in textual behavior. We would make essentially the same reaction to a picture of a man with a finger on his lips and a revolving red-and-white spiral, respectively.

These examples remind us of the fact that the behavior of the listener is not essentially verbal. The listener reacts to a verbal stimulus, whether with conditioned reflexes or discriminated operant behavior, as he reacts to any feature of the environment. Conditioned emotional responses to the visual stimulus *DEATH* resemble those to any stimulus associated with death in the practices of a community (such as a funeral wreath or grave stone) or any natural accompaniment of death (such as the appearance of a corpse). Operant behavior executed with respect to the same stimulus resembles behavior controlled by nonverbal stimuli entering into the same contingencies. The relevant properties of stimuli, the process of stimulus induction, the effect of "context," and so on, are not essentially verbal problems.

Since in English spelling there are alternative ways of representing speech sounds, it is possible to construct a text which evokes (1) a textual response generating vocal stimuli to which, as a listener, the reader responds in one way and (2) direct responses of a very different sort. The following fragment of a "poem" will, if read aloud at a steady speed and energy level, offer a fairly effective verbal stimulus to most listeners. It would do so to the reader if he were not responding directly to the text with other short-circuiting responses. The competing responses make it almost impossible for the reader to listen to himself and react appropriately. (The voicing of several consonants is incorrect, but the point is sufficiently made if the person who reads the poem aloud is less likely to understand it than another listener.)

Thus it ease lep't bean ethers know we man till.
Coal dance eye lent was thick wrist ill lair,
Why lone least are lie tanned a sing gull ant earn
Broke thug loom. A long thud rear erode
Ash abbey fig your maid it sigh lent weigh,
Sea king sum shell turn ear. Atlas teas topped
Tune ah cup honest rangers dark end o'er.
Up stare sub right league low wing lamb pup eared.
A mow meant air reap awe such ear eek all,
A doe run bard, thick lass puff rend leach ear . . .

A translation for the incurable short-circuiter:

The city slept beneath her snowy mantle.
Cold and silent was the crystal air,

While only star light and a single lantern
Broke the gloom. Along the dreary road
A shabby figure made its silent way
Seeking some shelter near. At last he stopped
To knock upon a stranger's darkened door.
Upstairs a brightly glowing lamp appeared.
A momentary pause, a cheery call,
A door unbarred, the clasp of friendly cheer . . .

Chapter 7

The Audience

VERBAL BEHAVIOR usually occurs only in the presence of a listener. When the speaker is talking to himself, of course, a listener is almost always present. But when this is not the case, a fairly simple relationship can be demonstrated: so long as a listener is present, verbal behavior will be observed provided other conditions are favorable. If the listener walks away or otherwise disappears, the behavior ceases. Thus, we stop talking when we discover that we are cut off on the telephone, or when a deafening noise interferes with face-to-face transmission. If the listener returns, verbal behavior begins again. When a situation arises which generates strong verbal behavior, the speaker usually remains silent until a listener appears. Exceptions to this rule, such as we have already seen in the extended mand, follow the principle of stimulus generalization. Under conditions of great strength, verbal behavior may be emitted in the absence of a listener.

The listener, as an essential part of the situation in which verbal behavior is observed, is again a discriminative stimulus. He is part of an occasion upon which verbal behavior is reinforced, and he therefore becomes part of the occasion controlling the strength of the behavior. This function is to be distinguished from the action of the listener in reinforcing behavior. Insofar as the listener stimulates the speaker prior to the emission of verbal behavior, we may speak of him as the audience. An audience, then, is a discriminative stimulus in the presence of which verbal behavior is characteristically reinforced and in the presence of which, therefore, it is characteristically strong. Discriminative stimuli become in turn reinforcing, and this is confirmed by the reinforcing effect of the appearance of an audience. Most repertoires contain mands which specify the appearance or attention of an audience, such as the vulgar *Hey!* or *Listen!*, the authoritative *Attention!*, or a vocative such as *My friends!*

In contrast with the discriminative stimuli which control tacts and echoic, textual, and intraverbal operants, an audience is usually a condition for the reinforcement of a large group of responses and therefore comes to affect the strength of such a group. Different audiences control different subdivisions of the repertoire of the speaker. (This control is always exerted in concert with stimuli determining more specific forms of response. The multiple causation of verbal behavior will be described in Chapter 9.)

Audiences which control the largest subdivisions of a verbal repertoire are the communities which establish the reinforcing contingencies of the so-called "languages"—English, French, Chinese, and so on. In a Chinese verbal community, only certain forms of response are effective; as an audience, any member or group of members of this community constitutes the occasion for the emission of forms called "Chinese." In the bilingual speaker, the Chinese part of a repertoire will be stronger upon such an occasion than in a community appropriate to another part, such as English.

Within a single language community many jargons, patois, cants, and technical vocabularies are controlled by special audiences. When these deal with special subject matters, they need not represent control by an audience. Thus, many objects encountered on a sailing boat are usually not encountered elsewhere. The jargon of sailing is in this case a subdivision of a repertoire isolated only because the occasion upon which it is appropriate is isolated. But when an engineer talks about the low tensile strength of a worn shoelace, he is speaking a language appropriate to a special audience rather than a special state of affairs. In some languages (for example, Japanese), certain forms of response are differentially reinforced by listeners belonging to different social classes or by listeners standing in different relations to the speaker. Each class or relationship thus defines a special audience controlling such forms. The "little language" with which we talk to children or they to us is a repertoire under the control of a special audience. Such a repertoire is reinforced in early childhood by indulgent listeners, but it may survive between friends into adulthood, as in Jonathan Swift's *Journal to Stella* with its *oo, zis,* and *im,* or its *deelest logues* for *dearest rogues.* There are special subdivisions of the community which also differentially reinforce bookish, pedantic, literary, archaic, polysyllabic, and polite vocabularies, and hence compose audiences in the presence of which these forms are particularly strong. Not to be entirely forgotten are animal audiences. We mand the disappearance of a cat with *Scat!* and of a fly or chicken with *Shoo!,* although we share our own language with dogs (*Go away!* or *Go home!*).

In analyzing these effects of an audience in determining the particular subdivision of a verbal repertoire, we assume that at least two alternative responses are available in a given situation, apart from the audience variable. The audience selects one set of responses in preference to another. When there is only one set, we need not appeal to the audience except as the all-or-none determiner of verbal behavior or silence.

The audience which determines a particular set of responses, as against another possible set in the same repertoire, raises an important question in semantic theory. The Frenchness of a French word does not seem to *refer* to any property of what is being talked about. The functional relation between a response and an audience does not fit the usual schemes of reference and is often omitted from semantic analyses. The audience variable always acts in concert with at least one other variable, which more specifically determines the form of the response. In the behavior of someone who speaks both English and German, a certain object plus an English-speaking audience evokes the response *bread,* while the same object plus a German-speaking audience evokes the response *Brot.* Another object evokes the responses *water* and *Wasser.* For most semantic purposes, the difference between *bread* and *water* is greater than the difference between *bread* and *Brot.* The notion of reference is therefore applied only to the relation which distinguishes *bread* and *water.* The difference, however, is simply that the variable which controls *bread* rather than *water,* or *Brot* rather than *Wasser,* is specific to these responses, while the variable which controls *bread* rather than *Brot* controls a large group of responses. The kind of control is the same.

The audience variable is important in interpreting the traditional notion of "proposition." If we define a proposition as "something which may be said in any language," then instead of trying to identify the "something," we may ask why there are different languages. The answer is that different contingencies of reinforcement involving a single state of affairs are maintained by different verbal communities. A proposition is not "free to be expressed in any one of many forms," for the form is determined by other variables, among them the audience. If there were only one standard and consistent verbal community, a proposition could be, though perhaps not happily, identified with "the response which expresses it." When there are many different communities and as many different audiences, the "something" common to all of the resulting alternative "expressions" cannot be identified with a verbal form. The only common factor is among the controlling variables. The argument that an idea must exist in some nonverbal form, since it may be expressed in many different ways—either within a single language or in different languages—may be answered in the same way. There is no true synonymy in the sense of a choice of different forms. When all the features of the thing described have been taken into account and when the audience has been specified, the form of response is determined.

A third function of an audience is to select a subject matter. Listeners differ in the extent to which they reinforce different types of verbal operants and, particularly, various classes of intraverbal responses and tacts. Given a single speaker with a specific history and a specific current situation, the audience will determine not only whether verbal behavior occurs, or the subdivision of the language in which it occurs, but also what types of responses are made and "what is talked about." Some audiences are suitable for behavior in the form of mands, others are clearly not. Others reinforce certain classes of intraverbals and tacts, not because the form of response is peculiar to a given language, but because of what we may roughly call thematic connections. The listener is interested in certain subjects and not in others. Moreover, in dealing with any given subject matter, listeners differ in the extent to which they tolerate and continue to reinforce distortions in the stimulus situation resulting from metaphorical extension or the special reinforcing contingencies discussed in the preceding chapter. Some audiences are the occasion for "imaginative," highly metaphorical speech designed to achieve emotional effects rather than to guide the practical behavior of the listener. The creative writer is under the control of this type of audience (Chapter 16).

The Physical Dimensions of an Audience

The verbal stimuli which control echoic, textual, and intraverbal behavior are usually easily identified. Many of the properties of objects which serve as stimuli in tacts also have substantial physical dimensions, although, as we have seen, the properties in control of metaphorical extensions and abstractions may be subtle. Even so, we look for some definite property correlated with control of the response in a given speaker. The audience presents a more difficult problem of dimensions. Through stimulus induction a wide range of "audiences" may be effective. We speak to strangers, to persons asleep or dead, possibly to clothing-store mannikins seen in a dim light, to animals, particularly if they resemble people, and so on. But the tendency to do so is usually slight.

An effective audience is hard to identify. The presence or absence of a person is not enough. Can he hear what you are saying, is he paying attention, does he understand your language, and is he an appropriate audience for a particular repertoire? These questions often cannot be answered by pointing to the physical properties of an audience. The control which a given individual exerts over the speaker is a product of a possibly long history in which his *audience character* has been established. This does not mean that every new acquaintance becomes an audience only through a long process, for the audience as a discriminative stimulus shows the principle of stimulus induction. The repertoire with which we are most likely to address a new acquaintance depends upon his resemblance to those who have reinforced our verbal behavior in the past. Except under conditions of extreme strength, an inappropriate audience is not likely to evoke a response. The precision of the audience control exercised by a new acquaintance continues to grow as verbal behavior is emitted and reinforced. Sometimes the growth is in the other direction. It may come as something of a shock to find that someone who looks very much like a familiar listener does not at all resemble him in his reinforcing practices. As an audience, however, he may continue to control the behavior appropriate to the familiar listener for a long time. The effect of a weak audience variable is evident in talking on the telephone. Frequent stimulation from the listener is necessary to support verbal behavior in strength. *Are you there?* is a mand for such stimulation.

Audience character is sometimes marked by special uniforms or other signs. Thus, at a convention a special badge worn by members of a local committee may function to indicate that such a person is an audience to whom questions about local arrangements may be successfully addressed. Clerks in a store wearing a special type of clothing also serve more satisfactorily as audiences to customers. In a store in which clerks dress like customers (let us say in weather in which customers enter the store without coats or hats), the customer may address a question about merchandise with an obvious uneasiness because of the uncertainty of the audience variable. The hero of Stendhal's *Le Rouge et le Noir,* Julien Sorel, was employed by a man of superior social status who nevertheless at times accepted his employee as an equal. To reduce the confusion arising from Sorel's ambiguity as an audience, his employer provided him with a special suit of clothes appropriate to his higher social position. Upon the occasions when Julien was to be spoken to as an equal, he wore this suit. When he appeared in other clothes, he was addressed as an employee.

The weakness of the physical representation of an audience presents a practical problem as well as a theoretical one. This type of variable is notoriously deficient. We are ill at ease in the presence of a new acquaintance, especially if he is unlike people we are familiar with, because he has not yet reinforced our verbal behavior and we find no behavior in strength. Even when we are speaking to a well-defined audience, it is easy to mix repertoires, to use foreign words where native words will do, to introduce technical terms into a casual account, to mix dialects or terms appropriate to different groups, and so on.

The distant audience. The reinforcement of letter-writing (or of dictating a recorded message to be sent to someone) is, as we have seen, deferred and hence likely to be weak. We are less inclined to write to a friend than to speak to him if he suddenly appears. Any discriminative stimulus associated with a deferred reinforcement would be weak if for no other reason, but in the case of letter-writing there are no strong current stimuli serving in lieu of the presence of the individual himself. What does control the repertoires and the subject matters of a letter? It is of no help to appeal to "mental images" of the person to whom one is writing, for we should have the same problem in explaining what causes the images. "Seeing a person" is an activity which is cognate with talking to him. Both may be executed in his absence, especially under conditions of exceptional strength.[1] We have no reason to argue that one is the cause of the other. We do not talk to a person because we see him or see him because we talk to him. When such a person is not present, the event or circumstance which "brings him clearly to mind" may also strengthen verbal behavior under his control as an audience. A favor-

1 *Science and Human Behavior,* Chapter 17.

ite bit of music, an episode in which he would be interested, or a letter from him may "remind us of him." We can achieve something comparable to his physical presence by putting a salutation at the beginning of the letter. Letter-writers frequently resort to pictures or mementos placed conspicuously before them at the time of writing. Once a letter has been begun, a substitute for a more specific audience variable is created, as we shall see in a moment.

THE NEGATIVE AUDIENCE

In the absence of an audience the probability of verbal behavior is low. But it may be low also in the presence of a type of listener who must be distinguished as an "occasion for not responding." This is the listener who, under certain conditions at least, does not reinforce verbal behavior in the accustomed manner. An ordinary audience under very noisy or distracting circumstances is an example: the speaker whose remarks have generated noisy laughter or violent protest waits for silence before continuing. A flittering bat may destroy the audience character of an otherwise attentive roomful of people. A person met for the first time, but who proves to be very deaf or unfamiliar with the speaker's language or simply unresponsive to verbal behavior which is currently strong, quickly loses any audience character he may have borrowed from similar persons through stimulus induction.

We may distinguish, however, between the listener who merely does not reinforce verbal behavior and the listener who actually punishes it. An audience in the presence of which verbal behavior is punished may be called a "negative audience." Kings, high government officials, powerful business executives, and others may become effective negative audiences in this sense. In their presence a speaker answers questions and, otherwise, speaks only if spoken to. Parents and other adults sometimes constitute such audiences for children who are to be "seen and not heard." Characters on the stage are also examples. Children, it is true, may take part in a Punch and Judy show by talking to the characters, warning them, giving them advice, and so on, but the adult audience is kept from similar participation by well-known punishments, such as ridicule or the mand *Sh!* The naïve Sir Roger de Coverley, who attended the theater only rarely, remained a child in this respect. That all audiences possess some such behavior, however, is shown by those instances in which, under extreme pressure, warning or advice is given to a character on the stage. In a murder mystery in which a sympathetic character was hastily removing any fingerprints which he might have left on the scene but was overlooking a pair of scissors which he had conspicuously handled, a very noticeable sibilance arose from the audience at each performance as the word *scissors* was whispered by many people.

Some negative audiences control only part of the repertoire of the speaker. A community which speaks French exclusively not only fails to reinforce the English repertoire of the bilingual visitor but may actually punish it. The child eventually learns that the "little language" of his home is not only ineffective in the world at large but punished by ridicule. The world at large thus becomes an effective negative audience for the "little language." Slang, patois, jargon, and poetic diction usually have their negative audiences as well as positive. There are also negative audiences for subject matters. Verbal behavior concerning the listener or persons important to him may be received aversively. We learn not to mention certain topics or certain events. With some listeners we come to avoid mands or use disguised mands instead. Punishment is also often contingent upon the extent of the stimulus control. A given listener may constitute a negative audience for metaphorical tacts, exaggerations, or lies.

Among the effects of excessive or inconsistent punishment are many neurotic symptoms, including the "repression" of some areas of verbal behavior. It is often necessary for the psychotherapist to establish himself as a nonpunishing audience. The behavior of the patient who is allowed to go unpunished is almost exclusively verbal. If the required change in audience control takes place, the patient may emit previously punished behavior, including behavior which he may appear to have forgotten. (See Chapter 16.)

THE SPEAKER AS HIS OWN AUDIENCE

People frequently talk to themselves. This can be observed when vocal behavior is overt—either because it has not yet been "repressed" to the covert level (see Chapters 15 and 19) or has returned to the overt level under conditions of limited feed-back (Chapter 16). In such cases, and probably when talking to others, the speaker reacts as a listener to his own behavior. Insofar as he automatically reinforces himself, he must be regarded as an audience affecting the strength of relevant parts of his behavior. At first glance, we may not seem to be able to demonstrate the effect of such an audience in the usual way—that is, by removing or presenting it while observing differences in amount of verbal behavior, repertoire exhibited, special subject matters selected, and so on. However, the speaker is effectively removed as his own audience under certain conditions of "automatic" speech or writing (Chapter 16), and responses then emerge for which the speaker himself constitutes a negative audience. He acquires this function when, as the result of special conditioning by the community, his own behavior has become aversive. When the resulting automatic punishment leads to "repression," the individual acts as if he were not hearing his own speech or not reading his own writing. We can encourage the suppression of the self-audience by preventing or reducing the normal feed-back of verbal behavior.

Other self-audiences are described in traditional parlance as "selves" or "personalities." [2] The individual talks to himself in the sense that one system of responses in his behavior acts upon another. His verbal behavior depends upon which "listening self" is dominant. The dramatic soliloquy often suggests a discussion among several speakers rather than intraverbal linkage in a single repertoire.

Verbal behavior primarily controlled by the self as an audience may show progressive changes. The diary-writer is affected by continuing automatic reinforcement, and the audience control which he exerts over himself may be sharpened. The probability of writing may increase, and special repertoires or subject-matters may emerge. The extent to which a speaker is his own audience may be worth noting, however, even when it does not change. The relative importance of this special audience may be observed when, in talking to others, the speaker is relatively insensitive to the conditions of the external audience—when, for example, he talks under conditions in which he cannot be heard or can be heard only with difficulty or continues talking even though the external audience has moved away or becomes clearly occupied with other matters. The self-speaker will be relatively insensitive to the language or sublanguages most effective on the other audience: that is, he will refer to people, places, and events with which only he himself is familiar, will use pronouns which have no antecedents, and may omit steps in an argument which are obvious to himself. He will not necessarily speak clearly and may

[2] *Science and Human Behavior,* Chapter 18.

frequently repeat. He will ride his own hobbies, talk nostalgically about his own history, and insist upon talking about pet themes with pet expressions. In all this we observe an insensitivity to external positive or negative audiences and may conclude that the individual is primarily talking to himself.

OTHER VARIABLES HAVING AN AUDIENCE-EFFECT

The kinds of control exercised by the audience follow from our simple three-term contingency of reinforcement. Any stimulating condition under which verbal behavior is reinforced eventually acquires some control over its strength. The listener, being necessarily involved in reinforcement (even when the listener is the speaker himself), becomes as an audience a variable which alters the strength of either all the verbal behavior of the speaker at once or special repertoires defined by form of response or by "themes" among the controlling variables.

Other stimuli may occupy the same position in the three-term paradigm. They may differ from the audience in not being closely involved in reinforcement, but the process of discrimination does not depend upon any "real" or "functional" connection. If verbal behavior is characteristically reinforced in a given place, for example, the place itself may acquire control. Thus we may observe an immediate change in the level of our verbal behavior upon entering a dining room, club room, or other place where we commonly talk. There are places—for example, churches and libraries—which function as negative audiences. In such places we may be aware of a low level of verbal behavior even though a circumstance may arise which elsewhere could generate a considerable output. Places which are quite unusual may not share any of this audience character through stimulus induction, and we may report under such circumstances that we were left speechless. Places may develop special control for the subdivisions of a repertoire which we call languages. The "little language" may be as much controlled by the home as by the people in the home. The bilingual speaker who speaks one language on his job and another in his home may talk to himself in the appropriate language in each place. In the same way, a place may specifically control verbal behavior appropriate to a given subject-matter. The scientist is more likely to talk shop in his laboratory than elsewhere.

The audience-effect of a mere place has been exploited by professional writers, who characteristically suffer the disadvantages of a deferred and ill-defined audience. Anthony Trollope [3] particularly recommended and scrupulously followed the practice of writing in the same place at the same time of day every day. Under these circumstances one may begin to write more quickly, write more readily, fall into a characteristic language, and deal more efficiently with a given subject-matter than when engaging in the same activities from place to place. Some writers have preferred to write in bed, others before a roaring fire. Buffon is said to have been able to write well only when elegantly dressed and surrounded by servants in his summer-house. The letter-writer may find an adequate substitute for the presence of the person addressed if he writes in the same place, with the same materials, at the same time of day, and preferably every day, for these circumstances tie together the behavior appropriate to a given correspondent.

Verbal behavior itself becomes just such a variable. Since responses seldom occur singly, early parts of a segment of behavior generate stimuli at the time of emission of later parts. When the stimulus control is specifically established, as in teaching a child to recite a verse, the reinforcing contingency is explicit, and a single response is controlled. The strict intraverbal response is not an example of the audience relation, and the general intraverbal tendencies revealed in the word association test, and presumably due to contiguous usage, may also be regarded as the mere averaging-out of many conflicting relationships. Nevertheless, some characteristics of a language may, as a result of sustained speech, acquire audience-control. From the obvious fact that we tend to speak in one language for substantial periods of time, it follows that English responses tend to be reinforced in the presence of stimulation supplied by other English responses, while French responses tend to be reinforced in the presence of stimulation supplied by other French responses. When speaking in French, we tend to continue doing so. The skillful bilingual, in borrowing a more appropriate expression from a second language, may find himself continuing in the second language.

The control exercised by the language is especially clear when an audience suddenly changes from English to French. Except for the very competent bilingual, a mere change in the listener who may be present does not bring about a complete change in the probabilities of repertoires. The appropriate repertoire becomes gradually avail-

[3] Trollope, A., *Autobiography*. His precept: *nulla dies sine linea*.

able as behavior progresses. Some of this may be due to self-echoic and explicit intraverbal responses, but it is also possible that a general condition closely resembling that of an audience gradually develops. Intraverbal behavior is mainly effective at the level of the operant unit, but French operants are also characteristically reinforced in the presence of the general Frenchness of recent speech constructed of a particular set of speech sounds. As one begins and continues to speak French, one therefore slowly reconstructs a characteristic condition under which French behavior is reinforced and in the presence of which it is of greater strength. Similarly, in letter-writing, the absence of the person addressed or of any characteristic place in which letters are written may be compensated for by the first few paragraphs of the letter. What follows is in part textual and intraverbal behavior comprising a special repertoire the probability of which is raised by the early part of the letter as it would be raised by the appearance of the person addressed.

Textual behavior often depends upon the audience-effect of previous behavior or of the text itself. When English is in progress we read *ALSO* as the English *also*; when German is in progress we read the same text as the German *also*. A fragmentary text may be read "in English" or in some other language depending upon possibly superficial characteristics of the text, such as commonly recurring groups of letters. An advertisement beginning with the text: *I.E.S. LAMPS RELIEVE* . . . leads to an abortive attempt to read it as French, with *I.E.S.* evoking the article *les*. Thus, in speaking French one emits a French form of response not only because of the presence of a given audience or of some situation which functions in lieu of an audience but because of adjacent French responses acting as controlling stimuli.

The effect of context in promoting the selection of one form of response where another verbal form might serve exemplifies the multiple causation which the audience-variable always involves and which will be discussed further in Chapter 9. We have seen that there are no true synonyms, for when all variables have been specified there is no remaining choice of terms. One of two alternative forms, however, may be evoked by part of a given situation depending on the rest of that situation. Adjacent verbal behavior may be relevant. Thus, in a familiar example, we speak of fish both as a form of food in discussing Lenten practices and as a class of the vertebrates in zoology, but we speak of a pig in talking about a farm and of pork in talking about the kitchen. We may refer to a group of animals as a school in talking about fish and as a herd in talking about cattle. There are many other terms which vary among species of animals for what are otherwise common features. We have, so to speak, different languages in speaking of different animals. Speaking in the Fox language, we say that all members of a *skulk* have *brushes,* while speaking in Rabbit, we say that all members of a *huske* or *down* have *scuts.*

Small groups of responses, among which other variables may make a selection, are sometimes differentially strengthened for special purposes, as we shall see in Chapter 10. For example, the mand *Give me the name of a President of the United States* provides an intraverbal stimulus for a small family of responses (the names of the Presidents) among which a possibly trivial variable will effect a choice. Assigning a topic for an essay has something of the same effect, and the writer may increase the extent and coherence of his own behavior by finding a successful title and keeping it clearly before him. Although the process here is probably identical with that which establishes an audience as a controlling variable, it would not be convenient to extend the notion of an audience to cover such cases or to use the notion of the intraverbal operant to embrace all audience effects.

Chapter 8

. . . .

The Verbal Operant as a Unit of Analysis

THE SIX TYPES of functional relations in verbal behavior so far defined may be summarized as follows.

In the *mand,* a given form of response which characteristically produces a given reinforcement varies in strength with the state of deprivation or aversive stimulation appropriate to that reinforcement. No prior stimulus determines the specific form of response.

In *echoic, textual,* and *intraverbal* behavior, the response is determined by a prior verbal stimulus—auditory in the first case, written or printed in the second, and both in the third. Control is concentrated in the stimulus by generalizing the reinforcement. In echoic and textual behavior there is a point-to-point correspondence between properties of stimulus and response, which makes possible a repertoire of minimal units. There is no comparable repertoire of intraverbal units, since the controlling relations are generally overlapping, conflicting, and usually weak.

In the *tact,* the stimulus which controls the form of response is usually nonverbal. Stimulus control is emphasized by generalizing the reinforcement. The control is shared by all properties of the stimulus, and a novel stimulus possessing one or more of the same properties may be effective. Responses controlled by some properties of a stimulus may show generic, metaphorical, metonymical, or solecistic extension. Through a special procedure of differential reinforcement, however, control may be restricted to one property or group of properties in abstraction.

Certain special consequences may affect the tact relationship. A special measure of generalized reinforcement may alter the extent or accuracy of the stimulus control, and this is even more likely to occur as the result of special effects upon the listener related to specific conditions of deprivation or aversive stimulation in the speaker.

The *audience* is a prior stimulus, usually nonverbal, which controls groups of responses. When two or more responses are under control of the same stimulus, the audience acts to select one of them. The repertoire under the control of an audience may be a language, a jargon, a cant, or some less sharply-defined functional subdivision of the behavior of the speaker.

These functional relationships are useful first of all as a mere classificatory scheme, functioning in this sense somewhat like the classificatory schemes of grammar. It is not a classification of forms of response, since we cannot tell from form alone into which class a response falls. *Fire* may be (1) a mand to a firing squad, (2) a tact to a conflagration, (3) an intraverbal response to the stimulus *Ready, aim . . .*, or (4) an echoic or (5) textual response to appropriate verbal stimuli. It is possible that formal properties of the vocal response, especially its intonation, may suggest one type of controlling variable, but an analysis cannot be achieved from such internal evidence alone. In order to classify behavior effectively, we must know the circumstances under which it is emitted. (This is true of traditional grammatical classifications as well, in spite of many efforts to establish purely formal systems. The standard grammatical practice when confronted with a record of verbal behavior is to reconstruct a plausible controlling state of affairs.)

The contingencies of reinforcement arising from the relations between speaker and listener also account for other distinctions in grammar, syntax, and the lay vocabulary. Just as we could classify mands as commands, requests, advice, and so on, by appealing to different aspects of the listener's behavior, so tacts can be classified as mentioning, announcing, proclaiming, stating, naming, and so on. The lay vocabulary has terms which are noncommittal as to the type of behavior (*utter, say, remark*), which distinguish states of strength (*insist, assure, doubt, guess*), and which refer to subtle arrangements of speaker and listener (*allege, vouch for, speak for, claim, disclaim, forswear, protest, promulgate, confirm, confess, tattle, disclose, lie, broach, denounce, promise, bid, bet, acknowledge, concede, admit, plead*). These distinctions are usually attributed to the "intention" of the speaker or to some other psychological state or activity. We can define subclasses of this sort by appeal to the same contingencies of reinforcement which characterize the principal types of verbal operants. We have no reason, however, to go into such detail here.

Classification is not an end in itself. Even though any instance of verbal behavior can be shown to be a function of variables in one or more of these classes, there are other aspects to be treated. Such a formulation permits us to apply to verbal behavior concepts and laws which emerge from a more general analysis. Before turning to this extension of the analysis, however, it will be well to consider some further aspects of the classification of verbal behavior and certain traditional problems which it raises.

THE "SAME WORD" IN DIFFERENT KINDS OF VERBAL BEHAVIOR

Traditionally it would be said that the same word may occur in all types of verbal operants. Thus, the word *snow* may appear as a mand, a tact, or an echoic, textual, or intraverbal response. A word is also said to appear in either vocal or written form. Moreover, as we have noted, it is characteristic of semantic theory to deal with both speaker and listener at the same time, and to say that the response of one contains the same word as the stimulus for the other. The traditional practice might lead us to look for a new unit of analysis—some common element in our different types or modes of verbal behavior or in the behavior of speaker and listener—and to suppose that the individual spontaneously acquires one type of behavior in the course of acquiring another. Let us see whether the traditional assumption is justified and whether we can set up any concept with the same generality.

The Same Form of Response in Different Types of Operants

In the terminology of meaning, we say that the word *doll* is used at one time "to ask for a doll" and at another "to describe or refer to a doll." When the response *Doll!* has been acquired as a mand, however, we do not expect that the child then spontaneously possesses a corresponding tact of similar form. If we find both types of operants in the repertoire of the child, we must account for them separately. This appears to make the task of explaining verbal behavior more difficult, but the advantage which appears to be gained by the traditional concept of the "word *doll*" is offset by the problem which remains of explaining how a child may learn to use a word both to "express a desire" and also to "describe an object." The total formulation has not been simplified; part of the task has merely been postponed. If we are to accept the full responsibility of giving an account of verbal behavior, we must face the fact that the mand *doll* and the tact *doll* involve separate functional relations which can be explained only by discovering all relevant variables.

In accounting for such instances we must not make the mistake of explaining too much. Precisely the same form of response is seldom if ever found in two operants. The skilled phoneticist will detect differences between the mand *Fire!* and the tact *fire*. Moreover, not all forms exist in both types of response. For example, there appear to be no corresponding tacts for the mands *Psst!*, *O!*, and *Lo!*, and we shall see that this is also true of a class of responses to be treated in Chapter 12. Responses which tact subtle properties of stimuli may never occur in the mand form, or at least only under circumstances in which the mands may be taken to include a form of specification which is not far removed from a tact.

However, a verbal response of given form sometimes seems to pass easily from one type of operant to another. The speaker commonly starts with a tact and then appears to possess a corresponding mand. The child in a toy store, unable to identify a particular toy, asks *What is that?* and is told *A doodler*. This is a stimulus for an *echoic* response—of the sort which is then commonly used to reinforce the response as a tact. But the child immediately says *Buy me a doodler!* He has never been reinforced for this response in the manner required to construct a mand. Does this represent the spontaneous origin of such an operant? The adult engages in similar behavior when, in a foreign country, he consults a dictionary to evoke a textual response which, emitted in the presence of a salesman, produces a particular result. The shopper does the same in consulting his own memorandum of items to be purchased. But such behavior has a rather complex history. The mand does not arise spontaneously, but only with the help of suitable behavior of transcription or translation. The child who "does not know the name of a toy" may be compared with a carpenter who is holding a nail in place when his hammer is out of reach. A verbal response to his apprentice produces the hammer. Such behavior is built up step by step. The behavior of "asking for the word needed to ask for a toy" is a mand reinforced by (and hence specifying) auditory behavior on the part of the listener which, when echoed, characteristically produces the toy. Once this has happened, the response exists as an independent mand because it has been reinforced as such. The general response *What is that?* is also reinforced and will be stronger on later occasions. (It is this kind of situation which encourages the notion of the word as a tool or instrument, but the analogy is of little help in formulating the case. It is ultimately no simpler to assert that "the child finds out what the word for the toy is and then uses it to ask for the toy.")

It is possible that all mands which are reinforced by the production of objects or other states of affairs may be interpreted as manding the behavior of the listener and tacting the object or state of affairs to be produced. Classifications of responses are useful only in separating various types of controlling relations, and some responses may show features of both mand and tact. In any case, we have to know the history of a particular form of response and of all the variables which have acquired control of it.

One connection may arise from the fact that the events which reinforce a mand often resemble the discriminative stimuli which control a tact. The milk which a child gets with the mand *Milk!* resembles the milk which controls the tact *milk* in response to the question *What is that?* This may facilitate the acquisition of whichever operant is acquired second. One could establish the mand *Milk!* through reinforcement with milk as a tactual, gustatory, and olfactory stimulus by feeding the child only from an opaque bottle. At the same time, one could establish a tact of the same form to the visual stimulation of milk in a clear glass. Under these circumstances a child would presumably not show any tendency to transfer the response from one type of operant to the other.

Another possible bridge may arise from the fact that the presence of the reinforcing object is an optimal condition for reinforcement. Thus the presence of milk constitutes part of the optimal occasion upon which the mand *Milk!* will be reinforced. Although the response remains a mand and is primarily under the control of the condition of deprivation, the presence of milk as a dicriminative stimulus is not entirely irrelevant. The mand will be more likely to occur in the presence of milk. This is one step toward the production of a tact which would presumably facilitate the eventual control of the response by such a stimulus under generalized reinforcement.

If there is no spontaneous development of one type of operant as the result of setting up another, then the only problem arising from the presence of the same form in operants of different types is a problem concerning the verbal community. The "word" as a unit of analysis is appropriate to the practices of the *community* rather than the behavior of the individual speaker.

Echoic and textual operants present no similar problems, partly because the form of the response is more closely determined by the minimal repertoire in each area. If it is usually safe to assume that the speaker who possesses a textual response also possesses an echoic response of the same form, it is only because echoic behavior is almost inevitably acquired before textual. Transfer in the other direction is never claimed; to be able to echo a response is no guarantee that a similar response will be evoked by a text. Nor is it often argued that because one is able to read or repeat a word correctly, he is then able to use it correctly in a mand or tact. The only other important issue involves intraverbal behavior, which is often so similar to the tact that a spontaneous transfer from one type to the other is assumed. For example, it is often argued that a response acquired intraverbally in studying a textbook is automatically available as a tact with respect to the subject-matter of the text. But a similar analysis would probably show that this is not true, and the assumption may well explain the weakness of many educational practices.

The pathological condition of verbal behavior called aphasia often emphasizes functional differences which are hard to understand in terms of the traditional account. The aphasic may not be able to name an object, though he will emit the name immediately in manding it; or he may be able to name an object although he cannot repeat the name after someone else or read it from a text as he once was able to do. But it is only traditional theory which makes this surprising. The aphasic has lost some of the functional relationships which control his verbal behavior. A response of a given form may no longer be under the control of one functional relation, although it is still under the control of another.

No matter how useful the concept of word may be in analyzing the reinforcing practices of a verbal community, it does not represent a functional unit in the behavior of the individual speaker. We must accept the responsibility of giving an independent explanation of how responses of the same form appear in different types of operants.

The Same Response in Different Media

The notion that the "same word" may be either written or spoken might lead us to say that the same verbal response may occur in different media. But speaking and writing are obviously different kinds of behavior, which utilize different parts of the body in different ways. Where we could paraphrase "the same word used in different ways" as "the same response in different types of operant," here we must attempt to bridge the gap between spoken and written behavior either by pointing to something common to the occasions upon which the behaviors occur or among the effects which they have upon the listener and reader. But common controlling variables, acting either prior to the behavior in the stimulating occasion or after the behavior as part of the event called reinforcement, will not permit us to get from one form of response to the other. The two forms of behavior must be separately conditioned.

There is another possibility, however. Every literate person possesses transcriptive behavior through which he quickly moves from a response in one medium to a corresponding response in another. That the possibility of conversion contributes to the notion of "the same response in different media" is supported by the fact that we are not so likely to appeal to it in a language which uses hieroglyphs. Here the transcriptive process lacks the point-to-point correspondence of the minimal repertoire of phonetic writing or reading. Moreover, the hieroglyph with its surviving vestiges of model-building has a closer affinity to the occasion for the response than to the response itself.

It is not argued, of course, that given the spoken form, one then "knows" the written. Nor is it implied that for every written form there is a corresponding spoken, and vice versa. These may be regarded as defects of transcription. Most alphabets are only roughly phonetic, and writing is therefore only roughly transcriptive. Most written languages contain many forms which are essentially ideographs or logographs—that is, written responses which are under the direct control of (usually) nonverbal stimuli but which correspond to relatively large units of vocal behavior with no minimal phonetic correspondence. In some cases, the written response is not controlled by the form of the vocal response alone (as might be true in the behavior of the skillful stenographer), but by its relation to controlling variables. Thus, the vocal response *second* leads to the written response *2nd* only when the vocal response is made to an ordinal numeral, not when it is made to a unit on a clock face.

Sometimes it seems to be implied that the spoken form *is* the word and that the written response is merely a way of representing it. This simply makes the transcriptive process unilateral. But we have no reason to assume that there is any basic medium of verbal behavior. One form of response is likely to be learned first by a given speaker and may remain so strong that it occurs first upon any given occasion, but written English, for example, is established apart from any vocal behavior in deaf-mutes, and could continue as a full-fledged language in its own right in a community of deaf-mutes. Even where there is a vocal parallel, it is often evident that parts of a written repertoire are still primordial. Separate speaking and writing vocabularies are the rule rather than the exception. Some parts of mathematical behavior are predominantly written, and corresponding vocal responses are usually textual in nature, at least for some mathematicians.

Since different musculatures are involved, both written and spoken verbal behavior may be executed at the same time. When one is speaking aloud while also writing "the same thing," the latter behavior may be regarded as a transcription of the former or the vocal behavior as "reading" the latter. An explicit order of occurrence—say, from vocal to written—may be detected, but errors sometimes reveal the superficiality of this control. In one such instance, the response *A second variable* was emitted vocally while *A certain variable* was written approximately simultaneously. If the two responses had followed the rules of transcription, any possibility of independent control might have gone unsuspected, but there was evidently a separate intraverbal relation controlling the written response, even though it showed transcriptive correspondences in the stress pattern, the sound of the initial consonant, and the sound *n* in the second syllable.

Even though repertoires of speaking and writing are separately acquired and may be exhibited concurrently, the question remains whether reinforcements in one area can have an effect in the other? For example, will a child who has learned to write and who has acquired the vocal mand *Water!* through reinforcement with water spontaneously demonstrate the written mand *Water!* without any specific conditioning of the written response? Something of the sort seems clear in the sweeping transfer to written behavior which occurs when vocal behavior is for any reason impossible—for example, when the speaker's vocal apparatus is injured or when the listener is out of reach of auditory stimulation. But it is difficult to interpret this so long as transcriptive behavior cannot be ruled out. It is quite possible that a child who has learned to write only in the sense of copying other writing will be unable to make this transfer, or that the child who has learned to write from dictation must also learn to "transcribe his own dictation." A child may very well learn to write, yet it may never "occur to him" to leave a note for someone whom he cannot wait to see or to resort to the written form when vocal behavior is otherwise impracticable or would be punished. Traditionally it would be said that the child must learn to *use* writing as well as learn to write. But "the use of writing" raises all the present issues.

When written behavior has been substantially modified through reinforcement, a change may be noted in the corresponding vocal repertoire. For example, one may acquire a particularly effective repertoire with respect to a correspondent whom one has never seen. When the correspondent is met in person for the first time and becomes an audience for vocal behavior, the effect of the earlier differential reinforcement will be apparent though it may not be as great as if the correspondent had always been an audience for vocal behavior. In any case the example presents no difficulty unless it can be shown that the written repertoire was fully autonomous—such as might have been the case in a correspondence between deaf-mutes. Vocal or subvocal responses must be ruled out as precursors or concomitants of the behavior of the letter-writer or as the very behavior of the letter-reader before the independent modification of the vocal repertoire need be assumed.

We may explain apparent transfers to other media in the same way. Pointing to a word in a dictionary is a form of verbal behavior which commonly appears to spring up without special conditioning when vocal behavior is for any reason ineffective. Thus we may point to a sign reading *SILENCE* in order to stop someone from talking in a reading room where a vocal response would be inappropriate. We may order a meal by checking appropriate items on a list which is then sent to the kitchen. Such behavior presupposes textual responses in both "speaker" and "listener." It also presupposes certain verbal responses on the part of the speaker which have the function of the transcriptive or translational behavior of Chapter 4. The separate stages may not often be easy to observe. When a meal is ordered by checking a list, a man may begin by emitting (possibly inaudible) textual behavior—that is, he reads the list. Some of his responses supplement latent responses in the form of mands. The list "probes" his repertoire of mands in the manner to be described in Chapter 10. The individual observes this when he discovers "what he wants to order." Checking the appropriate items on the list is another step which presumably must be separately learned.

These stages are obvious when the two mechanisms are in different skins. A reads the menu to B, and B's responses are now echoic rather than textual. Some of them supplement latent responses in the form of mands. B either repeats all of A's responses and demonstrates any special strength by repeating some with special energy, or he may repeat aloud only those responses which are particularly strong. He himself may comment on the special strength of certain items by saying *That is what I want,* or A may do this for him (as when A is a parent and B a small child).

The process of learning to point is sometimes quite explicit. We learn to "point" by pressing the doorbell button opposite the name of a friend in the vestibule of an apartment house. We "point" to the name of a piece of music we want to hear by pushing the button opposite that name on a "jukebox." We point to numbers in serial order in dialing a telephone. An audible textual response may often be detected in such cases, but an autonomous pointing response could be set up. There is no problem in explaining the verbal behavior of pointing to objects or to the imperfect models of objects called pictures, and it is seldom if ever claimed that such behavior follows spontaneously from the establishment of other verbal forms. (The possibilities here are seen in the operation of different types of vending machines. We push a plunger to point to (a) the article wanted (seen through a window), (b) a sample of the article wanted (also seen through a window), (c) a picture of the article wanted (a form of iconography), or (d) the printed name. Only in the latter case must we consider parallel verbal behavior of another sort.)

The independent functional control of behavior in two or more media is again demonstrated in the behavior of the aphasic. Vocal behavior may be lost while written behavior survives, or vice versa, where the defect is not due to paralysis of the appropriate response mechanisms. Sometimes both repertoires survive although one is slower or less accurate than the other. This is puzzling from the traditional point of view, in which verbal behavior is regarded as the use of language apart from any particular medium. What has been damaged in aphasia is clearly the functional control of the behavior, and the damage respects the lines of control.

Although it would be difficult to prove that changes in a response in one medium bring about changes in responses in another medium only through the mediation of processes of translation or transcription, at least the contrary has not been proved. Functional connections between two media must be carefully specified and analyzed in accounting for particular instances, and the traditional point of view offers no help in simplifying this analysis.

The Same Response Spoken or Heard

Although semantic theories frequently assume that meaning is the same for speaker and listener, the processes through which a man becomes a listener differ, as we have seen, from those through which he becomes a speaker. In acquiring a verbal repertoire the speaker does not necessarily become a listener, and in acquiring the behavior characteristic of a listener he does not spontaneously become a speaker. After "learning the meaning of a word" as a listener, one cannot then "use it" as a speaker, or vice versa. Large differences in the size and composition of speaking and listening repertoires are generally recognized. Since the responses of the speaker become the verbal stimuli of the listener, responses and stimuli have similar forms. Moreover, some of the conditions under which a man speaks are relevant to the effect of his behavior upon the listener. But these are facts about the practices of a verbal community and are to be explained in terms of the broader significance of verbal behavior. They do not suggest any process in the speaker which is derived from his position as listener, or vice versa, except through the explicit channels identified in a behavioral analysis. (Here again the aphasic often reveals the importance of insisting upon these distinctions. The fact that the individual may lose his power to speak but remain an effective listener is puzzling only if we have assumed that a special process of "understanding the meaning of a word" is common to both speaker and listener.)

The Same Response in Different Languages

It is possible to "say the same thing" in different languages (for example, in French and English, in technical and nontechnical jargons, or in synonymous expressions in the same language) in the sense that one state of affairs will lead to different responses in the presence of different audiences or contexts. This does not mean, of course, that having acquired a response in one language we automatically possess the corresponding form which says the same thing in another language. But when responses appropriate to two languages have been separately acquired, certain problems arise. Having "learned something" in French, does the bilingual speaker then "know it" in English? Or can the scientist describe to the layman something he has previously talked about only with a technical repertoire? If so, what is this "something" which, so to speak, seems to create behavior in a second language without the usual processes of explicit conditioning?

Not all types of operants present this problem. In echoic and textual behavior, the minimal repertoires suffice to bridge the gap between all sublanguages in the same phonetic or orthographic system. Having improved our skill in repeating or writing in one subdivision of a repertoire, we are not surprised to find a comparable improvement in other subdivisions. When different orthographic systems are involved, however, a change in one subdivision may actually hinder rather than help in the other. Extended practice in reading or repeating French may increase the errors of reading or repeating English.

The important cases are those in which no minimal repertoires are common to the two languages. Having learned how to order with the most satisfactory consequences in a given restaurant, we may transfer this "knowledge" to another language in ordering from a different waiter. Having read a book in French, we may be able to give the gist of it in English, or having acquired the multiplication table in English, we find it possible to multiply in French. A special case is the "erroneous" substitution of a synonym in recalling a poem or other passage.

Many such instances may be outright translations made possible only through the prior acquisition of an intraverbal repertoire established explicitly for this purpose. It is also possible that, although ordinarily only one response is emitted under the control of a given variable, many responses are characteristically strengthened by it, and such strengthening may not be without a future effect. We have seen, for example, that the stimulus word in a word-association experiment has a demonstrable effect upon many response words. The reader may emit only a single textual response to each printed word in a passage, but many collateral intraverbal responses may nevertheless be strengthened. Many such intraverbal responses belong in the translational repertoires already considered. Upon a later occasion, some change in the audience variable or some auxiliary source of strength may produce the recall of an intraverbal response rather than the textual response which was actually emitted upon the previous occasion.

A full explanation of this process depends upon collateral variables to be discussed in the chapters which follow, but an example may be given here. A young girl who had learned to sing a song containing the sentence *Run, run, run, with all your might* later sang this as *March, march, march, with all your might.* This is the kind of erroneous recall which suggests that what she learned in the first place was the "idea," and that she could express it in another way later. But a clear intraverbal connection between *march* and *run* is established by an English-speaking community. (In this particular case there were other variables which could have strengthened *march.* The song was called *March Wind,* and the child was accustomed to march about while singing it.) It is not so difficult to explain how a "fact" learned in one language can then be stated in another. A speaker who observes a girl in a red dress and describes the dress as *red* may later, when questioned by a French-speaking person, respond *rouge.* We need not suppose that this is an intraverbal translation, or that the earlier English response is essential to the later French. The speaker may make no comment upon seeing the dress and yet report it correctly at a later date in either language.

An apparent transfer from one language to another may result from the fact that responses in two languages may have the same effect upon the listener. Since the speaker is often his own listener, he may construct a verbal response having a particular effect upon himself. The response *March, march, march, with all your might* probably had much the same effect upon the child as the original response. The fact that the whole passage "made sense"—and, indeed, the "same sense" as the original—was almost certainly relevant not only in bringing the behavior of recall to an end (see below), but possibly in strengthening the recall itself. The child was faced with the task of constructing a verbal response to fit certain specifications (see Part V). A conceivable intraverbal connection between *run* and *drip,* established through common relations to faucets could have generated the erroneous response *Drip, drip, drip, with all your might,* but, in addition to the fact that contextual variables present at the time would favor *march* over *drip,* the response would not satisfy the test on the child as her own listener. In giving the gist of what one has read in a book or heard someone else describe, in the same or a different language, the speaker is often concerned with generating behavior having the same effect upon himself and will correct himself if he fails. Just as the skilled teacher acquires a set of paraphrases which he uses in "getting a point across to a class," so the speaker acquires special paraphrases which he finds helpful in getting the point across to himself. In reading fairly unfamiliar technical material, simple paraphrases may be developed for such purposes, just as in reading difficult material in another language one may fall back upon frequent translational responses for difficult terms. When one is asked to interpret a passage heard in another language, the simplest answer may not be translation but the construction of another set of responses having the same effect.

We should not overlook the possibility that verbal behavior in one language may give rise to private events within the individual which he may then describe in another language. Covert *nonverbal* behavior often occurs in solving problems, creating works of art, engaging in self-control, and otherwise manipulating variables affecting one's own behavior. The chess player may "think" of his next move in the absence of a chess board, and his behavior in doing so may or may not be verbal. When it is not, he can nevertheless describe the move, presumably as if it were made on a real chess board. Mathematical operations of a simple sort need not be verbal. Confronted with a verbal problem in arithmetic, a man may simply "see" a scale of numbers and add by advancing a given number of steps along it. The result may then be read as if he had manipulated a physical scale. A piece of mechanical apparatus may be designed nonverbally without the support of environmental events, and the result may be described as if the inventor had sketched the apparatus on paper or constructed a working model. Such private events raise difficult problems in an analysis of behavior within the framework of a natural science,[1] but we can give at least some indication of the different kinds of variables which lead to nonverbal thinking and which may therefore be involved in the transfer from one language to another.

[1] *Science and Human Behavior,* Chapter 17.

DYNAMIC PROPERTIES

A functional relation is more than a mere connection. The stimuli which control a verbal response not only determine its form and thus supply an equivalent for meaning, they increase the probability that the response will be emitted. Other variables having the same effect include reinforcement, deprivation, aversive stimulation, and certain emotional conditions. These are all independently manipulable events, and hence differ in an important way from the ideas, tensions, abilities, faculties, motives, and similar concepts which are often used to explain verbal behavior. One advantage is that we may now move on from a classification of verbal operants, in which our main interest is similar to that of semantic theory or grammar, to the complex processes which would traditionally be described as the "use of language." In particular we have to analyze the effects of combinations of variables, the composition of larger samples of verbal behavior, and activities commonly called verbal thinking. In recognizing the behavioral nature of the relations so far discussed, we have prepared the ground for these more complicated phenomena and may deal with them with the same principles and laws. Before extending our enquiry, however, it will be necessary to consider other conditions affecting the strength of verbal behavior as a whole as well as certain processes in the fields of conditioning, motivation, and emotion to which verbal behavior, simply as part of the total behavior of the human organism, is subject. This is also a convenient place to raise the question of what brings verbal behavior to an end.

The Strength of Verbal Behavior as a Whole

Some variables strengthen verbal behavior without respect to form. The attention of the listener as a reinforcer is an example. Any verbal behavior which evokes attention is reinforced apart from other specific actions of the listener. The mands which specify this reinforcement include the relatively formless *Ahem!,* which may get attention merely because it is a common antecedent of verbal behavior arising from the practice of clearing the throat before speaking, and responses which are emitted at the ends of sentences only for the sake of "holding attention," such as . . . *and* . . ., or . . . *so that* . . ., or . . . *I mean to say* . . . . We are concerned here, however, not with specific forms so reinforced, but rather with the fact that any verbal behavior is likely to be strong because of such consequences.

A distinction may be made between holding attention and keeping the floor. In the latter case, verbal behavior is strong because it prevents someone else from speaking. The examples just given may have this effect, as does the explicit mand *Wait a minute, I haven't finished!* Such behavior may occur when the speaker has indeed something to say; but it is likely to be generalized, so that the speaker continues to speak mainly to prevent another from doing so. A formalized example of this is the filibuster, where the rules of parliamentary procedure make the reinforcing effect explicit. Here there is no comparable mand; the only way to hold the floor is to continue to talk. The "content" of a filibuster usually demonstrates the main effect of such a variable: behavior is emitted which would be too weak to occur under other circumstances.

Holding the floor is an example of behavior under aversive control. The reinforcement of a filibuster is the avoidance of legislative action by the opposition. Another aversive condition avoided by verbal behavior without respect to form is simply silence. There are many situations, as we saw in Chapter 6, in which silence is used as a punishment, and it is therefore well to avoid any silence which may be interpreted as punishment. Certain standard responses—comments about the weather, the health of the listener, and so on—show a relatively high frequency mainly because they avoid silence. The threat of silence leads on the one hand to formless grunts, mumbles, hemmings, and so on, and on the other to an increased probability that *any* type of verbal behavior will be emitted.

One type of silence which is aversive to the listener, though not used as punishment, is the interruption of a sustained discourse. The speaker may be distracted, forgetful, or confused. The strength of the aversive condition built up in the resulting silence is shown in the energy of the response which finally becomes available. When a speaker forgets a name, something of the following sort may occur: *I ran into a friend of yours yesterday by the names of . . . m-m-m-, uh, I know it perfectly well—uh . . . Jones! Jones! That's it, Jones.* The unusual strength indicated by the force and repetition of the response *Jones* may be puzzling at first glance, since the response is recalled only after delay and must therefore have been *weak*. But the discrepancy is explained by the increasing aversive pressure which builds up during the silence which interrupts the sentence. Some escape is meanwhile provided by *m-m-m, uh,* and *I know it perfectly well.*

A special case of avoiding silence is stalling. Explicit responses which "play for time" are commonly set up. The troubadour has stock lines or refrains, the principal function of which is to permit him to recall or arrange the material to be emitted next. It has been shown that some of the stock lines of Homer probably served this purpose.[2] We have seen how echoic behavior permits the student to stall for an answer (Chapter 4); the same effect may be achieved with stock responses (*Now let me think, Do you mean...*, etc.) or with mumbled, relatively formless speech which brings a request for repetition after which a response of sharper form may be available. The television comedian usually has in reserve some verbal material to be used in case his program ends before the appointed time, as the experienced professor holds in reserve similar material to complete the hour when his lecture has gone too quickly. But apart from explicit responses reinforced through these consequences, such occasions are likely to strengthen any form of verbal behavior.

Another achievement of verbal behavior which is relatively independent of form is the concealing or suppression of other activities. An explicit example is the magician's patter, which may lead the observer away from an essential move. A less standardized example is Freud's observation that a patient may talk about one thing to avoid talking about something more aversive. Explicit responses may be acquired for this reason, but the same consequences tend to strengthen any behavior regardless of form.

Behavior continues without much respect to form under more trivial aversive conditions. The speaker usually finishes a sentence even though it is clear from the behavior of the listener that he has made his point. He ends the sentence to avoid aversive consequences which have followed in other instances when the end was important. The pressure to complete a metaphorical framework even though no metaphorical response is strengthened at the moment was noted in Chapter 5. In beginning a sentence *He was as cordial as...*, the speaker commits himself to a conclusion which may be otherwise undetermined. Stock phrases are often available (*... as you can well imagine*), but all verbal behavior may enjoy a slightly greater probability at such a time. Behavior is also emitted simply because it is verbal in supplying examples—as in discussing verbal behavior, in giving a sample of one's handwriting to be analyzed, in sketching in

2 Parry, Milman, "Homer and Hugo: I. The Singer's Rest in Greek and Southslavic Heroic Song," *T.A.P.A.*, *46* (1935).

printed matter when drawing a picture of a newspaper or magazine, or in testing a public-address system. Standard responses usually develop under all these circumstances (compare the technician's formula for testing a microphone) but behavior is also likely to be strong without respect to specific form.

The effects of such variables are well known. When a stock response is not forthcoming, behavior is commonly weak in energy level and almost formless. The speaker who has obviously made his point finishes by trailing off in an almost inaudible mumble. In holding attention or stalling for time the speaker may resort to the unformed voicing *uh* or the nasal *m* . . *m* . . . Vocal sounds are produced, but the behavior of the rest of the speech apparatus which ordinarily shapes them is lacking.

A second result is the emission of empty, trivial, or foolish behavior. Much of this becomes standardized, as in formulae like *Now, let's see* or *I mean to say*. Small talk and idle chatter may suffer explicit conditioning because they have this effect. In filling an embarrassing silence, our behavior is particularly likely to be of no importance. As Stendhal remarked, *"Le nombre des sottises que j'ai dites depuis deux ans pour ne pas me taire me met au désespoir quand j'y songe."* [3]

A third possible result is that the verbal behavior emitted under such circumstances will be inaccurate, ungrammatical in the sense of Chapter 13, or subject to the formal distortions of Chapter 11. One type of distortion under such pressure is exemplified by the well-known story of Mr. Morgan's nose.[4] Behavior strengthened without respect to form is likely to be determined by other variables in the history of the individual and hence regarded as "revealing." Psychoanalysts have been accustomed to pay particular attention to verbal behavior emitted under such circumstances. The principle underlies the analysis of literary works. The creative writer is reinforced by many things—among them money, prestige, and various forms of self-stimulation. Some of these may be contingent upon particular responses, but there is a large measure of generalized reinforcement for verbal behavior simply as such. The writer is, of course, under

[3] Stendhal, *De l'amour* (Editions Hypérion), p. 42.

[4] A woman who had invited J. P. Morgan to lunch cautioned her young daughter not to mention his rather prominent nose. The unforeseen result was that the little girl sat during luncheon staring at Mr. Morgan's nose. When the situation became unbearable, the mother sent the child away from the table and attempted to cover her embarrassment by a hastily contrived remark. Picking up the cream pitcher, she said, "Mr. Morgan, do you take cream on your nose?" The woman has been widely but erroneously identified as Mrs. Dwight Morrow.

many sorts of current external control, but the pressure to produce verbal behavior simply as such gives a rather free rein to variables in his history. Literary works may then be analyzed for the information which they supply regarding such histories.

Comparable material from the nonprofessional writer is obtained through various forms of Thematic Apperception Tests in which verbal behavior is reinforced without respect to form, perhaps through a reduction in aversive stimulation similar to that supplied by the crude mands *Say something* or *Write something*. In such tests the universe of available responses may be limited by supplying pictures, music, odors, and so on, to be "written about." The point of the test is to generate behavior without respect to form so that variables controlling form will have an opportunity to make themselves felt. Available responses are restricted in a different way by the "Verbal Summator" in which a similar mild aversive stimulus is employed. The modus operandi of such tests is discussed in Chapter 10.

A lack of formal control is accentuated by reinforcements which are contingent upon speed of response. Such contingencies arise in classroom recitation or discussion: the student who answers first is differentially reinforced by getting credit for the answer. The over-anxious student is likely to begin with a formless *uh . . . uh* or with stalling phrases and, other things being equal, with a greater probability of a wrong answer. The same contingency is seen at work when two speakers have stopped talking in an animated discussion and then begin to speak at the same time. This happens so often that starting together cannot always be a coincidence. Covert verbal behavior is under way in both speakers, although it is not strong enough to be emitted audibly. Some slight indication that the other speaker is embarking on a response supplies an added temporal contingency which brings any available response to the audible level. Behavior so generated is frequently likely to be unformed, trivial, inaccurate, or distorted.

GENERAL BEHAVIORAL PROCESSES RELEVANT TO VERBAL BEHAVIOR

Operant Conditioning

The process of operant conditioning naturally plays an important role in behavior defined in terms of the special way in which it achieves its effects. Differential reinforcement shapes up all verbal forms, and when a prior stimulus enters into the contingency, reinforcement is responsible for its resulting control. Appropriate contingencies of reinforcement define the repertoires of echoic, textual, and intraverbal behavior and bring verbal behavior under the control of the nonverbal environment. Differential reinforcement sharpens this control in abstraction.

It is customary to emphasize the *rate* at which such changes take place, and to record each case in a "learning curve." The learning process is a conspicuous effect of reinforcement, and practical problems of education make the rate of acquisition of verbal behavior important. But complex behavior is acquired at different speeds not because of great differences in the effect of reinforcement, but because of interactions among responses and stimuli. There is no "typical situation" which yields a general learning curve.

In emphasizing the effect of operant reinforcement in establishing a verbal repertoire, it is easy to overlook the fact that reinforcement continues to be effective after behavior has been acquired. The availability of behavior, its probability or strength, depends upon whether reinforcements *continue* in effect and according to what schedules.[4a] When reinforcements are abundant, the individual is likely to be called energetic, enthusiastic, interested, or, in the case of verbal behavior, voluble or talkative. When reinforcements are scarce, he is likely to be called phlegmatic, uninspired, lethargic, dull, discouraged, or, in the case of verbal behavior, taciturn or silent. These differences are often thought of as motivational, but insofar as they are due to differences in amounts or schedules of reinforcement, they may be distinguished from the effects of changes in the level of deprivation or aversive stimulation.

The reinforcement of verbal behavior through the mediation of a listener implies certain conditions which have important effects upon the dynamic properties of the behavior. For example, there is no relation between the energy of the behavior and the magnitude of the effect achieved. We sometimes shout to get action, but a whisper will have the same effect under other circumstances. The extent of the reinforcement depends upon the energy of the behavior of the *listener,* but only indirectly, if at all, on that of the *speaker*. This is not true of nonverbal behavior. A harder blow drives a nail farther. The distinction loses import as science develops systems of stored energy through which human behavior acquires expanding power and con-

[4a] Forster, C. B., and Skinner, B. F., *Schedules of Reinforcement* (New York, 1957).

trol. (It is possible that belief in verbal magic—the special power of words—declines for the same reason. The machine is the enemy of the word.)

Verbal behavior is also normally very fast, greatly exceeding the speed of nonverbal behavior with the same variety of forms and consequences. The limit appears to depend upon the mass of the musculature which is set in motion. Talking is faster than gesturing, and an external medium, as in writing or typing or smoke-signaling, exacts a penalty. Speed is also encouraged by the rapid serial chaining of behavior which is possible because the speaker need not wait for the physical reaction of the listener at each stage. Extensive segments of verbal behavior are reinforced only when completed. One advantage of speed is that temporal patterns become compact and hence more effective upon a listener or upon the speaker himself. This advantage is lost when we are forced to speak very slowly or to listen to a slow speaker. To put it roughly, we must speak fast to speak big thoughts.

Another consequence is that reinforcement of verbal behavior is not inevitable or even nearly so. Practical nonverbal behavior usually has an immediate and certain effect. We touch what we reach for, ascend stairs with a speed which is always about the same for a given rate of stepping, and so on. We do not always find what we are looking for, but at least we find the place in which we look. The exceptions are the ambiguous situations, as in a house of mirrors at an amusement park, which are so unusual as to be entertaining. In verbal behavior, the exception is the rule. An effect depends upon the presence and activity of a reinforcing organism whose behavior is not inevitable or often predictable. As a result, verbal behavior receives intermittent reinforcement, and this fact has many important consequences. For example, we behave verbally with a great deal less assurance than nonverbally, but we are less disturbed by occasional failures.

Since the reinforcing organism needs time, even the quickest mediation will introduce a delay sufficient to reduce the strength of the behavior of the speaker. Longer delays lead to extreme weakness. The ultimate reinforcement of written behavior may be delayed for days, weeks, or years, and behavior of this sort may have little strength. We immediately tell all the news to an old friend when we see him, perhaps in great excitement, though we have not recently written to him. Speaking is, of course, easier, but it is also more promptly reinforced, and the latter condition may be the more important. The "abulia" of most professional writers is legendary; that of the unsuccessful writer who gets no reinforcement at all is not so well known.

Somewhat offsetting the weakening effects of intermittent or delayed reinforcement is the fact that effects of verbal behavior may be multiplied by exposing many ears to the same sound waves or many eyes to the same page. Even without modern instrumental aid, verbal behavior may reach over centuries or to thousands of listeners or readers at the same time. The writer may not be reinforced often or immediately, but his net reinforcement may be great. The final condition of strength will be determined by all the factors in a given case. The difference between verbal and nonverbal behavior in this respect is reduced as technology amplifies and extends the scope of the latter.

Extinction

If the individual moves from one verbal community to another or if the community changes its practices, behavior may undergo extinction. Responses occur without achieving reinforcement. This has the effect of reversing the process brought about by operant reinforcement. It is to be distinguished from the loss of verbal behavior with the mere passage of time (*see below*) and from punishment, which, as we have seen, has a more complex effect.

Verbal behavior with respect to other listeners is extinguished when a man finds himself among strangers who do not speak his language or when he is isolated with a deaf person. His verbal behavior may first show the full strength resulting from earlier reinforcement, but responses become less common, and eventually he may show no overt verbal behavior, except as this is reinforced by himself as his own listener. Extinction is a much commoner process in its use in differential reinforcement. In order to shape up one form of response, we must extinguish responses of other forms. In order to shape up controlling relations with stimuli, we have to extinguish responses in the presence of other stimuli. This is particularly the case in narrowing stimulus control in abstraction.

Forgetting

The difference between extinction and forgetting is partly a difference in the actual process. Behavior may grow weak with the passage of time even though responses are not emitted. The presence or absence of reinforcement is not at issue. When verbal behavior has been extinguished in the presence of one audience, the fact that it has not been forgotten may be shown by producing a different audience. The forgetting to be discussed here should be distinguished from the forgetting due to punishment (Chapter 6) where a response may be lacking on what seems to be a suitable occasion but emitted on other occasions.

An extinguished response is not forgotten. It is simply not emitted in the circumstances in which it has been extinguished. This may be shown by changing the circumstances. Thus, we may no longer be reinforced for an outworn story, and it may seem to disappear entirely from our repertoire, only to be revived by a new audience, or by the moderate aversive pressure of such a question as *What was that story you used to tell?* Extinction produces a true weakening, while punishment either masks one response with another or, through differentiation, reduces behavior to an energy level at which it no longer generates the conditioned aversive stimulation which leads the speaker to do or say something else instead.

The loss of verbal behavior with the mere passage of time has been the subject of psychological studies of memory. These have generally been confined to intraverbal behavior, partly because, for reasons which we shall see in a moment, intraverbal behavior is more quickly lost. When there is no interference from similar forms of behavior or behavior appropriate to similar circumstances, an operant which has been well established shows very little loss in time. Returning to a special environment after many years, we may find most of the verbal behavior appropriate to it still intact, provided it had been extensively reinforced in the first place.

The verbal operants least likely to be forgotten are echoic and textual. The possibility of forgetting such behavior is often never considered. But if we can repeat a word we have not heard, or read a word we have not seen for twenty years, it is only because we have echoed and read many responses employing the same minimal repertoires during the intervening time. It is the minimal repertoire which makes forgetting so unlikely that the possibility is often overlooked. Now, something like a minimal repertoire can be detected in the case of tacts. The controlling relation between a specific object and its *common* name is supported by all instances in which similar objects lead to any type of extended tact and by all such extensions reinforced in their own right and thus part of the standard repertoire of the speaker. Moreover, the separate parts of some responses may find individual support elsewhere. We may retain such an operant as *intractable* in sufficient strength for occasional use because of the enormous number of other responses beginning with *in-* which have to do with the absence of a property, the enormous number of responses ending in *-able* showing the same adjectival force, as well as a substantial number of responses (*distract, tractable, extract, traction*) the circumstances of which share in common with the present situation some feature of drawing, or making do, or dragging.

The troublesome forgetting of proper names may be explained in part by the relative infrequency of reinforcement or by frequent interference from similar names or similar occasions having the same name. But proper names are a special kind of tact just because they do not ordinarily share a minimal repertoire. As we have seen, memory systems for the retaining of proper names often seek to relate a name to the minimal repertoire of common tacts—as by detecting some feature of a man which may be regarded as described by his name or some feature which evokes a response which in turn provides an intraverbal stimulus for his name.

Verbal Memory

In classical studies of memory interference from normal usage is minimized by choosing stimuli and responses which are as unlike standard behavior as possible and for this reason are called "nonsense." Responses are first generated as echoic or textual behavior but are brought under intraverbal control by making some sort of generalized reinforcement contingent upon the emission of a particular response in the presence of a particular stimulus. Such reinforcement is often not sharply identified, nor is the corresponding deprivation or aversive stimulation made clear.

The control which survives after a given period of time or after other responses have been similarly acquired or other conditions altered is tested by measures which are fairly closely related to response strength. For example, when a set of intraverbal operants has been thoroughly conditioned, the number of responses evoked by appropriate stimuli at a later date is taken as a measure of the surviving strength. It is assumed that in this condition of fractional strength incidental factors bring about the recall of some members but not others. Presumably each intraverbal connection has been weakened to the extent indicated by the ratio of the number of responses controlled before and after the passage of time. Sometimes the number of additional reinforcements needed to bring all responses under the control of the proper stimuli is compared with the number of reinforcements necessary to establish the series in the first place. Such studies are useful, not so much in permitting us to draw the curve according to which intraverbal connections are weakened with the passage of time, but in showing how various intraverbal operants interact with each other to facilitate or interfere with stimulus control.

The control exerted by an *audience* and by those audience-like conditions which facilitate verbal behavior also declines with the passage of time but the effect is usually not marked. It should be distinguished from the loss of intraverbal responses and tacts appropriate to a special field. Forgetting the technical term for something or not being able to recall a technical line of argument may not be due to failure of the technical audience. The effect of an audience in making a given repertoire more accessible probably declines in time, however.

CONTINGENCIES DETERMINING FORM

The properties of an operant response are specified by the contingency of reinforcement in the sense that only responses having certain properties achieve reinforcement. A response may show superfluous properties, however—it may have properties it does not "need." These often arise by accident in the early stages of conditioning. If a response is consistently executed with a given property, it is also consistently reinforced with that property, even though the property is not specified by the reinforcing system. Many examples would be called "superstitious." Unnecessary responses or properties of responses are maintained by fortuitous, but none the less effective, reinforcement. The forms of verbal responses may contain elements not demanded by the verbal community and these may persist for long periods of time.

In general, however, a response assumes a form close to the minimum which satisfies a contingency. It becomes as short as possible and as simply structured. *Why* form changes in this direction is not always clear. The net positive reinforcement is probably greatest for the simplest response which satisfies the contingencies, since such a response avoids the effort of executing a more complex form. Frequently we observe that a simple form emerges precisely because a more complex form is punished. Headline-writers, senders of telegrams, and those who must write messages with inadequate materials avoid lengthy responses, and their verbal behavior shows the properties to be noted in a moment. So do speakers in whom vocal behavior has been made automatically punishing—because of a sore throat, for example, or the danger of being overheard by a punishing audience. If the relatively greater effect of the more complex form can generally be regarded as a very slight but eventually effective aversive consequence, a trend toward simpler forms is explained.

We detect the effects of a relaxed contingency at several levels. The change may occur in the single speech-sound, in the single operant, or in the sequences of operants to be discussed in Part IV. We must distinguish carefully between changes taking place *in the individual speaker,* because of possibly temporary changes in the demands of a verbal community, and changes *in the reinforcing practices of the community as a whole,* which may require many generations. The latter, which are often called changes *in the language,* seem, in general, to be accumulations of slight changes in the behavior of individual speakers together with corresponding permanent changes in the reinforcing practices of the community. If the listeners of one generation reinforce a slight deviation from "standard" speech until that deviation becomes standard, then further slight deviations may be tolerated by listeners in later generations. There is presumably no limit to possible changes of form in such a system—as the transition from Latin to French, for example, suggests.

The change in reinforcing criteria responsible for the deterioration of form is exemplified by the general relaxation of the early educational reinforcements which are characteristically used to shape up verbal behavior. Those who arrange educational reinforcements are usually at pains to observe certain properties of response entering into the contingencies. Sounds are "pronounced correctly," the pattern of the operant is insisted upon in all its details, and explicit intraverbal sequences are set up. The verbal environment encountered by the speaker at a later date may not respect these contingencies. His repertoire of speech-sounds may become simplified and "sloppy", his *th*'s may become *d*'s, he may say *are* for *our,* and so on. It does not follow at all that the direction of deterioration will be the same in every speaker, for the change is determined in part by the verbal community. Above the level of the speech-sound we observe simplifications of larger operants in the dropping of unaccented syllables, especially at the beginnings or ends of forms, in the resort to nicknames and other expressions "for short," in the dropping of one of two or more identical syllables (haplology), and so on. If the response *photo* is as effective as *photograph,* the shorter form is likely to be stronger. Slight changes in these directions are accumulated historically in well-known examples of linguistic change. The effect in the individual speaker is described with such rhetorical terms as "syncope" and "apocope."

We observe the deterioration of longer passages in the cases described above in which length or complexity is automatically punishing. Verbal behavior under pressure of time is likely to show telescoping, omissions, a reduction in the range of pitch variation, and so on. Memorized speech which deteriorates when the contingencies are relaxed is exemplified by standard ritualistic verbal behavior—for example, the mumbling of *the truth, the whole truth, and nothing but the truth.* Ritualistic prayers are subject to this deterioration. In the Middle Ages, religious people commonly "gabbled" through prayers and other services to get them over with quickly. "They left out the syllables at the beginning of words, they omitted the dipsalma or pause between verses . . . they skipped sentences, they mumbled and slurred. . . ." [5] Possible punishment for these lapses was personified in a special devil (Titivillus) who was said to collect "failings and negligences and syllables and words" to be used against the guilty one at a later date.

All these trends toward deteriorated form will continue until the contingencies of reinforcement are no longer satisfied. When educational reinforcement has given way to the contingencies of everyday discourse, and in particular when these in turn have given way to the self-reinforcement of the speaker, the deterioration may be extensive. The point at which reinforcement is no longer forthcoming or at which aversive consequences may be forthcoming instead is not determined by the mere simplification of form. For example, in the course of deterioration, one form may begin to resemble another and to produce a reinforcement which is not relevant to the present condition of the speaker. The form of response may then be carefully elaborated in order to avoid such confusion. Indeed, elaboration for the sake of multiplying distinctive forms of response is possibly a

[5] Power, Eileen, *Medieval People* (Boston, 1929), p. 83.

more powerful trend, and it is obviously opposed to the deterioration due to relaxed contingencies of reinforcement.

Motivation

When an individual exhibits behavior in a sustained state of strength, it is common to describe him as "highly motivated." But a condition of strength may be the result of many different kinds of variables, and the term motivation is not appropriately applied to all of them. As we have just seen, behavior may vary in strength between fairly wide extremes simply as the result of conditions of reinforcement, other variables remaining constant, but to classify this with the effect of changes in deprivation, for example, is unnecessary and confusing. The term will be used here as a convenient classification for such variables as satiation and deprivation, the aversive stimulation used in generating avoidance and escape behavior, the effects of certain drugs, and certain uncontrolled processes of maturation or of aging in general.

The deprivation appropriate to a given reinforcement provides a means of changing the strength of verbal behavior. We can evoke a response which has been reinforced with food by making the organism hungry, other things being equal. But generalized reinforcement destroys the possibility of control *via* specific deprivations. Only the mand and the impure tact remain within reach of this variable. There are other conditions, however, which affect the general level of verbal strength, usually in concert with the level of nonverbal behavior as well. The active person tends to be active verbally as well as nonverbally, as the quiet or satisfied person remains quiet in every sense. In that special condition called sleep, most behavior is at a low ebb and this applies to verbal behavior as well. Cyclic changes during the waking hours, which may or may not be correlated with ingestion or other scheduled activities of the individual, are seen in both verbal and nonverbal behavior. A baby actively at play is also likely to be vocalizing. In the older child or adult a similar probability of verbal behavior is called a "talkative mood"—but this is usually a condition in which many sorts of nonverbal behavior are probable. If no listener is present, or if no suitable control is exerted upon specific forms of response, the individual may sing or hum a tune.

Aversive conditions which generate verbal behavior as a form of avoidance or escape often generalize to all verbal behavior without respect to form and to nonverbal behavior as well. The characteristics of the compulsive or driven man change as a whole as the aversive stimulation changes.

Professional writers have shown an understandable interest in the conditions which modify verbal behavior and have reported many interesting effects. Some have found a vigorous walk beneficial to verbal productivity. Shelley aroused himself verbally by overheating his head before a fire. Various stages of digestion seem relevant to verbal productivity, although no general rule has emerged. One writer may find himself most productive before breakfast, another after a heavy meal. Certain kinds of partial starvation resulting from special diets or special schedules of eating have been said to be favorable. (Some of these relations may have nothing to do with deprivation. When eating is closely associated with social behavior, much of which is verbal, the control may be more appropriate to the type of variable described in Chapter 7.)

Certain drugs have important effects upon verbal behavior. The so-called "truth serums" appear to reduce the anxiety or conditioned aversive stimulation generated by punishment. Behavior is made more probable by reducing its automatically punishing effects. The original truth serum, alcohol, has of course been widely used for the same purpose. A. E. Housman [6] reports that a single pint of beer at luncheon had a noticeable effect upon his poetic activity. DeQuincy [7] and Coleridge [8] have described the effect of laudanum on verbal behavior, and Aldous Huxley [9] has recently recounted the virtues of mescal. J. M. Barrie [10] preferred nicotine. Drugs also affect the mode of execution of verbal behavior, spoken or written. Drunken speech—with its distorted sounds, its explosive changes of speed and volume—is easily imitated and amusing to many audiences, and has been extensively used for dramatic purposes.

Age is another important variable. The schedule according to which verbal behavior matures in a standard verbal environment have been extensively studied. The age at which a child first makes speech-sounds or first acquires recognizable responses under the control of a verbal community and the growth of different kinds of verbal responses in his repertoire have all been recorded. At the other

6 Housman, A. E., *The Name and Nature of Poetry* (Cambridge, 1945).
7 DeQuincy, T., *Confessions of an English Opium Eater* (London, 1899).
8 Coleridge, S. T., Note in *Kubla Khan* (London, 1816).
9 Huxley, Aldous, *The Doors of Perception* (New York, 1954).
10 Barrie, J. M., *My Lady Nicotine* (London, 1890).

end of the age-continuum we find the verbal behavior of senility—slow halting speech under faulty stimulus control, "forgotten" intraverbals, the rambling of trivial intraverbals and self-echoics, the reduced audience-control which makes for irrelevance, unchecked repetition, and so on.

Emotion

The conditions which cause an organism to be "emotional" have never been exhaustively studied or even satisfactorily classified. Many are clearly related to reinforcement and to appropriate states of deprivation and aversive stimulation. Thus, dangerous or harmful stimuli not only make possible the reinforcement of avoidance or escape, they generate emotional conditions by virtue of which such behavior is more effective. Highly favorable reinforcing conditions produce a characteristic reaction (as in "joy"), and sexual behavior is accompanied by marked emotional changes. The existence of strong behavior which cannot be executed or, if executed, is repeatedly ineffective, generates the familiar pattern called "frustration." And so on.

The bodily changes in emotion which have been most thoroughly studied are the responses of glands and smooth muscles. These are primarily concerned with the internal economy of the organism, although they sometimes produce such visible "expressions of emotion" as weeping or turning pale. The vocal musculature is usually not activated, although vocal responses may be modified, as when one is "choked up" in anger or grief. These "expressions of emotion" can be conditioned according to the Pavlovian formula: a response may eventually be elicited by a stimulus which was originally ineffective but which has accompanied an effective stimulus. Such conditioning does not make the behavior verbal according to our definition. If one could actually learn to "cry real tears" because of the resulting effect upon someone, the process would illustrate operant conditioning and we should have to call the behavior verbal. But it is probable that all such efforts have to be achieved indirectly.[11]

A second type of emotional expression involves the muscular systems with which the organism deals with the external world. The so-called facial expressions are examples, as are certain responses of the whole body such as flinching or shuddering. The vocal apparatus may participate. The violent intake or expulsion of air from the

[11] *Science and Human Behavior*, p. 114.

lungs is likely to produce sounds, as in the startled "gasp," the grunt of "disgust," or the cries heard in extreme pain. While these are commonly observed under extreme emotional conditions, they also occur when the inference of an emotional effect is misleading. Thus, the cry of the epileptic is often interpreted as a cry of anguish and the first cry of the new-born babe is called a protest against birth, but it is more likely that both are simply by-products of the violent or spasmodic operation of the breathing apparatus. The later cry of the new-born baby appears to be reflex. Both vocal and lacrimal crying, in surprise, pain, sorrow, and so on, and the curious behavior called laughter are comparable forms which survive into adult life.

This second type of "expression of emotion" may seem to be conditioned on the Pavlovian pattern. A response comes to be evoked by a stimulus which was originally not in control. The wry face which is made first to the bitter medicine is eventually made to the sight of the bottle, and the laughter of surprise originally evoked by a novel stimulus is eventually controlled by the novel twist in a funny story. Usually, however, operant conditioning has occurred. This is especially clear when the form of such responses undergoes a change. Facial expressions of emotion are peculiar to a given culture. To some extent each verbal community has its own cry of pain (*Ouch!* or *Aie!*), its own forms of laughter, its own verbal expressions of contempt (*Pooh, pooh!*), and so on. (Expressions of contempt are often relatively formless, indicating that no well-formed behavior, either favorable or unfavorable, is at the moment strong.)

The extent to which the so-called emotional expressions become verbal—that is, acquire definite form because of the reinforcing practices of a community—is hard to establish. *Ouch!* may be a slight change in a cry of pain, or it may be wholly verbal if, in the absence of pain, it is emitted to restrain a dentist. Extreme states of pain usually yield more primitive forms. It is possible that most responses of this sort draw strength from at least two sources (Chapter 9).

Emotional variables have still another effect. When we "arouse an emotion," we alter the probabilities of certain types of responses. Thus, when we make a man angry we increase the probability of abusive, bitter, or other aggressive behavior and decrease the probability of generous or helpful behavior. The effect resembles that of a state of deprivation or satiation or a condition of aversive stimulation. The only difference is in the composition of the classes of responses affected. Why a particular set of responses all vary together as a function of the condition which makes a man angry has to be explained in terms of their consequences. The behaviors exhibited in anger are generally damaging to others; only those behaviors damaging to X are strong when we say that a man is angry at X. We make a similar point when we say that a man is hungry for sweets. Both behaviors may be generalized. Although angry at X, a man may show aggression toward Y, just as, although hungry for sweets, we may find him eating other foods.

One form of emotional expression may be simply a heightened probability of acting in a given way or to achieve a given effect. Some examples are verbal though nonvocal. Thus, a menacing posture and a clenched fist are expressions of anger as part of the behavior of striking. (They may be reinforced if they threaten the "listener" in their own right.) Vocal responses which express anger in the same way include mands which specify aversive conditions of the listener (e.g., damning him), tacts descriptive of the listener which have aversive effects (e.g. calling him names or applying pejorative adjectives), and responses which are directly punishing (*Pfui!* or derisive laughter). These are more clearly "expressive" than other forms of verbal behavior which may be equally punishing to the listener, as in telling him bad news or raising topics of conversation in which he is ill at ease. Since these responses depend on the individual histories of speaker and listener, any objective specification of such expressions seems hopeless. Nevertheless, when we infer from a single response that "a man is angry," we imply that the response is a member of a broad class, other members of which would be observed under other circumstances. We make the further assumption that his inclination to behave in this way is due to a specific inciting circumstance as the cause of his emotion. It is this relation between verbal behavior and emotional variables which is involved when, as in the composition of lyric poetry, level of productivity is sensitively affected by emotional circumstances. A great love or sorrow or hate may cause the "outpouring" of verbal behavior having an effect upon the listener or reader (perhaps the speaker or writer himself) appropriate to the emotion.

Some characteristics of verbal behavior often attributed to emotion are characteristic of any extreme state of strength. One may bubble over with joy or be struck dumb in surprise or silenced by grief, although comparable states of the behavior may arise for nonemotional reasons. Verbal responses closely associated with such emotional states are often classed as exclamations or interjections, a category or "part of speech" which has never been very happily received by grammarians. J. H. Tooke called it "the brutish inarticulate Interjection, which has nothing to do with speech, and is only the miserable refuge of the speechless." [12] Such responses are usually brief, frequently ill-formed, seldom inflected, and commonly occur in "noncommunicative" situations, as in talking to oneself. Many are, indeed, associated with strong variables, particularly in the fields of motivation and emotion. But in each case an explicit function may be detected by examining the controlling variables. As we saw in Chapter 3, some exclamations are mands—for attention (*Ahem!*), to direct the behavior of the listener (*Lo!*), for confirmation (*Eh, what?*), and so on. Others, as we saw in Chapter 6, function as reinforcements (*Good!*), punishments (*Pfui!*), or are useful in reinstating past conditions of a similar sort (*Tut, tut!*). The connection with emotion in all these cases is incidental.

The *manner* in which behavior is executed depends upon its strength. Some emotions, like extreme conditions of deprivation or aversive stimulation, are characterized by unco-ordinated behavior. The speaker may stammer, mispronounce, make mistakes in grammar, show solecistic extensions of the tact, and exhibit other signs of being "flustered." Exceptional muscular tension in the speech apparatus may increase the pitch and energy level of the behavior. But all this may occur in the absence of emotion.

Another class of verbal responses generated by an emotional condition is descriptive of the speaker's own behavior. A response such as *I am angry* is seldom called an expression of emotion. The public or private stimuli in control of such a response may fall within any of the classes just listed (cf. the discussion of *I am hungry* in Chapter 5). Thus, *I am angry* may be descriptive of the changes in glands and smooth muscles studied in the physiology of emotion; it may be a report of a facial expression (seen, perhaps, in a mirror) or of a cry of anger, possibly shaped by a particular community, or of an inclination to emit such a cry, or it may be a description of the speaker's own inclination to act aggressively. The community has set up the response *I am angry* on the basis of observable aspects of

[12] Tooke, J. H., *Diversions of Purley* (Edition of 1857), p. 30.

such behavior or other public concomitants, and the mature individual may use the expression with some accuracy when the controlling stimuli are now private.

"Damaged" Verbal Behavior

The ravages of age may be anticipated by other sorts of damage to the organism. The verbal effects of brain injury (say, from battle wounds, tumors, or hemorrhages) are usually discussed under the heading of aphasia. As we have noted, the phenomena are often surprising to one who has accepted traditional explanations of verbal behavior. When a man can pronounce a word "after" the physician but cannot use it for practical purposes, or cannot name an object upon demand but soon uses the name in another connection, or cannot "read" but can follow written instructions, or can follow written instructions only after reading them aloud, a functional classification of verbal behavior is dramatically set forth.

Changes in verbal behavior as a whole range from the complete loss of all behavior (due possibly, but not necessarily, to anarthria or paralysis of the speech apparatus) to a hyperexcitable state in which behavior is emitted rapidly and continuously, possibly for days. In the latter case, as usual when verbal behavior is strong for any *general* reason, the controlling variables may be trivial—the speech may be superficial, ungrammatical, illogical, and badly formed. Some effects may arise from damage to the sensory systems, but nonverbal behavior may be found to be still under sensory control. Thus, although a speaker can be shown not to be blind, he may suffer from "visual agnosia"—he cannot identify objects or colors though he may be able to deal with them practically. There are comparable defects in other sensory modalities. These will, of course, affect different types of verbal operants differently; textual behavior will suffer in visual agnosia (when it is called "alexia"), echoic behavior in auditory agnosia, and so on. But aphasic symptoms also seem to respect our classification for other reasons, mostly of a motivational nature.

The phenomena of aphasia are difficult to summarize because verbal behavior may be damaged at so many points in so many ways. In general we may hazard the generalization that aside from specific sensory and motor damage, aphasia is a condition of lowered probability of response. The symptoms of aphasia are valuable in emphasizing the property of "difficulty" inherent in all types of operants.

Damage is usually most severe in verbal behavior receiving generalized reinforcement. The order of damage seems to follow the order of "difficulty" deducible from the availability of a minimal repertoire. Textual and echoic behavior often survive (unless relevant sensory defects are involved) while intraverbals and tacts appear to be most vulnerable. Although names of letters may be echoed or read aloud, for example, the alphabet may not be correctly recited. Trivial intraverbal connections may disturb the chaining of responses. When a simple tact cannot be emitted, the generalized pressure from silence as an aversive condition may bring out a series of related responses. The first term in such a series (and perhaps others) cannot be an intraverbal if there has been no (at least covert) verbal stimulus. In such cases the response must be regarded as a tact in metonymical extension. Other things being equal the extent of conditioning may affect the result: a second language may be lost first, and so on.

Verbal behavior which has been reinforced in relation to some special condition of deprivation or aversive stimulation (including those effects upon others appropriate to various emotions) remains relatively accessible. The mand and the impure tact can often be evoked by arranging appropriate variables. On the other hand behavior which has been punished is likely to be relatively weak (for example, it may be difficult for the patient to repeat an untrue statement).

In addition to emphasizing the relative ease or difficulty of various types of verbal operants, damage to the organism may affect the second order activities to be discussed in Part IV. Grammatical and syntactical activities may be excessive and usually confused (paragrammatism) or lacking (agrammatism). The patient may be separately affected as speaker and listener, and among his behaviors as listener some may be affected and others not. In severe cases, all the behavior of the listener disappears, in which case we say that the patient no longer understands heard speech. All the behavior appropriate to the reader may be lost, but there are milder instances in which textual behavior is lacking altogether or in part although the patient can correctly follow written instructions. When instructions can be followed only if they can be read aloud and correctly pronounced, it appears that direct nonverbal responses to a text are missing, while responses to heard speech survive. By reading the text aloud the patient can generate the stimuli he needs.

WHEN DOES VERBAL BEHAVIOR CEASE?

Although we are especially interested in variables which generate and maintain verbal behavior, it is useful to consider the conditions under which behavior comes to an end. Sometimes a verbal response is actually emitted several times, either as the result of exceptional strength or because it provides its own stimulus for echoic behavior, but the more usual rule is that it is emitted only once. Evidently the response itself alters some of the variables which control it and hence immediately changes its own probability. What are these variables and how are they changed?

A verbal response may change the level of the appropriate deprivation. The reinforcement of a mand, for example, usually has this effect. The strength of the behavior may not subside at once. *For real pleasure, give me a cool glass of beer,* says the man in the advertisement, although he already holds such a glass in his hand. The young child who is emitting the mand *Me! . . . Me! . . .* to someone who is distributing gifts may emit one or more responses after receiving his gift. The declining strength may be evident in the fading energy of the response, the last instance being merely mumbled. More often a reinforcement produces a condition in which other behavior is evoked, and the mand is not repeated because of this competition.

The states of deprivation associated with generalized reinforcement cannot be altered in this way. The listener may instantly reduce a threat or other form of aversive stimulation as the consequence of a single response, but a single instance of *positive* generalized reinforcement must have only a negligible satiating effect. The change brought about by such behavior to prevent its own repetition must therefore be of another sort. We have already seen that the community does not continue to reinforce tacts except upon certain unusual occasions. It also stops reinforcing more than one instance, either of a tact or of echoic, textual, or intraverbal behavior. It does this because the function of verbal behavior for the listener is usually served with only a single instance. Once a response of this type has been emitted, it automatically establishes a condition under which, in view of the reinforcing practices of the community, it cannot be made and reinforced again. This aspect of the reinforcing contingencies of a community may not be equally effective upon the behavior of all speakers. The garrulous person has evidently been untouched by it; the laconic person may fail to repeat as often as necessary for an effect. (These characteristics of verbal behavior may be due in part to the defective practices of the community, although they also exemplify other effects.) In the sense of Chapter 6, we might say that one instance of a response converts the listener from someone who doesn't know to someone who knows. The audience-status of a given listener may be vague, but a listener to whom we have already emitted a tact is very obviously one who is not likely to reinforce a second instance. This is especially so if the listener makes his status clear with some such response as *Yes, I see, uh-huh,* or *Really?* In giving important orders (surgeon to nurse, captain to crew, waiter to chef) it is a common practice for the listener to repeat the order as an indication of his new audience-status. If he does not, the order is repeated. Pupils are sometimes required to repeat the responses of teachers for the same reason.

In talking about a complex situation or in presenting an involved intraverbal argument, it is by no means always clear that a single response has had the required effect, and verbal behavior of this sort tends to be highly repetitious. (It also tends to be marked by interjected responses which essentially mand the condition of the listener called "getting the point"—such as *You see!, So there you are!*) Unseen audiences encourage repetition—in letter writing, or in speaking impromptu on television, or in writing a book for which there is no way of predicting the reaction of the reader. An inattentive listener produces repetitious speech. Atypical audiences such as small babies, dogs, dolls, and so on, which may evoke behavior through stimulus generalization, show no sign of an effect, and the behavior is characteristically repetitious (*You're a cute little fellow, yes, you are, yes, sir, you're a cute little fellow, aren't you? a cute little fellow . . .*). The listener who wishes to stop a repetitive speaker does so by a clear sign that the behavior has had an effect, as in saying *Yes, you told me that!, You don't say!,* or *Yes, I know!*

The reaction on the part of the listener which brings verbal behavior to an end may be fairly specific. The speaker may not stop if the listener gives some other type of reaction. Suppose, for example, that a speaker emits a response in a loud voice under circumstances where quiet is demanded, and that the listener's only response is *Sh!* The speaker may then *whisper* the same response. This appears to be illogical, since the first response was obviously heard, but the listener's reaction was merely to the intensity of the response and repetition therefore follows.

The contingencies established by the community to oppose repetition obviously affect the use of frequency of response as a measure of strength. Since the strictures are not necessarily applied to synonymous forms of response, strong variables may lead to a sort of repetition with variation. Children not only repeat the same form, they often emit essentially synonymous forms in a thematic group. Two examples from a two-year-old are *They match just the same alike* and *I'm not through with it still quite yet.* Adults usually abide by the opposing strictures, but we are guilty of a similar lapse when, in response to a single state of affairs, we exclaim *Fine! Good! Excellent!* rather than *Fine! Fine! Fine!* Conrad was sensitive to this in the nonnative speaker and gives many instances—for example, *"Plenty too much enough of Patusan," he concluded with energy.* The pairing of synonyms is a common literary device which increases the likelihood of an effective response on the part of the reader in addition to eluding the taboo against repetition. Shakespeare has many examples (*the slings and arrows of outrageous fortune*), as does the King James Bible (*Rebuke me not in Thine anger, neither chasten me in Thy displeasure*). It is quite probable that the practice is reinforced not only by escape from repetition but by a more univocal reaction on the part of the listener under whatever common control such a group of stimuli possesses. The repetition which is encouraged when we are describing a difficult or complex state of affairs or driving home a difficult argument often takes on this sort of variation. Metaphysical treatises are sometimes reducible to a series of variations on a few elementary responses.

Verbal behavior which is strong because of some of the special consequences discussed in Chapter 6, over and above the special consequence of "letting the listener know," is brought to an end through a reduction in relevant states of deprivation, as is behavior in the form of the mand. The boy who cries *Wolf!* stops when his neighbors come running. The emotional behavior of the listener is not only a special consequence which cannot be effectively manded, it is not always obvious. Nor is the underlying condition greatly changed by a single response. We are seldom satisfied with getting one laugh or wringing one tear. Behavior which has this type of effect is characteristically repetitive. So is behavior with subtler effects: ... *in the dusty forgotten corner of a forgotten room,*[13] or *Something seemed to swell*

[13] Moore, George, *Confessions of a Young Man* (New York, 1901).

and grow and swell within his breast.[14] Compare, from the latter author, *The world may be wicked, cruel, and stupid, but it is patient. On this point I will not be gainsaid. It is patient; I know what I am talking about; I maintain that the world is patient.* Here, as in the poetic refrain and other kinds of rhetorical repetition, stylistic devices are possible because the literary community does not punish or fail to reinforce the repetition of a response with the same diligence as the practical verbal environment. Repetition is also encouraged because responses occur in the literary community with less strength.

Verbal behavior may come to an end simply because a few responses reveal the audience character of the listener. Someone to whom we speak for the first time may show through his first reactions that he is an example of an audience which does not reinforce verbal behavior—he is deaf, for example, or does not speak the language we are speaking. In such a case, behavior will cease much more rapidly than through the process of extinction itself. (Extinction was originally involved, of course, in bringing the behavior under the negative control of such an audience.) It is not necessary to extinguish our entire verbal repertoire each time we discover someone who speaks another language.

Verbal behavior which is primarily effective on the speaker himself is brought to an end only when an effect has been achieved. When this is not a punishing audience, or any variety of negative audience, the behavior may not come to an end, as diaries and notebooks sometimes show. The speaker who is talking to himself through someone else cannot be stopped by the ostensible listener merely by indicating that the behavior has been effective. Confession may require an external listener, but it is often primarily effective upon the speaker himself. Rousseau gave his reader fair warning: *"Je sais bien que le lecteur n'a pas grand besoin de savoir tout cela, mais j'ai besoin, moi, de le lui dire."* [15] Verbal behavior which arises primarily from anxiety or some other aversive condition of the speaker which is not effectively relieved by the behavior may be repetitious in a manner described by the Queen in *Hamlet* as "protesting too much."

It is a happy condition when the speaker who is talking primarily to himself achieves an effect upon himself at approximately the same time as upon his listeners. The commonest kind of failure makes for

[14] Machen, Arthur, *The Hill of Dreams* (New York, 1927).
[15] Rousseau, J. J., *Les Confessions,* Livre I.

repetition. Although the external listener may long since have undergone the appropriate change, the speaker continues to talk to himself. When the effect upon the speaker himself occurs before that upon the external listener, his behavior is called laconic. The external listener would have profited from repetition and amplification.

When there is a practical reason for preventing the cessation of verbal behavior, terminating consequences are avoided. The problem of the professional writer is to continue to react verbally. Many writers have found it a good rule not to talk about material on which they are working. To tell the plot of a novel or to go over the details of a scene weakens the behavior and makes it difficult for the writer to complete his task. Similarly, the psychological interviewer anxious to keep his client talking may avoid any indication that his behavior is effective, not only to avoid "shaping up" the behavior of his client along thematic lines (see Chapter 6), but to avoid bringing it to an end by appearing to agree or understand.

REFINEMENT OF THE DEFINITION OF VERBAL BEHAVIOR

Now that we have examined the variables of which a verbal response is a function, it will be helpful to restrict our definition by excluding instances of "speaking" which are reinforced by certain kinds of effects on the listener. The exclusion is arbitrary but it helps to define a field of inquiry having certain unitary properties.

When the mediating "listener" participates merely in his role as a physical object, there is no reason to distinguish a special field. The prizefighter or the physician achieves certain results only "through the participation of another person," but an uppercut to the jaw or an appendectomy is not usefully regarded as verbal.

To say that we are interested only in behavior which has an effect upon the *behavior* of another individual does not go far enough, for the definition embraces all social behavior. The artist, to take a particular example, is reinforced by the effects his works have upon people—himself or others—but much of his behavior is irrelevant here. A preliminary restriction would be to limit the term verbal to instances in which the responses of the "listener" have been conditioned. We could then exclude the behavior of painting a careful representation of a landscape as nonverbal, while accepting the use of a conventional symbol in a painting as a verbal response. But the artist who paints a realistic mother and child in order to evoke reactions appropriate to such a subject matter is appealing to conditioned behavior on the part of his audience, though his behavior is not usefully described as verbal. If we make the further provision that the "listener" must be responding in ways which have been conditioned *precisely in order to reinforce the behavior of the speaker,* we narrow our subject to what is traditionally recognized as the verbal field.

These distinctions can be illustrated by considering the different ways in which one may make a horse turn aside. When physical force is used—when the horse is simply pushed to the side—the result does not reinforce the pusher by virtue of the movement of a horse as a living organism. One might push a hobby-horse in the same way, and the behavior is of no interest here. If one makes the horse shy to one side by waving a frightening object, or attracts it to one side by holding up a novel object, the effect is achieved by eliciting *unconditioned* behavior. Similarly, when one waves a fly off the salad, the fly departs because of a characteristic unconditioned response to a moving object. The techniques and maneuvers of the bull-fighter have fairly predictable results because of the ways in which bulls tend in general to behave, though some specific conditioning goes on in the ring. Advertisers and merchandising specialists exert a similar control over human behavior: the buzzer in the bargain show-window is a primarily unconditioned stimulus which causes passers-by to look toward the window. Clearing the throat or saying *Psst!* to get attention may be effective for the same reasons. Conditioned stimuli are also used. A piece of sugar may induce the horse to turn primarily because turning and approaching similar objects has eventually been followed by reinforcing contact with sugar in the mouth. There appears to be no good reason to regard the "use" of such stimuli as verbal, for the controlling relations present no special problems.

A man engages in behavior requiring a further analysis when he turns a horse by letting the reins touch the skin lightly on the neck. The touch of the reins, unlike the waving of a frightening object, does not originally cause the horse to turn in a given direction, and there has been no *incidental* conditioning as in the case of the lump of sugar. The horse has been conditioned with respect to the touch of the reins *especially to create a means of control.* More particularly, it has been submitted to certain contingencies involving a touch on the neck and escape from, or avoidance of, aversive stimuli produced by whip or heel. This special conditioning eventually imparts to the behavior of the rider properties of special interest, as similar circumstances in the history of the listener give rise to important characteristics of the behavior of the speaker.

The special conditioning of the listener is the crux of the problem. Verbal behavior is shaped and sustained by a verbal environment—by people who respond to behavior in certain ways because of the practices of the group of which they are members. These practices and the resulting interaction of speaker and listener yield the phenomena which are considered here under the rubric of verbal behavior.

Part III
MULTIPLE VARIABLES

Chapter 9

. . . .

Multiple Causation

Two facts emerge from our survey of the basic functional relations in verbal behavior: (1) the strength of a single response may be, and usually is, a function of more than one variable and (2) a single variable usually affects more than one response.

An example of the first has already been given: the response *fire* may be a mand or a tact. It may also be an echoic, textual, or intraverbal response. (Since the form of echoic and textual responses is determined by verbal stimuli, they almost always have the same form as other operants.) The formal overlap need not be complete. In an example to be considered below, we shall find the response *discount* under the control of one variable and the fragmentary *disc-* under the control of another.

Evidence that a single variable may affect the strength of many responses is equally good. Different parts of the verbal community, or the same community upon different occasions, may reinforce different responses in the same way. The adult repertoire contains many mands varying with one state of deprivation or aversive stimulation; when a man is deprived of food, it is not simply the mand *Food!* which shows an increased probability. Reinforcing practices with respect to intraverbal behavior are even more complex. Just as a given stimulus word will evoke a large number of different responses from a sample of the population at large, so it increases the probability of emission of many responses in a single speaker. Many properties, each of which controls an abstract tact, are presented together in what we call a stimulus presentation or a stimulus situation, and through metaphorical, metonymical, or solecistic extension, each of them may encourage the emission of many others. Only echoic and textual behaviors fail to show a single variable in control of many forms of response.

Sometimes several members of a group of responses strengthened by a single variable are emitted. Certain idiomatic expressions consist of small "thematic" groups (*over and above, well and good, ways and means, part and parcel, safe and sound, odds and ends*). When verbal behavior is ineffective in altering the circumstances responsible for its strength, one response may yield to another (especially when straight repetition is punished), and the thematic group appears as a sort of repetition with variation. Groups of responses under a common variable are formally recognized under such rubrics as "attitude" or "opinion." When we use a measure of opinion to predict behavior, we argue that because one response in a thematic group has been made, other responses in the same group are probable. It is not necessary to identify the circumstances in the history and current condition of the speaker which are responsible.

A thematic group is the behavioral counterpart of a proposition. In the expression "the same thing may be said in several ways," "the same thing" refers to a common set of variables and "several ways" to a thematic group of responses. It is sometimes easier to predict that a man will "reply in the negative" than to say that he will emit a particular response, e.g. *Never!*, because the variables controlling a thematic group are only part of those to be taken into account in predicting a specific response.

Neither the fact that a single response may be controlled by more than one variable nor the fact that one variable may control more than one response violates any principle of scientific method. It does not follow that a specific functional relation is not lawful, or that the behavior occurring in any given situation is not fully determined. It simply means that we must be sure to take into account *all* relevant variables in making a prediction or in controlling behavior.

These two facts make it highly probable that any sample of verbal behavior will be a function of many variables operating at the same time. Any response under the control of one variable has a fair chance of being related to other variables also present. Now, it is a well-established principle in nonverbal behavior that separate sources of strength are additive. (Since some variables *reduce* the strength of verbal behavior, the addition must be algebraic.) As a result, multiple causation produces many interesting verbal effects, including those of verbal play, wit, style, the devices of poetry, formal distortions, slips, and many techniques of verbal thinking.

We have already appealed to multiple causation in dealing with the audience as a variable (Chapter 7). A large group of responses has a greater strength in the presence of a particular audience, and some member of that group has a greater strength in, say, the presence of a given object. The speaker emits the response which is both "appropriate to the audience" and "descriptive of the object." We have also used the principle to explain certain special effects in Chapter 6. A tact under the control of a particular stimulus which also achieves a special effect upon the listener has a heightened probability of emission. The tact *milk,* which is strong in the presence of milk, is more likely to be emitted when the speaker is thirsty for milk and inclined to emit the mand *Milk!* Except where stimulus control is altogether destroyed, as in fiction or lying, we have to take two sources of strength into account.

We turn now to a different type of multiple control, in which functional relations, established separately, combine possibly for the first time upon a given occasion. There are two sorts of evidence to be considered. In the study of verbal behavior we are often confined to records of the behavior of speaker or writer where the conditions under which the behavior occurred are not known. This is usually the case in the critical study of texts, in the linguistic analysis of recorded samples of speech, and in the explication of literature or scientific writing. We can reconstruct a probable verbal history of speaker or writer, but only rarely can our inferences regarding the relevant variables be directly checked. Nevertheless, the inferences are often plausible and the resulting analysis useful. A more direct kind of information is obtained from the deliberate manipulation of variables, where the resulting behavior is predicted or actually controlled.

In the present chapter, the first of these two kinds of evidence predominates. The functional relations demonstrated in Part II and the notion of multiple causation are used to interpret recorded instances of verbal behavior. In judging the validity of the analysis, the reader should bear in mind the possibility of a more direct kind of information to be discussed in the chapter which follows, in which the variables controlling verbal behavior are directly manipulated for practical purposes.

MULTIPLE AUDIENCES

In addition to the multiple causation which occurs when one audience combines with a different type of variable, we have to consider multiple audiences. The control exerted by each of two or more audiences is developed under appropriate circumstances, and the audiences then occur together, perhaps for the first time.

In a relatively trivial case, two or more audiences have the same effect upon the same response. The growing verbal strength of the soapbox orator as his audience increases is scarcely more than the intensification of a single variable. A similar increase in the magnitude of a negative audience is responsible for the complete suppression of verbal behavior in "stage fright," if that term may be extended to any situation in which an individual is speaking to a large number of people all of whom are potentially critical or otherwise negatively reinforcing.

Multiple audiences which control different responses or the same response in different ways produce more interesting effects. Different forms of response are established by different verbal communities when the ultimate reinforcement, as well as the external situation except for the audience, is the same. The audiences which separately control these forms of response then come together. The effect will be a severe reduction in the available repertoire if only responses common to both audiences are strong. For example, it is "hard" to discuss a topic before technical and nontechnical audiences at the same time. We may interpret "hard" in either of two ways. It may indicate the mere poverty of the available repertoire, as when we find it hard to speak in a language with which we are not very familiar. Or it may refer to the punishing contingencies which are probably present in such a situation; the speaker is subject to criticism from the technical audience if his responses are inaccurate or inefficient and from the nontechnical audience if his responses are obscure or unintelligible.

The presence of a negative audience can be detected only in combination with a positive audience, since its effect is felt as a reduction in the strength of behavior appropriate to the latter. Obscene responses reinforced by a child's playmates, for example, are punished by his family. So long as these audiences remain separate, no difficulty may arise; but both audiences together present a dilemma:

responses must be either emitted and punished by one audience or withheld with, let us say, a loss of prestige with respect to the other. Two scientists may stop talking shop while in a crowded elevator if they are sensitive to an additional audience which may react to their verbal behavior as gibberish. If the negative audience does not predominate, the result may be a loss of effectiveness with respect to the positive audience. When a seditious soapbox orator sees a policeman approaching from a distance, his behavior decreases in strength as the negative audience becomes relatively more important, perhaps eventually falling below the overt level. The student who mumbles an answer so that it is not clear enough to be wrong shows the effect of a positive audience (calling for *some* vocal response) and a negative audience, in the same skin, more responsive to details. Sometimes the combination of positive and negative audiences reduces the energy level of the response, so that only one audience is affected, as in whispering or passing notes surreptitiously. The behavior assumes an energy level or a form such that only one of two audiences is affected. The "aside" in the theater is a formalized device for speaking to only one of two audiences where the excluded audience may produce punishing consequences.

In these examples one verbal response is assumed to be effective upon two audiences in different ways. When two or more forms of response are effective on the positive audience but only one of them on the negative audience, the form which is effective only upon the positive emerges when the two audiences occur together. Parents may speak a foreign language to avoid effects upon their children which are punishing to the parents. One function of underworld cant is to serve as such a secret language. The thief in eighteenth-century London could say *Stow it, the cove's awake* and thereby warn his confederate that an intended victim was on the alert, the response having no effect upon innocent passers-by. Similarly, he could inform a friend that *The kiddy clapped his persuaders to his prad, but the traps boned him* with less danger of being overheard than if he had said *The highwayman put spurs to horse, but the police caught him.*[1] At one time it was common for physicians to transmit instructions to pharmacists via the patient in a secret language which the patient ordinarily could not understand. Thus the marks

[1] These examples are from Grose, F., *A Classical Dictionary of the Vulgar Tongue* (London, 1785).

℞
Sodii bicarbonatis
Sacchari — āā ʒij
Spiritus amonii aromatici — ♏xL
Aquae menthae piperitae q.s. ad — f ℥ viij

have an effect upon the pharmacist similar to that of the marks *sodamint solution,* but the latter might have an effect upon the patient aversive to the physician. In a well-known story by O. Henry, a telegram was composed in American slang so that it could not be deciphered by the South American police who intercepted it, even with the help of an English dictionary. Slang changes so fast that the modern American reader will probably be equally outwitted. The telegram read: *His nibs skedaddled yesterday per jackrabbit line with all the coin in the kitty and a bundle of muslin he's spoony about.* The vague terms in which we conduct an intimate conversation in a crowded streetcar or in the presence of a suspected eavesdropper also comprise a sort of secret language. The terms we use have a special effect upon the immediate audience because of other information available to him alone.

A single response may have different effects upon different audiences. A distinguished scholar used to acknowledge complimentary copies of books by writing immediately to the author: *I shall lose no time in reading the book you have so kindly sent me.* With respect to the audience of which the author was a member, this was synonymous with *I am anxious to read your book* or *I am going to read your book as soon as possible.* With respect to another audience, of which the scholar himself was a member, it was synonymous with *I shan't waste my time on such stuff.* Several types of irony exemplify this kind of multiple audience. Socrates encourages an innocent newcomer with a response which has one effect upon the newcomer (synonymous with *We are anxious to hear what you have to say*) but a very different effect upon the group (synonymous with *Show us how poorly informed you are*). In dramatic irony, the dramatist puts into the mouth of a character a remark which has one supposed effect upon the characters on the stage and a very different effect upon the spectators. When Macbeth reassures himself of his invincibility by repeating the prediction that he will be unharmed so long as Birnam Wood does not come to Dunsinane, he has a very different effect upon the audience, to whom the expression is no longer synonymous with the impossible. The artistic achievement in dramatic irony requires that the spectator respond to some extent as a member of both audiences.

In one form of mockery, the speaker's behavior appears to be strongly under the control of one audience but is so extravagant or outrageous to a second audience that the control exerted by the first is seen to be spurious. Let us say that a critic is to review a new play by the wife of the editor of his paper. What he says is in part determined by the play he sees, but its special effect upon his employer is not irrelevant. By resorting to fulsome praise, he may satisfy the latter contingency, yet salvage his reputation as a critic with his colleagues and with part of his public who, detecting the extremity of his review, will draw another conclusion about his reaction to the play.

Fable, satire, and allegory are composed of responses emitted with respect to one audience but effective upon another in a different way. At the time it was written, *Gulliver's Travels* had very different effects upon the young and the socially sophisticated adult reader, though it was not written in a secret language. As a description of, say, a disturbing social condition, a satire may be regarded as extreme metaphorical or metonymical extension. A stricter description would be punished, and the conditions are therefore ripe for metaphorical extension. But satire is not merely metaphorical extension; it takes a form appropriate to another audience. Many details may be appropriate, say, to a story for children and incapable of explanation as metaphorical extension with respect to the first audience. From a practical point of view, the part of the satire directed to the child as an audience acts as an additional guarantee against punishment. But both audiences are important for the satirical effect. The writer would not have written for the second audience alone, and an innocent member of that audience does not "get the point." The reader who "appreciates the satire" must be a member of both audiences.

Allegory commonly refers to two or more audiences of which none is necessarily negative. Bunyan's *Pilgrim's Progress,* as a metaphorical discussion of moral precepts, is directed toward an audience which might not require the allegorical form, but it is also a story of personal adventure and, as such, is directed toward an audience uninterested in moral precepts. The strategy of the allegory is to induce the second audience to respond with behavior appropriate to the first. Readers may vary considerably in the extent to which they are members of the two audiences. A child, reading the story, may be but little affected by the moral precepts; a moralist, reading it as metaphorical extension, may be scarcely touched by the personalities and episodes.

Fable, satire, and allegory resemble the behavior of the speaker who talks to someone "through" a second listener. The energy level and other characteristics of verbal behavior in, say, a crowded waiting room may indicate that the speaker is also talking to those who cannot choose but hear. The technique is useful with respect to potentially negative audiences. It is sometimes possible to speak to a person of real or ceremonial importance, to whom direct speech is forbidden, by speaking to a second audience in his hearing. One may complain of injustice in the presence of, but not speaking directly to, a magistrate. The second audience may be the speaker himself; the complaint may be mumbled to no one in particular. A child who has been punished for teasing may simply say to himself *I wish I had some candy* or *Candy is awfully good.* A doll or pet animal will serve the purpose of a second audience.

MULTIPLE VARIABLES IN THE IMPURE TACT

Under a carefully generalized reinforcement, the type of verbal operant called the tact approaches the condition in which its form is determined by only one variable. But insofar as the response is likely to have a special effect upon the listener, it varies in strength with the states of deprivation or aversive stimulation associated with that effect. Stimulus control is reduced, as we have seen, and in pure fiction may be altogether lacking. Between these two extremes we are necessarily dealing with multiple variables. The special effect of "letting the listener know,"—in particular, inducing him to behave appropriately to a given state of affairs—may combine with simple stimulus control. The response *Believe me, it's true* contains a mand and a tact. The function of the mand in coercing the listener to react "with greater belief" to the tact may be carried by a more urgent form of the tact (*It's TRUE!*) which must be attributed to multiple sources.

A special consequence may affect the choice of otherwise synonymous forms. The selection of one repertoire against another resembles the effect of multiple audiences. A sign displayed in a grocery store reading *Our weighing service is rendered by springless scales* suggests that the author was responding to certain properties of the scales but was also differentially reinforced for certain forms of response associated with a certain class of speakers or writers. The same condition of the scales might have evoked other responses in the absence of a special consequence—for example, *We use springless scales.* Fowler [2] classifies the special effects which influence the choice of synonyms under many headings: *dentifrice* in lieu of *toothpowder* is a "Genteelism," *meticulous* in lieu of *exact* exemplifies the "Love of the Long Word," *gainsay* in lieu of *deny* is a "Literary Word," *betterment* in lieu of *improvement* shows "Novelty-hunting," and so on.

PUNISHMENT IN MULTIPLE CAUSATION

Negative consequences are perhaps more effective in determining the choice of otherwise synonymous forms. Since mere difficulty of execution is an inherent punishment, the short response is preferred to the long (except when a special consequence of length is impending, as in Fowler's "Polysyllabic Humor"). The concrete may be preferred to the abstract for the same reason. Responses at lower levels of abstraction are relatively stronger, partly because of more frequent reinforcement, but also partly because extinction or punishment is commoner in the history of the abstract term. The hierarchy of abstractions corresponds to a hierarchy of potential negative consequences, and the greater likelihood of the less abstract operant shows the effect of the additional variable.

In the extreme case behavior which is automatically punishing may be simply "forgotten" in the Freudian sense. Instances in which there is "some reason for remembering" as well as "some reason for forgetting" show the algebraic summation of variables having opposing effects.

One of two possible responses is differentially selected because the other is also to some extent punishing when the speaker uses a "euphemistic" expression. The euphemistic response has fewer aversive effects upon the speaker, either directly or indirectly through the listener. The Freudian slip shows the same effect—when, for example, a former suitor calls a married woman by her maiden name because the name of her husband is aversive to him. The differential effect of a similar consequence is shown in the response which "avoids hurting the listener's feelings." An officer, coming upon a group of

[2] Fowler, H. W., *Modern English Usage* (London, 1930).

soldiers during a battle, asks *Who's in charge here?* but, as Tolstoy describes the scene in *War and Peace,* he means and is understood as meaning *Are you in a panic?* His question mands certain verbal responses on the part of the listener relevant to the condition of the group without suggesting cowardice or lack of discipline.

Punishments which are explicitly arranged by the verbal community have the same effect. When a response has been emitted, it may be punished if emitted again, and alternative responses in the thematic group are therefore relatively strong. There is a reverse effect. When verbal behavior is frequently criticized or otherwise punished, *first* responses may be rejected in favor of others (see Chapter 15). The first (possibly covert) response is automatically punished, because it shares one property with hasty "first thoughts," but any response which follows is strong because it shares a property of considered or improved responses.

In considering the algebraic summation of the effects of reinforcement and punishment we must not overlook the positive reinforcement of keeping silent. The child is approved for being silent, and the angry man is reinforced if his silence hurts someone. These "negative strengths" enter into the combined effects of multiple variables when, for example, we do not speak to someone with whom we have quarrelled because this would cancel our achievement of hurting with silence.

MULTIPLE TACTS AND INTRAVERBALS

An example of a double tact is the proper name which is appropriate to its subject. In Nomination (Chapter 5) a proper name is often in partial control of the person or thing to which it is applied when the name is "given to it" for the first time. When the proper name has been independently reinforced, as it will be whether it describes its object or not, the original relation may survive. Dickens' Mrs. Coiler "had a serpentine way of coming close . . . which was altogether snaky and fork-tongued." Her name is a response showing a nominative extension similar to metaphor and, at the same time, a "proper tact," the control of which would have been the same if the name had been, say, Mrs. Smith. The effect does not require nomination. If we know a man with white hair named Mr. Leblanc, the "common tact" will make it more likely that we shall call him by name, less likely that we shall forget his name, and so on.

Mixed intraverbals are exemplified by a telephone number or a car registration number containing the sequence *1, 2, 3, 4.* One can learn such a number more easily because of earlier contingencies establishing the same response.

The momentary combination of two tacts, two intraverbals, or a tact and an intraverbal may force the selection of one response against alternative forms. It is often difficult to prove the multiple sources, but examples are so common that anyone who has bothered to notice them can scarcely question the reality of the process. In a discussion of a political philosophy the response *If you're hungry enough, you can swallow anything* might have contained alternative forms such as *accept, believe,* or *fall for.* The form *swallow* appears to have prevailed either because of an intraverbal connection with *hungry* or as an extended tact descriptive of the situation. The term is irrelevant in this connection and could have a confusing effect on the listener. In the warning that *Those candy eggs will lay you out flat* the synonym for *make you ill,* apparently showing an intraverbal connection between *egg* and *lay,* is uncommon enough to suggest an additional source of strength, but in the response *Those no-trespassing signs are very forbidding* it would be difficult to prove the multiple sources of *forbidding.* Sometimes proof is scarcely needed. A young man complaining about the food served in a college dining hall insisted that the students should organize a *diet* to consider the matter. *Diet* is so unusual a synonym for *meeting* or *conference* that we do not need other evidence of an additional source of strength. (Perhaps *Diet of Worms* was not entirely irrelevant.)

These examples were all spoken, but comparable written material is abundant. A legend in a magazine beneath a picture of the Prime Minister's kitchen stated *A bad meal cooked here can derange British history,* where *derange* is so uncommon a member of a thematic group including *change, disturb, deflect,* and *alter* as to indicate auxiliary help from a prominent kitchen range visible in the center of the picture. In an advertisement showing a few bars of music with the caption *Noteworthy Music,* the response *noteworthy* seems to have been selected for obvious reasons from a group which contained *exceptional, distinctive, unusual,* and *outstanding.* In both these examples, the supplementary source could have been a tact to the accompanying picture, but, in general, examples from texts tend to be intraverbal. When a writer discussing the death of a famous woman aviator said *The round-the-world flight was to have been her last grave undertaking,* the last two words, as a synonym for *serious enterprise,* have additional intraverbal connections with death. *Grave* seems particularly forced by the extraneous relation. A reasonable inference of multiple sources seems to be justified in such an example as *One night, with the ship loaded with dynamite, a terrific storm blew up* or *This, the borers-from-within feel, augurs well for them* but is less convincing for the last three words in *Most theories of language run aground at this point,* even though it is especially easy to run aground near a point.

Sometimes the additional source of strength is combined with a variable which does not control a specific form of response. In choosing an example of verbal behavior out of the blue, we are likely to reveal an auxiliary source of strength which would otherwise be far too weak to produce verbal behavior. We cannot emit a random series of numbers because of the strong intraverbal stimuli generated by our own behavior, nor can we create pure nonsense. Even the finest work of Gertrude Stein, as we shall see in Chapters 14 and 15, shows various thematic groups suggesting or providing trivial supplementary sources which, under the circumstances, were powerful enough.

Revealing slips are often forcible intrusions of responses showing only a single source of strength. In Portia's *One half of me is yours, the other yours/ Mine own I would say,* the revealing second *yours* is due to an external source of strength but not to multiple sources. When the intruding word resembles the displaced, however, there are fragmentary multiple sources of the sort to be discussed in the next chapter. Nevertheless, the intruding response is not distorted and is appropriately classed with the present material. A minister was asked to officiate at the wedding of the daughter of a very close friend who was, to the family's great disappointment, marrying a ne'er-do-well. In reading the familiar lines to be repeated by the groom: *With all my worldly goods I thee endow,* he substituted *worthless.* Here is a combination of a fragment of the intraverbal or textual *worldly* with a full-fledged response to another variable. A guest who was being forced to look at a book of photographs taken during his host's summer vacation broke into a pause of embarrassing dimensions by saying *That's a most fatiguing-looking road!*

MULTIPLE CAUSATION IN LITERATURE

The notion of literary license, to which we have already appealed, leads us to expect especially rich thematic interconnections in verbal art. When T. S. Eliot writes

> .... What will the spider do,
> Suspend its operations, ...

suspend appears to be determined both by a variable which might have prompted such a response as *cease* or *desist in* and an intraverbal connection with spiders. In the same poem, the line

> The tiger springs in the new year

seems to show multiple sources of *springs. Leaps,* for example, would lack an intraverbal connection with *year.*

Some of the best examples of multiple sources of strength are puns and other forms of wit. The effect upon the listener or reader (see the following chapter) may be amusing or delightful, particularly in a period in which punning is fashionable, or it may share the sober profundity of dramatic irony. Jesus was presumably not joking when he said *Thou art Peter* (*Tu es Petrus* = *Thou art a rock*) *and upon this rock I will build my church.* Nor was Shakespeare when he wrote

> Golden lads and girls all must,
> As chimney-sweepers, come to dust.

Sometimes a response is repeated, as if under the control of multiple variables taken one at a time. Thus, Othello says *Put out the light and then put out the light,* responding to separate variables as if he were to say *Snuff the candle and smother Desdemona.*

Nonverbal behavior may, of course, have multiple sources of strength. For example, one may slam a door partly to close the door and partly to make a noise under the influence of emotional variables. If the emotional effect is to be felt by a second person, the sources of strength are both verbal and nonverbal. A verbal but nonvocal pun is made by the executive at his desk who rejects a proposition by turning "thumbs down" in the fashion of a Roman emperor at gladiatorial games and, with the tip of his thumb, pressing a button to have his visitor shown out of his office. Punning is easier in verbal behavior because forms of response are less dependent on the environment.

The pun as a form of humor is currently in disrepute. Its disfavor could be due to the fact that under multiple causation trivial and irrelevant sources make themselves felt. The irrelevant pun is a nuisance. The difference between good and bad puns seems to be just the difference in the relevance of the variables. In a "far-fetched" pun one source of strength would ordinarily have no effect. But if behavior due to multiple sources is specially reinforced—if the speaker is applauded for punning, for example—the feeble source gets its chance. The chimney-sweeper in the quotation from *Cymbeline* is dragged in to give *come to dust* a second source of strength; possibly it was *come to dust* which strengthened *chimney-sweepers*. But both sources of *Put out the light* are relevant. When Dr. Johnson offered to make a pun on any subject and "the King" was suggested, he immediately replied *The King is not a subject*. This is "good" because both sources of strength are relevant. Dr. Johnson was among those who felt that the pun was one of the "smaller excellencies of lively conversation." Many people have taken the opposite point of view, though few have gone as far as Victor Hugo's character in saying: *"Le calembour est la fiente de l'esprit qui vole."*

There are literary instances of multiple causation which are of a more subtle sort. The importance of "multiple meaning" has been widely recognized. Prescott discussed the principle in *The Poetic Mind* [3] and it has been elaborated by Riding and Graves,[4] by I. A. Richards,[5] and by William Empson.[6] These writers have been particularly concerned with the effects upon the reader to be discussed in the following chapter. Riding and Graves and Empson have emphasized the contribution of less rigid practices of punctuation. In Webster's line *Cover her face; mine eyes dazzle; she died young,* the response *mine eyes dazzle* may be related to the preceding phrase, as synonymous with *she is too beautiful to look upon,* or to the phrase which follows, as synonymous with *I am weeping because she died so young*. It was once customary to debate which meaning the author had in mind—that is to say, which source of strength was probably effective—but the doctrine of multiple meaning permits the critic to assume that both sources are relevant.

Empson's book contains many ingenious paraphrases suggesting multiple sources in poetry. His "ambiguity" refers to the effect upon

[3] Prescott, F. C., *The Poetic Mind* (New York, 1926).
[4] Riding, L. and Graves, R., *A Survey of Modern Poetry* (London, 1927).
[5] Richards, I. A., *Practical Criticism* (New York, 1929).
[6] Empson, William, *Seven Types of Ambiguity* (London, 1930).

the reader, but his analysis of examples may be interpreted as an attempt to reconstruct some of the thematic connections responsible for the behavior of the poet. Consider, for example, the fragment of one of Shakespeare's sonnets

> That time of year thou mayst in me behold
> When yellow leaves or none or few do hang
> Upon the boughs which shake against the cold,
> Bare ruined choirs, where late the sweet birds sang.

Bare ruined choirs is a metaphorical extension describing the branches of trees. Empson points to the following properties which might severally be responsible for the extension and suggests that perhaps all of them are involved: (1) choirs are places in which to sing, as were the trees in an earlier season, (2) choir boys sit in a row on benches, and birds on twigs, because of a basic geometry, (3) trees and choirs are made of wood, and choirs are often carved to resemble leaves, knots, and so on, (4) a ruined choir, like a tree in autumn, is no longer enclosed in a protective shelter—the leaves of the tree are the roof of the cathedral, (5) Gothic cathedrals, at least, are structurally similar to a forest of tall trees, (6) stained glass in a cathedral resembles the flowers and other bits of color in the forest in summer, but both tree and choir are now desolate.

In another type of "ambiguity," Empson considers such an example as *That specious monster, my accomplished snare,* where *accomplished* may be the equivalent of either *successful* or *talented.* The double meaning would be irrelevant unless the context revealed likely candidates for both sources.

An important additional source of strength in literature arises from the literary history of the writer, and has a bearing upon the behavior of the reader who shares a similar history. In Greek tragedy, for example, "both dialogue and lyrics are permeated with literary associations controlling the choice of words." [7] This does not refer to explicit references to other literary works, but to a sort of multiple causation acting upon the poet at the time of composition. An example, of which the poet was no doubt aware, is T. S. Eliot's

> The Chair she sat in, like a burnished throne,
> Glowed on the marble, where the glass
> Held up by standards wrought with fruited vines . . .

[7] Pearson, A. C., *Verbal Scholarship and the Growth of Some Abstract Terms* (Cambridge, 1922).

which is a fusion of intraverbal responses, including stress patterns, derived from Shakespeare's description of Cleopatra [8] and additional material serving as the subject of Eliot's poem.

The speaker need not be aware of an extra source of strength, in the sense of Chapter 5. When a response is under the control of a single stimulus, he can usually identify the stimulus and the controlling relation in answering such a question as *Why did you say that?* He is usually aware of what he is talking about in the sense of being prepared for such a question. But it is only in a very advanced verbal community that questions are ever raised about multiple sources of strength, which frequently pass unnoticed. A literary source was almost certainly not seen in Wordsworth's lines *Prophetic spirit that inspir'st the human soul of universal earth dreaming on things to come,* which is almost certainly borrowed from Shakespeare's *The prophetic spirit of the wide world dreaming on things to come.* Fragmentary intraverbal responses acquired in reading Shakespeare must have combined with other current behavior, but the line would probably have been rejected (Chapter 15) if this fact had been clear. Possible reasons why it was not clear are discussed in Chapter 16.

To "prove" that part of a literary work has been borrowed we must not only show a similar passage in a work which the author could conceivably have read but must show that the behavior is not probable for other reasons. The most conspicuous examples of borrowing are intraverbal. After a passage has been read or, better, memorized, any component response tends to bring out neighboring responses. The intraverbal behavior may appear when an actual occasion is being described. Lowes' study of the *Ancient Mariner* [9] is especially convincing because Coleridge was not writing from a first-hand experience of the sea. His descriptions must have been intraverbal, if they were not directly echoic or textual. The borrowing of a plot is, in the same way, most easily established as intraverbal if the plot is unusual and hence not likely to describe an actual event and if it is complex and hence not likely to have arisen from chance. Old plots, exhausted metaphors, and clichés are scarcely more "borrowed" than any other part of a verbal repertoire. Unusual collocations, however, show the intraverbal process at work.

[8] "The barge she sat in, like a burnish'd throne,
Burn'd on the water. The poop was beaten gold;"
Antony and Cleopatra, Act II, Sc. II.

[9] Lowes, J. L., *The Road to Xanadu* (Boston, 1930).

Borrowing usually shows not only the combining of multiple sources of strength but a certain distortion of form, an additional process to be discussed in Chapter 11. Parodies and travesties also show a fusion of current material and intraverbals generated by a literary work. The result is likely to be distorted. Multiple literary sources are clear in borrowed titles. The important effect is upon the reader, but we may also consider the behavior of the author at the moment of nomination. Faced with a book to which the title *A Tale Told by an Idiot* is appropriate, the author is likely to choose this title rather than a synonym lacking literary sources because of intraverbal connections acquired in reading *Macbeth*.

One of the uses of verbal art is to give added strength to responses which, if made for other reasons, would probably be punished. The behavior of a jilted maiden singing *Lover, come back to me* is on the one hand an extended mand and on the other an intraverbal sequence of responses acquired in learning the song. The homesick failure singing *Home, home on the range . . . where seldom is heard a discouraging word* or the lonely youth singing *I wish I had someone to love me* are similarly affected by multiple causation, where plain responses under the control of the same primary variables would be more likely to be punished. The singer may be a nuisance, but he is not called "moonstruck" or "cowardly" or "sorry for himself."

The behavior which is strengthened by such supplements need not be overt. Silent reading of preferred forms of verbal art may show a similar multiple causation, as we shall see in the following chapter.

FORMAL CONTRIBUTIONS OF STRENGTH

In many of these examples it does not matter whether a source of strength is to be classified as a tact or as an intraverbal response. It is convenient to group such variables under the rubric "thematic." Two responses are thematically related when they are controlled by a common variable with respect to which they lack the point-to-point correspondence seen in echoic and textual behavior. We may refer to sources involving echoic and textual responses as "formal" contributions to strength. The important difference concerns the minimal unit relationships available in the formal case.

If an echoic or textual stimulus acts when a response is strong for thematic reasons, the probability of emission is increased. The supplementary stimulus may simply cause the speaker to utter aloud a response which has already occurred subvocally. More often, the overt-covert distinction is not at issue. Thus, a forgotten name which is "on the tip of one's tongue" is instantly recalled (not merely read) when the name is seen in glancing at printed matter. In a noisy conversation we may overhear a verbal response which is currently strong in our own behavior, and the response may then "occur to us" although it would otherwise have remained latent. We say that we have been "reminded" of something. A textual example is supplied by a man who forgot to turn off an electric soldering iron in his basement workshop and who, thirty-four hours later, upon reading the word *solder,* immediately jumped up, went to the basement, and turned off the iron. "Remembering the iron" was not necessarily verbal, but the effect of the textual stimulus suggests that some response such as *The soldering iron! I forgot to turn it off!* was strengthened. The response might have occurred at any time during the thirty-four hours, but the textual prompt supplied by the printed text proved to be a necessary supplement.

FRAGMENTARY CONTRIBUTIONS OF STRENGTH FROM THEMATIC AND FORMAL SOURCES

One variable may control only part of the response controlled by another. In an example already mentioned, the remark *I know a store where you can buy disks at a discount* shows an unusual synonym (*disk*) for *phonograph record,* apparently under the influence of the variable responsible for *discount,* but *disk* and *discount* are not identical responses. The fragmentary response *lat* seems to be at work in *The new rules for lateral passes will provide a greater latitude for the development of new plays.* In the classical pun *traduttori traditori* (*translators are traitors*), the forms share only the fragments *trad-* and *-tor-* in common and both forms must therefore be emitted. In another classical pun *Barbari Barberini* [10] the two responses contain only one common fragment.

In many instances of folk-etymology a fragmentary echoic element (from a relatively unfamiliar echoic stimulus) is enough to evoke a response of some abiding strength, possibly in the nature of a tact. When *sparrowgrass* was first emitted for *asparagus,* a tact (*grass* under

[10] A reference to the Barberini family, who expropriated public monuments for their private use. The expanded form is *Quod non fecerunt barbari feceri Barberini.*

the control of grass sprouts) appears to have joined with a fragmentary echoic response. *Detect-thief* for *detective, beef-eaters* for *boufetiers,* and *stunk* for *skunk* lend themselves to similar explanations. Forms with no clear non-echoic stimulus control may not show multiple sources of strength (see the example of Rain Cloud for Reine Claude in Chapter 4). We are considering, of course, the origin of the folk-etymology in the behavior of one speaker, not the use of the established form. Similar tendencies in many speakers may, of course, be relevant to the survival of the form in a verbal environment.

Unconditioned vocal responses sometimes enter into multiply-caused verbal behavior. The form of the response *Ouch!* is modified by a particular verbal environment, yet an actual instance may be largely an unshaped cry of pain. A similar contribution has been recognized in Greek Tragedy in the appearance of words containing the sound of the cry ἄιαι. It has been argued [11] that a similar source is indicated in Burns' lines

> The wan moon is sitting ayout the white wave
> And Time is setting with me, O.

The sensitive ear is said to catch the *i*-sound of *Time* as in part a cry of despair.

Evidence for the strengthening of part of a synonym through what might be called self-echoic behavior appears in the frequent occurrence of idiomatic pairs such as *wear and tear, high and dry, spick and span, rack and ruin,* and in proverbs and mottoes such as *Haste makes waste.* Although these are undoubtedly acquired by most speakers as units in their own right, the second member of the rhyming or alliterating pair appears to be selected in lieu of alternative forms by an echoic element which is, however, less than the whole response. Some standard, but dead, metaphors such as *As bold as brass* or *As fit as a fiddle* also appear to show echoic sources of strength. The evidence is improved when the term affected is otherwise quite implausible (*As pleased as Punch*).

In rhyming argot,[12] one verbal response is substituted for another to which it bears both thematic and formal connections. Thus, a girl's hair may be called the *bonny fair.* The connection is not only by way

11 Rylands, George, *Words and Poetry* (New York, 1928), p. 53.

12 Maurer, D. W., "Australian Rhyming Argot in the American Underworld," *American Speech,* XIX (1944), 183-195.

of an extended (metonymical) tact or an intraverbal response but bears the partial echoic connection of the common form *-air*. The expression *cheese and kisses* in lieu of *the Mrs.* shows a similar intraverbal or metonymical connection plus the formal overlap of the rhyme.

Overheard rhythmic patterns may set up fragmentary echoic responses affecting the choice of synonyms. Responses are determined by multiple sources including the echoic stimulus. "Their conversation would have been different" says Tolstoy of two characters in *War and Peace,* "if they had not been talking while the song was singing. . . . 'I'm glad,' Dolokov made a brief, sharp reply, as was required to fit in with the tune." The effect is comparable to that of the "verbal summator" described in the following chapter.

FORMAL STRENGTHENING IN PROSE AND POETRY

In analysing the effect of internal formal supplements upon style we cannot assume that all instances of the clustering of sounds exemplify multiple sources of strength. Many instances will arise from chance. In poetry, the greater rigor of form makes a proof of the operation of a special process easier. However, a statistical analysis of the formal patterns in poetry has given surprising results.

The sound-patterning of poetry is one of the most important elements in the effect on the listener or reader. As a purely formal device it has sometimes been likened to music, but "meaning" is usually not omitted. It has been argued that sound-patterning is effective if the sound "fits the sense," not as in onomatopoeia but in showing correspondence in "character" between description and thing described. The multiple causation of verbal behavior makes possible still another interpretation.

The effect of formal multiple causation in literature should be a lack of randomness in the sounds of a given selection. The sounds should be to some extent grouped into clusters or patterns. Some grouping will arise from the variables of which the behavior is a function; any response, repeated because of some characteristic of a situation or a state of deprivation, will disturb randomness. But the principal devices of poetry are usually thought to show formal relationships beyond those due to the subject matter. A poet "uses alliteration" to the extent that his writing shows groups of responses in which stressed syllables begin with the same consonant. What is called assonance is inferred from a similar grouping of vowel sounds.

A rhyme usually involves both the vowel and the consonant which follows, generally at the end of a phrase, and rhythm is a lack of randomness in stress patterns. (We need not concern ourselves here with more subtle formal properties such as the matching of clause-length, nor is it possible at the present time to consider profitably the behavior of composing large responses with complex formal properties such as "acrostics" or "palindromes.")

The customary practice in literary criticism is to demonstrate such formal properties of poetry and prose by pointing to instances. There is justification for this when we consider the effect upon the reader or listener, of whom the critic is an example. But before inferring any process in the behavior of the writer, it is necessary to allow for the patterning of his verbal behavior to be expected from chance. In no case, perhaps, can we say that any one instance of alliteration or other formal similarity is due to a special process, but a general pattern may be demonstrated. Alliteration, for example, may be detected by a statistical analysis of the arrangements of initial consonants in a reasonably large sample. A tendency to alliterate is shown by the extent to which the initial consonants in a given literary work are not distributed at random.

Although we are often affected by random events, some of the things which may occur at random remain unexpected. Runs of luck in gambling may be nothing more than episodes in a random series but, possibly because the exigencies of gambling make them very important, they attract attention. The amount of alliteration which occurs by chance is similarly surprising. If we divide any sample of verbal behavior into words or syllables, record each part on a separate slip, and then "compose" a passage by drawing slips from a hat in which they have been well shuffled, we shall create many instances which would unquestionably be attributed to alliteration on the part of a poet.

A sentence like *Peter Piper picked a peck of pickled peppers* occurs so rarely by chance that we are probably right in suspecting a special process at work, and this is also true of poetry where the alliterating responses occupy special places. In Anglo-Saxon poetry, for example, we have to consider the chances, not only that two initial consonants will occur close together, but that they will occur at certain positions in the line or stanza. In much of what we think of as alliterative poetry, however, a statistical analysis yields little evidence of formal strengthening. One hundred of the sonnets of Shakespeare[13] were scanned according to arbitrary rules to determine the principal accented syllables. The initial consonants of these syllables were then tabulated, and a calculation was made of the number of lines to be expected containing two, three, or four of the same initial consonants. By comparing the actual frequencies with the calculated frequencies, the evidence for an explicit process of alliteration in the behavior of the poet was reduced to the following:

Although there are a considerable number of lines containing four like initial consonants (for example, *Born on the bier with white and bristly beard*), not oftener than once in twenty-five sonnets, or in 350 lines, does Shakespeare appear to have added or altered a word in order to change a line of three like consonants into one of four, except upon rare occasions when he repeats a whole word, presumably for thematic reasons. There are many lines containing three like initial consonants (for example, *Save that my soul's imaginary sight*), but there is no evidence that Shakespeare made any change in order to increase a line of two like consonants to one of three oftener than once in twenty-five sonnets, except when he repeated a whole word. There are many lines containing two like initial consonants, but there are fewer of these than are to be expected from chance alone, when we correct for the repetition of whole words. Allowing for the few lines extended to three or four occurrences, it appears that about once in every three sonnets Shakespeare *discarded* a word because its initial consonant had already been used in the same line.[14]

These numbers are not to be taken too seriously, particularly since we have no way of evaluating the formal and thematic contributions to the repetition of a whole word. But even so, this is very slim evidence for anything like a special process in the poet's behavior. The sonnets remain, of course, exactly as alliterative as they have always been, with respect to the sound patterns which affect the reader or listener, but the proof of an alliterative process in the form of a fragmentary formal strengthening of responses is quite inadequate.

In a poet like Swinburne, who could write

> The faint fresh flame of a young year flushes
> From leaf to flower and flower to fruit

[13] Skinner, B. F., "The Alliteration in Shakespeare's Sonnets: A Study in Literary Behavior." *Psychological Record, 3* (1939), 186.

[14] A similar study of twenty-five sonnets of Wordsworth's showed a very slight excess of lines containing three like consonants and a more severe shortage of lines containing two like consonants.

we expect another result, and get it. Here the alliteration is not only evident, but a statistical analysis permits us to represent it as a function of the distance between the first and second occurrences of the same sound. An examination of each pair of adjacent syllables in a block of 500 lines from *Atalanta in Calydon* showed a 55-per-cent excess of similar pairs over the frequencies expected from chance. In pairs of syllables separated by *one* intervening syllable, the excess drops to 47 per cent. When *two* syllables intervene, the excess is 32 per cent, and when *three* intervene, 20 per cent. All these figures are statistically significant in demonstrating a fragmentary strengthening of one response in each pair.[15]

A similar analysis may be made for assonance, in which vowel sounds rather than consonants are repeated. The proof of a special process determining the occurrence of *rhyme* is aided by the temporal or spatial patterning of rhyme in English verse. There is very little chance that the poet emits the rhyming word in the right form at the right time from sheer luck. Rhythm also seldom requires a statistical proof.

The actual behavior of the poet in accepting or rejecting an alliterative, assonant, rhyming, or rhythmic response involves something more than the mere strengthening of this response in his behavior and will be discussed in Chapter 15. The techniques which he may employ to encourage the appearance of responses having such properties are still another matter, to be discussed in Chapter 17. It is too late, of course, to reconstruct the process of composition with any hope of accuracy. We do not know the order in which the parts of a poem were first emitted or written down, what changes were made, how many opportunities for thematic connections were provided, or in what order self-echoic or other formal sources of strength could be effective. When there is evidence for a process such as that demonstrated in Swinburne's use of alliteration, two possible interpretations may, however, be noted. One response may be made and constitute the stimulus for a self-echoic fragmentary response which makes the occurrence of another response containing the same fragment more probable. Thus, having said *flame* we are more likely to say *flushes* in lieu of synonymous forms, or if *flushes* was actually written first, we are more likely to say *flame* or offer it as a substitute for a rejected

[15] An analysis of the first 500 lines of Wordsworth's *The Prelude* similar to the tabulation for Swinburne also gave considerable evidence that Wordsworth had discarded alliterative words.

word. On the other hand, such instances may be minimal tacts, in the sense of Chapter 5. The stimulus which evokes *flame* as an intraverbal or tact may act separately upon the initial *fl-* and the syllabic *-ame*. Under these circumstances, the response *flame* occurs with a high probability because it is composed of both these elements, but the separability of the elements is a possibility to be considered and one for which we shall find other evidence, particularly in Chapter 11. Hence, although we could perhaps demonstrate no "meaningful" connection between the state of affairs responsible for *flame* and the response *flush,* there is some reason to believe that *flush* is more likely to occur, let us say, in the presence of an actual flame than upon other occasions. The *fl-* does not need to be an *echoic* unit; it may be controlled by the same circumstances which led to the completed form *flame*.

Similar evidence is supplied by what is called partial recall. Perhaps we remember only that the name of an object begins with *t* or rhymes with *came*. Instances are commonest when a proper name is recalled, partly because of the lack of a minimal repertoire, but there is nothing about the process which is peculiar to proper names. A situation which does not adequately evoke a whole response in the form of a tact may evoke part of the response, perhaps in combination with other fragments. We say that a name we cannot recall "has an *a* in it" or "rhymes with a certain word," only because of a certain sophistication; a commoner result is to recall another ("wrong") name. Two examples from the behavior of young children may be given. A five-year-old girl, upon being served noodles for the second time in her life, called them *Yankee Doodles,* where the separate strength of the fragment *-oodles* is evident. Even though the response *Yankee Doodle* was strong for other reasons, its only connection with the current situation arose from the fact that the response *noodles* had previously been reinforced in a similar situation. Another child of ten said *merry-go-round* in lieu of *ferry boat*. The response was emitted weakly, with every indication that the child "knew it was wrong" (see Chapter 15); nevertheless it was made under circumstances which would, if clearer, have evoked *ferry boat*. The separate strengthening of the fragment *-erry* is evident.

There is no parallel problem in accounting for the fragmentary echoic source because, as we have seen, echoic behavior is either set up as a minimal repertoire or develops such a repertoire as the result of the independent strengthening of larger responses. We demonstrate the efficacy of an echoic supplement when we say to someone *Give me a word beginning with "t,"* or *Give me a rhyme for "friend."* These are mands for verbal action, and the answers which they generate show the combination of an echoic response which fulfills the condition of the mand and behavior determined without respect to form under the control of incidental variables in the situation.

In the above example, a more sophisticated person might have reported merely that the name had the sound *-erry* in it, but the erroneous recall demonstrates the separate functioning of a fragmentary tact just as clearly as the identification of the element. Usually identification is impossible. If in trying to recall the name *Denman Ross,* we recall *Russell Sage,* it may be impossible at that stage (before *Denman Ross* has been recalled) to point to the relevant stress pattern and length or the important element R_ss.[16]

In collecting examples of erroneous or partial recall, there is a tendency to note interesting cases and overlook trivial ones or those which seem to have no "significance." We have no adequate data to show the relative importance of consonants, vowels, position, stress patterns, and so on. A search for such data would be handicapped by additional sources of strength generated by the behavior of the recaller. For example, in trying to recall the name *Hale* from a list of students, a teacher first said *Dale,* then *Day,* which was another name on the same list. He then said *Hale*. It would appear that the competing form *Dale* may have derived strength from both *Hale* and *Day* and hence have emerged first. In noting merely the formal similarity of *Hale* and *Dale,* we miss the other contribution of strength to the latter name. A more extensive interference of this sort generated by the behavior of recall is recognized when we say *I keep thinking of "X" but that isn't it.*

Multiple sources of strength have a familiar effect upon sustained discourse. As soon as a man has begun to speak or to write, his own behavior generates stimuli for echoic, textual, or intraverbal responses. When these become too powerful or when they act in concert with weak variables, the result may be damaging. Too powerful an intraverbal contribution may convert speech into a mere flight of ideas. Too powerful a formal contribution will convert it into singsong or gibberish. The self-echoic repetition of a response as an unlikely member of a *different* thematic group is usually confusing to

16 Interesting examples of the erroneous recall of proper names are given in Woodworth, R. S., *Psychology* (New York, 1934).

the listener or reader.[17] On the other hand multiple sources of strength may contribute a certain integration or solidity to sustained speech, and they are likely to have an effect on the listener (as we shall see in the next chapter) which is reinforcing to all concerned.

The principle of multiple causation has its place in the more rigorous forms of verbal behavior seen in logic and science. The logical and scientific community is dedicated to the elimination of ambiguities and equivocalities, but it has not altogether eliminated metaphorical or even solecistic extensions or provided safeguards against multiple causation. We shall see later that some of the devices of verbal thinking necessarily involve the supplementary strengthening of responses through collateral variables. In any case the logician or scientist is subject to the limitations imposed upon him by his role as a behaving organism, and even here we must take into account the possibility of multiple sources.

[17] See Fowler, *Modern English Usage,* under "Repetition of Words and Sounds: Two Accidentally Similar but not Parallel Uses of a Word."

Chapter 10

. . . .

Supplementary Stimulation

One reason for trying to improve upon an analysis of verbal behavior in terms of ideas, meanings, information, attitudes, opinions, traits, abilities, and so on, is that such variables, even when acceptably defined, have little relevance to the practical control of verbal behavior. The formal descriptions of logic and grammar also leave the actual determination of verbal behavior out of account. The variables and controlling relations appealed to in the present analysis, however, can be applied to the problem of evoking verbal behavior. As the preceding chapter suggests, any two or more of these variables will be more effective in achieving this result than one taken separately.

Suppose we accept the engineering task of evoking a given response in a given speaker at a given time. To make the result important, let us suppose that a fairly large wager has been made: an English-speaking subject, unaware of the point of the experiment, is to be made to emit a common response, say, *pencil.* If we are reasonably free to arrange external circumstances as we please, what should we do? Obviously the quickest way to win would be to mand the response by saying to the subject *Please say "pencil."* The history of most English-speaking people with respect to such a verbal stimulus would almost certainly produce the desired result. But if this step has been ruled out, we shall have to introduce other variables characteristic of other operants having the same form of response. If the wager is a sizeable one, we shall probably introduce many of these at once in order to raise the probability of the response to the maximum.

To strengthen a mand of this form, we could make sure that no pencil or writing instrument is available, then hand our subject a pad of paper appropriate to pencil sketching, and offer him a handsome reward for a recognizable picture of a cat. We have not "created the need for a pencil" in the sense of generating a state of deprivation, but we have strengthened behavior which can be executed only with a pencil. Under similar conditions the response *pencil* has frequently been reinforced and hence will become more probable. Simultaneously we could strengthen other responses of the same form by providing echoic stimuli (a phonograph in the background occasionally says *pencil*) and textual stimuli (signs on the wall read *PENCIL*). We scatter other verbal stimuli among these to produce intraverbal responses: the phonograph occasionally says *pen and* . . . and there are other signs reading *PEN AND*. . . . We set up an occasion for a tact with the form *pencil* by putting a very large or unusual pencil in an unusual place clearly in sight—say, half submerged in a large aquarium or floating freely in the air near the ceiling of the room. We indicate our own audience-character as an English-speaking person by the simple device of speaking English. Under such circumstances it is highly probable that our subject will say *pencil*.

We do not, of course, often go to such extremes in generating a response, but we are nevertheless frequently interested in evoking verbal behavior, and the available techniques are all illustrated in this sample. In discovering the independent variables of which verbal behavior is a function we bring the behavior under practical control. The techniques of control which use multiple causation are applicable whenever we wish to evoke behavior already existing in some strength.

PRACTICAL CONTROL

We add a supplementary variable to existing sources of strength when, for example, it is important that someone recall a name or a fact, or speak up at an appropriate moment, or "get something off his chest." Why the behavior is not strong enough to be emitted without supplementation does not matter. A response may simply be poorly conditioned, or controlled by stimuli which are currently weak, or related to states of deprivation or aversive stimulation which are moderate or weak, or displaced by other behavior as a result of earlier punishment, or confused by other current variables. Sometimes the problem is merely to make previously subvocal behavior vocal, but usually it is to evoke behavior which will not otherwise be emitted, even subvocally. We cannot simply mand the required behavior, because we may not know what it is or because it will not be effective if it is due entirely to such a variable.

The processes of supplementary evocation may be classified in the following way. When the operator can identify the response to be evoked (for example, when the subject has forgotten a word which the operator knows), the supplementary stimulus is a "prompt." When the operator does not know the response even though it may be just as sharply specified by other circumstances (for example, when neither the subject nor the operator knows a word which, when discovered, will permit both of them to locate other information in a dictionary), the supplement is a "probe." The material employed may also be divided according to the distinction between formal and thematic strengthening discussed in the last chapter. We have to examine, then, (1) formal prompts, (2) thematic prompts, (3) formal probes, and (4) thematic probes.

Formal Prompts

Echoic prompts. The prompter at the rehearsal of a play holds the book in his lap and is always able to speak the next line as textual behavior. The actor on the stage is behaving intraverbally and with much less certainty. When an intraverbal connection is inadequate (when the actor forgets a line), the prompter supplies him with a *partial* echoic stimulus. When the actor then speaks the line, his behavior draws its strength from two sources: the original intraverbal conditioning and the echoic supplement. If the actor does not know the line at all, an intraverbal source is lacking, and his response to the prompter is then full-fledged echoic behavior and is not prompted. The two cases may conveniently be distinguished in terms of the size of the echoic stimulus. When the prompter supplies less than the whole line (perhaps only a few sounds or a word or two) the presence of an additional source responsible for the full line is obvious. When the whole line is given as a prompt and correctly echoed by the actor, the evidence of intraverbal conditioning has been obscured. (Although prompts are conventionally the beginnings of a verbal response, a rhyming prompt may be effective, and sometimes a mere stress-pattern is enough.)

Educational techniques which emphasize the memorization of verbal material lean heavily upon prompting. How the grade-school child acquires verbal behavior is often of little concern to the teacher. For example, a few lines of a poem are given to the child and he is told to "learn" them. In some little-understood fashion which the child is usually left to discover for himself, he must convert textual responses to intraverbals. The teacher then asks the child to recite the poem, rewards him if he does so correctly, and punishes him if he is unable to recite it or recites it incorrectly. In order to generate responses which may then be reinforced, the teacher may resort to a series of prompts. A partially learned poem is thus evoked and reinforced. The behavior eventually passes from a series of textual responses through echoic behavior to an ultimate intraverbal control. The amount of prompting required at any stage depends upon the strength which the behavior has acquired.

In what we may call a disguised formal prompt, an echoic stimulus is concealed within a larger verbal response. Thus, to evoke the response *addition,* a disguised prompt might take the form *Would you like a bit of ADvice?* If the concealed *ad-* is less effective than the undisguised *ADD-* it is because it does not as readily generate echoic behavior. The undisguised prompt is not only a formal stimulus for echoic behavior, it is essentially a mand, equivalent to *Say "add" and see whether the response does not occur to you.* The disguised prompt has something of the same effect if the *ad-* is emphasized, or pronounced archly in the manner of television quiz-masters.

A similar use of the echoic prompt is to restrict the listener's behavior to a small number of responses among which the determination is left to other variables. A trivial example is the mand *Give me a rhyme for "blue."* A more important practical use of the echoic (or in the case of the reader, textual) prompt is exemplified by the mand *Is this green or blue?* or *Answer "Yes" or "No."* Answers to such questions are under the aversive control implied in the mand, but a small echoic repertoire lies beyond the aversive contingencies. The mand *Repeat after me* . . . is an occasion upon which only a specific form of echoic behavior is reinforced.

Prompting is so common in social intercourse that we are especially inclined to echo any verbal stimulus under conditions in which prompting is useful. Frequently the result miscarries. For example, a speaker begins: *I have been interested lately in the situation in . . . uh. . . .* When a listener then prompts *Egypt,* the speaker echoes this energetically but corrects himself: *Well, no, not Egypt . . . uh . . . I was thinking of . . . Turkey.* Here the strength of Egypt was due exclusively to the echoic source. The speaker's incomplete sentence and the general conditions at the moment made an echoic response extremely likely because of the many occasions on which such a response had served as a useful formal prompt.

Textual prompts. The speaker who simply glances at his notes is using a textual prompt which has the same effect as the echoic prompt in the theater. Television indeed, has produced mechanical prompters, which present textual stimuli out of view of the television audience but available to the speaker. If the material is simply read, the behavior is not prompted, but the function of such stimulation is usually to supplement weak intraverbal behavior.

Advertising uses both echoic and textual prompts. A fairly common device is to arrange to have the name of a product appear before the customer in a store. A sign on the door or counter of a tobacco store simply gives the name of a brand of cigarettes or the name followed by *Please* or perhaps the whole phrase *I'll take a pack of Luckies, please.* The sign is a textual supplement which increases the probability that the customer will ask for a particular brand. The prompt may be disguised by showing a picture of someone uttering this response. Explicit mands (*Ask for "Luckies"* or *Say "Luckies, please"*) not only provide a supplementary stimulus for the name of a product but arrange some of the conditions which elsewhere in the life of the speaker are associated with the reinforcement of echoic behavior. A disguised form of the mand is exemplified by *Call for Philip Morris,* which may function as a mand although it is disguised as the response of a paging bellhop. (The behavior of crying one's wares probably has a comparable *echoic* effect. The peanut vendor at the baseball game calls *Peanuts! Popcorn!* not only to indicate that he has these for sale but to heighten the probability that potential customers will break into overt speech and ask for peanuts and popcorn.)

Abbreviations eventually become standard textual stimuli which control verbal responses in the absence of a strict point-to-point correspondence, but they usually begin as textual prompts. The text *ESQ.* could evoke the response *esquire* because of full-fledged conditioning unrelated to the fact that *ESQ.* is part of *ESQUIRE* (just as *and* is brought under the control of the text *&*). But *ESQ.* controls the response *esquire* in part because of the textual repertoire, and probably arose as an abbreviation because it did so. The hasty writer found that *ESQ.* achieved the same effect (upon either himself or another reader) as the longer form.

Like the echoic prompt, most abbreviations are simply beginnings of standard longer responses, but some may be the beginning and end (*MR.*) or samplings of letters or sounds covering the whole response (*MFG.* for *MANUFACTURING*). Initials in lieu of proper names for persons (*F.D.R.*), railroads (*The B and M*), or organizations (*The U.N.*) acquire the status of full-fledged verbal stimuli in their own right, but they also function as textual prompts, possibly as an additional source of strength after the independent response has been acquired. Spoken abbreviations and initials also serve as echoic prompts both before they have become established as full-fledged verbal stimuli and possibly afterward in a form of supplementary stimulation. Since abbreviations are mainly devices to avoid the labor of longer forms, they tend to occur in written verbal behavior. They are less common now than formerly (e.g. in manuscripts) because of the invention of easier methods of producing written verbal stimuli.

Thematic Prompts

A thematic prompt is a supplemental source of strength in the form of a tact or intraverbal response. It is better known as a "hint." Thus we may stimulate our hostess to ask *More tea?* either by inspecting our empty cup, or conspicuously draining the last drop, or by supplying an intraverbal stimulus containing forms such as *drink, beverage, coffee,* and so on. It is assumed that the response *More tea?* exists in some strength; if the supplementary stimulus is so strong as to generate the required behavior entirely on its own, the hint is too broad to be called a prompt.

The thematic prompt often functions in a manner close to that of the formal prompt. If a confederate has agreed that he will bring up a subject for discussion at a committee meeting and has failed to do so, we may resort to prompting. A formal prompt would be a whispered word or a word scratched on a pad. A thematic prompt would consist of verbal stimuli commonly evoking terms in the topic for discussion as intraverbal responses. A thematic prompt may be concealed in other verbal behavior less obviously than a formal prompt, but a thematic prompt is less likely to determine specific behavior on the part of the listener. The proper tone of voice or the arch look may, however, serve in lieu of an explicit *You were going to say something about such-and-such.*

Thematic prompts are also common in education. The teacher "directs" a discussion or encourages the student to talk about a given subject in a given way mainly through their use. Accidental thematic prompts also occur, as when we are "reminded of a topic about which we had intended to speak." We may translate an elliptical expression of this sort by saying that "behavior which existed in some strength receives an accidental supplement from related thematic materials."

Under conditions in which prompting has been especially effective (when the listener is "looking for a prompt"), the effect may depend upon at least two responses linked together in a chain. A thematic link may be followed by a formal, or vice versa. In strengthening the response *addition,* for example, the verbal stimulus *a particular printing of a book* might lead to a number of intraverbal responses, among them *edition,* which might act as a formal prompt to bring the response *addition* into sufficient strength.

Formal Probes

Echoic probes. The echoic stimulus may not always evoke a matching response. The stimulus itself may be unclear, the speaker may be hard of hearing, the echoic repertoire may not have been well conditioned, and so on. The plain mishearing of a verbal stimulus is common. But if the echoic stimulus is weak, it does not follow that the response is otherwise undetermined. Other variables are simply more likely to be effective as supplementary sources of strength. When such variables are apparent, we say that the mishearing is "revealing" in the Freudian sense. Thus, if someone hears his name mentioned in a noisy conversation when it is clear that there was, in fact, no corresponding verbal stimulus, we may ask what other variable could have been responsible for his tendency to hear his name called. The proud parent hears many more words in the babbling of his child than the skeptical neighbor. A relevant fact in interpreting such instances is that what is heard is reinforcing to the one who hears it. The fragmentary echoic stimulation has combined with some other variable to produce a verbal response which could not be evoked by either variable taken separately.

Sound patterns which are even more deficient as echoic stimuli will sometimes serve as supplementary variables, especially if they are repeated in rhythmic fashion. Since the weakness of the echoic stimulus must be matched by special strength from another source, examples of this kind are more clearly "revealing." They have frequently been used as literary devices. In Tolstoy's *War and Peace,* "it seemed to Prince Andrey [standing at the rail of a ferry-boat] that the lapping of the water kept up a refrain to Pierre's words: 'It's the truth. Believe it.' " And Arnold Bennett, in the *Old Wives' Tales,* describes a young girl running away from home in a railroad carriage: "And then the long, steady beating of the train over the rails, keeping time to the rhythm of the unanswerable voice within her breast: 'Why are you here? Why are you here?' "

A single instance of such a nonvocal auditory pattern seldom evokes an echoic verbal response. The fact that rhythmically repeated patterns do so is an example of a process called "summation," commonly observed in both reflex and operant behavior. It may be demonstrated in verbal behavior in the following way. Calling a man by name may be ineffective if the man is at a distance or if the background is noisy or if he is preoccupied with other behavior. But there is an intensity level at which such a stimulus, ineffective when presented once, will be effective if presented rhythmically at the same intensity several times. If we speak to someone who is reading a newspaper and he does not answer, we will be likely to speak again in a louder voice, but we can also achieve the same effect by speaking at the same intensity several times. It is this summation of ineffective stimuli which evokes a partially echoic response to a nonvocal stimulus pattern. When the stimulus is effective through summation, it is still necessary in most cases for other sources of stimulation to be present to determine the precise form of response.

An echoic probe based upon this principle is called the "verbal summator." It consists of a phonograph or tape recorder which repeats a vague pattern of speech sounds at low intensity or against a noisy background as often as may be needed to evoke a response. The material sounds like fragments of natural speech heard through a wall. For reasons which will be discussed in Chapter 15, the device evokes behavior more readily if the true nature of the patterns is concealed from the speaker. Under satisfactory experimental conditions, a subject will generally hear something being said for each pattern, and most subjects require no more than ten or fifteen presentations of each stimulus. Hundreds of responses may be collected in a few hours. These bear very little formal relation to the echoic stimuli (different subjects seldom give the same response) and therefore permit certain inferences about other variables. The responses tend to be unedited in the sense of Chapter 15 because the subject remains unaware of the controlling sources and is usually convinced that he is merely repeating what he hears, although possibly with some inaccuracy.

A partial list of responses obtained from one subject in such an experiment [1] follows.

> *Barley; have hold on that; do not do that; spell the party; have you pummelled him; how do you do; good-night; you know a part; cracker; have you anything; two four one eight; call station; sour pickles; calm down; keep out of it; hobo; do it again; you are mine; I knew her; Mannheim vis-a-vis; Lita hit . . . ; get over main jump; you tried them; he has you; he never hurts you; Heidi; a Bilderbuch; holding one over; why have you; Tabelletuch (reported only after repetition had been stopped); if I were you; are you old enough; have you forgot; who are you; I couldn't imagine; which am I; America; could I get on with you; who are you; will you come back; no may . . . do that; Dumas; don't go there; watch my margin; after all my duty; fly like a bee;*

Some of the nonechoic variables entering into the determination of such behavior may be identified. Since it is impossible, of course, to conduct such an experiment *in vacuo,* the immediate environment supplies some controlling stimuli. After watching the experimenter adjust two small knobs on the apparatus, one subject reported that the phonograph said *What wheels do you touch?* A distant clock striking the half hour led one subject to report *Half past.* Conditions of deprivation or aversive stimulation associated with such an experiment are also relevant and seem to account for responses such as *Call them louder, Make it closer, Force them harder,* and *Look out, you're going to sleep.*

As soon as a few responses have been emitted, self-echoic and self-intraverbal responses begin to occur. The response *Hire a bootblack* was followed immediately by *Have a bluebook.* The two responses have the same stress pattern, and the initial consonants are the same except for the reversal of *b* and *bl.* Moreover, *bootblack* and *bluebook* are words whose separate syllables are both words in their own right. They both end in *k* and contain the element *boo.* Additional strength may be supplied by a strong intraverbal connection between *black* and *blue.* Marked self-echoic strengthening is seen in frequent rhymes: *Blow that fuse up, No shoes up; Trial by another, Is he your brother?;* and *Over golden seas, There are men at ease.* The multiple sources sometimes produce a feeble sort of wit. *Harry Goldman* was followed by *In a gold mine,* and the forms *higher* and *hire* were interchanged over a long series of responses. After responding *Three*

[1] Skinner, B. F., "The Verbal Summator and a Method for the Study of Latent Speech," *Journal of Psychology,* 2 (1936), 71-107.

or four years ago, one subject then gave the response *An historical article,* and the incongruous juxtaposition of *three or four years* and *historical* may explain a later response in the experiment *Slightly historical,* which in itself may be a distorted form of the expression common at the time *slightly hysterical.*

Thematic groupings of responses without formal strengthening are exemplified by *Two four one eight, Call Station* (telephoning); *The music passed you, What's this motif?* (music); *Grand orchestra, You're musical* (music); *God of love, Come near the earth* (religion); *Make a full stop, Slow motion* (speed). (The last pair was followed by *Go to movie,* and the three responses, taken together, comprise a miniature flight of ideas.)

The intraverbal connections between some successive responses suggest patterns of everyday conversation: *Where are you going? Home as usual; Who are you? I couldn't imagine; Will you have tea? All right, I'll ring the bell; My eye's on the rope, What did he do? He pulled the rope; I love you, Do you love me?*

Occasionally there is evidence of an intraverbal sequence not all of which has been overt. One subject gave the response *You are a peanut* on one day of the experiment and on the following day *You are a peacock.* The latter was then followed by the response *Are you a nut?* It is possible that the response *You are a peacock* recalled the response *You are a peanut* and further covert verbal behavior then led to the question *Are you a nut?*

The intricacy of the formal and thematic interlocking of successive responses in the absence of any "prose meaning" is worth noticing because of its application to an analysis of poetry. A series of responses given by the subject responsible for the list above supplies a good example.

elle n'est partie
do not say your part
take leave of it
oh, are you
got your visa
elle ne sait pas
p-p-partie
are you going
who are you
vis-à-vis

Formal resemblances among these responses which are independent of thematic connection (and hence might be regarded as a sort of punning) are seen in: *partie, part; not say part, ne sait pas;* and *visa, vis-à-vis.* Both formal and thematic strength are evident in the pairs *elle ne, elle n'est; partie, partie; are you, are you;* and so on. Thematic interlocking with formal overlap is seen in *partie, take leave, are you going,* and perhaps *got your visa.* The stammered *p-p-partie* (the subject reported that the record was stammering) may be due to the fact that in transcribing the first response in the series, the experimenter asked whether the subject had said *partie* or *pas partie.*

Responses may be evoked in young children with vague echoic stimuli, but the material is heavily determined by the conditions of the experiment or, once a few responses have been emitted, by strong formal and thematic connections. A five-year-old girl gave the following:

> *I got my record; I got my record (it's making noise); My record makes lots of noise but I like it; I'm sitting on a stool; I got a pretty desk, though; Gee, I'm writing so hard; Gosh, I forgot my record; Who are those people knocking at my door?; Gee, my desk is lovely and my record too; (I think he's singing a nice fairy song); Gee, where's my wife? Where is it?; She's got my little girl along;*

followed by nineteen other responses in a total of ten minutes. This subject prefaced almost every response by saying *I think he's saying. . . .* Another five-year-old girl reported *Pigeon* for the first stimulus, and practically all subsequent responses were the names of birds.

Since identifiable sources of strength will not account for the greater part of the forms of response observed in the verbal-summator experiment, the rest must be attributed to other variables in the history of the subject. It is precisely in permitting us to infer these variables that the device has clinical use as a "projective test." When responses obtained in this way are broken into thematic groups and their grammatical structure analyzed, verbal predispositions may appear which could not always be discovered in the normal behavior of the subject because of the process of editing to be discussed in Chapter 15. In the summator experiment, to put it roughly, the subject need not take the responsibility for what he says. The present point, however, is simply that such a device works. By providing a very vague echoic stimulus as a supplementary source of strength, verbal behavior of otherwise undetermined form may be evoked. Miscellaneous relations to other variables, including internal echoic and intraverbal strengthening, serve merely to confirm the formulation.

The echoic stimulus is at a minimum (and other variables therefore relatively more important) in the psychotic behavior of "hearing voices." The mishearing of overheard speech is, of course, a common trait. The responses of psychotics to the verbal summator are relatively free of the pattern of the echoic stimulus.[2] In hearing voices we cannot assume that there is no echoic stimulus, since noises generated by physiological processes in the listener himself may suffice; and in many cases such hallucinations seem to be encouraged by external stimuli, such as the rustling of leaves.

Textual probes. Although a textual verbal stimulus is normally more stable than an echoic, it often evokes responses which fail to exhibit the point-to-point correspondence of the textual repertoire. The grade-school teacher is familiar with this effect. But even readers who have developed an extensive textual repertoire may *misread* when the textual stimulus is vague or very brief. In driving a car one may catch sight of a textual stimulus "out of the corner of one's eye" or as it quickly flashes by. In the laboratory textual stimuli may be presented for fractions of a second with a tachistoscope. Under all these conditions the textual response may be controlled in part by other variables.

A visual form of the verbal summator based upon this process has been designed by W. K. Estes.[3] Patterns of letters are exposed either for a short time or out of focus, and the subject is asked to make a textual response. Part of a sample protocol is as follows.

> *Left with me; his wife; tell me of; hit by the arm; guilty of the crime; to take this arm; light my way; boot planned; about my arm; get through the arm; feel the toe; tight on the arm; tied on the arm; on the side; letter by the hand; it on my head; real as they did; is statue on my left; graft on the side; found on its head; quarrel with; little girl all well; run down the hill; great man in the well;*

Self-echoic and self-intraverbal responses are again evident, as well as combinations of these in multiple causation.

When, at the beginning of an experimental session, the subject was permitted to see clearly a meaningful text, ostensibly as a sample of the material to be presented under less favorable circumstances later,

2 Rosenzweig, S., and Shakow, D., *Character and Pers., 8* (1940), 216-226.
3 Estes, W. K., *The Psychol. Record, IV* (1940), 174-180.

the theme of the sample persisted only briefly, and apparently as the result of successive intraverbal responses rather than any permanent "set." The grammatical structure of the sample persisted for a longer period of time. Thus, if the sample were a question, the next six or eight responses tended to be questions.

Other types of formal probes. We may generate verbal behavior with any of the variables which strengthen behavior without respect to form, or with any such variable in combination with purely formal variables. Thus, we may ask our subject to compose a list of words as rapidly as he can, or to write a poem in a suggested pattern, or to write highly alliterative passages using suggested initial consonants, or to write down all the words he can think of beginning with a given letter or rhyming with a given word, and so on. These are probes in the sense that the actual material obtained is not under powerful external control. All such material will be "edited" by the speaker in the sense of Chapter 15, since in contrast with the verbal summator of either auditory or visual form, the subject must "take the responsibility" for the responses generated.

Thematic Probes

An example of an early thematic probe is Jung's word-association test.[4] A series of verbal stimuli are presented to the subject, who is asked to report "the first word he thinks of" except for formally determined responses. The stimuli may be vocal or written and the responses vocal or written without seriously affecting the results. Some aspects of the behavior thus generated are significant apart from the responses generated or the evidence they offer of multiple sources of strength. If the subject "blocks" (that is, does not give a quick response), covert behavior may be inferred of the sort to be discussed in Chapter 15. Whether his responses are typical of the verbal community of which he is a member—whether they show "normal" intraverbal responses—may also be of interest. The actual responses (the "content" of the behavior) may reveal collateral variables. Different subjects give different responses, presumably because of differences in their verbal history or in current conditions or circumstances. Girls and boys give different responses, as we have seen in Chapter 4, as do students of law and medicine. Idiosyncratic responses, especially to "emotionally toned" stimulus words, may be especially useful. Self-echoic or self-intraverbal relations between

[4] Jung, C. G., *Studies in Word Association* (London, 1918).

succeeding responses are observed, as well as the persistence of grammatical or syntactic relations to the stimulus word.

In a test devised by John B. Carroll [5] key words are omitted from a prose passage although syntactical relations are preserved. Here is the first paragraph of such a test:

> The sky was __________ (adjective) as I walked to the __________ (noun). On the way I met Alison who looked very __________ (adjective). __________ (pronoun) spoke to me quite __________ (adverb). The last time I had seen Alison was the day my mother had __________ (verb), and this meeting brought back to me the memory of the __________ (adjective) event. Thinking of it brought a feeling of __________ (noun) over me and I wondered when anything like it would ever happen again.

The intraverbal stimulation supplied by the passage is somewhat less specific than in the word-association test. Once responses have been entered in the blanks, however, they function in a more important way in determining other responses.

The word-association experiment evokes intraverbal responses. Stimuli appropriate to tacts may serve a similar function. In the Thematic Apperception Test [6] the subject is asked to tell a story about a picture or to write something appropriate to given music, odors, flavors, and so on. As in the word-association test, some characteristics of the behavior thus evoked are not relevant here, but such tests illustrate the probing of behavior through inadequate stimuli where the behavior is inferred to be multiply caused and where additional sources of strength can therefore sometimes be inferred.

Compared with the formal probe, both the word-association test and the Thematic Apperception Test begin with fairly strong stimuli. The very fact that they are thematic suggests that they will exert a relatively powerful control. Collateral variables, however, still have relatively wide scope. In the Rorschach test, the black and white or colored "ink blots" are selected precisely because they do not evoke

[5] Carroll, John B., *Psychometrika, 6* (1941), 279-307.
[6] Murray, H. A., *Exploration in Personality* (New York, 1938).

standard responses with any consistency. The scoring of the Rorschach does not emphasize the "content" of the behavior thus generated, but the test nevertheless illustrates the use of multiple causation in the probing of verbal behavior. The effectiveness of vague visual patterns in evoking responses which, syntactically, name or describe the patterns or features thereof can only be explained in terms of collateral sources of strength. Much of this may be attributed to the visual stimuli themselves in the sense that many such responses represent metaphorical or nominative extensions of tacts. The material is therefore relevant to the tendencies of the subject to "see" patterns of given form.

The Question of Awareness in Formal and Thematic Probes

The clinical usefulness of a thematic probe depends upon the extent to which the subject is "unaware" of the action of collateral variables. When the subject "must take responsibility for what he says," he is likely to edit his behavior in the manner to be discussed in Chapter 15 and defeat the purpose of the test. Where the personal source of the behavior cannot be easily disguised, as in the Rorschach test, thematic material is minimized in "scoring" in favor of other aspects of the behavior. Sophistication may lead to editing in other tests as well. One who understands the point of the Thematic Apperception Test is often aware of editing his behavior and may, indeed, be unable to respond freely. When the real nature of the verbal summator is revealed, the test changes in clinical significance. The editing of the behavior generated does not place in question the reality of formal or thematic sources of strength or the multiple causation of behavior. It simply means that these processes may be obscured by an additional activity of the speaker.

In the auditory form of the verbal summator, a standard preface to each response may occur or be implied by the conditions of the experiment. When the subject's own response is strong he may preface his report with *It says* . . . or *He says*. . . . When his response is weaker, he may preface his report with *It sounds as if it were saying*. . . . When the echoic stimulus is clearly not verbal, as in listening to the click of the wheels of a train, the subject may report, *When I listen to the wheels, I find myself saying*. . . . Only in an obvious metaphor does the report take the form *The wheels are saying*. . . . Similarly, in the visual form of the summator, responses may be prefaced with *It says* . . . , *It looks as if it said* . . . , *I read it as* . . . , or *To me it says*

. . . . Responses of this sort, to be discussed in Chapter 12, are a description of the speaker's own behavior or of the variables controlling that behavior, emitted to qualify the effect of the response upon the listener.

A similar series of prefaces may be implied in responding to the Rorschach. The subject may essentially be saying *It's a . . . , It looks like a . . . ,* or *I see a . . . there.* There are parallel expressions when the speaker is aware that *no* stimulus is responsible for the behavior: *I heard voices, I saw words, Words flashed through my mind,* or *Even with my eyes closed, I saw a. . . .* We may note, however, a peculiarity of the vocal form of the verbal summator. The expression *I said to myself* has no exact parallel with respect to responses to visual stimuli, verbal or otherwise. We do not say *I read . . . to myself* or *I saw . . . to myself.* (The silent reading of an actual text is not, of course, involved.) The term *visualize* suggests a related notion of arranging visual stimulation for oneself. But when, under conditions in which the ringing of a telephone will be highly reinforcing, a man hears the telephone in the jingle of a bunch of keys, he does not report this by saying *I rang to myself.* One may engage in verbal behavior "to oneself" because the speaker may be his own listener.

STRENGTHENING VERBAL BEHAVIOR IN THE LISTENER

Supplementary stimuli play an important, and often neglected, role in the behavior of the listener (or reader). Traditional analyses of "meaning" are usually confined to those activities of the receiver of verbal behavior which we classify here either as conditioned reflexes (mainly emotional) or as discriminated operants. The speaker who responds to verbal stimuli with echoic, textual, or intraverbal behavior is also, of course, a listener and may show reflex or operant behavior in addition to the verbal responses of Chapter 4. The practical use of verbal stimuli as supplementary variables—as formal or thematic prompts—permits us to analyze still another aspect of the behavior of listener or reader.

Frequently the speaker "makes the listener say something he would not otherwise say." Both speaker and listener are under the control of essentially the same variables (they are, so to speak, in possession of the same facts) and nothing new is "communicated," but the speaker generates behavior in the listener to "make something clear to him," or "get him to see a point," or "help him understand" a state of affairs. Instead of reporting to the listener something which he alone sees, he gets the listener to "see something his way." He "says something for" the listener. The process is often exemplified by relatively intellectual scientific or philosophical discourse, and it is therefore perhaps all the more surprising that it may be reduced to echoic, textual, or intraverbal supplementation.

It is easy to demonstrate that the listener often says or can say what the speaker is saying, and at approximately the same time. The listener has no trouble in supplying a missing response when the speaker's behavior is momentarily obscured by a loud noise or a break in a telephone circuit, just as the reader fills in a small piece torn from a page. The listener reacts correctly even though the speaker's behavior is for some reason distorted (Chapter 11) and may even be unaware of the distortion. He completes a sentence for the speaker if his own behavior is more rapid or if the speaker is for any reason interrupted. He joins with the speaker in emitting an important word or phrase. Even when he does not emit the response, he may recognize his own participation by saying "He took the words right out of my mouth."

If both speaker and listener are in possession of the same verbal repertoire, there may seem to be little point in such a speech episode, but in instances which are useful enough to be reinforcing to the listener (and therefore usually indirectly reinforcing to the speaker), the speaker's responses are for some reason slightly stronger. The listener may not have been so thoroughly conditioned, say, or he may have to some extent forgotten. When, in a visit to the zoo, the speaker supplies the name of an animal which the listener possesses but in inadequate strength, he is not "instructing" the listener (in the sense to be discussed in Chapter 14) because he does not create a new functional relation. He simply adds a supplementary source of strength sufficient to evoke a response.

The fact that the response in this example was formerly of sufficient strength in itself is not essential. Two men may possess the same set of responses to a very complex set of variables (a difficult political situation, for example), but if one of them shows more powerful motivation, say, more active "composition" (in the sense of Chapter 14), or more extensive "thought" (in the sense of Part V), he becomes the speaker and the other the listener. The speaker characterizes the situation in a way which the listener immediately adopts because he has been close to making the same response himself. A similar case arises when a listener immediately "sees" that a metaphor is apt because the properties responsible for the extension in the behavior of the speaker have also been to some extent effective upon him. Again, two people working together on a problem in algebra may approach the solution by essentially the same path, having had similar intraverbal histories, but the one who emits the solution first becomes the speaker. The other is a well-prepared listener affected almost as strongly by the same controlling variables.

In this important effect upon the listener the speaker's behavior may be thought of as an *optimal* summating stimulus. Because it matches the behavior of the listener in every detail, only one stimulus presentation is generally required, though repetitions may sometimes be needed before the listener "gets the point." The parallel with the summator clarifies several features of the process. The speaker and listener do not, of course, emit the responses simultaneously. The time required for the echoic response may be of the order of a fraction of a second. There is only one verbal act on the part of the listener; it contains the echoic response and the response already existing in some strength. It is generally subaudible and hence difficult to examine. The *reader* usually participates in a more obvious fashion; he may be more clearly aware of his own subaudible verbal behavior, possibly because, unlike the comparable act on the part of the listener, it is not confused with the verbal stimulus.

In any given instance the behavior of the speaker has not yet been affected by, and does not depend upon, appropriate behavior on the part of the listener. The speaker may speak although his present listener shows no reaction or makes an erroneous response. Similarly, the listener may react in an appropriate fashion although the verbal stimulus is generated under irrelevant circumstances. The supplementary effect of the verbal stimulus is also independent of a current useful function. In one case the listener may be described as "saying something else with the same words." As Joseph Conrad's Lord Jim was being led away from the scene of his trial he overheard someone saying *Look at that wretched cur.* The speaker was responding to a dog wandering in the crowd, but Jim took it as a reference to himself. He did not see the dog, and hence did not possess the response under that control, but similar behavior with respect to himself was currently strong for other reasons. The general name for this is "eisegesis." An excellent example, pointed out by Upton Sinclair and quoted by Ogden and Richards,[7] is due to Lyman Abbott.

> Jesus did not say "Lay not up for yourselves treasures upon earth." He said "lay not up for yourselves treasures upon earth where moth and dust doth corrupt and where thieves break through and steal." And no sensible American does. Moth and dust do not get at Mr. Rockefeller's oil wells, and thieves do not often break through and steal a railway. What Jesus condemned was hoarding wealth.

A sort of fragmentary eisegesis is responsible for the difficulty of the reader who starts to say something with the first words of a passage and finds the balance not adapted to what he has begun. He misconstrues the beginning of a sentence and is helpless when he tries to continue to follow the text. Fowler [8] calls this "false scent." The process also goes awry in mishearing. An example is the unhappy experience of a gallant young man who had done more than his share of dancing with a middle-aged chaperon at a ball. The chaperon stopped in the middle of a dance and led the young man off the floor, exclaiming *I'm just too danced out!*, whereupon the young man replied *I wouldn't say you were stout at all!*

The extreme case of different controlling variables is what George Moore called echo-augury—"words heard in an unexpected quarter, but applying marvelously well to the besetting difficulty of the moment." [9] Here the simultaneous state of strength in both speaker and listener is due to chance and, as is often the case with chance, the listener may be especially impressed and even act upon the response with special belief. An overheard remark bearing some resemblance to the name of a race horse is taken as a "hot tip." Some of the same superstition is implied in the phrase *speak of the Devil,* which is appropriate to the case in which a man appears *after* his name has been mentioned. The same effect is felt when an object turns up shortly after its name has been mentioned.

When the same variables affect the behavior of both speaker and listener, the extent to which the same thing is being said is crucial. We do not enjoy hearing someone say what we ourselves also tend to say in full strength. If a lecturer says what we have been "saying all along," we are not helped nor are we pleased. Obvious remarks are neither useful nor delightful, nor are heavy doses of clichés, well-

[7] Ogden, C. K., and Richards, I. A., *The Meaning of Meaning* (New York, 1923).
[8] Fowler, H. W., *Modern English Usage* (London, 1930).
[9] Moore, G., *Confessions of a Young Man* (New York, 1901).

known stories, and so on. We could have said the same thing ourselves and did not only because an occasion was lacking upon which the behavior would be reinforced. At the other extreme, we cannot use and do not "like" behavior which has no appreciable parallel in our own repertoire. The discussion of an obscure detail, an account of a wholly unfamiliar subject, unrecognized literary allusions, far-fetched metaphors, intraverbal sequences which do not follow from the contiguous usages of our own experience, not to mention wholly unfamiliar verbal forms, are both worthless and dull. To some responses of this sort we may say *I don't get it,* in the sense of *I don't find myself saying anything like that.* To others, we may simply make no response whatsoever and eventually stop listening. (The same conditions govern nonverbal behavior. We are not helped by being shown how to do something we can already do, and we may strongly object to being shown. On the other hand, we also object to being shown how to do something which we never succeed in doing or have no interest in doing.) Between these extremes the speaker may be of considerable help. He is sought after because he supplies stimuli which permit us to engage in useful behavior. We are especially reinforced by speakers and writers who say what we are *almost* ready to say ourselves—who take the words "off the tip of our tongue." Significantly enough, we call such writers or speakers "stimulating." This does not mean that they make our mouth water or send us off on some practical errand; they merely make us think, in the sense of making us behave verbally with respect to some state of affairs.

We also find useful, though momentarily somewhat less reinforcing, a verbal response on the part of a speaker which we ourselves were less likely to emit. If we have been puzzling over a complex situation and someone suddenly makes a remark which is clearly appropriate, we make the remark with the aid of this supplementation almost as if we had arrived at the same conclusion ourselves. Similarly, the good metaphor or the apt remark may not be on the listener's tongue, although it is immediately accepted because of other considerable sources of strength. The listener may refuse credit and exclaim *Why didn't I think of that?,* but he must have "thought of it" to some extent if he accepted it immediately as an effective metaphor or a really apt remark. A merely echoic stimulus would not be valuable or reinforcing because it would not lead to "getting the point."

Speaker and listener will be most alike if they speak not only the same language but the same sublanguages. A common vocabulary is advantageous not only at the level of the word but in the larger functionally unitary responses which "say something." Slight differences in preferred forms will interfere with the summative effect, even though the listener may react appropriately in other ways. Similar intraverbal tendencies are helpful, particularly in the ordering of responses and the adding of grammatical tags to be discussed in Chapter 13. For example, broken English may fail to supplement effectively the behavior of the listener who speaks good English even though it serves well enough the other functions of verbal stimuli. Roughly the same speed of utterance is important. We fall behind a fast speaker, and grow impatient with a slow one—a fact which raises a special problem for the slow speaker or stutterer. Length of response is also a factor; other things being equal, the longer a verbal stimulus the less likely it is to find a corresponding pattern in the behavior of the listener. Whether the stimulus is vocal or written is also important, for there may be considerable differences in sensitivity to supplementary sources of strength in the two modalities.

Thematic Correspondences between Speaker and Listener

The themes of literature have been extensively analyzed, especially within the framework of psychoanalysis. The "personality" of the writer is reflected in what he writes to the extent that the behavior from which we judge both personality and literary behavior are functions of the same variables in the writer's history. It was not so commonly recognized before Freud that the relation between a literary work and the *reader* is partly of the same sort. We may enjoy a poem or book simply because of the reactions discussed in Chapter 6, but it is probable that our enjoyment comes in larger measure from the fact that the literary work says what we, the reader, tend to say. Literature enables the reader to behave verbally in an appropriate fashion. The lover has only to read or recite the sonnets of Elizabeth Barrett Browning to speak as a lover in a convenient and effective way. Just as the jilted maiden has a special reason for singing "Lover, come back to me," the reader who is himself in love may be particularly affected by a novel about someone in love whose verbal behavior, transcribed as part of the "conversation," supplies the same kind of auxiliary stimulus.

Among the reasons why the reader does not speak without textual help is simple lack of opportunity, particularly the lack of an appropriate audience. Under strong states of deprivation a man may, of course, talk to himself without any other audience, but reading a text to oneself is not under audience-control at any motivational level. Another common reason is that the reader is himself less energetic verbally, or less gifted and imaginative. It is easier to emit the behavior of someone else, as prompted by a text, than to engage in the same behavior without auxiliary help. Psychoanalysis has emphasized another reason. Some forms of verbal behavior—concerned, for example, with sex or with aggressive action toward other persons—are frequently punished in everyday life, though the same forms of behavior generated by a text go unpunished. Thus, one may be punished for a verbal attack upon a parent or sibling, though not for reading of such an attack in a novel. To Freud, the behavior "repressed" by punishment was released through "identification" with a character in a novel, but the facts may be represented without using the Freudian conceptual scheme.[10]

Although the punishments at issue are generally associated with the ethical practices of the group, some grounds are relatively trivial. Excessive repetition is an example. One may complain of a lost love only a few times before some sort of punishment sets in, but one may sing a love song many times or read many works of literature on the same theme without running a comparable risk. Some of the devices employed by the speaker or writer to escape punishment will be discussed in Part V. To the extent that the reader is simply saying what the writer says, the same analysis applies to him.

The personal involvement of both writer and reader in a literary work has led to many analyses of the themes of literature according to particular systems of personal psychology. Psychoanalysts have analyzed hundreds of literary works either to exemplify the principles of psychoanalysis or to demonstrate a correspondence between the biography of the writer and the themes of his works. The details of these correspondences are of interest only with respect to a particular system of personal psychology. Which themes are most important and why they are most important are questions which are independent of the verbal processes which lead to their expression in literature.

A reader seeks out other works of a given writer or other literature of a given type because of the reinforcement he has received. The reinforcement depends upon his own verbal behavior. A thematic correspondence between a reader and a literary work is likely to

[10] *Science and Human Behavior,* Chapter 24.

involve a matching of variables in the fields of motivation and emotion. The universality of a literary work refers to the number of potential readers inclined to say the same thing, at least in some measure. The writer who seeks universality will try to match strong latent verbal repertoires. The success of a book is some indication of the number of people who possess a given kind of verbal behavior in strength. But books which are "universal" are less likely to be "favorite" books in matching most accurately the idiosyncracies of a particular reader. Gordon Allport [11] has pointed out that autobiographies seem to be especially interesting because they satisfy the reader's own self-love. We might translate this by saying that most people possess strong behavior of talking about themselves and that only autobiographies or novels written in the first person supply the appropriate verbal supplementation.

Ambiguity, in Empson's sense,[12] should increase the chances of a successful match between the reader and the literary work. If at least two sets of variables are responsible for the behavior of the writer, the reader is more likely to share at least one set. In general, however, multiple causation in the behavior of speaker or writer has another more appropriate effect upon the listener or reader, as we shall see in a moment.

Building a Correspondence between the Behaviors of Speaker and Listener

The speaker or writer may work on the listener or reader in order to increase the likelihood that a later response will be a successful match. A novel achieves one of its main effects by preparing the reader to join in with the remarks of its characters. Novels with "lots of conversation" are especially effective in this way. When we read a description of a merely nonverbal event, or an indirect quotation, our verbal behavior is not accurately supplemented with textual stimuli, but when we read conversation, the textual supplement is more likely to be effective. The great character writers prepare the reader in such a way that a given remark seems inevitable. The conditions for a good match are then ideal and "identification" is easy. A similar effect is achieved in the theater, where the spectator is

11 Allport, G. W., "The Use of Personal Documents in Science," *Soc. Sci. Res. Council Bull.*, *49* (1942), p. 78.

12 Empson, W., *Seven Types of Ambiguity* (London, 1930).

prepared for responses which are later strengthened by an echoic supplement as he hears a character speaking.

Building similar verbal behavior in the listener or reader is often recognized as an explicit goal. When a listener "agrees" or "concurs," he may take various practical steps which are important to the speaker, but first of all he must "say the same thing." *I agree* can generally be translated *I also say*. The same goal may be thought of as creating, strengthening, or changing an "opinion," which may be defined as a thematic group of responses emitted with respect to a particular controlling state of affairs. The speaker reveals his interest in getting the listener to respond in a suitable way when he emits the simple mand *Say to yourself . . . ,* followed by the particular verbal response which he wishes to strengthen. He may check on his success by asking *Don't you think so?* or *Wouldn't you say?* He may try to create a spurious sense of strength with frequent responses such as *Of course* or *Naturally*. If these are echoed by the listener, they will go far toward concealing the fact that a given response is perhaps almost wholly echoic and hence not a matter of course or natural at all.

The speaker or writer may also resort to rhetorical devices. One of the commonest of these is repetition. As the verbal summator shows, a repeated stimulus may eventually be effective even if its summating power is originally slight. Children often react more and more appropriately to repeated tellings of a story, and may insist upon precise repetition. Where simple repetition has undesirable collateral effects, the rhetorically inclined speaker must repeat in disguise. Fragments of the required response—especially certain key words—are worked into other sentences. Classical rhetoric had names for many devices in which repeated responses were interwoven with other material for ornamental or persuasive purposes. Simple repetition was called "epanalepsis"; the repetition of a word or clause after other matter was called "epistrophe"; a double repetition at the beginning and end of successive clauses was called "symploce"; the repetition of a word in a different syntactical frame was called "polyptoton"; and so on.

Creating a match between the behavior of listener and speaker is often useful for ulterior purposes. An echoic or textual supplement prepares the listener to say the same thing but not "for good and sufficient reason." Variables involved in tacts and intraverbal responses can be used with more justification: when the speaker engenders appropriate behavior by emphasizing the important aspects of a situation, or when he rearranges various features to yield more clear-cut assertions, he may be strengthening useful behavior. The listener eventually agrees, if at all, for good reason. The commoner case in which the speaker makes intraverbal preparations—by reviewing data, describing cases, and so on—is also justifiable in this sense. A venerable example is the fable or parable, where a story is told in order to build a strong disposition to join with the speaker when the moral is reached. An episode in a Greek tragedy prepares the audience to agree with the summing up by the chorus. But these "thematic" preparations may also be spurious, as when agreement with a final proposition is rendered more likely through the use of wholly irrelevant thematic materials.

Understanding

The listener can be said to understand a speaker if he simply behaves in an appropriate fashion. The behavior may be a conditioned emotional response. When, for example, the listener blushes at the mention of a social error, he can be said to have understood what was said to the extent that his reaction was appropriate to the original event. A remark in a language which he did not "understand" would not have affected him in the same way. A verbal stimulus which is the occasion for successful action is understood in much the same way: the listener understands to the extent that he tends to act appropriately. In "instruction" (Chapter 14) we shall see that he understands to the extent that his future behavior shows an appropriate change. These are all ways in which we are said to "understand a language"; we respond according to previous exposure to certain contingencies in a verbal environment.

But another process is involved when we understand or come to understand a remark about something which is familiar to us. In a trivial sense "to understand" is "to be *able* to say the same thing." This is the sense in which we say that we can or cannot hear over a noisy telephone. Scientists who study conditions of vocal communication usually accept an accurate restatement as evidence that a vocal response has been understood. This is possibly something more than a purely echoic response either as auditory mimicry or as a reproduction of conventional speech sounds. The listener probably says *I understand* only when he can emit corresponding behavior such as might occur in the language in response to nonverbal or intraverbal stimuli.

The best examples of this are in the field of scientific and philosophic discourse. Suppose we start to read a fairly difficult paper. We respond correctly to all the words it contains, so far as dictionary meanings go, and we are familiar with what is being talked about; still, we may not understand the paper. We say that we do not "get it" or do not "see what the writer is driving at" or why he says what he says. What we mean is that we do not find ourselves responding in the same way. The paper does not supplement verbal behavior in us which exists in any considerable strength. We possess each of the responses in the sense that it is part of our verbal repertoire, but we do not tend to emit it under the same circumstances as the author of the paper. This meaning of understand is in accord with the layman's use of the word. We understand anything which we ourselves say with respect to the same state of affairs. We do not understand what we do not say. We *mis*understand when we say something *else* with the same words—that is, when we behave in a given way because of the operation of different variables.

Suppose, now, we go over the paper again—as we must if we are ever to understand it. What processes will explain the changes which take place? Intraverbal sequences established during the first reading will, of course, leave their effect: the paper will now be familiar. To some extent, therefore, we will tend to say the same things. Through this process alone we might eventually memorize the paper. But that would not be enough; we might still say that we do not understand it, though we should probably say that we now understand it to some extent. Other processes must take place if we are to get the point the writer is making. Instruction in the special sense to be discussed in Chapter 14 will probably occur. Some sentences in the paper will present two or more verbal stimuli together in what we call definition; the resulting change in our behavior will be felt when these responses occur separately elsewhere in the text. Other sentences, through predication, will produce other transfers of response by increasing our "knowledge." Our behavior will be altered on subsequent readings in the direction of increased understanding because our usage will then be closer to the writer's. There will also be an effect similar to that of the verbal summator: we will "come to understand" the text as we come to make suitable textual responses which supplement responses made for other, and in the optimal case better, reasons. Slight thematic tendencies to respond (that is, to emit tacts or intraverbal responses) come into their own through repetition, and eventually they are made "on their own" with or without echoic or textual supplementation. The process is obvious when we hear a subtle metaphor many times before seeing that it is apt. It is also clear when we are trying to decipher bad handwriting, a poorly recorded vocal stimulus, or a passage in an only partly familiar language. Our only recourse in such a case is to reread or relisten until we find ourselves making a "plausible" response—that is, a response under the control of other variables. This result of simple rereading is that we come to make responses not simply as textual behavior but for other reasons.

A remark or a text is relatively easy to understand if the listener or reader receives help from incidental intraverbal sequences. A heavily reworked text may lack the flow of intraverbals found in the first version. A style such as Conrad's is often difficult because a word, correct enough in a single sense, may lack intraverbal support —possibly in this case because Conrad was writing in a second language.

The analysis of a passage, as in literary criticism, is made more difficult by the very process which makes the passage easier to understand. When the critic has reread a poem or a novel many times, he is no longer able to react to it as a naïve reader. He is no longer able to judge it, therefore, in its original effect as a work of art. What he has to say about it may be understood only by those who are willing to reread it sufficiently often to generate the same set of conditions.

A listener may, of course, understand a remark in a language which he does not speak, but his understanding is less likely to include "saying it himself." The process of coming to understand by becoming more familiar with the remark may be conspicuous. There may be an intermediate stage in which the listener may share Alice's reaction to The Jabberwocky: "Somehow it seems to fill my head with ideas—only I don't exactly know what they are."

I understand, like the more casual *I see,* describes the strength of a verbal response with respect to the sources of that strength. The exact conditions under which it is emitted are not easily specified (but see Chapter 12). *I understand* is not merely a description of strength, such as *I am sure* and *I know,* nor is it a matter of a correspondence with the behavior of the speaker, as *I agree*. It calls for a subtle distinction among the variables responsible for the listener's own behavior. He can say *I understand* only after he has identified the variables which were mainly effective in leading him to make the same response. In particular he must be sure he has not "understood" because of spurious techniques of rhetoric or style which have built predispositions to respond through irrelevant devices.

One of the principal effects of verbal behavior, then, is the strengthening of corresponding behavior in the listener. The verbal stimulus does not impart information available only to the speaker because of his special point of vantage, nor does it create new behavior in the listener. Instead, it clarifies and strengthens behavior which has already been available in some degree. This is often for the benefit of the listener; but it may have indirect effects in shaping and maintaining the behavior of the speaker. We learn to speak to be understood.

The process is especially important when one is talking to oneself. So far as communication or instruction is concerned, talking to oneself would be idle if not actually pathological, since verbal behavior is scarcely productive in this way when both speaker and listener are inside a single skin. But the supplementary effect upon the self-listener may be important. The full extent of this can be appreciated only when we have considered some of the special achievements of verbal behavior in the field of thinking (Part V).

Tricks of Strength

In addition to promoting "understanding" the speaker (or writer) may be interested in altering the strength of the listener's (or reader's) behavior for other reasons. It may even be important to weaken his response, or to make it for him before he is ready. The speaker is most effective if he simulates the verbal characteristics of the listener as closely as possible, in what classical rhetoric called "schesis." By anticipating objections ("prolepsis") or answering imaginary objections ("anthypophora"), the speaker reduces the tendency of the listener to emit responses which might provoke disagreement or misunderstanding. In the somewhat different technique of anticlimax, a response is made to appear weak by contrasting it with strong verbal material.

Another technique consists of letting the listener make a key response entirely on his own. This is in fact the only recourse of the speaker who has overprepared his case and built up behavior past the point where his response will be received as useful or delightful. A shop-worn phrase is frequently clipped because the complete response would find the listener too well prepared. We may say *A word to the wise* but omit *is sufficient* because its intraverbal support is too strong. Similarly, when the listener may be assumed to have the answer to a "rhetorical question," some of the effect will be lost if the writer then supplies it. In allusion, innuendo, insinuation, and implication, the strength of a response is raised to the point at which it may be safely left to the listener. The speaker may simply break off a sentence at the point where the reader is able to complete it for himself (the classical technique of "aposiopesis"). (In "paraleipsis," the speaker pretends to pass over material which the listener can presumably say for himself, but his statement contains the behavior at issue in a thinly disguised prompt.) The "surprise ending," as in the type of short story associated with de Maupassant, gets its effect by strengthening a response which the reader is left to emit without textual aid. The effect is greatest if the response is never actually made. Something is lost when the naïve reader completes the point: *The jewels were false? Why, then the poor woman was paying for their replacement all those years for nothing!*

In still another technique the writer sets down a passage which is so weak that the reader is led to emit a stronger form, or so contrary to the evidence that the reader is led to deny or correct, or so ridiculous that the reader is led to protest. In irony or sarcasm, for example, a statement is made which is obviously untrue or the opposite of a true statement: a troublesome difficulty leads to *A pretty fix* and a personal injury to *Very kind of you, I must say*. In understatement, or "meiosis," the writer says less than the reader is prepared to say. Humorous collocations of terms (*horsefeathers*), nonsensical flights of ideas, "oxymorons" (*the gentle art of murder*), or the *Wildean* epigram in which a carefully prepared response is replaced by its opposite, play upon the fact that the reader is *not* likely to emit the behavior. He is led to emit a response which he is surprised to hear himself make. Something of the same sort is achieved in a *reductio ad absurdum,* where by what seem to be logical steps the reader eventually finds himself assenting for the moment to an absurd proposition. (In reconsidering the premises, he goes beyond the present process.) There are several games in which children induce their fellows to emit verbal behavior which they are surprised to find themselves saying. A child may, for example, be told to read the following words rapidly and repeatedly,

bell-lie-mud-um

only to find himself saying *I'm a dumbbell.*

Style

The advance preparation of the responses of listener or reader is involved in what is called style. The style which is "the man" need not detain us; everyone has idiosyncrasies of verbal behavior which are more or less useful and reinforcing to others. The style which, according to Walter Pater, is "a certain absolute and unique manner of expressing a thing, in all its intensity and color" represents an attempt to deal with the problem as a matter of successful expression. Various forms of expression will be more or less exact, more or less difficult to understand, and we may choose between styles on that basis. But most of the ways in which the stylist works upon the reader are to be classified as instances of the present process. The writer plays cat and mouse with the verbal strength of the reader—building it up, allowing it to fall away, holding it in abeyance (as in a periodic sentence), or exhausting it suddenly with an apt remark. The "happy phrase" is not one which expresses a thing well (the reader usually has no independent evidence of this), it is a phrase which is exactly suited to the present verbal tendencies of the reader. If these are due to the same thing, so much the better; but other reasons for the match are commoner. *Le mot juste* is not the word which best describes something apart from the context; it is the word for which we are optimally prepared by all that precedes it. The preparation is largely a matter of intraverbal tendencies. Since the reader's disposition to respond must reach a critical value just as a word is reached, the interpretation explains why timing is so important in style, why we lose the thread when we are interrupted, and why we cannot begin in the middle of a paragraph and get the effect of style even though the content is perfectly clear.

Many stylistic tricks are most easily demonstrated in the poetic devices of rhyme, rhythm, alliteration, and assonance. The multiple causation which produces these effects in the behavior of the poet carries through to the listener or reader in the form of fragmentary strengthening through echoic or textual responses. The reader is already prepared, for example, to emit the second of a pair of rhyming words because of a fragmentary textual (or self-echoic) response to the first member. In hearing the couplet

And other strains of woe which now seem woe
Compared with loss of thee will not seem so

the echoic response to *so* combines with an echoic fragment from the preceding *woe. So* is not only thematically determined by the preceding *will not seem. . .*, it is also formally determined. This preparation can be demonstrated by asking people to complete couplets from which the last word has been omitted. Practically all readers of

And so sepulchered in such pomp dost lie
That kings for such a tomb would wish to __________.

will be able to add *die,* where the thematic preparation from *sepulchre, lie,* and *tomb* is added to the formal preparation from *lie.* Although the "goodness" of poetry depends on many things, overpreparation of the rhyming word is usually condemned, as are rhymes which are far-fetched in the sense of having implausible thematic connections, or terms which belong to an older literary tradition and therefore fail to achieve the expected effect.

The echoic contribution from the first of a pair of rhymes would be effective regardless of the position of the second member, but the "rhyme scheme" heightens the effect through a special intraverbal device. The inveterate poetry reader develops a temporal discrimination which makes the echoic contribution greatest at a particular point. The specialist in Alexander Pope, for example, gets an effect from the rhymed couplet which is lacking in the novice who reads Pope for the first time. The verbal repertoire of the specialist contains a set of skeletal lines with characteristic last syllables. It is roughly the same intraverbal repertoire which makes it possible for the skilled person to produce rhymed couplets with ease.

In alliteration and assonance, the first instance of a sound contributes some strength to the instance which follows and which the reader can therefore say to some extent "on his own." The advanced strengthening due to rhythm is rather vague and does not greatly predispose the reader to make any one response. The rhythmic stimulus must therefore be repeated, as in the verbal summator. One instance of the stress pattern ˘ – does little toward strengthening responses with similar patterns, but several repetitions ˘ – ˘ – ˘ – may establish so strong a tendency that a response which does not show this stress pattern is unlikely. Alliteration, assonance, and rhyme are improved by repetition, but do not need it.

A parallel thematic preparation shows the reader's side of multiple meaning. Because of interlocking variables in the behavior of the writer the reader is likely to be affected by at least one of the sources of strength, but multiple sources are available for the reader with similar behavior. The reader may find the descriptive name of Mrs. Coiler or Col. Bully as useful as the writer. When the second of a pair of rhyming words takes some measure of strength from the thematic material which precedes it, we say that it is an appropriate response or that it "makes sense." If a textual fragment is added from the first rhyming word, three variables contribute to the reader's behavior when he reads the second rhyming word. In reading the lines from T. S. Eliot noted in Chapter 9

The tiger springs in the new year

the preparation for *new year* from the intraverbal response to *spring* is added to the thematic preparation from the whole passage. The textual response at the moment the poem is read is the third source of strength.

Not all responses showing multiple variation prepare the reader *in advance*. Thus, the response *Cut this knot intrinsicate* may be strong in the reader for much the same reason as in Shakespeare, for separate sources of the blending forms *intricate* and *instinsic* may be discovered in the text. The resulting behavior is not built up step by step as in the formal devices of poetry. A writer like James Joyce, however, builds thematic predispositions much as a poet builds formal predispositions. The analyses which have been made of *Ulysses* and *Finnegans Wake* reveal the extent to which multiple thematic sources entered into the behavior of the writer. These works also reveal the relative weakness of thematic verbal play. Intraverbal supplementation often depends upon similar verbal histories in writer and reader, which may be lacking; while the poet, working with formal supplementation, can count on appropriate echoic or textual repertoires.

The formal preparation of the listener or reader which develops as a poem is heard or read bears upon a problem of long standing in literary criticism. It is generally assumed, in line with traditional conceptions of verbal behavior, that there are only two elements in a literary work—form and meaning. Some works, particularly poems, seem to be enjoyable because of their form: they are nice noises, and they can be enjoyed in this sense by one who does not know the language. Literary works are also enjoyable because of their meanings: they describe things which are pleasant or interesting. But there is obviously something more in good writing—something not far from wit or verbal play. This has been argued to be a subtle connection between form and meaning, but a more likely possibility is that it has to do with how a reader's behavior is prepared and released by a text. A parallel distinction has been made [13] between "melopoeia," or the musical art of literature, "phanopoeia," or the art of images and meanings, and "logopoeia," the artistic use of the reader's disposition to emit words. In logopoeia the writer utilizes strong patterns arising from the reader's verbal history and constructs others on the spur of the moment. Joyce's line *Wring out the clothes, wring in the dew* borrows strength from the latent intraverbal sequence *Ring out the old, ring in the new,* as well as from a current theme of women washing clothes in the open air. The line may or may not be musical, it may or may not evoke emotional or practical responses, but it clearly manipulates verbal strength. It is this verbal play which is reinforcing to the reader and hence indirectly to the writer.

Supplementary Stimulation and Verbal Humor

Logopoeia is most obvious in verbal play or wit. The reinforcing effect of a clever style is hard to analyze; we usually simply report our delight and prove it by returning to the same writer for more of the same stimulation. But the laughter generated in verbal play is more objective. Laughs can be counted and even, as in a television audience, measured in decibels. Each of the literary effects already described has a parallel in the field of humor, where the response of the listener or reader may be more closely followed.

There are many reasons why men laugh, and they do not all apply here. Even in the verbal field, some behavior may be laughable merely because it is clumsy, awkward, surprising, or otherwise amusing in character. Stuttering or lisping and marked dialects are stock devices in humorous writing. The tongue-twisting distortions discussed in the next chapter are often laughable. Verbal behavior is also amusing when it describes an amusing episode. Such effects upon the listener have been discussed in Chapter 6. The effect of wit as a

[13] See, for example, Ezra Pound, *How to Read* (Toulon, 1932).

form of verbal play, however, involves the listener's verbal behavior.

The supplementary evocation of any *feeble* response is usually funny. A trivial feature of a stimulating situation may be responsible for a tenuous metaphorical extension, as in the classical anecdote about the dentist who, in repairing his car, took a firm grip on a sparkplug with a pair of pliers and said *Now this is going to hurt a little.* Far-fetched intraverbal sequences, nearly senseless flights of ideas, are usually amusing, and many non-sequiturs are funny. The classical "bull" offers an example. The exchange:

> SOLDIER: I've caught a tartar.
> SERGEANT: Bring him along.
> SOLDIER: I can't.
> SERGEANT: Then come along yourself.
> SOLDIER: He won't let me.

is funny possibly not because it is illogical but because *He won't let me* following upon *I've caught him* is very weak. We describe the condition of the reader by saying he doesn't "expect" the response.

Multiple variables produce funny results not because they are variable but because the supplementation encourages a tenuous source of strength. The newspaper clipping:

> Fertile, Minn., June 27.—Aged 83, Henry L. Gaylord, Fertile attorney, is the father of a bouncing son, his eighteenth child....

is amusing because of a remote thematic supplement.

The wit which depends on a trick of strength is often too subtle to be easily reconstructed. When a street car stopped with a squeak which could be written:

His companion, also familiar with Bach's *Toccata and Fugue in D Minor,* found this funny because of a similar, *and similarly far-fetched,* tendency to complete the phrase. Very weak tendencies define "zany" humor: when the orchestra at an open-air concert began to play Rimsky-Korsakov's *The Flight of the Bumblebee,* a listener began to brush away an imaginary bee. These examples are on the fringe of the verbal field. The "speaker" emits a very feeble response which supplements an imitative response in the "listener" which was too weak to appear without aid. If no parallel tendency had existed in the listener's behavior, the results would not have been amusing. Innuendo, understatement, and "dumping" the behavior of the listener with a surprising remark are familiar techniques in humor as well as in style. The importance of the strength of the listener's response is shown by the possibility of "spoiling" a joke or witty remark by emitting a key response too early in the telling.

The devices of poetry are all amusing when the multiple contributions of strength lie within proper bounds. Rhyme is ordinarily not funny, but if it is far-fetched it may be. Polysyllabic rhymes are likely to be far-fetched in this sense, and can scarcely be used in serious poetry.

W. S. Gilbert, following the distinguished precedent of *Ingoldsby Legends,* made the most of this sort of humor:

> I know the Kings of England and I quote the fights historical
> From Marathon to Waterloo in order categorical.
> I'm very well acquainted, too, with matters mathematical,
> I understand equations, both simple and quadratical . . .

The distortion produced by too strong a rhyme, as in the Ogden Nash effect (see Chapter 11), is almost invariably funny. Excessive rhythms and alliteration have become a part of folk-humor: *Peter Piper picked a peck of pickled peppers.* The rhythmic scanning of poetry presents many opportunities to play with the strength of a response. A forced delay in reaching a strong response, as in the unduly prolonged last line of a limerick, is often humorous.

Although supplemental strengthening of weak verbal responses seems to be reinforcing in itself and to explain much wit, as well as the success of witty people, we must not overlook a more serious function. Freud has emphasized the fact that witty responses are often (a) automatically reinforcing to the speaker and (b) punishable by the listener or community. Humor is preoccupied with tabooed subjects, in particular sex, and with having aversive effects upon the listener or others. Freud argued that wit permits the "release" of repressed responses, but the point can be made by saying that the response receiving supplemental support is weak because of punishment. Both interpretations miss an important point. Consider the witty remark of an English woman who had helped Napoleon the Third when he was in exile in England and who was virtually ignored by him after he had returned to the throne. On a chance encounter he casually asked *Restez-vous longtemps à Paris?* and to her reply she added *Et vous, sire?* The aggressive nature of the remark no doubt accounted for much of its strength; the function of the wit was to make an aggressive response unpunishable. But it is not enough to say that the speaker could appeal to the "harmless meaning" in a legalistic extenuation (*I was only adding a rather thoughtless conversational remark*) because the "aggressive meaning" (*You may not be on the throne long* or *You will be in England again soon, asking for my help*) was clear to everyone. Rather we have to appeal to a particular characteristic of the witty verbal community. Just as the literary community tolerates weak determiners of strength, so the witty community exacts a *quid pro quo* for otherwise offensive behavior. It is almost as if the community had agreed: You may be aggressive *provided* you are also amusing. This is now an established practice, but we may search for its origins in the well-known fact that the amusing is generally only a small measure of the annoying and that an event is less annoying if taken with a sense of humor. The witty person can be aggressive or otherwise offensive by inducing the listener to "laugh it off."

VERBAL PUZZLES AND GAMES

Many verbal games and puzzles appear to be effective simply as complex arrangements of probes and prompts. A riddle or conundrum is often more than a mere question in that the answer will show unusual sources of strength. Many riddles simply demand a metaphorical answer which is reinforcing for that reason alone:

> Down in the meadows there was a red heifer
> Give her hay she would eat it,
> Give her water she would die.[14]

[14] Taylor, Archer, *English Riddles from Oral Tradition* (Berkeley, Calif., 1951). The answer is *fire*.

Sometimes two or more thematic prompts are given and the answer must be a single intraverbal response to both. Formal prompts are common. A formal element enters when thematic prompts are given for each syllable separately and also for the answer as a whole, since any part of the solution then supplies a formal prompt for another part.

Charades are riddles using nonverbal stimuli as thematic prompts. The solver's responses begin mainly as tacts, metaphorical or otherwise. Separate prompts are "acted out" for each syllable and for the whole answer. In one version the answer is a familiar short passage. Each word is "acted out," while the response as a whole is assumed to have some resting strength.

Many conundrums are not asked in order to get an answer, but simply to set the stage for the wit of the answer supplied by the asker. It is not likely that anyone will answer the conundrum *What is the difference between a cat and a comma?* by saying *A cat has claws at the end of its paws while a comma denotes a pause at the end of a clause.* The intraverbal stimulation supplied by *cat* and *comma* is inadequate. One who has made an effort to do so, however, is an ideal listener when the answer is vouchsafed. Difficult charades, and in particular those with answers involving far-fetched puns, are also often designed to point up the wit in the answer rather than to evoke it.

The crossword puzzle consists of a pattern of squares which restricts the formal properties of the responses emitted in solution. A group of definitions supply intraverbal stimuli for responses to be entered into rows and columns. As the puzzle is solved, formal prompts are generated by the letters shared in common by intersecting words. The more difficult intraverbal responses pick up supplementary formal strength. Thus, the intraverbal stimulus "a saying" may be ineffective until the formal prompt PR__E_B has been composed, whereupon the response PROVERB appears—to reinforce the solver. In difficult crossword puzzles (particularly the sort popular in England), usable responses can often be arrived at only through chains of intraverbal or echoic responses.

The complex "Double-Crostic" of Mrs. Elizabeth Kingsley begins with a set of definitions serving as intraverbal stimuli for responses of specified length. The letters composing responses to these are then redistributed in a series of spaces representing the letters of a short passage from a book or poem, as in a cryptogram. Partial formal stimuli generated by the easier intraverbal prompts lead to tentative completions of parts of the passage. Letters added in the process then supply formal supplements for intraverbal responses satisfying the definitions which remain. The initial letters of the words defined give the author and title of the work from which the passage was taken. These responses may arise either through the growing recognizability of the passage, in which case they are intraverbal, or through the increasing number of initial letters, in which case they arise from a formal prompt.

In the game of anagrams a group of letters must be rearranged until the text for a standard verbal response is composed. When a group of letters is identified as the anagram of "the name of an animal," for example, a thematic variable is added.

A simple puzzle related to anagrams, in which responses are generated by both thematic and formal prompts is the pyramid of words. A single letter is given or guessed. Letters are then added one at a time to compose a series of words satisfying a set of definitions. The solver is subject to formal stimulation supplied by the letters already obtained at a given stage and thematic stimulation supplied by a definition.

A somewhat similar puzzle is illustrated by the following. All blanks in the couplet are to be filled with the same group of letters rearranged in different patterns.

> Come, waiter, fill the ______ until the ______ run over.
> Today we ______ upon this ______, tomorrow ______ for Dover.

Except for the specification that the same letters must be used for each blank, the puzzle contains only thematic stimuli. But formal prompts contribute to the solution. An intraverbal response in any one blank supplies formal stimulation which in combination with other intraverbal material may (if correct) strengthen a response suitable to another blank. Since the thematic stimulation is relatively weak, this may require several trials. (The behavior of the solver in trying, rejecting, rearranging, and so on, is properly to be classified with the material of Chapter 15.)

The "resting strength" of a familiar passage—for example, a proverb—is used in a game in which each member of a group gives a sentence containing one word of the passage. The words may or may not appear in order. It is usually necessary to repeat this badly disguised formal prompt many times to evoke the passage in question. An "easy" answer is a passage existing in considerable strength.

The game of "Categories" uses both thematic and formal material. The player is required to write down several names of flowers, cities, animals, and so on, beginning with an arbitrarily selected letter. The "category" is an intraverbal prompt which combines with the textual prompt of the initial letter to evoke the required answers.

Formal and thematic materials share about equally in another game which has an effect particularly close to that of wit or verbal play. A definition is given for a response composed of two words which must rhyme. If, for example, the definition is *Little difficulty,* the solver must make an intraverbal response to either *little* or *difficulty* to obtain formal stimulation which, in combination with an intraverbal response to the remaining word, will complete the solution—in this case, *slight plight.* In an actual sequence of events *difficulty* might evoke the intraverbal response *plight,* which provides a self-echoic supplement to *slight* as an intraverbal response to *little.* The game is often effective because of the surprising speed with which the definition evokes a unique, complex response.

Some games involve thematic prompts only. In the familiar "Twenty Questions," yes-or-no answers to tentative questions create a series of intraverbal stimuli which progressively reduce the universe of discourse. If the first question reveals that "it" is an animal, further questions are thematically related to animals. Eventually a response is uniquely determined by the stimuli thus generated. Several forms of the game require identification of a fictional or historical person. When the first letter of the name is given, a small formal source is effective in reducing the universe of discourse. Each question-and-answer creates other intraverbal stimuli which progressively reduce the number of possibilities.

In another game a person is to be identified from the answers to questions which call for far-fetched metaphorical or metonymical extensions. The answers to such questions as *What music does the subject remind you of?* or *What flower might the subject wear or be interested in?* may provide intraverbal stimuli which combine to determine a name. A variation consists of determining the occupation of an unknown person from a series of puns. The player is told that X is "one of the best boxers in town," that he is "the last man you want to have serve you," and so on. From this he must identify X as an undertaker.

In a game commonly called "Teakettle," a story is told in which a single word occurs frequently, but the word is replaced by the expression *teakettle*. Upon each occurrence, intraverbal sources are generated which eventually determine the word for which *teakettle* has been substituted.

Games and puzzles involving formal material alone are not common. In the familiar "word ladder" the player is to construct a series of anagrams, each differing from the preceding by only one letter, but producing another specified word in a specified number of steps. For example, we are to get from *eye* to *lid* in three steps. A solution is

EYE–LYE–LIE–LID

There are no thematic determiners as such, but the specification that each step must consist of a recognizable English word goes slightly beyond sheer formal manipulation.

Formal tricks such as "palindromes" may exploit multiple sources of strength but only indirectly and usually only with the aid of the manipulative behavior of Part V. Some of the "delight" in a good palindrome—for example, *A man, a plan, a canal—Panama*—may be traced to the formal strength of the behavior of spelling it backward derived from the behavior of spelling it forward, but there is evidently much more involved. Only by a very complex checking procedure can we establish the beautiful formal interlocking of the Latin sentence

Sator arepo teret opera rotas

where the first word is composed of all five first letters, the second word of all five second letters, the third word of all five third letters, and so on, and where the sentence is also a palindrome.

Chapter 11

. . . .

New Combinations of Fragmentary Responses

THE OPERATION of two or more variables in the multiple causation of verbal behavior is especially clear when the behavior is composed of fragments of responses. When two operants are of approximately the same strength at the same time, their responses seem to blend or fuse into a single new, and often apparently distorted, form. Material of this sort not only supplements the analysis of multiple causation in Chapters 9 and 10 but tells us something more about the control of all verbal forms. Fragmentary or minimal units of response appear in a new light.

Not all new or distorted forms of behavior are recombinations of fragmentary responses. The defective *execution* of verbal behavior, as in drawling, lisping, mirror writing, or the phenomena of motor aphasia, is generally not relevant. Stuttering, stammering, and "neurotic" handwriting may be related to supplementary variables, but as commonly studied they do not contribute to our knowledge of the present process. Nor are we concerned at the moment with new forms of response resulting from a miscarriage of the compositional processes to be discussed in Part IV. The intrusion of a wholly irrelevant response into verbal behavior in progress is also more appropriately discussed elsewhere (Chapters 15 and 16).

A response composed of fragments under the control of separate variables may never be observed if the speaker or writer rejects it in the process of editing. The fact that most of the examples to be considered are vocal does not necessarily mean that vocal behavior is more vulnerable to fragmentation; it simply offers less opportunity for editing. On the other hand, although written behavior leaves a more permanent record and supplies a less evanescent "feed-back" to the writer, visual stimulation can be more easily interrupted than auditory. Hence, it is easier to reduce the feed-back from written behavior to produce the special conditions of editing, such as those of automatic writing, discussed in Chapter 16. Under such conditions, fused or blended responses are as common in written as in spoken form.

Recombinations of response fragments are usually nonsense, and they interrupt or disturb discourse. For this reason the listener eventually learns to discount or ignore them, just as, except in unusual cases, he eventually overlooks stammerings, mannered repetitions, and so on. A psychological theory may reverse the process. When, for example, distorted responses or "slips of the tongue" are regarded as "revealing," they are noticed and collected, as has been the case under the Freudian influence. This is selective observation if only those instances are recorded which are conceivably revealing. Similarly, slips which have been collected for their bearing on the origin of linguistic forms or on linguistic change tend to be restricted to effective and surviving instances. Funny slips or distortions are obviously also a biased sample. In analyzing the normal relevant processes we must discount instances created by the routine manipulation of fragmentary responses specifically because of the resulting stylistic, witty, or funny consequences. Distortions such as *mirthquake* (describing a comedy) and *Reno-vated* (describing someone who has obtained a divorce in Reno) do not represent the same processes as the spontaneous recombination of response fragments.

A careful study of large samples of recorded speech would be necessary to determine the relative frequency of different types of fragmentary recombination and the extent of such recombination in normal discourse. Part of the following material comes from articles and books on distorted verbal behavior or "linguistic lapses." Most of it is derived from casual observation. No premium has been placed on distorted forms which, because they are effective upon the listener, may become part of an established language, nor upon distortions which are revealing or amusing. Nevertheless casual observation is necessarily selective.

The conditions necessary for the production of a blend were described by Lewis Carroll in the Preface to *The Hunting of the Snark*,

. . . . Take the two words "fuming" and "furious." Make up your mind that you will say both words, but leave it unsettled which you will say first.

> Now open your mouth and speak. If your thoughts incline ever so little toward "fuming," you will say "fuming, furious"; if they turn, by even a hair's breadth, toward "furious," you will say "furious, fuming"; but if you have that rarest of gifts, a perfectly balanced mind, you will say "frumious."

Since we have at the moment no quantitative measures of verbal strength delicate enough to prove a perfectly balanced mind, we cannot be sure that two responses must have the same strength in order to blend into a distorted form. We may agree, however, that if the strengths were very different, one response would be emitted in its entirety before the other.

The conditions under which fragmentary responses recombine are somewhat easier to identify. Responses which are poorly conditioned are presumably more subject to fragmentation. Recombinations are frequent in the behavior of young children and in adults learning a language for the first time. A well-established repertoire may suffer recombination under the conditions of illness or fatigue and as the effect of certain drugs, of which alcohol is the best known. Strong competing behavior, as when the speaker is "paying little attention to what he says," has a similar effect. Speech which is emitted under strong aversive pressure or as a function of any of the variables strengthening behavior without respect to form (Chapter 8) tends to suffer this kind of distortion. These variables may act directly upon the fusing process or upon the behavior of editing, rejecting, or encouraging such products.

Recombined responses have attracted attention for many reasons. We are concerned here with three things: (1) the types of operants contributing fragments, (2) the geometry or mechanics of rearrangement, and (3) the possible effect of resulting forms upon the listener, of whom the speaker himself may be an example.

MECHANICS OF BLENDING

Blends may be studied as mere forms of response apart from the controlling variables. A response may contain approximately equal parts of the contributing responses, or one response may predominate. *Intricate* and *intrinsic* are represented in approximately equal amounts in Shakespeare's *intrinsicate,* as are *winding* and *wandering* in the same author's *wind'ring.* But in *grapeline,* which is a blend of *grapevine,* in the sense of an undercover system of communication, and *line* (of communication) or in *taunts* (from *haunts* and *teases*) the first source contributes by far the greater part of the resulting form. Generally one response contributes the first part of the blend and another the latter, as when *snarl* and *tangle* make *snangle.* The combining forms frequently contain a large common element—as in the *Hindian rope trick* or the prolix *especified,* from *especial* or *especially* and *specified.* A smaller common element is seen in *mizzling* (from *mist* and *drizzling*), *scap* (from *scalp* and *cap*), and *bläge* (from *blazing barge*). In *interturb* (from *interrupt* and *disturb*), the combining syllables *-rupt* and *-turb* contain the same sounds except for the voicing of *b* but in different orders.

Some fused responses are recombinations of syllables which are likely to have independent status as autonomous responses. Thus, the response *wasteling* appears to be a recombination of elements of *wasteful* or *wastrel* and *changeling,* but the relative separability of *-ful* and *-ling* may have encouraged the new form. In the whimsical *beguincement,* the combining forms *beginning* and *commencement* show only the *n* in common.

Although blending is often discussed only at the level of the word, perhaps a commoner result is the fusion of larger responses containing several words. The blending of phrases is so common in the speech of very young children that it is usually overlooked. A two-and-a-half-year-old girl who had acquired the responses *You made a mistake* and *You missed it* said *You miss-take* upon an occasion when someone failed to catch a ball which she had thrown. This response would probably not have been emitted by an adult because of the violation of standard grammatical patterns. The following examples may be distinguished from distortion due to a miscarriage of the process of composition by the fact that in each case two responses larger than the single word may be identified:

in favor with (in favor of, in sympathy with)
you're probably true (you're probably right, it's probably true)
do you matter (do you mind, does it matter)
a nice piece of job (a nice job, a nice piece of work)
for that matter of fact (for that matter, as a matter of fact)
you'll have more end of fun (you'll have no end of fun, you'll have more fun)
you have been telling whispers (you have been whispering, you have been telling secrets)
in the nick of his teeth (in the nick of time, by the skin of his teeth)
a turning stone in his career (a turning point, a milestone)

put any weight in his opinion (give any weight to, put any faith in)
there is no crime against it (it's no crime, there's no law against it)
I say to hang with it (I say hang it, I say to hell with it)
scores of more (scores more, scores of others).

If these occur more frequently than the blends of single words, it is possibly because they are less likely to be rejected by the speaker in the process of editing.

Phrase-blends account for many subtle malaprops. Several examples from written verbal behavior, which have escaped the editing process, follow. In a sign in a restaurant reading *We are zealous of our reputation, zealous* appears to have arisen from two states of affairs which might have led separately to *We are jealous of our reputation* and *We are zealous in maintaining our reputation.* In a committee report the sentence *We were besieged to arrange interviews, besieged* appears to have been controlled by two states of affairs which might have led separately to the responses *We were beseeched to arrange interviews* and *We were besieged by persons requesting interviews.* In *Can You Forgive Her,* Trollope [1] writes: *She could not refrain herself from making it,* here *refrain* appears to be a blend of *refrain from making it* and *restrain herself from making it.* An apparent blend of two phrases which would not be detectable in vocal speech occurs in a prologue to a play [2] written by C. M. Dodgson (Lewis Carroll), which begins: *"Ladies and Gentlemen" seems stiffened cold,* where *stiff and cold* would suggest less morbid sources of strength. The prolix fusion of phrases is exemplified by *That's what I think so* (from *That's what I think* and *I think so*) and *For that matter of fact* (from *For that matter* and *as a matter of fact*).

Multiple causation is responsible for a formal blending which involves elements below the phonetic level. Whining appears to be a blend of crying and speaking. An emphasized onomatopoetic response may function both as a conventional tact and as mimicry, as when the word *sizzling* is pronounced so that it sounds especially like something sizzling. Multiple sources of strength may be responsible for minor distortions of form in written behavior. This is generally true in hieroglyphic or pictorial writing, in which conventional responses combine with the representational repertoire of the artist. A fusion of a standard response and a pictorial element is sometimes used in

1 Trollope, A., *Can You Forgive Her* (London, 1864), II, p. 156.
2 Dodgson, C. M., *Logical Nonsense* (New York, 1934), p. 159.

children's books, for example, in printing the word *tall* in very tall slim letters. It has been pointed out that mathematicians often show their trade in their handwriting by changing forms of letters to make them resemble figures, as musicians do to make them resemble notes, rests, and other musical marks. In an objective examination in which answers were to be indicated with a *D* or *O,* responses often took on a blended form which could not be recognized by the instructor as either a *D* or an *O,* presumably because both responses were equally strong (i.e., the student did not know the answer). We blend a stress pattern and a verbal response when we forcibly scan a line. We blend the intonational pattern of one response with the speech-sounds of another when we deal with an interruption by continuing the verbal behavior in progress in a manner which would be appropriate to the response *Please be quiet for a moment.* The writer of *A Few French words* was exemplifying a blend of *few* and the behavior of capitalizing appropriate to the word which followed. Misspelling may be a sort of blend. The sentence *Perspiration oozed from his pours* shows multiple sources of *pours* which would be missed (or possibly nonexistent) in a vocal response.

In most of the examples given above, the combining responses are alternative forms appropriate to a single occasion. Normally only one response would appear. In haplological blending, the combining fragments are parts of a larger response all of which would normally be emitted. The blend results from the omission of intervening material. Sometimes the result is similar to the "cognate" blend, as in *Sarling* for *Sorry, darling, quiddy* for *quite ready, slatter* for *slightly fatter, honorship* for *honorary membership,* and *generalities* for *general uniformities.* These appear to exemplify the combining of forms of response having separate sources of strength. This is not true, however, of standard examples of syncope. Distortions such as *crism* for *criticism, nonse* for *nonsense,* and so on, as well as the now-accepted forms *narcism* and *pacifism* show the omission of elements but not the fusion of different responses. For the same reason, a separate category is necessary for the so-called "brachylogies" in which one or more elements are simply omitted. The response *Today's to do it* is not a blend of phrases but the residue of a longer response (*Today's the day to do it*) part of which has been omitted. Whimsical haplologies such as *cinemactor* may also be distinguished from genuine word or phrase blends.

F. L. Wells,[3] in "Linguistic Lapses," suggested a classification of lapses as Regressive and Progressive Assimilation, Regressive Dissimulation, Metathesis, Omission, and Substitution. The terms regressive and progressive refer to the normal sequential order of the blending forms (an example of regressive assimilation is *blass plate*), but many blends involve responses which would not normally occur in any sequential order, and order itself seems to be less important than the fact that two responses are strong at the same time. Metathesis refers to a reciprocal displacement to be discussed later. Omission would include many of the examples just given. Substitution includes an intruding distortion to be discussed later.

SOURCES OF THE FRAGMENTS ENTERING INTO RECOMBINATION

Two responses are likely to be strong at the same time if they are both functions of the same variable. Many blends are mixtures of two or more tacts under the control of the same stimulus—for example, *lore* for *lame* and *sore,* or *rone* for *rock* and *stone*. Different aspects of the same stimulus may evoke different responses, but these seldom seem to blend. When a single property is vague, two or more responses which are not synonymous may be strengthened. The response *teablespoonful* occurred under circumstances in which a given magnitude was not large enough to evoke *tablespoonful* nor small enough to evoke *teaspoonful*. The response *I believe he graduated with a cumma* appears to indicate an uncertainty between a *summa* and a *cum laude* degree. Slightly different properties of the same stimuli generate the components of the facetious *twinfants,* as well as the behavior of the small child who reported *Esquimos eat slobber*. Some folk-etymologies are rearrangements of fragments. There is internal evidence of the intraverbal source which explains the slip in the following sentence from a newspaper: *Breaking the glass with a chair he climbed through a window and clung to the sill by his fingerprints until three detectives called on him to jump.* It is possibly relevant that all the letters of *tips* are contained in *prints*.

Many blends show the interaction of tacts and intraverbals or two or more intraverbals. A child reciting the days of the week and

3 Wells, F. L., *Archives of Philosophy, Psychology and Scientific Method,* No. 6 (New York, 1906).

ending *Thursday, Friday, Sixday* was blending *Saturday* and the response *six* which was intraverbally determined by the similarity between *four, five* and *-ur, Fri-*. The erroneous recall *Vain, inglorious Milton* appears to fuse *Mute, inglorious Milton* with *vainglory*. The erroneous recall of a child's song as *Old Macdonald had a farm, C-I, C-I-O* shows at least two intraverbal sources: the correct version *E-I, E-I-O* and *C-I-O.*, the labor organization whose leader was at the time trying to organize a farmers' union. A sentence beginning *There are two sets of anterior conditions which give the adult case* was actually written *result* rather than *adult,* where the thematic strength of *result* appears to be related to the terms *anterior* and *give*. The written response *populary usage* seems to contain a combination of *popular* and *vocabulary* as a synonym for *usage*.

Malaprops are often blends containing material from adjacent thematic sources. Mrs. Malaprop [4] falls victim to a barrage of intraverbal responses composing a grammatical theme as follows:

> Long ago I laid my positive *conjunctions* on her, never to think on the fellow again;—I have since laid Sir Anthony's *preposition* before her; but, I am sorry to say, she seems resolved to *decline* every *particle* that I enjoin her. (Italics added.)

Multiple intraverbal blends include instances in which a response is distorted by the anticipation of a later response. When an amateur actor reads a line as *Cecere—Cecelia, please take me seriously,* the fairly widely separated *Cecelia* and *seriously* seem to have become entangled. *The white rat in the maze* emitted as *the white raze* and the corrected responses *Will the gentleman from Yale—from Maine—yield,* and *The many strong Cases—courses—given by Professor Chase* are other examples.

Echoic and textual stimuli may contribute fragments if appropriate stimuli occur at the right time. In a conversation in which several people were taking part, a speaker began to say *When you were born,* but hearing another speaker say *birth,* said instead *When you were birthed.* In a similar discussion, *the last straw* became *the last word* because the word *word* was "in the air." A man dialed the telephone number of a Mr. Brenner, heard the answerer say *Linwood speaking,* and said *I'd like to speak to Mr. Brenwood.* A newspaper headline *Mercury rising after dipping to 30 in north west* was read as *dripping* presumably because a more characteristic response to *mercury*, namely, *dropping,* combined with the textual response *dipping.*

[4] Sheridan, *The Rivals,* Act III, Scene 3.

Self-echoic and self-transcriptive tendencies may produce perseverative distortions (*idle chattle*). Blends of synonymous forms may be attributed to a mixture of audiences or a weakness of audience control. Occasionally this is obvious. A song beginning in German *Morgen rot* and in English *Morning red* was sung *Morgen red.*

Mishearing and misreading usually represent a recombination of fragments, one source of which is the echoic or textual stimulus which is "misheard" or "misread". A simple error—an echoic or textual response under inadequate stimulus control—need not show another source of strength, but when a vague echoic stimulus such as supplied by the verbal summator is "heard" as, say, the subject's own name, a special source of strength may be inferred. The same is true of hearing one's own name when another name was actually uttered.

In mishearing it is not always clear that the distorted form is the echoic behavior of the listener rather than "what he hears" and then reports, but in the parallel textual case the response is usually more easily identified. When the auxiliary source of strength is clear, we may say that the response is "revealing" in the Freudian sense. Thus, after a narrow escape from a serious accident, a motorist was astonished to see a sign reading *ONE MILE TO DEATH.* Upon closer inspection, it appeared that the sign actually read *ONE MILE TO BATH.* (Note that *B* "contains" an *E* or two *D*'s.) Rough geometrical arrangements are often relevant. Shortly after reading of the death of Bernard DeVoto, an acquaintance was startled to see the name *DeVoto* in raised chromium letters on a passing automobile. Closer inspection revealed *De Soto* with a large intruding *V:*

A general geometrical reshuffling of the fragments of a textual stimulus plus a strong intraverbal contribution of strength was illustrated when the words *A Strange Idyll* were "read" as *The Strange Case of Dr. Jekyll and Mr. Hyde* shortly after the book by Stevenson had been read. More trivial variables are apparently responsible for the rearrangement in reading the roadside sign *Sahara Coal* as *Scarlet O'Hara,* or *Butternut Coffee* as *Peanut Butter Coffee.*

Erroneous recall of a poem is the intraverbal parallel of mishearing and misreading. The fusion of poorly recalled material with responses to current variables, under multiple causation, creates novel forms. Sometimes the collateral variables supplying fragments are obvious. In the erroneous *Feed pepper to your little boy and beat him when he sneezes, Feed pepper* has displaced *Speak roughly* because of other parts of the original passage, and possibly because of the presence of *sneezes.* (Compare the example of *Run, run, run* in Chapter 9.)

Perhaps the best-known type of distortion is the tongue twister, a phrase or sentence—for example, *rubber buggy bumpers*—which can be spoken correctly only slowly or with great effort. The actual stimulus may be echoic (when one is asked to repeat such a phrase), textual (when one is asked to read it), or intraverbal (when one has memorized it). The original form of stimulation is unimportant because the multiple sources which lead to distortion arise from the behavior itself as a self-echoic supplement.

The momentary self-echoic tendency in the tongue twister is responsible for other distortions. A young girl, spending the summer in the country, explained to a new friend: *I have a prettier doll which I left in the citier.* The same child also once referred to her *pocketbooket.* The president of a temperance organization once started to explain a new program with the words: *Our old slogan was "The saloon must go"; our new saloogan is . . . . .*

Among the multiple sources of strength which produce distortion are certain "negative" variables—that is, variables which operate to suppress parts of a response and therefore to encourage the appearance of other fragments. The effect of punishment in encouraging recombinations of fragments involves the process of editing to be discussed in Chapter 15, but the material which presents itself for editing is relevant here. In the response *I knew that person peopally* punishment for repetition has suppressed a second instance of *person* (*I knew that person personally*) and given rise to the characteristic substitute *people.* Similar processes of editing may account for the distorted response *pawl pearing,* written in describing a piece of apparatus containing a pawl bearing. The distortion could be a simple example of self-echoic strengthening, but there are several ways in which the response *ball bearing,* current under the circumstances, could have affected the result. There are dialects of English, particularly among people who have originally spoken German, in which *b*'s go unvoiced. *Pall pearing* is a German-American form of *ball bearing.* In learning to imitate the dialect, one learns to substitute an unvoiced *p* for a voiced *b* in every case. The editing necessary to avoid calling a pawl bearing a ball bearing may have continued in force to produce the second change from *b* to *p*. Perseverative distortion (for example, writing *slame* for *same* just after having written *slander* and *slain*) is possibly nothing more than the effect of the self-echoic or self-transcriptive tendencies responsible for alliteration, but the possibility should not be overlooked that they also show a process of editorial substitution.

THE RESULTS OF RECOMBINATION

Recombined fragments of responses are usually nonsense. A wholly new and ineffective form of response emerges or, if the speaker sees it is nonsense in time, is caught before it is completed. What may appear to be stammering or stuttering is sometimes the beginning of a fragment in recombination. In answer to the question *What time is it?,* a man looked at a clock face showing the hands at 5:16, began to reply *Fif-,* and then corrected himself to *Five-sixteen.* It is possible that the edited response *fifteen* was a blend of *five* and *sixteen,* perhaps supported by a loosely controlled response to the position of the minute hand, but nevertheless unusable at the moment. Similarly, a nonsensical response has been edited when *riduc-* is broken off and corrected to *ridiculous.*

Sometimes the result is a standard form of response which is nevertheless inappropriate. Thus, fragments of *heresy* and *sacrilege* may compose *heritage,* which is not only nonsense under the circumstances but possibly misleading. Other examples are *table* from *telegraph cable* and *became* from *because I came.* It is quite possible that the standard form contributes to the recombination, acting in this respect as a third source of strength. The distorted form contains intraverbal sequences which have been established earlier by miscellaneous reinforcements.

Occasionally fragments may recombine to produce a standard form attributable to a current variable. A young lady being taken to dinner by an eligible young man looked at the menu and exclaimed *I am simply ravished!* We may be content to regard this as a normal blend of *famished* and *ravenous,* but it is difficult not to consider the possibility that *ravished,* possibly even *simply ravished,* had some current strength. There was little doubt of the collateral variable responsible for a phrase blend reported by Brill.[5] A guest who was somewhat of-

[5] Brill's translation of Freud, S., *Psychopathology of Everyday Life* (Pelican Books, 1938).

fended by the frugal repast to which he had been invited began to discuss a political figure. *However,* he concluded, *he always gives you a square meal,* which was hastily corrected to a *square deal.*

Occasionally a response, though seen to be a neologism by both speaker and listener, is permitted to stand and may be effective. This is especially true of blends of phrases. In a heated argument, such a phrase as *This is a cold-boiled violation of human rights* may be allowed to stand, although *cold-boiled* appears to be a recombination of fragments of *hard-boiled* and *cold-blooded.* (Note that *cold-boiled* is also a standard expression, as in referring to meats.)

The blend attracts most attention when it supplies a new response. Only fairly late in the history of Western civilization has a combination of fog and smoke become common enough to generate the response *smog,* but the standard response is now useful, and the word passes into the language. The response may no longer represent the recombination of fragments, though it probably gains strength from its formal similarity to *smoke* and *fog.*

The normal accompaniments of the fragmentary responses entering into a recombination are usually not emitted. Sometimes, however, they turn up. When the textual stimulus *a distinguished path in psychology* is read as *a distinguished man in pathology,* we have to note not only the displacement of *path* by *man* in a possible blending of *a distinguished path* and *a distinguished man* but the combination of that fragment with the *ology* of *psychology* to produce *pathology.* Examples in which all fragments find their place in new combinations are familiar to everyone. A child of six spoke of *a thown of crorns,* a lecturer on economics had difficulty in avoiding the phrase *ways rages,* a radio announcer recommended a way of baking *muttered buffins,* a toastmaster presented *Hoobert Herver* as a guest speaker, a professor once quoted from the *Omayat of Rhubar Kyam,* and a lecturer on astronomy asserted that a given effect *upon the orth's erbit would main a reminor problem.*

When these so-called "metatheses" produce effective though irrelevant patterns, they are commonly associated with the name of the Reverend W. A. Spooner, once Warden of New College in Oxford University, who was famous for his talent in producing recombinations of standard forms. Though he is credited with meaningless but amusing examples (*many thinkle peep so, I believe*), he is better known for the examples in which the recombined fragments compose standard forms (*the queer old Dean, a glutton dropped from above,* and a journey to London *on the town drain*).

WITTY AND STYLISTIC EFFECTS

The pun which is distorted in form may be easily traced to multiple sources of strength. Being more probably nonsensical, it usually appears only when editing is weak (Chapter 16), and it demands possibly greater skill in managing the problems of sentence construction (Chapter 14). We are concerned here only with the production of the material out of which the joke is made. When a sailboat which has cost more than the owner can afford is named *Spinthrift,* we recognize a personal conflict in the two relevant sources: *spendthrift* and *spindrift.* Nor are we at a loss to account for the conclusion of a letter addressed to a mistress who has rejected the writer:

> ....for I am, with the greatest ad-whoration, most deivine creature, Iour most passionate admirer, adwhorer and slave, Jonathan Wilde.[6]

A witty blend of phrase, *As Maine goes, so goes Vermont,* was claimed by several writers after the 1936 presidential election, when only two states, Maine and Vermont, voted for the Republican candidate. The circumstances were optimal, since the phrase *As Maine goes, so goes the nation* was a familiar aphorism appropriate to a national election, and various current tacts and intraverbals contained *Maine and Vermont.*

When a humorous distortion acquires currency in a verbal community, it need no longer represent the present process. At one time it was fashionable for young people to use distortions of geographical names in lieu of conventional expressions. In taking leave of someone the speaker might say *Abyssinia,* in lieu of *I'll be seeing you.* Although such a response may continue to have some of its original effect upon the listener and may represent a special state of editing on the part of the speaker, each instance does not show the process of fusion. (It is a "bad" joke because of the irrelevance of the geographical response, although there is a spurious relevance if the practice is fashionable.)

An original example of a phrase blend in which very little time was consumed in arriving at the witty response depends upon intraverbal borrowing from Keats' sonnet which ends

6 *History of the Late Mr. J. Wilde the Great,* Book III, Chapter 6.

Or like stout Cortez, when with eagle eyes
He star'd at the Pacific—and all his men
Look'd at each other with a wild surmise—
Silent, upon a peak in Darien.

A young man was once describing to an eminent logician an episode which had occurred during a walk along a section of the Maine coast. He had emerged from a group of trees to find himself standing upon a large boulder at the top of a bank, with the surf striking the rocky shore below him. *There I stood,* he said *looking out over the sea, silent on a peak in Darien. Suddenly I felt the boulder under me begin to move* .... The logician immediately exclaimed: *Imagine your wild surprise!* The fusion of the intraverbal *wild surmise* and the conventional tact *Imagine your surprise!* must have occurred within a matter of one or two seconds.

We have seen that far-fetched rhymes, especially those involving several syllables, have some of the humorous effect of the far-fetched metaphor evoked in multiple causation. When the formal sources of strength produce an outright distortion, there is no doubt of the underlying process. In a type of light verse popularized by Ogden Nash, the poet appears to be submerged by multiple sources of the sort responsible for normal rhyme.

If called by a panther
Don't anther.

Poetry written before the standardization of English spelling often appears to us now to suffer from the Ogden Nash effect. In the couplet

For gain, not glory, wing'd his roving flight,
And grew immortal in his own despight

despight appears to the modern reader to be misspelled through an overpowering self-transcriptive tendency to match the earlier form.

Giving in to the forces of distortion is characteristic of a kind of "zany" humor. S. J. Perelman has supplied many examples: *The hickory I've been lickory for, I mean the hickory I've been looking for.* It is also an ingredient of television humor: the question *Do you enjoy Debussy?* evokes the response *De-who-ssy?*

The multiple sources of the behavior of the serious writer produce distorted forms, as some of the examples of blends or recombinations of fragments already given suggest. Some of the examples analyzed by Empson [7] involve distortion, although changes in pronunciation or spelling, or both, may conceal this fact. Thus, in analyzing the line

> In the dead vast and middle of the night

Empson argues that *vast* may be multiply determined by sources which severally would have evoked *vast, waste,* and *waist.* Some of the responses which Coleridge borrowed in composing the *Ancient Mariner* [7] entered into the blending of phrases. The borrowed material might be merely the rhythm or cadence of a passage, plus a few key terms, or a grammatical frame upon which other current responses were arranged.

It is sometimes plausible to argue that a grammatical frame has been preserved from earlier intraverbal material even though all important forms have been replaced. The unusual strength needed to hold such a frame together may be available in thoroughly memorized material. Thus, grammatical paradigms sometimes provide a sort of figured bass against which new themes are played, as in the poem read at the trial of the Knave of Hearts in *Alice in Wonderland.* Both Gertrude Stein and James Joyce used grammatical paradigms in the same way.

A more obvious literary borrowing with distortion is the paraphrase or parody. Whether a parody is amusing depends upon the extent of the contribution of the passage parodied and upon whether the resulting recombination of fragments is amusing for other reasons. The use of intraverbal connections from earlier literary works has been raised to the position of a philosophy of composition, particularly by Ezra Pound and T. S. Eliot. Eliot's lines:

> But at my back from time to time I hear
> The sound of horns and motors, which shall bring
> Sweeney to Mrs. Porter in the spring...

contain responses determined by other parts of the poem and by the circumstances under which it was written, but also fragments from two other poems—Andrew Marvell's

> But at my back I always hear
> Time's wingèd chariot hurrying near...

and Day's *Parliament of Bees,*

> A noise of horns and hunting, which shall bring
> Actaeon to Diana in the spring.

[7] See Chapter 9.

Another kind of blend involving intraverbal sequences acquired from literary works is imitative writing. Robert Louis Stevenson advocated the deliberate use of borrowed verbal material in learning to write. By playing "the sedulous ape" the young writer ekes out his own meagre repertoire with patterns of response characteristic of an established author. Intraverbal aping may serve as a probe in raising fragmentary behavior above the strength required for emission. A further, possibly permanent, strengthening may follow from self-reinforcement (Chapter 6). Apart from the question of its mode of operation, the practice represents a blend of fragmentary responses from two sources—the literary source of the intraverbal frames or sequences and the variables controlling possibly original verbal behavior in the writer.

Finnegans Wake, by James Joyce, is and may well remain the classic example of the recombination of borrowed verbal fragments, including extended intraverbal frames. In

> *Hadn't he seven dams to wive him, and every dam had her seven crutches, and every crutch had its seven hues, and each hue had a differing cry,*

several local themes and standard intraverbal sequences are combined with the intraverbal frame of the nursery rhyme *As I was going to St. Ives.*

In another well-known passage, through a remarkable series of puns and blends, Joyce tells two stories at the same time—one of Nuvoletta, a little girl who climbs over the bannisters and falls, and another of a drop of rain precipitated from a cloud and falling into a river. Some of the responses which tell both stories at once are as follows:

> *Then Nuvoletta reflected for the last time...*

(Nuvoletta *thought* and the cloud *shone*)

> *...she made up all her myriads of drifting minds in one, she cancelled all her engauzements.*

(Nuvoletta reduced all her plans to one; the drifting, gauzy particles of the cloud collected in a single drop)

> *She climbed over the bannistars*

(*-sters* for the child, *stars* for the cloud)

...A light dress fluttered. She was gone.

(*Night dress* for the child, *light dress* for the cloud)

> *And into the river that had been a stream... there fell a tear... a leaptear...*

(strength borrowed from the traditional *leap year,* which may have a possible connection with desperation, with *leap* picking up the earlier theme of jumping)

> *But the river tripped on her by and by, lapping as though her heart was brook.*

(This has extraordinarily complex sources, a few of which may be noted. *Lapping* and *brook* are thematically connected with *river. As though her heart was brook* is a distortion of *as though her heart was broken.* An inferred intraverbal *crying* appears to be displaced by *lapping* as a distortion of *laughing.* A river which laughs is acting as if it had the heart of a child—that is to say, of a child river or *brook.* The hysterical mixture of laughing and crying, of being both old and young, is appropriate to the whole passage.)

FORMAL DISTORTION AND THE UNIT OPERANT

Separable fragmentary verbal operants are implied by the minimal repertoires of echoic and textual behavior, and fragments of tacts and intraverbal behavior may be under separate functional control, even though these do not always show comparable minimal units. A large intraverbal or tact may be reinforced as a whole, for example, when it is composed of separable parts which are also independently reinforced. The additional facts of multiple causation presented in Chapter 9, the *modus operandi* of the practical devices of Chapter 10, and the functional autonomy of the fragmentary responses entering into the recombinations of the present chapter extend the evidence for these minimal units of verbal behavior.

Samuel Butler emphasized the multiple causation of his own verbal behavior in the preface to the second edition of *Erewhon:*

> It may be said that I must have misquoted from design, from ignorance, or by a slip of the pen; but surely in these days it will be recognized as harsh to assign limits to the all-embracing boundlessness of truth, and it will be more reasonably assumed that each of the three possible causes of misquotation must have had its share in the apparent blunder.

Part IV
THE MANIPULATION OF VERBAL BEHAVIOR

Chapter 12

The Autoclitic

THE PRECEDING CHAPTERS have presented verbal behavior as a repertoire of responses, some of them minimal in size, others complex but susceptible to fracturing, existing in various states of strengths under the control of variables in the environment and history of the speaker. The speaker himself may seem to have been left out of account. We have not had to assume that there is anyone who "knows what he is saying" or "wants to say," or "how to say it."

Converting the speaker into an interested bystander is certainly the direction in which an analysis of behavior will first move. As a causal agent responsible for the structure and character of verbal behavior, the speaker is threatened by the causal relations identified in the course of a scientific analysis. Whenever we demonstrate that a variable exerts functional control over a response, we reduce the supposed contribution of any inner agent. For example, if we can show that the occurrence of a response is due to the presence of a stimulus of specified properties, then it is not necessary to say that a speaker uses the response to describe the stimulus. If we can show that a response is stronger when we deprive the individual of food, then we do not need to say that a speaker uses the response to describe or disclose his need. If metaphorical extension can be shown to take place because a particular stimulus property has acquired control of a response, we do not need to say that a speaker has invented a figure of speech to express a perceived similarity between two stimuli. If an audience can be shown to strengthen a particular subdivision of a verbal repertoire, we do not need to say that a speaker chooses words appropriate to his audience. Even if we regard each of these pairs of statements as interchangeable translations, in which all terms are assumed to be definable by reference to behavior, the place of the speaker is obviously greatly reduced or obscured in the first of each pair.

But we have not got rid of the speaker entirely. There are verbal responses still to be accounted for—responses such as *if, that, as, therefore,* and *some*—many of which strongly suggest the behavior of a directing, organizing, evaluating, selecting, and producing system. These are the terms, so troublesome in working out semantic correspondences, which are commonly explained by reference to the speaker's "intention," his "propositional attitudes," and so on. We have not yet demonstrated any superiority in dealing with them.

The aspect of verbal behavior called "assertion" also remains to be considered. The verbal operant is a lively unit, in contrast with the sign or symbol of the logician or the word or sentence of the linguist, but it does not fully account for the active nature of verbal behavior. We may show that a chair as a stimulus increases the probability of, and perhaps evokes, the response *chair,* but we cannot for this reason say that the response "asserts the existence of the chair." The mere emission of a response, no matter how dynamic, will not serve as a substitute for assertion and will not account for responses such as *is* or the final *s* of many verbs.

We have also not yet discussed the order to be observed in large samples of verbal behavior, or other evidence of what might be called "deliberate composition." Some order among verbal responses may arise from their relative strengths, from intraverbal linkages, and from certain corresponding orders in the environment and history of the speaker, but the larger design evident in most verbal behavior cannot be explained in this way.

The verbal operants we have examined may be said to be the raw material out of which sustained verbal behavior is manufactured. But who is the manufacturer? We cannot satisfactorily answer this question by pointing to a special subdivision of the speaker as a controlling self or personality, because no ultimate explanation would thus be achieved. We should still have to explain the behavior of such a "speaker," and our problem would only be made more difficult because *that* speaker is inaccessible. Order, design, and "deliberate" composition are observable features of verbal behavior which can most effectively be studied with the instruments of analysis already in our possession. What are the actual data and what can be done about them?

The important properties of verbal behavior which remain to be studied concern special arrangements of responses.[1] Part of the behavior of an organism becomes in turn one of the variables controlling another part. There are at least two systems of responses, one based upon the other. The upper level can only be understood in terms of its relations to the lower. The notion of an inner self is an effort to represent the fact that when behavior is compounded in this way, the upper system seems to guide or alter the lower. But the controlling system is itself also behavior. The speaker may "know what he is saying" in the sense in which he "knows" any part or feature of the environment. Some of his behavior (the "known") serves as a variable in control of other parts ("knowing"). Such "propositional attitudes" as assertion, negation, and quantification, the design achieved through reviewing and rejecting or emitting responses, the generation of quantities of verbal behavior merely as such, and the highly complex manipulations of verbal thinking can all, as we shall see, be analyzed in terms of behavior which is evoked by or acts upon other behavior of the speaker.

The speaker is the organism which engages in or executes verbal behavior. He is also a locus—a place in which a number of variables come together in a unique confluence to yield an equally unique achievement.

DESCRIPTIVE AUTOCLITICS

The speaker may acquire verbal behavior descriptive of his own behavior. Although the community can establish such a repertoire only by basing its reinforcing contingencies upon observable behavior, the speaker eventually exhibits it under the control of private events. The behavior so described may be verbal: the speaker may talk about himself talking. He may describe the responses he has made, is making, or will make. For example, he may say *I said "Heads"* or *I am now saying "Heads"* or *I will say "Heads."* He may also describe the state of strength of such a response, as well as its controlling relations. In doing so, he may use any of the vocabularies designed for the description of verbal behavior, including that in

[1] Chapter 18 in *Science and Human Behavior* is relevant to this discussion.

which the present book is written. The events available to him as stimuli consist of the products of his own behavior as speaker. He may hear himself or react to private stimuli associated with vocal behavior, possibly of a covert or even incipient form. In a more obvious case, he may read what he has written. Self-stimulation has already been appealed to in discussing self-echoic, self-textual, and self-intraverbal behavior, as well as certain effects of the speaker acting as his own listener and audience. Such stimulation may also assume control of the verbal operant called the tact.

The contingencies necessary for self-descriptive behavior are arranged by the community when it has reason to ask "What did you say?," "Did you say that?," "Why did you say that?," and so on, for the answers are useful in many ways. It is unlikely that such behavior would arise in the absence of explicit reinforcement; indeed, it remains uncommon even though strongly encouraged by the community. As Russell [2] points out,

> When you see a black object and say "this is black," you are not as a rule noticing that you say these words: you know the thing is black, but you do not know that you say it is.

Although it is possible that such "knowing" may be nonverbal, the contingencies which generate a response to one's own verbal responses are unlikely in the absence of social reinforcement. It is because our behavior is important to others that it eventually becomes important to us, as we have seen.

The possibility that we may tact our own verbal behavior, including its functional relationships, calls for no special treatment. We may study and describe what we said or wrote yesterday just as we study and describe what someone else said or wrote at some other time. True, we are at a special point of vantage in describing our current or potential behavior, but we can also describe the current or potential behavior of anyone about whom we have similar information. The kind of self-descriptive behavior which needs further study arises from a special effect on the listener. The ultimate explanation of any kind of verbal behavior depends upon the action which the listener takes with respect to it. Effective action requires a verbal stimulus which is "intelligible" in the sense of loud and clear and which stands in a reasonably stable relation to the conditions under which it is emitted. When we ask "Did you see it, or did

[2] Russell, Bertrand, *An Inquiry into Meaning and Truth* (New York, 1940), p. 72.

someone tell you?", we are asking for more information about controlling relations. We are essentially asking, "Was your response a tact or an echoic or intraverbal response to the verbal behavior of someone else?" Because controlling relations are so important, well-developed verbal environments encourage the speaker to emit collateral responses describing them. These responses are in a sense similar to other tacts descriptive of the speaker's behavior (at the moment or at some other time) or even of the verbal behavior of someone else, but the immediate effect upon the listener in modifying his reaction to the behavior they accompany establishes a distinctive pattern. We shall refer to such responses, when associated with other verbal behavior effective upon the same listener at the same time, as "descriptive autoclitics." The term "autoclitic" is intended to suggest behavior which is based upon or depends upon other verbal behavior.

One type of descriptive autoclitic informs the listener of the kind of verbal operant it accompanies. If the speaker is reading a newspaper and remarks *I see it is going to rain,* the *I see* informs the listener that *it is going to rain* is emitted as a textual response. Behavior which is acquired as textual or echoic behavior, but retained and emitted as intraverbal, is often prefaced by *I see* or *I hear* or, without indicating the original source, *I recall* or *I am reminded.* A mand is more clearly effective as such if prefaced with *I demand* or *I ask you,* and various sorts of tacts are prefaced with *I tell you, I'm telling you, I declare* (*a state of war*), *I observe* (*that he is absent today*), *I call it* (*a shame*), and *I pronounce* (*you man and wife*). *I remember* indicates a tact (or intraverbal response) made to a stimulus no longer present. *I recall* is more likely to indicate the action of a former *verbal* stimulus. In each case, the autoclitic which describes the speaker's behavior could be omitted, but the response would be less effective on the listener.

Another group of autoclitics describe the state of strength of a response. *I guess, I estimate, I believe, I imagine,* and *I surmise* all indicate that the response which follows is based upon insufficient stimulation or has been poorly conditioned. *I can't say, I hesitate to say,* and *I am tempted to add* suggest other sources of weakness. *I submit, I suggest,* and *I suppose* acknowledge the tentative nature of the response which follows. A controversial autoclitic of weakness, to which we shall return in Chapter 19, is *I think.* The strength of the response which follows, and hence indirectly the adequacy of the variables responsible for it, is suggested by the autoclitics *I know, I assure you, I insist, I swear, I promise,* and *I will say*. All these autoclitics of strength could be omitted without changing the *nature* of the effect upon the listener, but they make that effect more precise by permitting the listener to modify appropriate action accordingly.

Another group of autoclitics describe relations between a response and other verbal behavior of the speaker or listener, or other circumstances under which behavior is emitted. Important examples are *I agree, I confess, I expect, I concede, I infer, I predict, I dare say, I must say, I can say, I admit, I reply, I should say,* and *I mean to say*. All of these permit the listener to relate the response which follows to other aspects of the current situation, and hence to react to it more efficiently and successfully. Another controversial autoclitic is *I wish*. When the response which follows specifies the behavior of the listener (*I wish you would tell me what you want*), it has the effect of a softened mand equivalent to *Would you tell me what you want?* or *I am inclined to ask you what you want*. When the response which follows describes merely a condition (*I wish it were spring again),* the autoclitic suggests an extended or magical mand similar to *O to be in England now that April's there*.

Another group of descriptive autoclitics indicate the emotional or motivational condition of the speaker but affect the listener not so much in modifying his reaction to the accompanying response as in emphasizing his personal relation to the speaker. Examples are *I am happy to say, I regret to inform you, I hate to say,* and *I must tell you* (*that I don't agree with you*).

So important is it to the listener to have some indication of the sources of the behavior of the speaker that in many communities it is simply good manners to begin speaking with an autoclitic of one of these types. Sometimes the character of the speaker's behavior is obvious, and no autoclitics are needed; but in "striking up" a conversation under what one might call neutral circumstances, a descriptive autoclitic is almost required: *They say, I am reminded,* or *I heard the other day* (*about a new scheme . . .*).

Almost all these examples contain words referring to verbal behavior, such as *say, repeat, admit,* and so on. They are all applicable to the behavior of other speakers and to the behavior of the speaker himself when they do not serve an autoclitic function. For example, they may all describe past behavior of the speaker, or the behavior of the speaker with respect to other listeners. In *I hesitated to say that you might fail the examination* the response *hesitated to say* does not clarify or modify the listener's reaction to the original instance of *You may fail the examination.* This could even be true in the present tense. *I am quite ready to say that you will pass the first examination but I hesitate to say that you will pass the second (and this will give you some idea of my uncertain state of mind*) may not show the autoclitic effect of the normal *I hesitate to say* since it is merely a report of a state of affairs relatively unaffected by the possible reaction of the listener.

Negative autoclitics qualify or cancel the response which they accompany but imply that the response is strong for some reason—for example, that it has been made by someone else. Even the simple negative autoclitic in *I don't think he has gone* is more than *I think he has not gone,* since it is characteristic of circumstances in which someone may have said *He has gone.* Some autoclitics suggest that the accompanying response is not strong but merely exaggerated—for example, *I would not go so far as to say . . ., I wouldn't call (him actually foolhardy), I don't say (it's serious).* The reference to other sources of the response is more explicit in *I don't recall* and *I won't admit.*

Autoclitics which indicate that the speaker is not emitting the accompanying response on his own include *I doubt* and *I deny.* The negative forms of these (*I don't doubt, I cannot deny*) therefore indicate that the accompanying response is asserted by the speaker in spite of being placed in doubt by other circumstances.

Negative autoclitics sometimes function in connection with the process of editing to *permit* the speaker to make a response although under present circumstances it may be at least mildly punished. Thus *I don't suppose you have a match* is a concealed form of *May I have a match?* which is itself a rather softened form of the mand *Match, please! I need not tell you . . .* defers to the strength of the listener's behavior and avoids the punishment contingent upon being too obvious. A similar device is to describe one's behavior purportedly with respect to another listener: *I sometimes say to myself* or *I sometimes say to my wife,* but where the effect is not to apprise the listener of one's verbal habits but to let him hear the response which follows. In some degree all these devices are equivalent to the autoclitic *I should like to ask, I should like to mention,* or *I should like to say.*

Although most autoclitics are normally followed by sentences, they may be followed by pronominal forms standing in lieu of sentences (such as *that* in *I deny that,* or *so* in *I think so*) or single responses the position of which in more extended speech is clear (*I say Yes, I vote No*).

Autoclitics which do not describe the type, strength, or manner of a response but merely indicate that the response is being emitted may serve several functions. The almost idiomatic *I say,* as in *I say, old chap,* is scarcely more than a mand for the listener's attention, comparable to *See here* or *Look here, old chap.* It is an announcement that the speaker is preparing to speak. Sometimes it is a gesture of deference and essentially points out that what is being said is being said only by the speaker. In this case the pronoun *I* is often omitted: *To my way of thinking, In my opinion.* On the other hand, an autoclitic may indicate that what is said is not merely the speaker's contribution but is already agreed to by the listener or by people in general (*They say, One might suggest, You might say, You will agree, So to speak, It may be said, It is true that, As my wife always says*). Negative forms are *I hope you won't think* and *You don't mean to say.* Deference to the listener is indicated in *Let me just say, Let me ask, If I may suggest, It might seem to you, Without wishing to contradict, Though you are undoubtedly right, still . . . .* Anticipation of the verbal behavior of the listener is indicated in *You may well object, You may imagine, One might reply, We might say, You will be inclined to answer, I can hear you saying.*

Some autoclitics indicate to the listener that what is to be said should have the same effect as what has just been said (*that is to say, in other words, I mean . . .*). Another common autoclitic indicates that what is to follow stands in a subordinate relation to what has been said (*for example, for instance*).

As in some of these examples, the speaker may not be specifically mentioned. Adverbs or adjectives which "modify" the response they accompany and are clearly autoclitic in function are *happily, seriously, fortunately,* and *needless to say. So to speak* indicates that the accompanying expression is unusual or perhaps not to be taken literally, while *to coin a phrase* indicates that the accompanying response is either a neologism or, ironically, very well known. An intraverbal source is indicated by beginning *Speaking of the transportation of vegetables,* and a restricted audience by *Between you and me.* The autoclitic function may also be carried by an arch look or a tone of voice. A certain type of nervous laugh has an autoclitic function, equivalent to *I say, but I hope you won't think I mean . . . .*

A distinction is sometimes made between a language which talks about things and a language which talks about language. This is essentially the force of Carnap's distinction between object language and metalanguage.[3] This is not, however, the distinction carried by the term autoclitic. Once verbal behavior has occurred and become one of the objects of the physical world, it can be described like any other object. We have no reason to distinguish the special vocabulary or syntax with which this is done. The forms of response used in autoclitic expressions are also used in the description of verbal behavior as an object, and this makes the autoclitic distinction difficult. Nevertheless, it is an extremely important distinction, as we shall see in what follows. Orthographically, we cancel the autoclitic function with quotation marks. *I say he's right* contains an autoclitic. *He's right* might stand alone and be effective, but the accompanying *I say* specifies a special current effect upon the listener. *I say "He's right"* shifts the emphasis to *I say;* the speaker is telling the listener something about his current verbal behavior, but he may have no interest in whether the listener reacts to the state of affairs described by *He's right.*

The *I say* in the indirect quotation *I say that he's right* is also not strictly an autoclitic, though it may occur as one. A convenient test is to ask whether the response could occur in the same way in a statement describing, for example, past verbal behavior. *I said "He's right"* is identical in every way with *I say "He's right"* except for the time at which the remark *He's right* occurred. The indirect quotation *I said that he was right,* with the change in the tense of both verbs, reveals the nonautoclitic function of the case in the present tense. This may be splitting a hair, but a single example will show how necessary it sometimes is to do so. The response *It is true that I was absent* contains an autoclitic (*It is true*) which modifies the effect of the accompanying *I was absent* by indicating that it is emitted in spite of variables which tend to suppress it. In this sense, it is fairly close to *I admit.* But *true* occurs under other, and very important, circumstances. Since it refers to verbal behavior, it cannot be in the primary or object language, as Tarski first showed. In Carnap's terms, it is in the metalanguage. But the metalanguage is not necessarily autoclitic, though it shares the same terms and may contain responses having an autoclitic function. The sentence *My remark "I was absent" is true* is different from *It is true that I was absent.* The former

[3] Carnap, Rudolph, *Logical Syntax of Language* (New York, 1934).

is designed to achieve an effect upon the listener related to the truth of a sentence, whereas the latter is designed to achieve an effect upon the listener related to the absence of the speaker. The distinction is clearer under less controversial circumstances. The sentence *I admit that I was absent* is autoclitic, but the sentence *"I was absent" is an admission* is not only not an autoclitic but more obviously serves a different function. Similarly, the sentence *I hesitate to say he is a liar* has an autoclitic function in modifying the effect on the listener of the response *he is a liar,* whereas *"He is a liar" is said with hesitation* has an effect upon the listener concerning the behavior of the speaker. (As we shall see in a moment, the distinction which Bertrand Russell makes between a primary and secondary language is closer to the distinction between nonautoclitic and autoclitic behavior than Carnap's distinction between object language and metalanguage.)

Logicians have been interested in languages which describe language partly in order to solve certain paradoxes. Consider the heterological paradox, for example. Some words appear to describe themselves. Thus *short* is a short word and *English* is English. Call such words homological. *French* is not a French word and *infinitesimal* is not a very small word. Call such words heterological. Then *homological* is itself homological, but what about *heterological*? If *heterological* is heterological, then it does not describe itself and must be homological, but in that case it is heterological. This issue has nothing to do with autoclitic behavior. The difficulty arises from asserting that a word can describe itself. No word describes anything; at best, it is "used to describe something," but we have seen that even this expression has its difficulties. In an analysis of verbal behavior, we should have to proceed in something like the following way. Let us consider a small universe of printed words, such as *SHORT, INFINITESIMAL, ENGLISH,* and *FRENCH,* and assume a speaker possessing both textual responses and tacts. Then with respect to some of these verbal stimuli the textual responses and the tact both have the same form. One may read the marks *SHORT* by saying *short* and one can describe them by saying *short.* One may read the marks *FRENCH* by saying *French,* but one describes them by saying *English.*

This does not dispose of the heterological paradox, however. There are certain tacts related to verbal behavior which describe not form alone but relationships to controlling variables. For example, a word is "appropriate" not with respect to its form alone but in relation to a situation. While we can read the word *APPROPRIATE* by saying *appropriate,* we cannot call the word appropriate without knowing something else about it. *Homological* and *heterological* are words of this sort. The literate person can read both of these instances by saying *homological* and *heterological,* but he cannot describe them with these terms without knowing the circumstances under which they occur.

MANDS UPON THE LISTENER

The autoclitic function begins to emerge in a clearer light when a more specific action upon the listener is specified. The autoclitic begins to function specifically as a mand. The moderate *I announce* may under certain circumstances be replaced with the more ceremonial *Lo!* or *Behold!* The generalized mand *O!* may be regarded as intensifying the mand function of what follows. A strong tact may be preceded under certain circumstances by *Know, then. . . .* The idiomatic *I say* is, as we have already pointed out, similar to *Listen* or *See here,* which have the form of mands. So have *Take it from me, Note that, Take* (*for example*), and *Think of it this way*. Punctuation is an autoclitic device and is sometimes used in vocal discourse for a clearly autoclitic function. The response *Quote, unquote* inserted near a word which is perhaps also pronounced with a special intonation clearly modifies the listener's reaction, and a sentence ending with *Period!* could as well have ended with the autoclitic *That is all I have to say; make what you will of it.*

Some mands enjoin the listener to construct additional verbal behavior and to react to it as if it had been emitted by the speaker. The whimsical use of *Ditto* in lieu of a repeated phrase is an example. The tag *. . . and vice versa* enjoins the listener to construct a sentence in which the principal terms are reversed and to react to it as if the speaker had emitted it also.

A special class of responses which do not directly specify the behavior of the listener but have a similar function in starting, stopping, or deflecting his reactions are often difficult to paraphrase and are almost impossible to translate from one language to another. They are also likely to be used by different speakers in different amounts and possibly with slightly different effects. Examples are *Then, too; Now, then; So!; Oh, well; Why . . .* (as in *Why, you ras-*

cal!); *No! You don't say!;* and the terminal *So there you are!,* which has the effect of *Now react to that, please.*

A more businesslike type of mands upon the listener specifies certain behavior involved in verbal thinking (Chapter 19): *Assume . . . , Let X equal . . . , Consider the equation . . . ,* and so on.

QUALIFYING AUTOCLITICS

The descriptive autoclitic indicates something of the circumstances in which a response is emitted or something of the condition of the speaker, including the strength of his verbal behavior. Somewhat more explicit mands upon the listener are concerned with the practical problem of making a response effective upon him although they do not alter the nature of his reaction. He may react more positively or more hesitantly, but the action he takes is unchanged because the autoclitics do not qualify the relation between the accompanying response and a given state of affairs. A very important group of responses, which have been the subject of extensive logical and linguistic analysis, serve this autoclitic function of qualifying the tact in such a way that the intensity or direction of the listener's behavior is modified.

Negation

Possibly the example most often discussed is *no.* What is the referent of this response (or of its related forms *not, never,* and *nothing*)? In a logical or linguistic analysis, we may perhaps say that the referent of *no rain* is the absence of rain, but this is clearly impossible in a causal description. If the absence of rain evokes this response, why do we not emit a tremendous flood of responses under the control of the absences of thousands of other things? The traditional solution, which seems to apply here, is that there must be some reason for saying *It IS raining* whenever we say *It is NOT raining.* Russell thinks that the reason is always verbal. Someone asks *Is it raining?* and we reply *No, it is not raining.* "Thus," says Russell, "negative propositions will arise when you are stimulated by a word but not by what usually stimulates the word.[4] "

But the stimulus which controls a response to which *no* or *not* is added is often nonverbal. *Rain* may be a response to a similar stimulus—a few drops from a lawn sprinkler beyond a hedge, for example.

[4] Russell, *op. cit.,* p. 62.

The response *It is raining* then shows generic or metaphorical extension. Or a common accompaniment of rain—say, a threatening sky—may evoke the response as an example of metonymy. The extended nature of the tact is suggested by the commoner alternative response *It looks* (or *feels*) *LIKE rain* (see below). Other responses to which *no* or *not* is added may be intraverbal; some irrelevant contiguity of usage has strengthened a response which, if not qualified, would have an inappropriate effect upon the listener. In each instance a response in some strength is emitted, but it is emitted under circumstances in which it is not reinforced as a tact by the verbal community and may even be punished. This additional condition, acting upon the speaker, is the occasion for adding the autoclitic *no* or *not*.

The effect of *no* is clear when it is emitted as a mand specifying the cessation of nonverbal behavior on the part of the listener. We observe that someone is about to perform a dangerous act and cry *No!* A singer misses a high note by a full half-tone and we cry *No!* also. We say *No!* to children to halt various undesirable acts—for example, the handling of fragile objects. By a sort of magical extension, we also emit the mand when it is too late and the object has been shattered. The response is naturally extended to verbal acts. A child says *Two and two are five* and we say *No!* This does not stop the present instance, just as it does not save the fragile object, but it may prevent repetition and permit a correct response. (It may also function as punishment, as we have seen.) Under the same circumstances, we might expand the mand into the form *Don't say that!* As we shall see in Chapter 19 we sometimes mand our own behavior as listeners, as when we reach for a cigarette or piece of candy, say *No!*, and stop. We do the same thing with respect to our verbal behavior, as in the response: *It was during the administration of President Roosevelt—no, Truman* . . . where the *no* serves, as it were, to stop or cancel the response *Roosevelt* and clear the way for *Truman*.

The response is acquired from the reinforcing practices of the verbal community. The child first hears *No!* as the occasion upon which some current activity must be stopped if positive reinforcement is to be received or aversive stimulation avoided. When the child later engages in the same activity, he recreates an occasion upon which the response *No!* is strong. Upon such occasions he is especially likely to receive a generalized reinforcement for the verbal response. If, as the result of his own *No!*, the child ceases to behave in the specified way, he may be automatically reinforced by the reduction of conditioned aversive stimulation. A two-year-old girl had been taught not to touch objects by parents who, instead of saying *No!*, merely shook their heads. The child acquired the behavior of approaching a forbidden object, reaching, stopping, and shaking her head. The movement of the head was transferred to her own verbal behavior precisely as *No* is transferred.

Later the behavior of saying *No* is extended to verbal responses. If the child finds himself saying *Red* under circumstances in which the response is characteristically followed by the listener's *No!*, he himself says *No!* This may serve first as a correction following the actual emission of a response, but it may later accompany a response as a genuine autoclitic. Because of the standardizing practices of the verbal community, a response such as *Red—no* or *No—red* eventually assumes the form *Not red.* In the example just cited, the child would emit a response—say, *This is mine*—under inappropriate circumstances, and accompany it by a shake of the head. The combined response was equivalent to *This is not mine.* (The stimuli which continue to strengthen *Red* and which therefore continue to produce the qualified *Not red* are only those situations which are similar to red. Blue will not only not evoke *Red,* it will not evoke *Not red.* A strong reddish-orange may, however, do so. Additional verbal stimulation—for example, the echoic prompt *red*—may, of course, evoke the response *Not red* in the presence of a blue object.)

The response *no,* as an example of a qualifying autoclitic, has the force of a mand. It may be roughly translated *Don't act upon this response as an unextended tact.* The response becomes intimately associated with the response it qualifies, but its surviving independence is seen when it is used "absolutely" as in the examples given above. That it does not "refer to a property of a state of affairs, but rather to a response made to a state of affairs" may be shown by considering three examples: (*a*) *Jones is ill,* (*b*) *Jones is not well,* (*c*) *"Jones is well" is false.*[5] Although all three of these responses may be emitted with respect to the same state of affairs so far as Jones is concerned, they are not instances of the same response, and only one of them, (b), contains an autoclitic. They differ in their momentary effects upon the listener (and indirectly upon the speaker) and also in the collateral circumstances which generate them. In (a), *ill* refers to an observable property of a stimulus, just as *tall* or *standing on his head* would do;

[5] See a somewhat similar discussion by Quine, W. V., *Journal of Philosophy, 39* (1942), 68-71.

(b) may be evoked by the same state of affairs, but it implies that there is also a tendency to say *well*. A tendency to avoid *ill* may be enough. For example, the speaker has previously reassured the listener that Jones would not be ill, so that *Jones is ill* has special punishing consequences; or someone else may have said *Jones is well*. (The autoclitic *not* has slightly different functions in the two cases, serving in lieu of *I admit that I was wrong in saying that Jones would be well* in the first case and as *I deny that Jones is well* in the second. The response (c) is emitted when the speaker is discussing the response *Jones is well* as an objective thing. He himself may have said it, the listener may have said it, or it may be a common rumor. Nothing in the listener's behavior with respect to Jones or Jones' illness need be important to the speaker at the moment. A listener who had been acting upon the assumption that Jones was well might change his plans upon hearing the response *"Jones is well" is false,* and under very exceptional circumstances the speaker might emit such a response because of this effect upon the listener, but the circumstances under which the three responses are normally made permit a useful distinction.

Descriptive and qualifying autoclitics may be combined, and more than one instance of either may occur in a single response. The distinctions are usually of a practical nature. Thus, *It is true that he is not handsome* and *It is not true that he is handsome* are different responses made under different circumstances. We have no reason to analyze or paraphrase such material further.

Standard expressions including *not* and acquired as unitary responses may not indicate any autoclitic activity in a given instance. *He is not at all well* may function as a standard response under the control of a state of affairs which might also control *He is ailing*. It may still carry some suggestion of "an unwillingness to say *ill*," but this is not essential. If, in commenting upon a performance, one says *Not bad, not bad!* rather than *Good, good!* (the rhetorical practice called "litotes"), it may show some surviving tendency to say *bad,* but often probably does not. In addition to standard forms of response containing *not,* there are many intraverbal sequences which are responsible for responses in which an autoclitic function is very slight or lacking. Genuine negation is perhaps as rare as genuine metaphorical or metonymical extension. In particular, the affixes which serve an autoclitic function tend to become assimilated in standard forms. A sunless sky is a kind of sky, and the response *sunless* may be as simply determined as *cloudy*. The response must have originated under circumstances (which doubtless still recur) in which the response *sun* was emitted and to which the speaker then added the autoclitic *-less*. Eventually the response is controlled, not by the absence of sun, but by the presence of a gray sky.

Assertion

Just as *No!* may stop the listener, so *Yes!* encourages him to continue. *No!* serves as punishment, *Yes!* as positive reinforcement. As *No!* cancels a statement (*Vote for X? No!*), so *Yes!* emphasizes it (*Vote for X? Yes!*). Unfortunately *Yes* preserves its individuality by appearing only in "absolute" position. Its autoclitic function is served in larger samples of verbal behavior by fragmentary responses which are difficult to interpret because they also serve other functions. The kinship of *is* with *Yes* is apparent in the common coupling *Yes, it is.* Its function as a descriptive autoclitic is shown by comparing such examples as *I think it's Joe* and *It IS Joe.* The first response suggests weakness with the descriptive autoclitic *I think,* the second suggests strength with its emphasized *is.* The simple assertive function of *is* is usually clear when it occurs in such responses as *It is* or *There is* (*It is an ancient mariner* or *There is a man for you*).

But *is,* like the other autoclitics of assertion in English, serves other functions. For example, it is controlled in part by temporal characteristics of the stimulus (it indicates, as we say, the present tense). The two functions can be separated. The assertive force is common to *is* and *was,* but different temporal aspects of the stimulus control the two forms. If someone says *It was raining* and we reply *It IS raining,* our response is equivalent to *It is raining NOW.* We emphasize the *is* to describe a temporal aspect. But when someone says *It isn't raining* and we reply *It IS raining,* we emphasize it as we might add the colloquial *so* (*It is SO raining*) to bring out the autoclitic function. Both *so* and a strong *is* have the effect of *certainly* (*Certainly it's raining!*), *of course* (*Of course it's raining!*), and other descriptive autoclitics already mentioned.

Although the response *is* is a function of other variables, some of which we have yet to discuss, the autoclitic component acts upon the listener to strengthen his reaction to the response which it accompanies. The assertive autoclitic enjoins the listener to accept a given state of affairs. It must therefore, like *no,* be classified as a special sort of mand. Any collateral condition which is likely to weaken the listener's response (for example, a denial by someone else or a doubtful set of circumstances) leads the speaker to intensify the assertive autoclitic. Children, less constrained by the intraverbal grammatical paradigms to be noted in Chapter 13, use *is* in its purely assertive function in such an antiphonal contradiction as (A): *He is so!* (B): *He is not!* (A): *He is!* (B): *Isn't!* (A) *Is!* . . . Such behavior may remain in strength even after the response which was asserted and denied has been forgotten.

It is sometimes said that the word is inanimate but that language comes to life in the sentence. Words by themselves say nothing; it is the sentence which asserts. This is not the present distinction. The primary responses to which an assertive autoclitic is added are by no means inert. They are verbal operants resulting from a history of reinforcement and existing in given states of strength. Under suitable circumstances, responses occur without autoclitic qualification. This is recognized by Russell,[6] who states that in the object language, "every single word is an assertion," but this use of the term tends to confuse two functions. Russell argues that the assertion of the single word is different from the assertion of the secondary language because it has no antithesis, but this is a logical device which has no close parallel in a functional analysis. Through the reinforcing contingencies analysed in Part II, the verbal community makes it probable that under specific circumstances the speaker will emit specific forms of responses. So much for the "assertion of the word." Any given instance of such a response is of little importance to the listener without some indication of the circumstances under which it was emitted. If I know that someone has said *wolf* and nothing else, the response will be of very little use. The speaker may be calling for help, describing an animal at the zoo, reading a sign, repeating what he has heard, or completing the phrase *Big, bad*. . . . An autoclitic will sharpen the effect by indicating some of the sources of strength, as well as the degree of strength. The assertive autoclitic has the specific function of indicating that the response is emitted as a tact or, under certain circumstances, as an intraverbal. Other verbal operants are characteristically not asserted. The mand does not need to be, because of the reinforcing contingencies which are responsible for it, and in echoic and textual behavior the important conditions for the listener are those which prevailed when the echoic or textual stimulus was produced by someone else. The assertive autoclitic also indicates that

[6] Russell, *op. cit.*, p. 92.

certain limits of stimulus control have been respected—in the present case that the response is not made merely to a picture of a wolf, a wolf-like creature, a shadow, and so on. (The situation is further described in predication and in the construction of more elaborate sentences, as we shall see in the chapters which follow.)

Another kind of autoclitic affects the reaction of the listener by indicating the kind or degree of extension of a tact. When we respond to a novel stimulus with a response under the control of the contingent property, although the stimulus is otherwise unusual, we indicate the extension with such an autoclitic as *sort of* or *kind of* (*It's a kind of chair* or *It's a sort of brown*). The appropriateness of the terms *kind* and *sort* to *generic* extension may be noted. Such an autoclitic asserts the presence of a chair or the color brown but qualifies the assertion in such a way that the listener is prepared for an unusual instance. Extension of the tact along a continuum of intensity or magnitude is indicated by the colloquial usage *It's kind of hard* or *It's sort of heavy*. When the extension is metaphorical, we use an autoclitic such as *as* or *like* or the suffix *-like* or *-ly*. Thus *a ghostlike apparition* advises the listener that the apparition isn't actually a ghost. *He is like a lion* suggests that the property leading to the response *lion* is not the property respected in a zoological classification. In *bright as the sun, as* qualifies the *sun* but not *bright;* whatever is being described *is* bright but is merely *like* the sun.

There are autoclitics suggesting other types of approximation. When correspondence with an appropriate stimulus is to some extent a matter of chance, a form of *happen* is likely to be used. Many instances involve the "description of future events." The obsolete colloquial *happen,* as in *Happen he won't come,* survives in the obsolescent *mayhap* and the current *perhaps.* Descriptive autoclitics which indicate the state of strength of the speaker's behavior may also be shifted to indicate the probability of the event described. *He is truly noble* may be interpreted as equivalent to *Truly, he is noble,* or even *I'll say he's noble,* in which the emphasis is on the speaker's inclination to emit the response *noble* with respect to the subject under consideration. It may also suggest more directly the reason why the speaker is so inclined: the aspects of the subject's behavior are clearly aspects of nobility. It is the distinction between *Verily, he is noble* and *He is very noble.* Such responses as *probably, surely, maybe, undoubtedly, truly,* and so on, are often qualifying autoclitics rather than descriptive. The distinction is whether the effect on the listener is related to the speaker's inclinations or to the properties of the stimuli responsible for these inclinations.

QUANTIFYING AUTOCLITICS

An autoclitic affects the listener by indicating either a property of the speaker's behavior or the circumstances responsible for that property. The distinction is important in interpreting logical processes. In a logical or linguistic analysis of the response *All swans are white,* it may be admissible to say that *all* refers to, or modifies, *swans.* In a scientific account of verbal behavior, however, we cannot suppose that anyone ever responds to all swans. At best a man can respond to all the swans in his personal history. In describing such a history *all* is more appropriately taken as equivalent to *always* or *always it is possible to say*. As an autoclitic it "modifies," not *swans,* but the whole sentence. Similarly, *some* may be translated as *Sometimes it is possible to say* and *no* as *It is never possible to say.* Logic is concerned with interrelations among autoclitics, usually without respect to the primary verbal behavior to which they are applied. It does not care about swans but about sentences. For the moment, we are interested only in noting that *all, some,* and *no* have autoclitic effects in modifying the reaction of the listener to the responses which they accompany. Predication is not essential. If, after examining an aviary, a man says *All swans,* he suggests the extent to which his response *swan* applies to the situation. If he says *Some swans* or *No swans,* he suggests different extents. (Problems of quantification arise in predication, as we shall see, because the extent to which two or more responses are made to properties of the stimulus, as well as the extent of their association, must be indicated to the listener.)

As in all autoclitics, when many responses involving quantifying forms are acquired as units, no current autoclitic activity is necessarily implied, *May I have some butter?* is a concealed mand producing a special effect, in which *some* functions in lieu of a sharper specification of amount. *May I have a pound of butter?* produces a different consequence. Both may be emitted upon occasion without specific autoclitic activity.

Two very common quantifying autoclitics are the articles *a* and *the,* which function to narrow the reaction of the listener by indicating the relation between a response and the controlling stimulus. The circumstances under which we say *book* are different from those under which we say *the book* and both are different from the circumstances under which we say *a book.* These differences may all be important to the listener.

We sometimes add autoclitics to the verbal behavior of another speaker: we emphasize what he has said by saying *True!,* we qualify it by saying *Maybe,* and we deny it by saying *No!* These are all forms which we also apply to our own behavior. A special form of assertive autoclitic used with respect to another speaker is a modification of *is* in the form *So be it* or the Hebrew *Amen.*

In the absence of any other verbal behavior whatsoever autoclitics cannot occur. We do not simply say *almost* or *perhaps* or *some* or *the.* It is only when verbal operants of the sort discussed in Part II have been established in strength that the speaker finds himself subject to the additional contingencies which establish autoclitic behavior.

Although autoclitics are set up by the verbal community because they are useful to the listener, we must not forget that the speaker is himself a listener and that he himself may eventually find his own autoclitics useful. For example, they have an important effect in verbal thinking, as we shall see in Chapter 19.

Chapter 13

. . . .

Grammar and Syntax as Autoclitic Processes

An extension of the autoclitic formula permits us to deal with certain remaining verbal responses (for example, *shall, of, but,* and *than*) and certain fragments of responses which occur in "inflections," as well as with the order in which responses appear in larger samples of verbal behavior. Traditionally these comprise the subject matter of grammar and syntax. It is no part of our present plan to analyze in detail the grammatical and syntactical practices of any one language, but the nature of such practices needs to be pointed out.

Purely formal analyses of grammar and syntax (in which, for example, parts of speech are defined in terms of formal properties, including frequency or order of association with other parts so defined) are of little interest here, where no *form* of verbal behavior is significant apart from its controlling variables. Traditional views of grammar and syntax, as concerned with "the study of the relations of the ideas comprehended in a thought," are perhaps closer to our present concern, but again we have little to gain from the traditional treatment. It is now fairly widely recognized that the mingling of grammar and logic has been unfortunate for both fields. The accidental features of Greek and Latin grammar left their mark upon logic for many centuries, and logic had the unhappy effect of suggesting the rationalizing of grammar in terms of thought processes. We may make a fresh approach to both fields by analyzing the behavioral activities involved in the emission of larger samples of verbal behavior. In addition, while accounting for the verbal operants and activities which compose the subject matter of grammar, we lay the groundwork for a treatment of verbal thinking.

The autoclitics discussed in the preceding chapter describe, qualify, or otherwise comment upon verbal behavior and thus clarify or alter its effect upon the listener. Some responses which in this sense also "modify" verbal behavior have by no means so obvious a function. They do not occur except when they accompany other verbal behavior—they are "meaningless" by themselves—but their autoclitic function is often obscure. Examples are the responses traditionally called prepositions, conjunctions, and articles, as well as certain fragmentary responses employed in inflection. Many of these serve as minimal tacts, but they also have an important autoclitic function.

The manipulation of verbal behavior, particularly the grouping and ordering of responses, is also autoclitic. Responses cannot be grouped or ordered until they have occurred or at least are about to occur; and the process of putting them in order has the effect upon the listener of an autoclitic. Some of the relevant behavior, such as punctuation, has the dimensions of verbal *responses*; but this is not always the case. In general, autoclitic devices are interchangeable. A given effect may be achieved in different ways, although not necessarily within a single language.

The autoclitic function of the devices of grammar and syntax must be distinguished from their other functions. In the verbal response *The boy runs,* the final *s* in *runs* is in part a fragmentary tact under the control of specific features of a given situation. The relevant properties are subtle but include (1) the nature of running as an *activity* rather than an object or property of an object (2) the singularity of what is running, and (3) the currency of the activity. As an analysis of the stimulus control of *-s* this statement can scarcely be said to be an improvement upon the traditional statement that *run* is a "verb in the third person singular and the present tense." It will serve, however, to distinguish referential from autoclitic functions. The fact that the final *s* in English verbs indicates assertion was pointed out in the preceding chapter. Another autoclitic function remains to be treated.

The ordering and grouping of responses also have several functions. In the first place, speech sounds are ordered in the patterning of responses. Apart from the spectra of single speech sounds, the only dimension of verbal behavior is temporal, and order is therefore an important property. *Tip* and *pit* are different responses, as are *lookout* and *outlook.* Secondly, verbal responses may be ordered to correspond to the order of the relevant stimuli. The responses of an announcer in describing a boxing match stand in a fairly simple temporal relation to the events described. The three responses *Veni, vidi, vici* occur in that order for good reason.[1] Thirdly, order may arise from the order of *verbal* stimulation in the behavior of the speaker. A "train of thought" in free association follows the order in which verbal stimuli evoke other verbal responses. In the recitation of a long passage the order is due to a similar intraverbal linkage. Fourthly, order may be traced to the relative strength of responses in the current repertoire of the speaker. Other things being equal, the strong response occurs first. Lastly, we have to note rhetorical order. In the response *Him I despise* the position of *him* may be in part a function of relative strength, but the rhetorical pattern has been designed for a special effect upon the listener. The periodic sentence is a well-known device in which an important word is held until the listener or reader is thoroughly prepared for it, in the sense of Chapter 10.

RELATIONAL AUTOCLITICS

An additional autoclitic function of such a grammatical tag as the final *s* in *runs* is to indicate "agreement" in number between the verb and the noun which serves as its subject. In our example, the *-s* indicates that the object described as *the boy* possesses the property of running. The fact that the boy and the running go together and that these are not isolated responses occurring together accidentally is made clear to the listener by the grammatical device. In the response *The boys run,* the *-s* has other functions as a minimal tact, but it also serves as a relational autoclitic in its "agreement" with the form of the verb. In *The boy's gun, 's,* as distinct from *s',* is a minimal tact indicating singularity, but it also serves the autoclitic function of denoting "possession." It is the boy who owns the gun. (The "agreement" in number, gender, and case between noun and adjective in such a language as Latin is a much better example of the relational autoclitic.)

Inflections appropriate to "mood" are seldom involved in relational autoclitics. Mood is often merely a device for classifying types

[1] Violations of this principle are classified in rhetoric as "hysterologia" or "hysteron proteron"—inversions in the order which "conveys meaning" as opposed to merely conventional or autoclitic order.

of operants. As we have seen, imperatives and interrogatives are two classes of mands. Mood sometimes also refers to the strength of a response (indicative *versus* subjunctive) and may even suggest a condition responsible for the difference. Thus, the optative mood describes mands which "express wishes," but the response *He may go* as a statement of the probability of his going contains an autoclitic of strength comparable with the descriptive autoclitic in *It is probable that he will go.* We use mood as a descriptive autoclitic specifying a causal condition when we say that a particular subjunctive implies a condition "contrary to fact."

Even within a single language, such as English, there is considerable freedom to interchange devices. Possession may be indicated by a tag, as we have just seen, or by a prepositional phrase (*The gun of the boy*). The tags which indicate the belonging together of noun and verb need some support from grouping. The responses cannot be too far apart because the English tag is weak and will not permit such a wide separation of subject and predicate as Latin.

In Latin, ordering and grouping serve much less often as relational autoclitics. They are used primarily for rhetorical purposes. Rhetorical effects based upon order greatly exceed anything possible in English where order and grouping have been exhausted for the autoclitic purposes achieved in Latin by tags. Robert Bridges has commented on the use of order in Latin as follows:

> . . . an example from the second collect at Evening Prayer in the [Church of England] Prayer Book—'Give unto Thy servants that peace which the world cannot give' . . . is a translation. . . of the Latin *da servis tuis illam quam mundus dare non potest pacem.* 'The English is good [says Bridges] but the artistic order of the Latin words, which in English would be unintelligible disorder, assists and enforces the meaning without the slightest obscurity, and the words group themselves in a sort of dance figure, instead of a "march past"!' [2]

Predication

Predication is effected by a relational autoclitic to which has been added an autoclitic of assertion. Let us say that a single object evokes the two tacts *chocolate* and *good.* These may be made separately (*Chocolate!* and *Good!*) under circumstances which lead us to classify the responses as separate "announcements" or as a sort of double-barreled announcement (*Chocolate! Good!*). The common source of the two responses, the fact that they are made to the same object, can

[2] Quoted by Logan Pearsall Smith, *Milton and His Modern Critics* (London, 1940)

be indicated by the relational autoclitic of order. *Good chocolate* is appropriate only to a single type of situation; it is a response to good chocolate. It shows neither assertion nor predication. *The chocolate is good* shows a relational autoclitic of ordering and grouping and it also contains an autoclitic of assertion. Taken together these make it a predication. The assertive and relational autoclitic function of predication was suggested by Thomas Hobbes in this way: "Perhaps *Judgment* is nothing else but the composition or joining of *two names of things or modes* by the verb IS." [3]

Predication may involve more than two terms, and relational autoclitics then become especially important. The sentence *The boy runs a store* is under the control of an extremely complex stimulus situation, most features of which may be important to the listener. The relational autoclitic of order in English carries a heavy burden: roughly speaking, it must be clear that it is the boy who does the running and the store which is run. Where the order of items in a two-term predication may be reversed with only minor violations of standard order, a reversal in the case of a three-term response may be disastrous. *Good is the chocolate* is allowable English and a conceivable response if a rhetorical effect upon the listener, or powerful echoic or thematic prompting, is involved. But *The store runs the boy,* while English, is not reinforced when evoked by the same situation as the reverse order. In a language which employs tagging rather than grouping and ordering, a change in order is usually not troublesome.

Relational Autoclitic Behavior

It is not enough to point to the presence of autoclitic forms in a language. What are the processes which lead to their emission? Here again we must make a distinction between the purposes of a linguistic or grammatical analysis and an analysis of verbal behavior. A very important property of the verbal operant of Part II is its size. We have only to demonstrate a unitary contingency of reinforcement to suggest the unitary function of a part of verbal behavior. Frequently the part does not correspond to a lexical or grammatical unit. Although *boy* and *hat* may upon appropriate occasions be simple tacts, it does not follow that *the boy's hat* is therefore a compound expression. It may have a simple functional unity. In the response *the book on the table* the phrase *on the table* may have the same simple dynamic control exercised by a property of the environment exem-

[3] Quoted by Lee, I. J., *Language Habits in Human Affairs* (New York, 1941).

plified by the response *red* in *the red book.* Indeed, the whole expression *the book on the table* or *the red book* may function as a unit. The behavior of the lumber-camp cook in calling *Come and get it!* is as unitary as the response *Food!* or the ringing of a large metal triangle. We do not need to analyze grammatical or syntactical processes in accounting for such behavior. *Tally ho!* is the equivalent of *There's a fox!* and it would be idle to speculate about the function of the fragment *ho* or *There's* in the behavior of the current speaker. We can imagine a situation in which the response *There's a fox!* would require grammatical analysis, although this is unlikely in the case of *Tally ho!* In general, as verbal behavior develops in the individual speaker, larger and larger responses acquire functional unity, and we need not always speculate about autoclitic action when a response appears to include an autoclitic form. It also seems reasonable to suppose that, as a verbal environment undergoes historical development, it reinforces larger and larger units. At least, the environment must be prepared to reinforce larger units as units before the parallel process will occur in the development of the individual speaker.

Something less than full-fledged relational autoclitic behavior is involved when partially conditioned autoclitic "frames" combine with responses appropriate to a specific situation. Having responded to many pairs of objects with behavior such as *the hat and the shoe* and *the gun and the hat,* the speaker may make the response the *boy and the bicycle* on a novel occasion. If he has acquired a series of responses such as *the boy's gun, the boy's shoe,* and *the boy's hat,* we may suppose that the partial frame *the boy's* ________ is available for recombination with other responses. The first time the boy acquires a bicycle, the speaker can compose a new unit *the boy's bicycle.* This is not simply the emission of two responses separately acquired. The process resembles the multiple causation of Chapter 9. The relational aspects of the situation strengthen a frame, and specific features of the situation strengthen the responses fitted into it.

Specific relational autoclitics are more easily understood when the situation is complex and several verbal operants are strengthened. If the separate features of a situation evoke appropriate responses in an order determined only by relative strength, the result will probably be gibberish. Effective behavior demands, to put it roughly, that an appropriate first response be chosen, and that other responses be related to this and to each other with appropriate autoclitics. If, when a response or two have been emitted, intraverbal responses are generated, these must be taken into account and appropriate relational autoclitics added in composing the larger sample.

The standard practice in English gives priority to objects over action, and to single properties over objects. There is a fair probability that a prominent object in a situation will evoke the first response or, if that object has a conspicuous property which also strengthens a response, that the latter will be emitted first. Grammatical tags must still be added. In English the kinds of stimuli called things or objects usually evoke responses with tags appropriate to nouns, whereas the kinds of stimuli called actions usually evoke responses with tags which indicate verbs. This is by no means inevitable. It has been pointed out that, although we usually say *The horse neighs,* we could as well say *The neigh horses.*[4] Ultimately the distinction is meaningless. It is only because words referring to action conventionally carry distinctions of tense, person, and so on, that we conjugate them, and it is only because words referring to things need to "agree" with the adjectives describing them, or need to be designated as acting or being acted upon, and so on, that we decline them. And it is only because of the grammatical and syntactical practices of conjugation and declension that we call the responses verbs and nouns respectively. The speaker responds to a common property of the situation and gives it a tag. This alters the status of, and the available grammatical practices with respect to, the responses which remain. If the first response has been tagged as a noun, a fragmentary intraverbal pattern will supply the appropriate tag for, say, the verb to follow.

The part played by convention is shown by the difference between English and American newspaper headlines. When a king dies, two aspects of the situation, the king and death, control strong responses. In English headlines, it is customary to report an action with a noun if possible, and the headline will read *Death of the King.* In America the verb form is retained for action, and priority is given to the response to an object or, in this case, a person. The comparable headline reads *King Dies.*

In Chapter 3 we saw that a mand may specify an ultimate reinforcement (often a state or object) or the listener's behavior in mediating that reinforcement. In the response *Give me a cigarette, cigarette* is called a noun. In the response *Cigarette!* it is perhaps still a

[4] Gardiner, A. H., *The Theory of Speech and Language* (Oxford, 1932).

noun. But in the whimsical *Cigarette me!* it has become a verb, comparable to the verbs in *Water the horses* or *Air the room.* In a language with more marked inflection, the response would begin to pick up tags appropriate to verbs as the transition is made from object to action.

Faced with a blue sky, the English speaker does not hesitate to put the responses in the order *the blue sky* just as the French speaker does not hesitate to put his responses in the order *le ciel bleu.* (By indicating the agreement in gender the French writer adds a rather unnecessary reassurance that it is the sky which is blue and not something else which may have been mentioned.) That this is a matter of an established pattern rather than an explicit act of composition upon a given occasion is shown when the process goes wrong. *French Paris* was emitted as a mistake for *Paris French* possibly because *French* is usually an *adjective* and hence has priority while *Paris* is usually a *noun* and hence takes second place.[5]

The initial control exercised by a property of the situation which commonly evokes a first response may be subject to many disturbing influences, such as the special consequences of rhetorical order or traces of formal and thematic strengthening arising from earlier behavior. When a line of verse is inverted so that the rhyming word falls at the end, a skeletal formal contribution of strength is made to a particular order of responses.

In complex circumstances the first response evoked may prove unprofitable or wholly unsuccessful in generating new material. The speaker must begin again if a larger sample of verbal behavior is to be successfully completed. Much rewriting consists of trying different starts, in the sense of responding to different aspects of the situation and adding different grammatical tags. In the sentence *Before the reinforcement of a verbal response can be effected, the response must be elicited,* an action evoking the response *reinforce* took early control and a tag (*-ment*) appropriate to a noun was added. This forced the rest of the behavior into an awkward form. The empty response *can be effected* was needed to compensate for the action lost by saying *reinforcement* rather than *reinforce.* The sentence was recast: *Before a verbal response can be reinforced, the response must be elicited.* This contained an unfortunate repetition of *response* which was not greatly improved by the substitution of a pronoun. A further improve-

[5] Possibly also because of intraverbal strength from Chaucer's "...For Frenssh of Parys was to hir unknowe."

ment came from dropping the *Before* as an explicit relational autoclitic referring to temporal properties of two events, and allowing the temporal order of the responses to carry the same effect: *A response must be elicited to be reinforced*. (For reasons which will be clearer in the following chapter the appeal to order may be made explicit by adding, significantly, the response *in order to*—making the sentence *A response must be elicited in order to be reinforced*). To keep the notion of reinforcement in a prominent position the new form could be recast to read *To be reinforced a response must be elicited.* The force of *before* was recaptured by adding the response *first,* giving *To be reinforced a response must first be elicited.* It is too late to reconstruct the materials originally entering into the sentence, but the "broken" form *Elicit response, then reinforce* probably carries them all. The required temporal relation represented by *then* is expressed more generally by a different autoclitic: *No elicit, no reinforce.* The example shows the range and relatively arbitrary character of the autoclitic activity of "putting in the grammar."

Occasionally a sample of verbal behavior suggests alternative grammars which would be more acceptable to the reader. In a passage from a detective story *They know I'm too much for them with my good common streak of hard sense and determination,* the responses *good, common, streak, hard, sense,* and *determination* could have been arranged in several other orders, some of which might be closer to standard English. From a story by Sinclair Lewis the phrase *then he discovered with aghast astonishment* . . . suggests another order in which *aghast* is related to *he* rather than to *astonishment: then he discovered, aghast with astonishment.* Shakespeare's *sicklied o'er with the pale cast of thought* could easily have assumed other orders in which the action described could be *overcast with thought* and hence *sickly and pale.* One who has begun a sentence *As a matter of fact* . . . has probably been close to beginning it with *The fact of the matter is.* . . .

The effect of one grammatical tag in setting up another with a sort of skeletal intraverbal response is clearly seen when the process miscarries to produce "bad grammar." The classical example *The wages of sin is death* finds the intraverbal connection between *sin* and *is* overcoming the more remote relation between *wages* and *are.* In a hastily written sentence on an examination beginning *Paresis increase rapidly* . . . the final *s* of *paresis* has controlled a verb appropriate to a plural subject because *-s* is a common ending of plurals.

When a sentence is well under way, with tagging irrevocably established, there are often certain leftover scraps of responses which need to be worked in. Sometimes new responses need to be generated to fill gaps, but apart from this, available materials need to be arranged in some kind of order. Several rhetorical figures or "tropes" refer to more or less acceptable solutions. "Tmesis," "anastrophe," and "hyperbaton" refer to unusual orders of responses which, in a language which uses order for autoclitic purposes, may be disturbing. In saying *He came to uswards* rather than *towards us,* the undue strength of *to us* appears to break up the response *towards,* with the second half being emitted when time permits. In the classical example *that whiter skin of hers than snow* the special strength of *whiter skin,* determined in part by the relational autoclitic of grouping, breaks up the metaphorical expression *whiter than snow,* with the surviving fragment bringing up the rear.

MANIPULATIVE AUTOCLITICS

An extraordinary book written in the late eighteenth century by John Horne Tooke is the best introduction to the autoclitics which remain to be considered.[6] Tooke held that the "two great purposes of speech" were carried out by two kinds of words respectively. In the first place he recognized nouns and verbs as "necessary for communication." He is referring here to the stimulus control of verbal behavior on the pattern of the tact. The grammatical distinction between noun and verb is, as we have seen, arbitrary and unnecessary so far as reference is concerned. All other words he took to be "abbreviations" employed for the sake of dispatch. This notion is represented in the Greek title of his book ἐπεα πιεϱοεντα (*"winged words"*). For Tooke the term "abbreviation" carried something of the meaning of "saying much more than it appears to say." This was important to him, for he undertook to reveal the concealed significances of these words. The term also seems to have referred to a historical process in which older and usually much longer forms were gradually changed and contracted. Tooke's method was to demonstrate the function of an abbreviation by an appeal to etymology, in which he was an early, if by no means infallible, specialist. He himself pointed out that etymology was not essential to his argument. In expanding abbreviations so that their function was

[6] Tooke, J. H., ΕΠΕΑ ΠΤΕΡΟΕΝΤΑ: *The Diversions of Purley* (London, 1857).

more easily recognized it was simply necessary to find what would be accepted as equivalent expressions of a more obvious sort. That many of the words he analyzed revealed such expanded forms in their etymological history was reassuring.

Tooke does not seem to have appreciated the full significance of his work. He missed the modern point that some parts of language deal with other parts of language, and that his abbreviations were simply terms which had to do with the manipulation of the nouns and verbs which he recognized as primarily concerned with communication.[7]

The words which Tooke analyzed have to do with responses to rather complex situations in which the reader is enjoined to arrange and relate his reactions in the most efficient way. Thus the word *but*, which Tooke argues to be etymologically derived from *be out*, enjoins the listener to exclude something, or to make an exception of either a single response (*All but Henry left the room* may be "expanded" to read *All—except Henry—left the room*) or a sentence (*All left the room, but Henry returned*). The first *but* makes an exception of a noun, the second of a verb. In the second, *and* may be substituted with only a loss of emphasis on the opposition between leaving and returning. In the first case, however, the substitution of *and* for *but* would make the sentence redundant and wrong.

The response *and* enjoins the listener to add to what has already been said, whether a single response is to be added (*This is for you* and *me*) or another sentence (*This is for you* and *that is for me*).

If, according to Tooke, goes back to *give*. *We shall go tomorrow given it does not rain*. The logical *if-then* relation raises other problems. *If you see an honest man, then you see a happy one* might be paraphrased: *If you can say "honest," you can always say "happy."* The equivalent form *All honest men are happy* contains the quanti-

[7] He was undoubtedly influenced by contemporary discussions of parts of speech, but by attempting to reduce prepositions, conjunctions, particles, and so on, to nouns and verbs he tended to obscure their special function. A sample from the *Diversions of Purley* which shows his concern with the contemporary interpretation of the function of speech is worth reproducing.

> 'First he [Harris] defines a *Word* to be a "sound significant." Then he defines *Conjunctions* to be words (i.e. *sounds significant*) "devoid of signification."—Afterwards he allows that they have—"a kind of signification." But this kind of signification is—"*obscure*" (i.e. a signification unknown).... Not contented with these inconsistencies, which to a less learned man would seem sufficient of all conscience, Mr. Harris goes further, and adds, that they are a—"*kind of middle beings*"—(he must mean between signification and no signification)—"*sharing the Attributes of both*"—(i.e. of signification and no signification) and—"*conduce to link* them both—(i.e. signification and no signification)" '*together.*'

fying autoclitic *all* in lieu of *if*. Both deal with verbal responses but in a deceptive way. No one can emit a tact in response to all honest men or to all instances of saying *honest*. The statement really concerns the defining properties of the stimuli controlling the responses *happy* and *honest,* or some relation between them.

(Tooke is concerned with explaining the force of certain well-known words, particularly prepositions and conjunctions. He has nothing to say about the manipulative function of the autoclitic when it is served by grouping or by order. The expression *If we had world enough and time* can be carried by a change in order without the autoclitic *if: Had we but world enough and time.*)

As a rather different example, we may let Tooke present the case for the preposition *through.*

> But of what *real object* is 'through' the name?. . .Of a very common one indeed. For as the French peculiar preposition *chez* is no other than the Italian substantive *Casa* or *Ca,* so is the English preposition *Thorough, Thourough, Thorow, Through,* or *Thro',* no other than the Gothic substantive 𐌳𐌰𐌿𐍂𐌰, or the Teutonic substantive *Thuruh:* and, like them, means *Door, gate, passage. . . .*
>
> After having seen in what manner the substantive *House* became a preposition in the French, you will not wonder to see *Door* become a preposition in the English.[8]

The goal of a Tookean analysis is not to reach a logically equivalent paraphrase nor to reduce all expressions to a minimum of logical terms. It is simply to get back to a form of response which has a more readily identifiable effect upon the listener. The paraphrase generally converts a brief response of obscure function into a longer, explicit, and, as it were, more muscular equivalent. Tooke is in general supported by modern linguistic and logical trends. Sapir's [9] analysis of the word *for* is in the Tookean spirit, as is W. B. Quine's very revealing *Elementary Logic* [10] where many important autoclitics are carefully analyzed. Both Sapir and Quine are concerned with an empirical analysis of the function of verbal behavior. We must make

[8] Tooke, *op. cit.,* p. 180. We could analyze a given instance such as *The dog went through the hedge* by saying that the relation between the going dog and the hedge is characterized by emitting a common response, *door,* closely associated with a similar relation. The response under the control of the relation can undergo historical changes which need not affect the same response controlled elsewhere by the original generic stimulus.

[9] Sapir, Edward, *Language* (New York, 1921).

[10] Quine, W. B., *Elementary Logic* (Boston, 1941).

a distinction, however, between the explanations at which they ultimately arrive and the present analysis.

What Tooke lacked was a conception of behavior as such. He was still under the influence of British empiricism and, in spite of an heroic declaration of independence, of Grammar. Perhaps he came closest to the present position when he wrote:

> The business of the mind, as far as it concerns language, appears to me to be very simple. It extends no further than to receive impressions, that is, to have Sensations or Feelings. What are called its operations, are merely the operations of Language. A consideration of *Ideas,* or of the *Mind,* or of *Things* (relative to the Parts of Speech), will lead us no further than to *Nouns:* i.e., the signs of those impressions, or names of ideas. The other Part of Speech, the *Verb,* must be accounted for from the necessary use of it in communication. It is in fact the communication itself: and therefore well denominated *'Ρῆμα, Dictum.* For the Verb is *QUOD loquimur;* the Noun, *DE QUO.*

Here, struggling against an enormous weight of tradition, Tooke is talking about verbal behavior. He has "disabbreviated" the puzzling terms which cannot be accounted for as object words or by appeal to images—terms which we would classify here as autoclitics—and has found that they are verbs. This leads him to an important generalization which we could paraphrase in this way: some verbal responses are evoked by external states of affairs. These Tooke wants to call nouns. Other responses are communication itself. They affect the listener and have no function aside from that effect. Tooke wants to call them verbs. Writing more than a hundred and fifty years ago, he had perhaps no alternative, but a fresh formulation is possible today.

Many instances of verbal behavior which contain grammatical or syntactical autoclitics may not represent true autoclitic activity. We do not actually tell the listener to leave something out of account every time we say *I have read all but the last two chapters.* The response *all but two* is frequently a standard form controlled by a standard situation. An alternative expression would have been *I still have to read the last two chapters.* It is only upon genuinely novel occasions that the listener is specifically manded to modify his behavior. But these occasions do occur, and the explicit autoclitic activity of the speaker in manipulating his behavior must be taken into account as an important verbal function. Further activities of this sort together with a summary of the effect upon the listener will be described in the following chapter.

Chapter 14

Composition and Its Effects

We are concerned here with what Emerson called the "shuffling, sorting, ligature, and cartilege" of words. The speaker not only emits verbal responses appropriate to a situation or to his own condition, he clarifies, arranges, and manipulates this behavior. His activity is autoclitic because it depends upon a supply of verbal responses already available.

The ultimate explanation of autoclitic behavior lies in the effect it has upon the listener—including the speaker himself. In general the reactions of the listener at issue are those which can be wrong—that is, which may be ineffective in dealing with the environment responsible for the speaker's behavior. Much of the emotional and imaginal behavior of the listener (and reader) has little to do with grammar and syntax. An obscene word has its effect regardless of its location or grammar. So do most of the words which give an emotional character to speech. T. S. Eliot has argued that it is the function of the prose meaning of a poem to induce the reader to continue reading so that the collateral effects which do not depend upon prose significance may have their opportunity. Poetry can be wholly ungrammatical so far as part of its effect is concerned, but the reader will seldom read for that part alone; he must be carried forward by a prose meaning.

Autoclitic behavior is concerned with practical action or with responses on the part of the listener which depend upon a correspondence between verbal behavior and a stimulating state of affairs. The scrambling of poetry, such as in the example from Lord Chesterfield in Chapter 6, destroys both the autoclitic order and the effect of autoclitic responses. The "meaning" which it destroys is the meaning about which the poem may be right or wrong—that is, with respect to which the reader may take effective action, even if only verbal. The "meanings" which survive are emotional and connotative conditioned responses, including those appropriate to seventeenth-century writing and didactic verse.

The larger segments of verbal behavior resulting from autoclitic activity are usually called sentences. It is commonly said that the sentence, not the word, is the unit of speech, but we have no reason to use the notion of sentence to obtain a unit of verbal behavior more active than word. Verbal behavior is characteristically dynamic regardless of size or complexity. Nor does the autoclitic "assertion" of Chapter 12 or the "predication" of Chapter 13 call for a new term. Efforts have been made to define a sentence in terms of what it says. The *Concise Oxford Dictionary* defines sentence as a "set of words complete in itself containing subject and predicate (either, or part of either or both, somet. omitted by ellipsis), and conveying a statement, question, or command." Note that the verbal response itself (or the record it leaves) is not the statement, question, or command, but merely "conveys" it. This suggests the expression of an idea or proposition. Characteristically, a sentence is said to be complete only if the "thought" is complete, and so on. But while we may find criteria for the properties of a sentence, possibly in its effect on the listener with respect to a given state of affairs, the definition does not help to explain how sentences are emitted.

Some simple sentences are generated simply by adding autoclitics to available verbal operants. Let us assume that a speaker observes a hungry man and that there is a listener available who is interested in hungry men—that is, who reinforces speakers who tell him about hungry men or does things about hungry men which are indirectly reinforcing to the speaker. The principal properties of the situation strengthen the responses *man* and *hungry*. In broken English the speaker may simply say *hungry man* as an announcement (assuming a special predisposition on the part of the listener) or *man hungry* as a rudimentary predication. Falling back upon a tendency for pronouns to occur in predication, he might amplify this to *Man, he hungry*. Anyone more practiced in English will use the more appropriate assertive autoclitic *is: Man is hungry*. A further designative autoclitic is needed. *Man is hungry* may be a sweeping generalization, but the specificity of the current situation can be indicated by the autoclitic *the*. The complete form *The man is hungry* is optimally effective on the assumed listener.

Nothing as explicit as this necessarily occurs when a sentence is uttered. Some sentences are standard responses to situations comparable to well-memorized verses or maxims or oaths. Others are nearly complete skeletal "frames" upon which an exceptional response or two may be hung. In general we are reinforced for complete sentences and punished for broken or fragmentary expressions, and variables strengthening only a few responses tend to evoke complete sentences through multiple causation. This is clearly the case when there are no external sources of strength for the added responses. For example, if we have overheard the verbal stimuli *man* and *hungry* in that order and if the situation demands an echoic response (if we have been asked *What did he say?*), we are more likely to reply *The man* (or *Some man*) *is hungry* than merely *man hungry*. Similarly, in recalling poorly memorized prose or verse we are more likely to emit erroneous but complete sentences than the mere fragments actually recalled. Literary borrowing turns up as completed sentences even when only a few key words are borrowed.

The verbal community which makes the distinctions carried by various types of autoclitics generates this tendency to respond in larger characteristic units. Some sentences are more than mere key responses on strong skeletal frames, or fragmentary responses completed under the pressure to produce whole units. A set of variables may be so unusual or so complex that the past verbal behavior of the speaker yields no appropriate standard pattern. He must then manipulate his responses, with the help of special autoclitics. The resulting creation of larger segments of verbal behavior is an activity which may be called composition. Assertion and predication are not necessarily composition because, although they are usually involved in the organization of verbal behavior in response to complex arrangements of variables, they do not in themselves characterize either the larger unit or the particular state of affairs which gives rise to it.

Formal evidence alone will not show whether sentences have been composed. Memorized sentences emitted as purely intraverbal sequences, sentences reproduced as echoic or textual behavior, or the blends of a few key responses with stock patterns are not composed in this sense. The "unity" which we recognize in most sentences may have some basis in the unity of the "facts" described or the "ideas" expressed, but much of it is conventional.

The responses evoked by a situation are essentially nongrammatical until they have been dealt with autoclitically. They may be already ordered or tagged because of other considerations, or standard units requiring no special act of tagging in the present instance. Behavior is sometimes emitted in this essentially grammarless form. Hasty speech, where there is no time to supply autoclitics, is not always completely ordered and may lack grammatical tags. In composing a cablegram we may not be able to afford the autoclitics, though order is free. In headlines, lack of space frequently squeezes out autoclitics. A sore jaw has the same effect. Broken English is usually close to the latent form, for most autoclitics are not acquired in the early stages of learning a language. Only a few autoclitics found their way into the speech of Mr. Jingle in the *Pickwick Papers:*

> Played a match once—single wicket—friend the Colonel—Sir Thomas Blazo—who should get the greatest number of runs—won the toss—first innings—seven o'clock A.M.—six natives to look out—went in; kept in—heat intense—natives all fainted—taken away—...

Here the order is determined primarily by the original order of events, assertive and manipulative autoclitics are few, and the adjustment of the behavior to the listener is at a minimum.

As with relational and manipulative autoclitics in general, there is great leeway in the application of grammar and syntax to latent material. Suppose a speaker is primarily concerned with the "fact" that "Sam rented a leaky boat." The "raw" responses are *rent, boat, leak,* and *Sam.* The important relations may be carried in broken English by autoclitic ordering and grouping: *Sam rent boat—boat leak.* If we add the tag *-ed* to *rent* and *leak,* as a minimal tact indicating "past time," and the articles *a* and *the* to serve a subtle function in qualifying *boat*—in answer, say, to the anticipated query, *What boat?*—we get: *Sam rented a boat. The boat leaked.* Other manipulative autoclitics, including punctuation, produce at least seven other versions.

Pronouns are autoclitics when they have antecedents in the verbal behavior itself; like Tooke's abbreviations they are used for "dispatch," as in *He rented a boat. It leaked.* Slightly additional help is given the reader when relations between the two parts of the behavior are emphasized: *He rented a boat, but it leaked.* Or *He rented a boat, and it leaked.* If *it* is replaced by *which*—a stronger autoclitic function in tying the *leak* clause to the *rent* clause—we have *He rented a boat, which leaked.* The relation formerly shown by *and* and *but* must be carried by other autoclitics (such as *moreover* or *how-*

ever). An even closer relation is suggested by dropping the comma: *He rented a boat which leaked,* where there is little room left for an autoclitic representing *and* or *but.* Lastly, ruling out the possibility of any equivalent of *but* or *that,* we may avoid the pronoun by using the adjective-noun relational device: *He rented a leaky boat.*

The changes which may be rung on four verbal operants in such an example are scarcely to be compared with the possibilities in more complex verbal behavior. Consider, for example, the following sentence: *In its long apprenticeship to theological dogma, classical humanism has created a type of philosophy which is inimical to the temper of scientific inquiry.* There are possibly only three basic responses here, *humanism, opposition, science,* expressed in broken English as *Humanism oppose science.* But it would be better to point out that *oppose* is the result of an association with *theology* and that the *dogma* and *philosophy* of theological humanism are opposed to the *inquiry* of science. A very large number of sentences may be composed with this material, depending upon the choice of minor autoclitics—*Classical humanism is inimical to science because it has served a long apprenticeship to theological dogma, Theological dogma has imparted to classical humanism a philosophical temper opposed to the temper of scientific inquiry,* and so on. All such sentences "say the same thing" if the same basic operants are retained and if the autoclitics have the same force.

Most errors in sentence construction discussed in works on grammar and syntax illustrate weaknesses of autoclitic activity: a pronoun suggests a relation with an unrelated response; autoclitics are used to excess (*He saw that when he arrived at his destination that he found. . . ,* or *He may perhaps have gone,* or *He denied that he had not said it* [for *He denied saying it*]); or the autoclitics disagree (*I am sure that perhaps he went*); and so on. These are relatively sophisticated problems. Rougher difficulties are encountered by the young speaker. Here are five examples from a two-and-a-half-year-old girl: *When you untry to do it (try to undo it), Shoes are to put on—to keep the floor cold from, Why did you put milk and coffee to the same gether? (together in the same cup), I will buy a great big big big bug as you are, I use my red toothbrush to my night* (after being told "I used my yellow toothbrush this morning and I will use my red one tonight.") Unfortunately weakness is never fully outgrown. Here are some examples collected from everyday adult speech: *What business of it is theirs? The own course of your ideas. If for nothing just but to talk. On there in the table. What begins with your name? Things about the papers in them. A nice group of looking children.*

The special contingencies involving whole sentences often require that additional material be dredged up to achieve an acceptable product. (Where and how the additional material is found will be discussed in Chapter 17.) A good example of composition which requires filling in is the writing of "commercials" on radio and television. Often the only assignment is that the name of the product and two or three relevant adjectives shall be emitted a number of times in a short passage. Sentences must be composed containing the name and the adjectives, but the other material is essentially undetermined. A somewhat similar task was discussed in Chapter 5 in the completing of metaphorical frames, where a comparison is begun although no response has been suggested to satisfy it. The achievement of the witty speaker is not only the production of responses having relevant multiple sources of strength, it is equally the composing of sentences in which these responses seem to be at home. To do this, additional verbal material must often be found.

Analysis of Segments of Verbal Behavior

In a rather speculative way we may reconstruct the process of composition by analyzing a segment of behavior into (1) its essential operants, (2) the intraverbals possibly arising from these operants in the course of emission (often composing thematic groups of responses), and (3) the autoclitic framework. In a well-known passage from the King James version of the Bible we may isolate a response *blessèd* which is placed in opposition to the responses *ungodly, sinner,* and *scornful.* A second unrelated thematic group contains the three responses *walketh, standeth,* and *sitteth,* and each of these has an intraverbal mate *counsel, way,* and *seat,* respectively. The passage reads: *Blessèd is the man that walketh not in the counsel of the ungodly, nor standeth in the way of sinners, nor sitteth in the seat of the scornful.* The force of this passage is largely due to the thematic preparation which builds up steadily as the members of the thematic groups are ticked off.

Groups of responses may be rearranged autoclitically although the relational and manipulative autoclitics do not serve their usual purposes. In other words, there may be no relation asserted or predicated among the basic operants or their intraverbal groups. Gertrude Stein has supplied a rich store of examples:

> Seat a knife near a cage and very near a decision and more nearly a timely working cat and scissors. Do this temporarily and make no more mistake in standing. Spread it all and arrange the white place, does this show in the house, does it not show in the green that is not necessary for that color, does it not even show in the explanation and singularly not at all stationary.

The passage is mainly a series of mands: *Seat a . . . , do, make, spread, arrange,* followed by three questions or mands for verbal action: *does this show, does it not show, does it not even show.* The rest of the passage can be broken into several thematic groups: (a) *near, very near, more nearly;* (b) *timely, temporarily;* (c) *seat, standing, stationary;* (d) *knife, scissors;* and (e) *white, green, color.* Certain formal prompts were probably effective. There are four words ending in *-ly,* two in *-ary,* with one instance of *-ari-* within a word. There also appears to be an excess of initial *n*'s and *s*'s in accented syllables.

As another example from which we may try to infer some of the processes involved in composition let us consider the Shakespearean sonnet:

> Th'expense of Spirit in a waste of shame
> Is lust in action, and till action, lust
> Is perjured, murd'rous, bloody, full of blame,
> Savage, extreme, rude, cruel, not to trust,
> Enjoyed no sooner but despisèd straight,
> Past reason hunted, and no sooner had
> Past reason hated, as a swallowed bait,
> On purpose laid to make the taker mad;
> Mad in pursuit and in possession so;
> Had, having, and in quest to have, extreme;
> A bliss in proof, and proved a very woe;
> Before, a joy proposed; behind, a dream.
> All this the world well knows; yet none knows well
> To shun the heaven that leads men to this hell.

Here the principal autoclitic activity is in emphasizing a set of opposites, epitomized by the opposition between *heaven* and *hell,* and echoed in *enjoyed-despised* and *hunted-hated.* On the side of *hell* is *lust,* which has associated with it four thematic groups: (a) *waste, shame, expense, full of blame;* (b) *perjured, not to trust;* (c) *murderous, bloody, savage, cruel;* and (d) *extreme, rude.* On the side of *heaven,* we have *bliss* and *joy.* Another group of opposites has to do with the passage of time: *in action–till action; no sooner–straight; in pursuit–in possession; had–having; before–behind.* The moral is introduced with a third opposition—between *world well knows* and *none knows well.* This is the material from which, together with the formal sources of strength from the writer's experience with traditional sonnets, and with the formal sources generated on the spot, the poem appears to have been composed. There are many possible autoclitic variations on the material in any given line. The first line, for example, might have read, *A waste of spirit in the expense of shame, A shameful and expensive waste of spirit,* or *A shamefully and expensively wasted spirit.* The final selection is heavily influenced by the skeletal stress pattern of iambic pentameter.

As a final example, consider the following passage from Thoreau's Notebooks: [1]

> As I stand under the hill beyond J. Hosmer's and look over the plains westward toward Acton and see the farmhouses nearly half a mile apart, few and solitary, in these great fields between these stretching woods, out of the world, where the children have to go far to school; the still, stagnant, heart-eating, life-everlasting and gone-to-seed country, so far from the post-office where the weekly paper comes, wherein the new-married wife cannot live for loneliness, and the young man has to depend upon his horse for society; see young J. Hosmer's house, whither he returns with his wife in despair after living in the city,—I standing in Tarbell's road, which he alone cannot break out,—the world in winter for most walkers reduced to a sled track winding far through the drifts, all springs sealed up and no digressions; where the old man thinks he may possibly afford to rust it out, not having long to live, but the young man pines to get nearer the post-office and the Lyceum, is restless and resolves to go to California, because the depot is a mile off (he hears the rattle of the cars at a distance and thinks the world is going by and leaving him); where rabbits and partridges multiply, and muskrats are more numerous than ever, and none of the farmer's sons are willing to be farmers, and the apple trees are decayed, and the cellar-holes are more numerous than the houses, and the rails are covered with lichens, and the old maids wish to sell out and move into the village, and have waited twenty years in vain for this purpose and never finished but one room in the house, never plastered nor painted, inside or out, lands which the Indian was long since dispossessed [of], and now the farms are run out, and what were forests are grain-fields, what were grain-fields, pastures; dwellings which only those Arnolds of the wilderness, *those coureurs de bois,* the baker and the butcher visit, to which at least the latter penetrates for the annual calf, —and as he returns the cow lows after;—whither the villager never penetrates, but in huckleberry time, perchance, and if he does not, who does?—where some men's breaths smell of rum, having smuggled in

[1] Shepard, Odell, *The Heart of Thoreau's Journals* (Boston, 1927).

> a jugful to alleviate their misery and solitude; where the owls give a regular serenade;—I say, standing there and seeing these things, I cannot realize that this is that hopeful young America which is famous throughout the world for its activity and enterprise, and this is the most thickly settled and Yankee part of it.

The autoclitic frame of the passage begins with the writer's report of the circumstances under which he is speaking: *I stand, I look, I see.* It ends with the autoclitic *I cannot realize* (which we may perhaps translate *I do not find myself saying* or *I cannot say*). Thoreau cannot assert two incompatible thematic groups. The first of these can be broken up into several subgroups: (solitude and loneliness) *houses half a mile apart, few, solitary, great fields, stretching woods, out-of-the-world, far to school, so far, loneliness, horse for society, a sled track winding far, depot a mile off, solitude, only butcher and baker visit or villager in huckleberry time;* (stillness) *still, stagnant, all springs sealed up and no digressions;* (misery and despair) *men smell of rum, misery, heart-eating, life-everlasting, despair, old men rusting it out, young men pining for post office and lyceum, world going by and leaving him, sons not willing to be farmers, old maids wanting to sell out,* and *cow lowing for departing calf;* (time's decay) *gone to seed, trees decayed, rails covered with lichens, farms run out, forests become grainfields, grainfields become pastures, Indians long-since dispossessed, rabbits, partridges, and muskrats multiplying, and owls serenading.* The other thematic group, which Thoreau finds it impossible to say under the same circumstances, consists of *hopeful young America, famous for activity and enterprise, most thickly settled and Yankee part of it.*[2]

In analyzing a sample of written verbal behavior we cannot, of course, identify the actual order in which one response evoked another. For example, we cannot tell which of two intraverbally related responses was the stimulus and which the response. The material may have been extensively reworked, and some intraverbal sources may have been lost. In short, we lack the information needed for anything but the most superficial interpretation. Nevertheless, some notion of the complex process of composition may be suggested by a thematic and autoclitic breakdown.

[2] Thoreau was aware of his penchant for apparent paradoxes. His notebook for September 2, 1854, contains this item: "My faults are:—paradoxes, saying just the opposite,—a style which may be imitated."

LARGER ARTICULATIONS

In addition to that part of composition which is concerned with the autoclitic relations among the parts of a substantial segment of verbal behavior, we have to consider the difficult problem faced by the speaker or writer in working within narrow dimensional limits. Vocal verbal behavior has only one important dimension: time. Within this dimension the speaker must describe multidimensional scenes or episodes and present complex arguments. For this purpose he may use special manipulative autoclitics which connect remote responses, signal temporary digressions, pick up dangling threads, and so on. *Incidentally, by the by, meanwhile, we shall return to this in a moment, but first, parenthetically, to go back for a moment* are examples. Sometimes a response is repeated after other behavior in order to pick it up for use in connection with other responses, as in the classical figure called "anadiplosis": *He retains his virtues amidst all his misfortunes—misfortunes which no prudence could see or prevent.* A similar function is served by special pronouns referring to verbal behavior—for example, *the former, the latter,* or *that,* as in the expression *He said THAT?*

Several unusual orders of words have been identified and labeled in classical rhetoric. In "hypallage" an adjective may modify the wrong noun—*who rushed like lions to the roaring slaughter* (from e e cummings). In "hyperbaton" words occur out of order without necessarily suggesting other relations—as in the example, already noted, *that whiter skin of hers than snow.* In "anastrophe" a normal order is simply reversed—*the country over.* Any demonstrable reinforcing effect of the passage on the listener may be taken into account to explain the use of such devices, but as common characteristics of literary works we may take them to show how some of the circumstances of literary composition disrupt normal processes. Among these the effect of formal strengthening is obvious: of the examples just given, the first may have been furthered by the alliteration of *like lions,* the second by the fact that the normal order would not scan, and the third by the fact that reversing the order brings a rhyming word into position.

"Chiasmus" may show the effect of a strong intraverbal. In *A Boston man and a woman from New Bedford,* the intraverbal connection between *man* and *woman* could have reversed the normal *A Boston man and a New Bedford woman.* We should not, of course, say that the speaker—or more likely the writer—"changed the order to get an effect." Given certain supplementary formal variables, the unusual order has a greater likelihood of emission. (If "the writer tried out various orders and selected one because of its effects, on himself or someone else," his behavior in doing so is of the sort to be discussed in Chapter 15.) The frequency of unusual, and not necessarily effective, orders in literature is a further indication of the relaxed criteria of the literary community. Unusual, illogical, or confusing orders are likely to appear (are not likely to be edited) because of the special verbal environment of the world of letters.

The order of the parts of a sentence has been the subject of much speculation. It has been pointed out that the order in Chinese is the reverse of that in an address on an envelope; the most general term is followed by a succession of more specific responses. A sentence has been characterized as an exercise in "progressive correction"—a response is made and possible misunderstandings are then corrected. We have little reason to suppose, however, that all sentences will show such a pattern or that they are designed to serve any one general function. The primary operants in a sentence are due to complex and changing variables, and many other responses are strengthened as soon as a sentence is begun. The speaker may later find himself with unused responses which must somehow or other be incorporated into the sentence, or with lacunae which must be filled by a search for new material. It is scarcely worth dignifying the result of all these activities with a special name which might be taken to imply a single process.

Written verbal behavior can be two-dimensional or, rarely, three-dimensional. Tables, lists, charts, systems of indices, and so on, are all verbal devices in which autoclitic arrangements are carried out in space. In the periodic table of the elements, spatial relations serve to represent the adjacency of elements, the identification of an atomic weight with an element, the common properties of subgroups (for example, the rare earths), and so on. These relationships could be expressed vocally only with the heavy use of articulative autoclitics.

The spatial properties of pictorial forms of writing are, of course, obvious. Occasionally a pictorial element may be introduced into phonetic writing. In the following poem by e e cummings, the response *slowliest* is interwoven with a more complex response, and the whole poem goes slowly as the reader pauses slightly at the end of each line.

un
der fog
's
touch
slo
ings
fin
gering
s
wli
whichs
turn
in
to whose
est
people
be
come
un

Autoclitics of Composition

Some autoclitic responses enjoin the listener or reader to compose verbal behavior having specific properties. *Vice versa* is the equivalent of *change the order and react.* In *It is discussed in the third or fourth chapter or both* the *both* enjoins the listener to combine the separate responses which precede in an additional sentence or phrase. *And so forth* enjoins the listener to add further responses of the same sort at will. *Take England, for example* mands a reaction with respect to a given subject or theme. A special act of articulation is enjoined by *rather* or *on the other hand* which prepares the listener for a contrary response.

The "punctuation" of written verbal behavior is perhaps the best example of compositional autoclitic behavior. It satisfies our criteria because it cannot occur until primary behavior is available to be punctuated, and it amplifies, clarifies, and modifies the effect on the reader. It corresponds, in part, to temporal and intonational patterns in vocal verbal behavior, which must also be regarded as autoclitic. Punctuation is "read" in such patterns.

The separateness of verbal operants is shown by slight pausing in vocal behavior and by spacing in written. Conventional standards somewhat mask this evidence of the unity of the parts of a remark. A memorized passage, as a single operant, is likely to be run together in vocal behavior, but it is separated in a conventional way when written, except when running together is used whimsically or with literary license to suggest unity of response. Commas, semicolons, periods, capitals at the beginning of sentences, and so on, correspond to more marked pauses in speech, separating larger segments of behavior.

Some punctuation serves a minor autoclitic function in indicating the type of operant (! and ? mark special kinds of mands) or of controlling relation (proper names capitalized in English, all nouns in German). Quotation marks are obviously associated with the autoclitic *he said.* The effect is carried vocally by intonation and timing. The colon has a sophisticated function equivalent to that of the autoclitic *as follows.* The apostrophe, both in the possessive *'s* or *s'*, is a relational autoclitic with no vocal parallel. Parentheses have an almost pictorial character in separating one response from another, as do dashes used either as the equivalent of parentheses or as a sign of breaking off.

DIFFERENCES IN THE DENSITY OF AUTOCLITICS

The extent to which communities encourage autoclitics varies over a wide range. Literary English has shown periods in which sentences were long and heavily articulated and other periods in which the reader was left to surmise the relations among responses. Hemingway and Proust differ with respect to the density of autoclitics as much as Mr. Jingle and standard conversational English.

Special subdivisions of a given verbal community may act as separate audiences to determine the level of autoclitic behavior, as we shall see in Chapter 16. In addition to the practices of the community, the individual speaker may employ or avoid autoclitics for personal reasons. For example, it is characteristic of the timid or conservative person to qualify everything he says to avoid possible misunderstanding. We have seen, also, that momentary conditions may influence the density of autoclitics—when, for example, there is no time or space for more than the basic operants.

CONDITIONING THE BEHAVIOR OF THE LISTENER

In the behavior of the listener (or reader), as we have so far examined it, verbal stimuli evoke responses appropriate to some of the variables which have affected the speaker. These may be conditioned reflexes of the Pavlovian variety or discriminated operants. The listener reacts to the verbal stimulus with conditioned reflexes, usually of an emotional sort, or by taking action appropriate to a given state of affairs. The autoclitic of assertion makes such action more probable. Relational autoclitics, especially when combined with assertion to compose predication, have a different and highly important effect. Since it does not involve any immediate activity on the part of the listener (although responses of the other sorts already noted may take place concurrently), we detect the change only in his *future* behavior.

Respondent Conditioning

In a standard experiment on the conditioned reflex, a glandular response—say, sweating in the palms of the hands (the "galvanic skin reflex")—is conditioned by repeatedly presenting a neutral stimulus—say, the sound of a bell—at about the same time as an unconditioned stimulus, such as a fairly strong electric shock. The previously neutral sound of the bell eventually elicits a response somewhat like that to the shock alone. We can, of course, substitute a verbal stimulus—say, *shock*—for the bell. The result will be more predictable if we supply an autoclitic amplification *When I say "shock", you will feel this.* The listener's *future* behavior with respect to the verbal stimulus *shock* will then be changed. Responses appropriate to an impending shock will be evoked by the verbal stimulus *shock*.

When *shock* has become an effective conditioned stimulus, it may be paired with another verbal stimulus in a situation which is wholly verbal. By saying *When I say "three", you will receive a shock,* we change the future behavior of the listener with respect to the stimulus *One, two, three.* In another variation on this theme, the pairing of verbal stimuli may make a *nonverbal* stimulus subsequently effective. By saying *When you hear a bell, you will feel a shock,* we construct a future response to a bell. The new stimulus here is nonverbal, as in the original example of bell and shock, but a response to it has been set up without using either the bell or the shock in a conditioning situation.

Since this effect follows the pattern of the conditioned reflex, it is mainly of importance in the field of emotion. Instances in everyday life are commonplace. If *X* is someone who arouses a strong emotional reaction in us, then the remark *X is going to telephone you shortly* will alter our subsequent response to the sound of the telephone bell. The mere juxtaposition of verbal responses has this effect. A government is careful to associate the names of its heroes only with press announcements generating favorable emotional reactions, and advertisers show the same concern for the names of products. A story or poem may build up strong emotional reactions to proper names, wholly within the verbal framework of the story or poem, through a similar pairing of stimuli. This may be done merely in order to achieve literary effects of an emotional sort, or for purposes of propaganda. In a well-known passage from James Joyce's *The Portrait of the Artist as a Young Man,* an emotional response to the word *eternity* is generated with the following passage:

> Forever! For all eternity! Not for a year or for an age but for ever. Try to imagine the awful meaning of this. You have often seen the sand on the seashore. How fine are its tiny grains! And how many of those tiny little grains go to make up the small handful which the child grasps in its play. Now imagine a mountain of that sand, a million miles high, reaching from the earth to the farthest heavens, and a million miles broad, extending to remotest space, and a million miles in thickness: and imagine such an enormous mass of countless particles of sand multiplied as often as there are leaves in the forest, drops of water in the mighty ocean, feathers on birds, scales on fish, hairs on animals, atoms in the vast expanse of the air: and imagine that at the end of every million years a little bird came to that mountain and carried away in its beak a tiny grain of that sand. How many millions upon millions of centuries would pass before that bird had carried away even a square foot of that mountain, how many aeons upon aeons of ages before it had carried away all. . . . At the end of all those billions and trillions of years, eternity would have scarcely begun.

By piling up words which refer to periods of time and words describing things which occur in vast numbers, the verbal stimulus *eternity* (scarcely capable of ostensive definition) is given a power which may then be used in phrases such as *an eternity of happiness* or *an eternity of punishment* for purposes of religious control.

The Conditioning of Discriminative Stimuli

The verbal stimulus *When I say "three", go!* may have no immediate effect classifiable as a response, but it changes the subsequent behavior of the listener with respect to the stimulus *Three*. We are not concerned here with an elicited conditioned response, as in the example given above, but with the operant behavior of "going" evoked by the discriminative stimulus *three*. In a slightly different example, the later effect of a nonverbal stimulus is changed. Thus, *When the fire burns out, close the damper* leads to subsequent behavior under the control of a nonverbal stimulus arising from the condition of the fire. Both of these examples are what might be called conditional mands—the behavior manded is brought under the control of a future stimulus. However, a tact may provide a discriminative stimulus for operant behavior. By saying *When I say "soup's on", dinner will be ready,* we give the verbal stimulus *Soup's on* the same discriminative function as *Dinner is ready*. The same control is imparted to a nonverbal stimulus by saying *When the kettle whistles, tea will be ready.*

Other effects which a composed verbal stimulus may have upon the listener include some of the most subtle and at the same time some of the most important properties of human behavior. Ali Baba sees a thief standing before a door, hears him say "Open, Sesame," and sees the door open. There is no observed immediate effect upon Ali Baba as a listener, but later, alone before the door, he himself says "Open, Sesame!" To say that he has now "discovered how to open the door" is elliptical. He now possesses behavior which will open the door, and this behavior is likely to occur upon any occasion when an opened door is reinforcing. But young Ali Baba must have been taught to execute imitative responses and when to execute them. We have already seen this process at work in the acquisition of echoic behavior, and we have seen how this may be narrowed down so that the child echoes only when he is likely to be reinforced for doing so. But the present example is not echoic behavior, although covert echoic behavior may well occur. Ali Baba acquires a useful mand simply by hearing someone emit a response of the same form when this event is followed by the reinforcing opening door.

We impart behavior of this sort to a speaker with the aid of autoclitics. Thus Ali Baba might explain to a confederate *To open the door, say "Open, Sesame!"* or *If you want to open the door, say "Open, Sesame!"* This will be effective only if the new listener possesses an echoic repertoire and has also been conditioned to respond appropriately to the autoclitic frame *If . . . , say. . . .*

A tact may be acquired in the same way. Thus, we hear a man called

Jones and see him respond appropriately to this "vocative." As a result, we may also address him as *Jones,* or later reply *Jones* to the question *Who was there?* or correctly designate him when asked *Which man is Jones?* But this does not all happen in the naïve speaker or listener; it is the end result of a long process of verbal conditioning. The young child hearing someone called *Jones* many times does not therefore himself call him *Jones,* nor for this reason report that *Jones was present,* nor point to Jones in reply to the question *Which is Jones?* All these stages are developed through the use of autoclitics. An "introduction" is a species of autoclitic which enjoins the listener to respond in certain ways with respect to a proper name. *This is Mr. Jones* contains the autoclitic *is,* which makes the sentence more effective than the mere emission of the response *Jones* in Jones' presence. A more explicit autoclitic is the form *They call him Jones. Call me Ishmael* is the equivalent of *My name is Ishmael,* or *I am Ishmael.*

Ostensive definition operates through the same process. We pick up the names of objects without autoclitic help when we observe someone manipulating objects while also naming them. Thus we may "learn the name of" a Jones-plug by watching someone working with electrical apparatus while describing his own behavior as he does so. The same correlation of verbal and nonverbal events plus an autoclitic occurs in the ostensive definition *This is a Jones-plug.* The effect upon the listener is not only to establish *Jones-plug* as an appropriate tact but to set up nonverbal behavior in response to similar stimuli, for example, behaving correctly when asked *Please hand me a Jones-plug.*

A purely verbal definition appears to use the same process. Thus *An amphora is a Greek vase with two handles* has at least three effects upon the listener. As a result of having heard this response he may (1) say *amphora* when asked *What is a Greek vase with two handles called?,* (2) say *A Greek vase having two handles* when asked *What is an amphora?,* and (3) may point appropriately when asked *Which of these is an amphora?* Again, these are not results which occur spontaneously in the naïve speaker but rather as the product of a long history of verbal conditioning. Education is largely concerned with setting up the behavior necessary to permit these changes to occur.

An interlinear translation has the same effect as a definition, as do the more awkward translations called "vocabularies." By seeing a French and an English word in juxtaposition (with the implied autoclitic ______ *means* ______), the reader acquires, though possibly not efficiently, appropriate behavior (1) as reader of the term in the new language, and (2) as speaker of the term in the new language.

A clue to the additional verbal processes which have this effect upon the listener is the advantage gained when explicit autoclitics are used. To return to an example involving simple conditioning, when we bring a naïve subject into a laboratory and present pairings of bell and shock, it may take him some time to "learn the connection," as we say. We may achieve a quicker result by telling him *When you hear the bell, then you will receive a shock.* This contains the important autoclitic frame *When . . . , then. . . .* In a sense, the autoclitic enjoins the listener to respond in a given way. This is especially clear in a conditional mand. *When I call your name, answer "Present"* is a mand comparable to *Say "Present"*, except that the listener withholds the response until the condition in the *When* clause is satisfied. This cannot occur until such clauses have become effective in the verbal behavior of the listener, as the result of a long and difficult process. The process is not obscure. We understand how a child, as a member of a group, comes to respond to a mand only when it is coupled with his name. Originally there is some tendency to stand up whenever the verbal stimulus *Stand up* is heard, but eventually he stands up only when hearing *Charlie, stand up.* This is scarcely different from responding to the conditional mand *If your name is Charlie, stand up.* It is only a slight further step to a conditional mand of the sort *When you get the answer, stand up.* The child responds appropriately only if the discriminative function of getting an answer controls the response of standing up because of the conditional instruction *When you get the answer, ...*

What might be called a conditional tact operates through the same process. The verbal stimulus *When the light is on, the door is unlocked* affects the listener by bringing behavior appropriate to an unlocked door under the control of a light as a discriminative stimulus. The autoclitic frame could be exchanged for a more obvious form: *"Light on" means "door unlocked,"* which might be expanded to the form *Respond to the light's being on as to the verbal stimulus "The door is unlocked."*

It is the function of predication to facilitate the transfer of response from one term to another or from one object to another. A sign on a telephone reading *Out of Order* has a simple effect upon the reader: he does not use the phone. If he is told *The telephone is out of order* (say, when the telephone is not present), this pairing of the two verbal stimuli *telephone* and *out of order* with the autoclitic *is* has the same effect: he does not approach the telephone or engage in any behavior appropriate to using it. If this is the result of previous occasions upon which a similar state of affairs has been associated with the same verbal stimulus, the entire response *The telephone is out of order* is functioning as a unit. But when such a response is first effective, *out of order* must already have become an important verbal stimulus, possibly in such responses as *The radio is out of order* or *The car is out of order.* The response *The telephone* must also have been effective in such combinations as *The telephone is ringing* or *The telephone is in use.* The verbal stimulus *The telephone is out of order,* heard in this form for the first time, brings behavior formerly controlled by the stimulus *out of order* under the control of the stimulus *telephone* and the nonverbal stimulus supplied by the telephone itself. As a result of having heard this response, the speaker not only does not use the telephone, he may warn a third party that it is out of order. Similarly, when we say *That kind of mushroom is poisonous,* we effectively alter the listener's behavior by bringing under the control of a particular kind of mushroom all the behavior previously controlled by poisons. The effect upon the listener is verbal if he then simply repeats what we have said, or talks about the mushroom as poisonous. It is practical and nonverbal if he avoids eating that kind of mushroom and makes sure that others avoid it also.

INSTRUCTION AND KNOWLEDGE

The change which is thus brought about in the behavior of the listener is appropriately called "instruction." This is the sense in which the term is used in educational institutions. The student comes to emit certain kinds of responses, both verbal and nonverbal, because of verbal stimuli occurring under specific circumstances. Lectures, demonstrations, texts, and experiments all increase the verbal and nonverbal repertoires of the listener or observer through processes of this sort. In the field of history, the effect is almost exclusively a modification of the student's future *verbal* behavior, and he carries much of this change in his behavior as a speaker in the form of intraverbal sequences. In the practical sciences, a more important effect may be to establish nonverbal modes of response.

One immediate effect is traditionally described by saying that the reader now "knows something he did not know before." To return to an example discussed in Chapter 5, we might say that the most important result of hearing someone say *Fox,* under circumstances where this is clearly a tact or with the autoclitic support *There is a . . . . ,* is that the listener now "knows there is a fox in the neighborhood." But what do we mean by "knows"? In what sense does our listener know Jones' name or the name of a Jones-plug or that the telephone is out of order? The term "know" refers to a hypothetical intermediate condition which is detected only at a later date. We are said to know that a telephone is out of order even before we exhibit behavior appropriate to telephones which are out of order. We are said to know that a man's name is Jones before we exhibit behavior appropriate to a man named Jones. But this use of the term is not confined to changes induced verbally. We may discover that a telephone is out of order by trying to use it, as we may discover that there is a fox in the neighborhood by seeing one. To the extent that the two sorts of changes are the same, we may say that being told there is a fox in the neighborhood has the same effect as seeing one, just as being told that the telephone is out of order has the same effect as discovering that it is out of order in trying to use it. In both cases it is potential behavior which is called knowledge. (A verbal stimulus may lead the listener to "see" the thing described in a sort of conditioned seeing,[3] and this has often been identified with "knowledge." However, such a condition does not always obtain when the term knowledge applies. We may infer that conditioned seeing, when it occurs, provides another similarity between verbal and nonverbal instances.)

But is there no immediate effect? The reader of a novel may never do anything about what he has read. Changes in his future behavior —such as the change in attitude generated by a propagandistic novel— are incidental. Yet the immediate effect is not wholly composed of conditioned and discriminative reactions to the separate verbal stimuli. The reader behaves with respect to the description of a novel scene in some measure as he would behave to the scene itself— with novel behavior. The description is "composed" of separate verbal ingredients just as a scene is composed of separate events, and

3 *Science and Human Behavior,* Chapter 17.

one's reaction to both is in part determined by how they are put together in this instance. When Dickens reports that Little Nell is dead, the reader's emotional reaction is not merely the separate conditioned reflexes evoked by *Little Nell* and *dead.* This problem is more than merely verbal. We react to the death of a pet dog with more than separate conditioned responses to the dog and death.

Knowledge, rather than the behavior of knowing, is said to be *communicated* in a speech episode. The notion of communication is somewhat more appropriate here than in the effects upon the listener discussed in Chapters 5 and 6. Nevertheless, it remains a misleading metaphor. Consider the "fact" that there is gold in the Klondike. A person may be said to know this nonverbally if, when he needs gold, he goes to the Klondike. Commoner evidence of his knowledge is that he says *There is gold in the Klondike.* The verbal response may have arisen from an act of composition on the spot in the Klondike, or echoically or textually (possibly carried intraverbally) from the behavior of someone else. The response may be valuable simply as such, either to the speaker or someone else, if it produces an expedient change in the behavior of someone who needs gold. The response *There is gold in the Klondike* alters behavior with respect to the *fact* that there is gold in the Klondike, but this is nothing more than the original stimulating circumstance responsible for the autoclitic coupling of the responses *gold* and *Klondike.* The fact is not transmitted from one speaker to another. What is "made common"to both listener and speaker (to take the etymology of *communicate*) is either a verbal response or a resulting nonverbal tendency (to go to the Klondike when gold is reinforcing).

The notion of communication breaks down, as we saw in Chapter 10, when both the speaker and the listener are in possession of "the same facts," or, more precisely, of "the same behavior." The traditional conception of language would lead one to believe that in such a case total silence would prevail, yet perhaps the greater part of scientific and philosophical discourse is of this sort. We shall deal with this extraordinarily important effect of self-instruction in Chapter 19.

In comparing the behavior of speaker and listener in a given instance, it must also be noted that the behavior of the one is relatively independent of the behavior of the other. A speaker may instruct the listener even though he does not himself possess the "knowledge" imparted. To alter a classic example [4] slightly, when Father So-and-so tells an assembled company that his first confessant was a murderer and Mr. Y then enters and says that Mr. X was Father So-and-so's first confessant, the change brought about in the behavior of the assembled company with respect to Mr. X (to whom behavior appropriate to a murderer is now shown) may not occur in Mr. Y himself. The distinction between an established larger pattern of verbal behavior and a first instance of the composition of such a pattern also need not apply to both speaker and listener. A response which is painfully composed by the speaker in a pattern which thus occurs for the first time in his behavior may prove to be a standard stimulus to which the listener reacts without exemplifying the process of instruction. On the other hand, the crudest cliché on the part of the speaker may profoundly alter the behavior of the listener. This may even happen when the speaker is his own listener, as when we "suddenly see the significance of" a copybook maxim. Here an intraverbal chain of long standing—say, *haste makes waste*—suddenly becomes effective in inducing the listener who is inclined to avoid waste to avoid haste also.

Conditions Limiting the Instruction of the Listener

In addition to the usual factors affecting the listener's behavior (such as clarity of the verbal stimulus or the extent of conditioning of separate responses), successful instruction is subject to several conditions. One of these is the "prestige" of the speaker or the listener's "belief" in what he says. The listener reacts to the behavior of a given speaker to an extent determined by the consequences of past reactions. The speaker can build confidence or belief by saying many things which are obviously true or quickly confirmed, or by resorting to rhetorical devices. The listener is instructed by repetition, by the prompting and probing techniques of Chapter 10, and—of special relevance here—by the skillful use of autoclitics: *You will agree . . . ., I needn't say . . ., Of course, . . .,* and so on. Other relevant autoclitics are mands, and the listener reacts in ways resulting from contingencies previously arranged by the current speaker or someone like him. He responds to a definition (*Let us call this type of operant a tact*) or a conditional mand or tact (*If the resulting number is less than 2000, try again*) as he responds to any order. Effective teaching depends in part upon the ability of the teacher to generate prestige

[4] Thackeray in "On Being Found Out" (*Roundabout Papers*) calls it an "old story."

relationships which make his mands effective in this kind of instruction.

The often dramatic behavior of the listener under hypnosis is an extreme case of instruction. Techniques for inducing the hypnotic state are rich in mands, and hypnotic suggestions usually take the same form. If we give the hypnotized subject a flyswatter and say *This is an umbrella,* he transfers what we may call his umbrella-behavior to the flyswatter. Our response is a sort of magnified definition or instruction: *Act as if this were an umbrella.* If we then say *It is raining,* he may transfer his rainy-day behavior to the present scene and perhaps hold up the flyswatter as an umbrella. (These statements are, of course, no more or less an *explanation* of hypnosis than the preceding statements are an explanation of verbal behavior; they simply classify hypnotic instructions according to more general verbal contingencies. Hypnotic procedures intensify verbal control to the exclusion of other forms of stimulation. The exceptional results obtained under hypnosis do not differ in kind from the normal behavior of the listener.)

Verbal instruction is limited by the extent of the change demanded. As a verbal response becomes more and more complex a point will be reached at which the listener is unable to act appropriately. Good examples are frequently discussed by logicians. The listener may indicate the instruction which has taken place by saying *True* to the statement *Paris is the capital of France* or to *"Paris is the capital of France" is true.* He may also respond appropriately to *" 'Paris is the capital of France' is false" is false,* but he may find it difficult to respond, at least immediately, to more complex arrangements of these autoclitics. This is no more surprising than any failure to respond to complex instructions. The listener who responds correctly to *Put your right hand to your left ear,* may show signs of confusion in responding to *Put your left hand to your right ear, your right hand to your nose, wink your left eye, and put your right foot forward.* The appropriateness of *right* and *left* depends upon the order and adjacency of terms, and at some point the resulting behavior breaks down. In some forms of semantic aphasia, the capacity of the individual to maintain even normal sizes of patterns is impaired, and the range of effective speeds is restricted.

The extent of the instruction which occurs may be in part a matter of the instruction needed. An expert easily understands a novice because he must make very little change in his behavior. The commonplace is more easily understood than the novel. *"Malheur à qui invente en parlant."* [5] The time available to the listener also affects the extent of the instructional change of which he is capable. Difficult material may be understood, in this sense, if it is presented slowly. Written verbal stimuli have a great advantage over vocal in this respect because the reader may control the rate of presentation. Almost any material which involves instruction becomes unintelligible in this sense if presented (or read) too rapidly—even though it remains intelligible in the sense that any given part may be correctly echoed. Speed-of-reading tests measure the optimal speed at which changes of this sort may be brought about.

The "difficulty" of a verbal stimulus—say, a text—obviously may mean many things: its clarity, the familiarity of the terms it contains, the supplementary strength it generates with echoic, textual, and intraverbal stimuli, and the density and nature of its autoclitics. To these we may add the kinds of changes it is designed to bring about in the behavior of the listener or reader.

[5] Attributed to "Faublas" by Stendhal, *Le Rouge et le Noir: "Une idée un peu vive y a l'air d'une grossièreté, tant on y est accoutumé aux mots sans relief. Malheur à qui invente en parlant!"*

commonplace is more easily understood than the novel, "[illegible] *[illegible] en perles*."[5] The time available to the listener also alters the extent of the instrumental change of which he is capable. Difficult material may be understood, in this sense, if it is presented slowly. Written verbal stimuli have a great advantage over vocal in this respect because the reader may control the rate of presentation. Almost any material which involves instruction becomes unintelligible in this sense if presented (or read) too rapidly—even though it remains intelligible in the sense that any given part may be correctly echoed. Speeded-reading tests measure the optimal speed at which changes of this sort may be brought about.

The "difficulty" of a verbal stimulus—say, a text—obviously may have many dimensions: its length, the familiarity of the terms it contains, the supplementary stimulation it generates with echoic, textual, and intraverbal stimuli, and the density and nature of its autoclitics. To these we may add the kinds of changes it is designed to bring about in the behavior of the listener or reader.

[5] Attributed to [illegible] by Stendhal, *Le Rouge et le Noir*. [illegible]

Part V
THE PRODUCTION OF VERBAL BEHAVIOR

Chapter 15

. . . .

Self-Editing

VERBAL RESPONSES are described and manipulated by the speaker with appropriate autoclitics which augment and sharpen the effect upon the listener. They are also often examined for their effect upon the speaker or prospective listener, and then either rejected or released. This process of "editing" is an additional activity of the speaker.

THE REJECTION OF VERBAL BEHAVIOR

A response which has been emitted in overt form may be recalled or revoked by an additional response. The conspicuous external record of *written* verbal behavior may affect the "speaker" before it reaches any "listener" and may be crossed out, erased, struck over, or torn up. The writer has reacted to, and rejected, his own behavior. The process has interested literary critics. For example, Ridley,[1] after a careful examination of Keats' manuscripts, came to the conclusion that "the great bulk of Keats' corrections were made in the moment of composition; a word is discarded before it is even completely written." When a writer does not revoke, it may still be necessary to distinguish between the act of allowing the text to reach an ultimate reader and the original behavior of writing it.

Comparable "editing" of *vocal* behavior is more ephemeral and hence harder to describe. Withholding audible speech may seem to be nothing more than not emitting it. Some restraining behavior may, however, be detectable, such as biting the tongue or lips or

[1] Ridley, M. R., *Keats' Craftsmanship: A Study in Poetic Development* (Oxford, 1933).

holding the hand over the mouth. In extreme instances people have apparently bitten out their tongues in order to keep from engaging in verbal behavior which might be damaging to themselves or others.[2] The act is effective, of course, only in a nonliterate person. A formalized refusal to speak, as to a court of law or legislative committee, is known as contempt.

If a vocal response has not been heard, it can be "revoked" simply by not repeating it upon request. The response has, so to speak, been crossed out. A response which has already reached the listener can be "taken back" with an appropriate manipulative autoclitic. To the stenographer in the office or courtroom, the speaker simply says *Strike that out.* To the everyday listener he may say *Forget it,* or *Skip it.* He may add a belated *No* or substitute a corrected version beginning with an autoclitic such as *I meant to say. . . .*[3] When Falstaff, angry with Prince Hal, says *God save thy Grace—Majesty I should say, for grace thou wilt have none,* the response *Grace,* as part of a common intraverbal sequence, has an incongruous automatic effect upon the speaker, who then rejects it and substitutes the equally common *Majesty,* which is free of the collateral effect. The formalized revocation of verbal behavior is exemplified by retractions and recantations.

Subvocal behavior can, of course, be revoked before it has been emitted audibly. As we shall see in a moment, that is one of its advantages. The speaker tests his behavior on himself before offering it to the ultimate listener. Inadequate withholding, when there are strong reasons for emitting a response, may lead to whispered or mumbled or hesitant behavior of low energy and speed. In "lip-speaking" to someone at a distance or through a heavy window—that

[2] W. E. H. Lecky, in *A History of European Morals,* ii, p. 296, cites Plutarch, *De Garrulitate,* and Pliny the Elder, *Historia Naturalis,* xxxiv 19, in referring to a courtesan who evidently did this to avoid revealing the conspiracy of a friend.

[3] How is it possible, from the point of view of a functional theory of meaning, for one ever to "say what one does not mean" or "not to say what one means to say"? The autoclitic expression *That is not what I meant to say* is easy to explain when the *listener* has reacted inappropriately, as if to another response. *I meant "light" in the sense of illumination, not as opposed to "heavy"* is a further specification of the variables responsible for the speaker's behavior, which will presumably have a more appropriate effect on the listener. But the speaker is not likely to misunderstand *himself* in this sense. When he discovers that he has not said what he meant to say, he is acting in his role as self-listener. His verbal slip, for example, comes as a surprise, and he reports that he "meant to say" another word. Or when a subtle or difficult state of affairs exerts only tenuous stimulus control, but general conditions of strength nevertheless produce verbal behavior, he may comment upon the inadequacies of his behavior by saying *That isn't quite what I mean.* He reacts to, and comments upon, the appropriateness of his behavior to certain controlling variables.

is, behaving with the lips as if speaking—vocalizing may be inadequately withheld; some words may be vocalized, or exaggerated lip movements may be accompanied by a sustained vocalization of low energy level and little or no change of intonation. It is sometimes possible to watch audible behavior, in the very course of producing unforeseen effects, retreat to the subaudible level—as when one embarks upon an untactful anecdote and abandons it when half told. The expression "making a man eat his words" is not too far-fetched a metaphor. Behavior which has not been tested subvocally is so often aversive to others that the speaker who neglects to test may be enjoined to "stop and think" before speaking.

Much of the self-stimulation required in the autoclitic description and composition of verbal behavior seems to occur prior to even subaudible emission. In both written and vocal behavior changes are made on the spur of the moment and so rapidly that we cannot reasonably attribute them to an actual review of covert forms. This sort of editing is sometimes also accompanied by physical movements of self-restraint, as in biting the tongue or jerking the pen away from the paper. Evidently stimulation associated with the production of verbal behavior is sufficient to enable one to reject a response before it has assumed its final form. The subject is a difficult one because it has all the disadvantages of private stimulation.

Why Behavior is Rejected

The speaker usually rejects a response because it has been punished. As we saw in Chapter 6, punishment does not directly weaken behavior; it merely strengthens incompatible forms.[4] A child acquires an obscene response at school, emits it in his home, and is punished. The effect is not to reduce the probability of that response, but to make it, as well as the circumstances under which it is likely to be emitted, a conditioned aversive stimulus. When the response is again strengthened to the point of emission, it generates aversive stimulation (the "threat" of punishment). This special consequence alters the apparent strength of the verbal operant, but it has another distinguishable effect in generating a kind of behavior conveniently called rejection. Rejecting a response reduces the conditioned aversive stimulation generated by it and is reinforced because it does so. The behavior is to be classed as either escape or avoidance, depending upon whether the unconditioned aversive stimulation has yet

[4] *Science and Human Behavior,* Chapter 12.

occurred. Clapping the hand over the mouth in time to prevent an overt response is clearly avoidance, as is saying something else instead. "Taking a response back" is a form of escape.

In addition to setting up avoidance or escape behavior, the conditioned stimulation generated by punishment has an emotional effect. We not only "take back" a punishable response or catch it on the tip of our tongue, we undergo a reaction of fear or guilt. As Conrad puts it in *Lord Jim, I . . . was afraid to speak, in the same way that one dares not move for fear of losing a slippery hold.* In reducing the aversive aspects of a situation we may, at the same time, reduce the emotional reaction, and this may be an additional reinforcement. But the emotion (whether it is "felt" or not) is not essential to rejection; it is, for one thing, too slow to produce quick, on-the-spur-of-the-moment, subvocal editing. (It may alter the strength of the punished response by conflicting with motivational or emotional variables of which the response is a function.)

The emotional by-product of punishment need not occur if aversive effects prevent the emission of the response even in subvocal form. This is what Freudian psychologists call "successful" repression. The punished response never reaches the stage at which it generates the emotional pattern of anxiety, and successful repression is therefore less troublesome than a less effective form. It is also more successful from the point of view of the punisher, since it may eliminate objectionable behavior from a repertoire without creating harmful side effects. But if at this stage there is no conditioned aversive stimulation, there is presumably no act of withholding to be considered here.

The effect of punishment in reducing the frequency of punished responses by a sort of editing can be demonstrated in lower organisms. In a demonstration experiment a pigeon is taught to "name" four colors by pecking printed words. If a colored area is red, the hungry pigeon is reinforced with food for pecking the word *red;* if the color is yellow, pecking the word *yellow* is reinforced; and similarly for blue and green. Under these conditions the pigeon is reinforced, on the average, for one out of every four pecks regardless of color, and accurate "naming" therefore develops very slowly if at all. There are two ways to solve this problem. The pigeon can be forced to "look at" the color just before responding to the appropriate name: for example, the printed names can be kept inaccessible until the pigeon pecks the colored area. This practice guarantees a strong stimulus just before a response is made to a name, and stimulus control quickly develops. Another technique is to punish wrong responses. When the pigeon pecks the correct word, food is presented, but when it pecks the wrong word, the apparatus is turned off and the pigeon is forced to wait a few minutes before making another response. This mild punishment has a dramatic effect. The pigeon begins to hesitate in striking the name and then begins to look at the color before responding to the words. Its performance is greatly improved. Here punishment improves the relationship between a response and its controlling variables so that editing is eventually unnecessary.

Why Verbal Behavior is Punished

Verbal behavior may be objectionable to the listener simply as noise. Punishment for this reason usually drives the verbal behavior of children to the covert level. When the community has made sure that a child possesses an effective repertoire, it often has no further interest in what the child says. A period follows during which "children are to be seen and not heard," and punishment is frequently invoked. Useless tacting of commonplace stimuli, uncontrolled intraverbal behavior in the form of idle chatter, illogical sequences of ideas, and frequent intraverbal sequences which are idiosyncratic and hence "hard to follow" are suppressed. The contingencies which set up echoic behavior are not intended to establish such responses to all verbal stimuli; and the child may need to be punished for repeating rather than answering a question, or for excessive repetition. No sooner is a child taught to read than he is taught to read silently, often by being punished for reading aloud. In libraries, churches, theatres, and so on, people are to some extent punished for all verbal behavior regardless of form.

Certain properties of responses are aversive to others and likely to bring punishment. Among these are too loud a voice, a rasping tone, undue sibilance, heavy alliteration, singsong, and such defective execution as bad spelling, stuttering, or incompleteness.

Verbal behavior is frequently punished because of deficient *stimulus control*. Poor conditioning, forgetting, interactions among somewhat similar responses, and many other conditions may lead to "the wrong word"—to mands and tacts, and echoic, textual, and intraverbal responses which do not satisfy the reinforcing contingencies of the community. The deficient control in the impure tact—lying, exaggerating, wishful thinking, and so on—invokes punishment in most communities. Behavior which is strong primarily because of its effects upon the speaker himself, because he is "talking to himself," is likely to be punished by others. "Illogical" speech, far-fetched intraverbal sequences, and the irrelevant intraverbal responses called "flight of ideas" are commonly punished, especially by practical and scientific verbal communities. The resulting "fear of uttering nonsense" [5] poses problems for the technique of psychoanalysis. Responses taken without acknowledgment from the verbal behavior of someone else, as in plagiarism, are also subject to punishment.

Verbal behavior is usually punished—if only by its ineffectiveness—when it is under poor *audience control.* Both vulgar and highbrow expressions are punished in the contrary environments. Some responses—such as obscenities, blasphemies, and so on—are fairly generally punished, but evidently not by the verbal environments which set them up. In general, movement from one group to another fosters punishment. The child of an immigrant family finds that the language of his home meets with ridicule or suffers other disadvantages in the outside community. Most children experience a similar change with respect to the "little language" of the nursery. Familiar expressions appropriate to one's peers are punished when emitted with respect to one's superiors. The weakness in audience control may be a matter of either form or theme—exemplified in the former case by the excessive borrowing of words from another language and in the latter case by the revealing of commercial or governmental secrets or by "tattling" or "squealing." Another punishable insensitivity to the audience is exemplified by the response which is too obvious, too commonplace or shopworn, or simply too often repeated by the present speaker.

Verbal behavior may be punished in a sort of retribution if it has punishing consequences for the listener. Reference to a painful state of affairs which "hurts the listener's feelings" is a kind of "bad break" which is revoked if it generates aversive self-stimulation in time. Once emitted, it may leave the speaker with a conditioned emotional reaction of guilt. The alacrity with which the "bad break" is revoked is in striking contrast to the insensitivity with which the speaker may continue to hurt a listener with criticism or burden him with repeated mands. The return punishment in such instances often

[5] Freud, Sigmund, *Basic Writings* (Modern Library), p. 718.

seems substantial (*Oh, for heaven's sake, stop nagging!*) and far in excess of any demonstration of "hurt feelings" after a tactless remark. When this is the case, we must conclude that hurting the listener with criticism and nagging is not punishing to the speaker. On the contrary it then appears to be a special form of positive reinforcement appropriate to the emotional condition called aggression.

Verbal behavior may be automatically self-punishing. The names of disliked persons and responses appropriate to embarrassing, dangerous, or gruesome episodes generate punishing consequences in the process of being emitted. A speaker (especially a child or superstitious person) will often obviously reject or revoke a response when asked to emit a sentence in which the name of a loved one is coupled with a blasphemous, obscene, or pejorative adjective, or in which the loved one is elaborately damned. The response will be either not emitted or soon revoked with an autoclitic such as *I didn't mean it,* often with clear signs of anxiety generated by the automatic conditioned aversive stimulation. In somewhat the same way it may be difficult to get a child to bless an enemy or describe him with affectionate or flattering adjectives.

A subtle form of punishment follows when a response "gives something away"—when it spoils the point of a joke by presenting the key word too soon, reveals an ulterior motive in propaganda, or presents the point of an essay in such a simple form that the rest of the essay becomes superfluous. Verbal behavior is also punished when it exposes the speaker to punishment for other reasons—as when a sin or crime is confessed or inadvertently revealed. Particularly since Freud, a response may be punished because it exposes the operation of objectionable variables. When passing a litter of pigs while walking with a friend, a sudden inquiry about the friend's children is scarcely apropos. A writer's choice of themes may be subject to punishing consequences at the hands of critics influenced by psychoanalysis. But if the post-Freudian has an additional reason for weighing his words, the change is nevertheless one of degree. Gross "revelations" have probably always been grounds for editing. In Anthony Trollope's *The Last Chronicle of Barset,* published in 1866-67, Grace Crawley has received a written proposal of marriage from Major Grantly, but because of her father's current misfortune and disgrace she is compelled to reject him and to conceal her own feelings. She writes to him:

"I know that a gentleman ought not to marry any girl to do himself or his family an injury by it, and I know that if I should make such a marriage, I should be unhappy ever afterward, even though I loved the man ever so dearly with all my heart." These last words she had underscored at first, but the doing so had been the unconscious expression of her own affection and had been done with no desire on her part to convey an expression to him. But on reading the words, she discovered their latent meaning, and wrote it all again.[6]

The Effects of Punishment

Concealing the identity of the speaker. In a group the speaker may *murmur* his dissent or protest or *hiss* his disapproval. These responses do not conspicuously employ the speech apparatus, and the sounds are not easily traced to their source. (The *whisper* is a different kind of modification of response because it involves multiple audiences.) The anonymous letter is the written counterpart of the murmur or hiss but susceptible to the normal variety of forms. In all these ways the speaker avoids punishment. A related technique is to leave a manuscript to be read or published after one's death. Roman wills often contained vicious comments on public men and affairs.

Recession to the covert level. There are many reasons, as we shall see in Chapter 19, why behavior drops below the level of scope or energy at which it affects the surrounding world, but much behavior is covert simply because it would be punished if overt. The speaker talks to himself to avoid the punishments mediated by the external environment. Children generally talk aloud until punished for doing so, and adults who are characteristically resistant to punishment—for example, certain types of psychotics—also do so.

Talking to oneself. The usual punishing contingencies permit certain modes of avoidance or escape in which behavior is actually emitted. The behavior may be overt but concealed from listener or reader. One may talk aloud when alone; or one may keep a diary, under lock and key. The overt behavior may be restricted to the writer as the only audience by being put in coded form. Samuel Pepys could not sufficiently escape the various subtle punishments which threatened him by speaking only covertly or by trusting his diary to lock and key; he resorted to writing in a form which remained undeciphered for many years.

Disguised speech. Punishment based upon form of response may generate other techniques of evasion. One method is illustrated by

[6] Trollope, Anthony, *The Last Chronicle of Barset* (Everyman's Edition), p. 324.

the story of the two nuns who purchased an ass, only to discover that the one word which made the beast move forward was obscene. Fortunately it was composed of two syllables, neither of which by itself was objectionable. The nuns solved their problem by a nice division of labor: one emitted the first syllable and the other the second. Another device is possible when an echo has a short reverberation time and can be heard to repeat only a final syllable or two. Erasmus used this technique in a form of wit: "he twice uses oblique forms of ὄνος (Greek for *ass*) as an echo, first for *eruditionis,* and then for *Cicerone*." [7] Another form of evasion is exemplified by the acrostic—the timid lover conceals the name of his beloved in, perhaps, the initial letters of a poem.[8] Other forms are made possible by resorting to multiple audiences—as in satire (Chapter 9). And it is only a short step to the use of metaphor or symbolism—a device studied in great detail by Freud. In general, symbolic behavior lacks the punishable properties of the unsymbolic counterpart but retains properties which are positively reinforcing.

The Autoclitics of Editing

All the effects so far listed may be regarded as the immediate result of the combined action of positive and negative consequences of behavior. We do not need to suppose that the speaker makes any deliberate effort to avoid punishment. Under conditions in which both reinforcing and aversive consequences prevail, certain forms of behavior are relatively strong as a result of algebraic summation. Often, however, the speaker hits upon these forms only after punishable behavior has reached at least an incipient stage of development and has been rejected. (How the speaker finds behavior which is still reasonably appropriate to the situation and need not be rejected will be discussed in Chapter 17.) When this has occurred, punishment has done more than generate a "negative strength" to be assessed in multiple causation.

One form of editing which involves an obvious process of review and revision consists of emitting the response but qualifying it with an autoclitic which reduces the threat of punishment. Having rejected a response because it will injure the listener, we may never-

[7] Hudson, W. H., quoted in notes by Leonard Dean on Erasmus, *The Praise of Folly* (University Classics, Chicago, 1946).

[8] A commencement hymn written by a graduating senior at Harvard was found after publication to be an embarrassing acrostic. The initial letters of four four-line stanzas composed a scatological comment on all commencement hymns.

theless emit it after prefacing it with the autoclitic *If I were in a more aggressive mood, I might say. . . .* Many autoclitics express the speaker's faith that he will receive a *nihil obstat: Perhaps you will not take it amiss if I say . . . , If you will pardon the expression . . . ,* and so on. The compounding of qualifying autoclitics so obviously shows that the speaker is sensitive to the possibility of aversive consequences that it is a powerful device for portraying character. In Trollope's *Dr. Thorne,* the doctor has just said, "I don't know whether you can condescend to be civil to Thumble. I could not." Mr. Robarts replies: "I am not quite sure that incivility would not be more efficacious." We can reconstruct a series of responses from the most bold to the most hesitant, as follows:

a) Incivility is more efficacious (when used)
b) Incivility would be more efficacious (if used)
c) I say that incivility would be more efficacious (but I may be wrong)
d) I do not say that incivility would not be more efficacious
e) I do not say with certainty (am not quite sure) that incivility would not be more efficacious.

The rhetorical device called "paraleipsis" consists of emitting a response together with an autoclitic which asserts that the response is not being emitted: *I will not mention the obvious lack of logic in what my opponent has just said.* Another device is the pretended slip. In the Presidential campaign of 1952 efforts were made to associate the Democratic candidate, Adlai Stevenson, with Alger Hiss, who had been convicted of perjury in testifying in an inquiry into Communism. A Republican speaker affected a *lapsus linguae* by calling Stevenson *Alger.*

A response which may be mildly punished—because, for example, it is slightly inaccurate or inappropriate to a particular verbal community—is often emitted with the autoclitic "nervous laugh" indicating to the listener that the speaker has felt the effect of punishment but is responding in spite of it. Insecure people may qualify most of their remarks, at least with respect to potentially punishing listeners, with an autoclitic giggle.

Sometimes a response which is "known to be wrong" will be emitted with a colorless intonation or with low unmodulated energy. When several people are trying to recall a name, one may "hopelessly" emit an obviously incorrect response. Children occasionally emit malaprops in this manner, especially when they are due to obvious fragmentary sources of strength. In the example noted in

Chapter 9, the child who had only recently seen her first ferry-boat and had not yet acquired a well-defined tact referred to the boat as a merry-go-round in a manner clearly indicating that the expression was incorrect.

In describing this effect of punishment, such expressions as *withholding, releasing, permitting, repressing, rejecting,* and so on, are generally figurative. We cannot always point to a special activity of the individual which physically constrains verbal behavior, pushes it around, or sets it free. What usually happens is that an incompatible response displaces a punished response, the net productive effect of punishment being to provide for the reinforcement of the incompatible response forms. This principle is sometimes used to explain the strength of verbal behavior for which there is no other explanation: the behavior is strong because it displaces punishable responses. This is the explanation of the patient in therapy who talks excessively on one subject to avoid talking on another, but the process was recognized long before Freud. The hero of Benjamin Constant's *Adolphe* reported that, as tension between himself and his mistress mounted, *"nous parlions d'amour de peur de nous parler d'autre chose."*

It is sometimes necessary, as we have already seen (Chapter 6), to regard "doing nothing" as a response if it has identifiable reinforcing consequences. But doing nothing is obviously incompatible with punishable behavior, and among the consequences of "not speaking" is often the avoidance of punishment. There is a distinction, albeit a tenuous one, between rewarding a child for keeping silent and punishing him for talking; but in the second case the punishment arranges for the automatic reinforcement of keeping silent. In "snubbing," one person punishes another by refusing to speak to him. The effect of snubbing is very close to that of insulting, but the two behaviors must be described as "not speaking" and "speaking" respectively. When a child is punishing his parents by remaining silent, he may break into unedited speech when an exciting event occurs, but this automatically punishes the child by destroying the advantage he enjoyed in punishing by silence. One may continue to remain silent in snubbing an acquaintance in order to avoid the punishment automatically generated by the loss of the snubbing advantage.

The various effects of punishment do not seem to warrant the extensive use of this technique to reduce the strength of verbal responses. If punishment is administered skillfully enough to produce "successful repression," the result may be satisfactory, and in general there is a considerable gain if punishment generates a process of editing through which verbal behavior is emitted with "deliberation." This is particularly true with respect to the practical consequences of verbal behavior to be considered in Chapter 18. The value of "deliberation" is seen in the experiment in which a pigeon "names" colors. The human speaker's performance is also improved by a mild punishment. If all one's verbal responses were invariably reinforced, one would be almost constantly occupied with verbal behavior. A mere reduction in the relative frequency of reinforcement [9] would reduce this activity, but probably not to a reasonable level. The process of extinction, as employed in discrimination, brings verbal behavior under appropriate stimulus control, but the conditions under which verbal behavior is reinforced are so extensive and so confusing that something more is probably needed. The processes of editing generated by punishment greatly increase the appropriateness of verbal behavior to all features of an occasion, including the audience.

Unfortunately, however, the consequences are not always so happy. Stuttering, stammering, mutism, stage-fright, emotional confusion, and a general low level of verbal behavior with a loss of all its advantages may follow. Milder consequences are familiar. It is often only because of the rejection of a first response that a second objectionable form gets its chance. Because of punishment for clipping final g's the correct response *mountain* may be rejected in favor of *mounting*. In Chapter 11 the rejection of repetitious forms was found to lead to distorted neologisms. The high-flown phrase proved too strong in the composition of a poster supplied by an insurance company: *Please post this card in your garage with a view of having your co-operation in lessening automobile accidents,* where a commonplace version (ending, perhaps, *and help us avoid automobile accidents*) seems clearly to have been rejected.

POSITIVE CONSEQUENCES LEADING TO THE RELEASE OF A VERBAL RESPONSE

The automatic reinforcement of verbal behavior also plays a role in the process of editing. If the subvocal test reveals simply that a response generates no conditioned aversive stimulation, the response

[9] Ferster, C. B., and Skinner, B. F., *Schedules of Reinforcements* (New York, 1957).

is then "released." But the test may have a positive effect which encourages overt emission. This will be important if the covert response is weak because it has been poorly conditioned or has suffered extinction, or because the speaker is fatigued or ill, or because the controlling situation, including the audience, is not clear, and so on. By reinforcing the speaker at the covert level, the response acquires additional strength and may be overtly emitted.

"Testing for correctness" is a case in point. A person who has acquired a second language mainly as a listener or reader and then begins to speak it is for a long time a more discriminating listener than speaker. He produces responses in the language with some difficulty but readily distinguishes between effective and ineffective forms or patterns. This leads him to reject mistakes, but an equally important result is that correct responses are reinforced. In speaking one's native tongue with respect to new or confusing circumstances a comparable reinforcement of effective behavior may occur. Autoclitics, grammatical tagging and ordering, rhetorical ordering, and so on, may be tested subvocally and successful instances reinforced to the point at which they are emitted overtly. In reviewing behavior at the covert level, one may for the first time "see what one has to say, and judge it worth saying."

Many other positive consequences come into play when verbal behavior is produced to satisfy specifications (see Chapter 17). A familiar but not necessarily verbal example is mimicking the behavior of another person. The poor mimic has an inadequate imitative repertoire; nevertheless, he may be capable of discriminating between a good and bad imitation. His only recourse is to emit a variety of responses and to select those which have the appropriate effect upon him. Although poor attempts are automatically punished, improvement is mainly achieved by the reinforcement of good attempts. The verbal parallel is, of course, echoic behavior. In both the original acquisition of a verbal repertoire and, possibly much later, the acquisition of a new language, the echoic behavior of the speaker develops later than his behavior as a listener. This makes possible the automatic reinforcement discussed in Chapter 4, and it also provides for momentary reinforcement which may affect the outcome of an editorial review. The special effects of Chapter 6 may also alter the strength of behavior in momentary reinforcement.

THE PROCESS OF EDITING

Although original manuscripts supply some information about written behavior, the covert editing of vocal behavior is not easily observed. Frequently there are external evidences—for example, the time required by a process of review—and the speaker may describe at least part of the process with autoclitic comment when the behavior is eventually emitted. The general process appears to be as follows. The production of raw verbal behavior, following the principles outlined in Parts II and III comes first. Autoclitic responses or activities (Part III) then occur. The resulting behavior may not immediately reach the ultimate listener. Because of punishment of other behavior, it is held up for review by the speaker or writer. Changes occur in the act of review which lead to rejection, to emission in qualified form, or to full-fledged emission. Often the process is not complete until the speaker has resorted to other activities to produce alternative forms of response (Chapter 17).

The functions of the speaker in generating and editing the raw material of his verbal behavior suggest the traditional distinction between ecstatic and euplastic composition. Wholly unedited behavior is ecstatic. The heavily wrought and thoroughly considered end-product is euplastic. Sometimes these functions are usefully separated in time. A writer may find it most effective to produce large quantities of behavior under the relaxed conditions of editing to be discussed in the next chapter and then to work this material over under totally different circumstances. There is a comparable separation in time when a writer refashions material he has dreamed—as R. L. Stevenson is said to have done. Drugs which favor the emission of verbal behavior act mainly upon the ecstatic phase. Tacitus reported that the Germans made their decisions at night when drunk and acted upon them the next day when sober. Something of the same sort is done by the poet who, in an ecstatic phase, produces material which is later considerably reworked.

Sometimes the two activities go on in different skins. The manner in which Talleyrand was accustomed to prepare state papers is an example. He would

> limit himself to giving to his aides a general idea of the document they were to write. He might indicate certain expressions to be inserted in the text which was to be submitted to him, and for his part that was about all. When the work was brought to him, he read it carefully. If

he was not fully satisfied he refolded the paper and, handing it back to the writer, said either *That's not it,* or *That's not it, yet* or, possibly, *That's not quite it* with no further explanation. It was up to the writer to guess how he might achieve the ultimate triumph: *That's it.*[10]

[10] Lacour-Gayet, G., *Talleyrand, 1754-1838* (Paris, 1930).

Chapter 16

Special Conditions of Self-Editing

VERBAL BEHAVIOR is not always subjected to the review discussed in the last chapter. Some variables are too powerful to wait for editing. A response is "blurted out," and the speaker may later report *I couldn't resist saying. . . .* Behavior of more moderate strength also remains unedited for a number of reasons which we must now examine.

DEFECTIVE FEED-BACK

If editing is to occur, the speaker must react as a listener to his own behavior. If he cannot do so, he cannot edit. When behavior is executed with speed, either because it is very strong or because speed has been differentially reinforced (compare the student answering a question rapidly in order to be the first to answer it), the response affects the listener as soon as the speaker himself. The speaker cannot prevent the response, though he may later revoke it. The slip which is not "caught" but immediately "seen" after emission is characteristic of rapid speech.

The feed-back from the speaker's own behavior may be physically interrupted. Deaf persons are more likely to talk aloud, particularly when alone, because it is more difficult for them to make the distinction between covert and overt behavior upon which punishment is based. A synthetic deafness may have the same effect. Hairdressers are familiar with an example. The beauty "parlor" has revived the etymology of the term in a curious way. One type of hair-dryer stimulates the customer with what is technically called "white noise." The rushing sound of the warm air used to dry the hair is an effective masker of auditory stimuli. When self-stimulation is thus effectively prevented, a customer will occasionally begin to talk aloud, to the possible amusement of others whose hearing is not affected by the dryer. Written behavior is usually fed back as a visual stimulus, but the writer may write in the dark or may not look at what he is writing. This condition commonly encourages the "automatic writing" described below. The movement of a planchette which traces letters on paper or spells words as it moves about a "Ouija board" bearing letters of the alphabet may be due to slight responses of which the operator himself is unaware. When two people place their hands on the planchette, it is easy for each to attribute any movement to the other.

Defective Self-observation

Even when return stimulation is not lacking and when there is time to respond to it, the speaker may nevertheless fail to respond. He does not edit because, to put it roughly, he "does not know what he is saying." The stimulation generated by the speaker's own behavior, whether public or private, has simply not been effective. The spoken slip may not only not be seen when emitted, it may even be denied when pointed out later. This is not particularly surprising since only a small part of the stimuli impinging upon the organism evoke responses, verbal or otherwise. However, reinforcing contingencies play their part. Some verbal environments do not demand much self-descriptive behavior, while others produce the familiar "introspective" person. Similar contingencies may explain differences in editing. In a relatively permissive environment, the stimulation generated by the speaker's behavior is not sufficiently aversive to lead to editing. When failure to edit is due to the lack of such contingencies, we do not usually say that the speaker *cannot* describe his own behavior because, when the proper contingencies are introduced, he usually does.

Under these conditions the speaker usually accepts a correction as to what he "meant to say." Occasionally his own further behavior provides additional stimuli leading to a belated editing. A repetition of the response which has emerged as an unseen slip may have this effect: *In the north you had a leader of humble origin like Lee; in the south, a man like Lee—I mean, in the north you had a man of humble origin like Lincoln. . . .* Here the erroneous response *Lee* passes unnoticed until the same response is made a second time under suitable circumstances. The fact that the speaker finds it already strengthened from self-echoic sources seems to act as a sufficient supplement to generate retraction.

Textual errors are perhaps more often permitted to stand than spoken. A psychologist had prepared an examination question by listing the names of important men which his students were to arrange in historical order. The question was captioned: *Who followed whom?* The name Hume was on the list. One hour after preparing the question it occurred to the psychologist that he might enliven the examination by substituting the pun *Who followed Hume?* Upon returning to the manuscript, he found that he had already written *whom* as *Hume.* Another instance supplied by the same psychologist involves misspelling. In writing a paper which referred especially to some experiments on anthropoid apes, he had complained of the unorganized and opportunistic ways in which the problems of a science of behavior were being attacked. *Instead of an organized campaign,* he wrote, *such investigators seem content with a sort of gorilla warfare.* Several weeks later a colleague raised the question of whether the humor in *gorilla* was appropriate in a scientific paper, but the writer had not noticed the misspelling or the multiple variables.

Misspelling and misprinting involve deficient editing, but they are of little interest except when they show the operation of other variables. One edition of a well-known book on psychoanalysis contains the passage *The father's action* (in coitus) *may be construed as sadistic—the posture perhaps being associated with fighting. . . . This sadistic conception of coitus may affect later martial relationships.* The authors may have permitted *martial* to stand, where it appears to have replaced *marital,* because of a thematic connection with fighting.

Defective Responses to Controlling Variables

It is perhaps commoner for the speaker to respond to his own *behavior* but not to the variables which control it. The relation to controlling variables may be tenuous or obscure, or not seen because punishment has been contingent upon it. One who is accustomed to explaining his behavior may express his puzzlement by saying *I can't understand what made me say that.* More often, however, no explanation is felt to be necessary. Most Freudian slips involve a failure to see the controlling variable rather than the behavior itself. The phenomenon was known before Freud. Trollope describes many instances of it. In *The Last Chronicle of Barset,*[1] for example, the dominating Mrs. Proudy has come to a sudden end, leaving her husband master of his own house for the first time.

> He could have [his letter bag] when he pleased now;—either in his bedroom or left for him untouched on the breakfast table till he should go to it. "Blessed be the name of the Lord", he said as he thought of all this; but he did not stop to analyze what he was saying.

Controlling variables are commonly overlooked in literary borrowing. A writer usually possesses extensive verbal repertoires generated by reading other writers. These are usually rejected or emitted only with appropriate autoclitics acknowledging the source. When it is inferred that the writer is aware of the source but, by not mentioning it, takes credit for the behavior, the result is called plagiarism.

Controlling variables are especially likely to be overlooked when they enter into multiple causation. We have already noticed how the projective test may be used to evoke verbal behavior which is less likely to be edited by the speaker because he does not recognize the location of the controlling variables. In the verbal summator, for example, the subject is less likely to edit his behavior if he believes himself to be repeating fairly accurately what he hears. Repetition is less likely to be punished than behavior emitted by the subject with respect to other variables.

Two intellectual movements in Western culture have greatly increased the individual's sensitivity to controlling variables by reinforcing behavior descriptive of such variables and punishing its absence. One of these is the literary movement of self-analysis culminating in the writings of Marcel Proust, as a result of which the reader is led to search for the causes of passing moods, capricious memories, or fragmentary verbal behavior. Shortly after reading the words *gutta percha,* the writer once found himself repeating *With love's light wings did I o'erleap these walls.* This was recognized as a line from *Romeo and Juliet,* but there seemed to be no reason for its recall. Only after prolonged scrutiny was it discovered that *o'erleap* was incorrect and that the word was *o'erperch.* Had it not been for the influence of Proust, this devious causal relation might well have gone unnoticed.

The other cultural movement is, of course, psychoanalysis. Freud's interpretation of revealing slips and other anomalous behavior of

[1] Trollope, Anthony, *The Last Chronicle of Barset* (Everyman's Edition), p. 248.

everyday life has forced the speaker to react more sensitively to the variables which may be inferred from his behavior and, as we saw in the last chapter, to reject responses which reveal objectionable variables. It is possible that Samuel Butler would not today so obviously give vent to his father-hatred by writing a book in which a father figures in an unfavorable light, nor would Lewis Carroll torture young children on the verbal rack called *Alice in Wonderland.* In a causal account we have to explain simply why behavior of this sort is emitted. The behavior, whether in literary disguise or not, is strong for reasons which can at least be suggested if not proved. Whether or not it is edited is a separate question.

Among the variables controlling behavior to which one may be unable to respond is the stimulus. A stimulus may be effective enough to evoke a response although the relationship between the two cannot be identified. When we say *He reminds me of so-and-so, but I don't know why,* we are saying essentially *When I see him I find myself saying "So-and-so," but I can't identify the controlling features of his appearance.* In the same way, we cannot always retrace the intraverbal steps which have led us to the solution of a problem or the recall of a line of poetry.

"Automatic" Verbal Behavior

An inability to respond to one's own verbal behavior or to controlling variables is most marked in certain conditions of the organism, of which sleep is the commonest example. Most people speak occasionally while asleep; but the behavior does not affect the speaker as listener and is not edited. Similar conditions exist in the spontaneous or hypnotically induced trance. Verbal behavior under such circumstances is called "automatic." The commonest case is automatic writing, where it is easy to prevent the subject from being stimulated by his own behavior and where the result is also more readily available for analysis, but automatic talking is also possible. Spontaneous automatic writing frequently suggests an escape from powerful repressing forces. A student who had done well at a small college, in close contact with sympathetic members of the faculty, went on to graduate school, where he found things much more difficult and the faculty quite indifferent to his problems. During a particularly difficult lecture he stopped taking notes and very slowly covered a page of his notebook with a scrawl in large, childish letters: *I can't go on, please, I want to go back.* At the end of the lecture he looked at the page and exclaimed *See what I've done!* What he had written "automatically" would, of course, have been rejected prior to emission in a "normal" condition. Automatic writing is not always clearly punishable, however. Hadamard [2] reports that in high school, faced with a task which did not interest him, he found he had written across the top of his paper: *Mathématiques*—the name of his favorite subject. The response was strong but not because it could not be emitted elsewhere.

Writing under hypnosis may not affect the writer as reader and frequently takes forms which would be rejected in the waking state as potentially punishable. Feed-back from the writing arm may also be interrupted although the individual is not out of contact with other features of the environment. In a psychological experiment conducted at Harvard University, Gertrude Stein and Leon M. Solomons found it possible to generate automatic writing simply by allowing the subject to make random writing movements while engaging in other activities such as reading a book. It has been pointed out elsewhere [3] that the automatic productions which they reported with Miss Stein as subject strongly resemble some of her later literary works. For example, the automatic passage

> Hence there is no possible way of avoiding what I have spoken of, and if this is not believed by the people of whom you have spoken, then it is not possible to prevent the people of whom you have spoken so glibly. . . .

resembles the passage beginning *Seat a knife near a cage* analyzed on page 350.

The fact that the automatic writer is eventually surprised to discover what he has written clearly suggests that he was not being stimulated by it at the moment of writing. As a result, automatic writing is often ungrammatical, childish, obscene, hackneyed, or trivial. All these features would have led to the rejection of the behavior in normal writing.

Automatic writing is frequently well *composed,* however. The self-stimulation needed for the autoclitic functions of Part IV must be available. What is lacking seems to be the self-stimulation associated with punishment. But there are conditions under which self-

[2] Hadamard, Jacques, *The Psychology of Invention in the Mathematical Field* (Princeton, 1945).

[3] Skinner, B. F. "Has Gertrude Stein a Secret?" *Atlantic Monthly* (January, 1934).

stimulation is reduced, and editing therefore deficient, which involve a deterioration in composition. "Delirium" could almost be defined as unedited behavior. Verbal behavior in illness or great fatigue is less likely to be edited, not only because it is not clearly enough characterized, but because the editing function is also weakened. Something of the same effect is produced by various drugs, including alcohol and the so-called truth serums, which have in addition the effect of allaying the anxiety associated with punished behavior and therefore reducing the tendency to withhold responses.

Some of the pathology of verbal behavior may involve editing. The aphasic patient may be unable to withhold an inappropriate response although its inappropriateness is obvious to him. In palilallia (mentioned in Chapter 4) there is a similar inability to restrain behavior, in spite of obvious punishable properties. Under gross physiological derangement a patient may talk continuously for days. Unrestrained verbal behavior is also common in the postepileptic.[4] It is not clear whether the behavior is too strong to submit to editing or whether the withholding process is deficient.

SPEAKER AND LISTENER AS "SEPARATE PERSONALITIES"

When feed-back from verbal behavior has been lacking at the time of emission and when the speaker or writer is then faced with evidence of that behavior, he is likely to attribute it to another person. He not only has no memory of having produced it, but the unedited material may be so strange or objectionable as to be unrecognizable. In Dickens' *Great Expectations*, Joe, the blacksmith, makes up a couplet for a tombstone:

> "I made it," said Joe, "my own self. I made it in a moment. It was like striking out a horseshoe complete, in a single blow... Couldn't credit my own ed—to tell you the truth, hardly believed it *were* my own ed."

Similarly it was reported of Keats

> that he has often not been aware of the beauty of some thought or expression until after he has composed and written it down. It has then struck him with astonishment—and seemed rather the production of another person than his own... Such was Keats' sensation of aston-

[4] Rosett, J. "Synthetic Conceptions in Neuropsychology." *Sci. Mon., N.Y., 53* (1941), 417-426.

ishment and pleasure when he had produced the lines "His white melodies" and so on.[5]

When evidence of personal participation is inescapable, there is a tendency to assign the work to supernatural forces. The Greek and Roman oracles, often apparently speaking in a trance state similar to that of automatic writing, were accepted as speaking for the gods. Poets have often been assumed to be possessed by gods or daemons. The modern spiritualistic medium often claims to be speaking with the voice of a dead person. Great religious works are often said to have been dictated by God.

In works which are not clearly prophetic or revelatory, the supernatural character of the other speaker is more clearly a figure of speech. Writers, from the most ecstatic to the most prosaic, have testified to the feeling that someone else is writing for them. From time to time it has been fashionable to "invoke" the Muse at the beginning of a literary work—to call upon the creative personality to appear and go to work. Frequently a poem is reported as coming out of the air, or at least from nowhere, already constructed and often surprising to the writer. Thus George Russell (AE) [6] writes

> ...To me it was only after long reverie that a song would come as a bird might fly to us out of the vast hollows of the air...There was always an element of the unexpected in the poetry itself, for it broke in upon and deflected the normal current of consciousness. I would be as surprised at the arising within me of words which in their combination seemed beautiful to me as I would have been if a waterlily had blossomed suddenly from the bottom of a tarn to make a shining on its dark surfaces. The words often would rush swiftly from hidden depths of consciousness and be fashioned by an art with which the working brain had but little to do.

A. E. Housman [7] describes essentially the same process in less imaginative terms as follows:

> Having drunk a pint of beer at luncheon—beer is a sedative to the brain, and my afternoons are the least intellectual portion of my life—I would go out for a walk of two or three hours. As I went along, thinking of nothing in particular, only looking at things around me and following the progress of the seasons, there would flow into my mind, with sudden and unaccountable emotion, sometimes a line or two of

5 Woodhouse, as quoted by C. I. Finney in *The Evolution of Keats' Poetry,* II, p. 532, from a manuscript in the Lowell Collection in Harvard College Library.

6 Russell, George, *Song and Its Fountains* (London, 1932).

7 Housman, A. E., *The Name and Nature of Poetry* (Cambridge, 1945).

> verse, sometimes a whole stanza at once, accompanied, not preceded, by a vague notion of the poem which they were destined to form part of. Then there would usually be a lull of an hour or so, then perhaps the spring would bubble up again, I say bubble up, because, so far as I could make out, the source of the suggestions thus proffered to the brain was an abyss which I have already had occasion to mention, the pit of the stomach. When I got home I wrote them down, leaving gaps, and hoping that further inspiration might be forthcoming another day.

Even a relatively pedestrian novelist such as Galsworthy [8] reported a similar phenomenon:

> I sink into my morning chair, a blotter on my knee, the last words or deed of some character in ink before my eyes, a pen in my hand, a pipe in my mouth, and nothing in my head. I sit. I don't intend; I don't expect, I don't even hope . . . Suddenly, my pen jots down a movement or remark . . . When the result is read through it surprises me by seeming to come out of what went before, and by ministering to some sort of possible future.

Prescott, in *The Poetic Mind*,[9] has collected many such instances. Some are treated rather mystically by those who report them, others (for example, Goethe) naturalistically in the language of somnambulism. Frequently the "other writer" has been given a name or otherwise personified—often, no doubt, whimsically or figuratively, but so commonly as to indicate a substantial tendency. George Eliot spoke of a "not-self" which took possession of her. Alfred de Musset described writing as listening, "as if some unknown person were speaking in your ear." James M. Barrie gave the name McConnachie to his "writing half." Milton mentioned a celestial patroness who dictated his poems.

Often the contribution of the "other one," being the result of a lowering of editorial standards, suffers imperfections which are subject to later editing by "one." The ecstatic comes to terms with the euplastic. As Robert Graves has somewhere described it:

> Many poets of my acquaintance have . . . observed that on laying down their pens after the first excitement of composition they feel the same sort of surprise that a man finds on waking from a "fugue," they discover that they have done a piece of work of which they never suspected they were capable; but at the same time they discover a number of trifling surface defects which were invisible before.

[8] Galsworthy, John, *The Creation of Character in Literature*, Romanes Lecture (Oxford, 1931).

[9] Prescott, F. C., *The Poetic Mind* (New York, 1926), p. 34.

Even the work of Stevenson's "dreamer" needed touching up:

> The stories must now be trimmed and pared and set upon all fours, they must run from a beginning to an end and fit (after a manner) with the laws of life: the pleasure in a word had become a business; and that not only for the dreamer but for the little people of his theatre . . . These understood the change as well as he. When he lay down, he no longer sought amusement, but printable and profitable tales.

In clinical studies of similar results, it was at one time common to identify several "personalities" within the individual. A classical example is Morton Prince's *The Dissociation of a Personality.* A patient, "Miss Beauchamp," writes first under hypnosis and later spontaneously with the personality of a younger, socially defiant "Sally." The verbal productions of Sally are childish, occasionally badly spelled, and preoccupied with certain simple themes, such as resentment at being restrained and a fondness for candy and a certain Mr. W. J. The fact that Miss Beauchamp was not stimulated by her behavior—that, roughly speaking, she did not "notice" it at the time of emission—seems to be related to the fact that such behavior would have generated conditioned aversive stimulation, with concomitant emotional states of guilt or anxiety. She would have punished herself by "noticing." In the sense that she was not noticing it, her behavior is called "automatic." The term is unfortunate in that it suggests the absence of creator rather than critic.

Verbal behavior frequently occurs in dreams. As Dickens [10] reported: "Language has a great part in dreams. I think, on waking, the head is usually full of words." Coleridge's account of the composing of Kubla Khan in a sleep induced by opium is, of course, well known. The alter ego of Robert Louis Stevenson, as already noted, frequently composed when Stevenson was asleep; the core of *Dr. Jekyll and Mr. Hyde,* for example, occurred first as a dream. Although dreamed speech may be edited upon waking (as when we do not report it to others), the original production is relatively free of the effects of punishment and in this respect resembles automatic writing. The speaking and listening functions are, so to speak, assigned to different personalities. The dreamer is the listener. Dreams in general are "enjoyed" rather than "produced." The "dream-work" is done by someone else, and the "listener" is not threatened.

The "other one" to which verbal behavior is assigned by the actual

[10] Nonesuch Dickens, xii, Letter to Dr. Stone, p. 269.

speaker may not be fanciful, even though erroneously identified. In the verbal-summator experiment the response is assigned to the phonograph record or the speaker who made it. In mishearing, the response is assigned to the speaker overheard. A curious case is reported by Brill.[11] The remark of a woman patient to her doctor *Do not give me any big bills; I cannot swallow them* is analyzed as a slip revealing a financial worry. Since *p* and *b* differ only in voicing, and since the previous *big* could easily account for the intruding slip *bills,* it would be hard to prove such a specific contribution. It is possible, moreover, that the woman actually said *pills* and that the slip was committed by the doctor in mishearing it—possibly because of supplementary strength due to his fear that he was being accused of overcharging. If this was the case, the doctor successfully avoided the mildly punishing recognition of this possibility by attributing the slip to his patient.

EDITING AS A FUNCTION OF SPECIAL AUDIENCES

The traditions and practices of editing which prevail within a verbal community are in part responsible for the extent of the verbal behavior shown by its members. The reticent or laconic differs from the voluble or effusive, in part at least, because of differences in the consequences of verbal behavior. Within a given community a speaker will show various degrees of editing in the presence of various special audiences. This fact is used by the speaker himself in encouraging his own verbal behavior when he seeks out a favorable audience, as we shall see in the following chapter. Here we are concerned merely with certain audiences distinguished by the extent to which a speaker is released from the customary editing of his verbal behavior.

When a speaker serves as his own audience, he is relatively free of the threat of punishment. Subvocal behavior is less sharply edited than vocal, and he is freer to talk to himself than to others. Diaries written solely for the writer are likely to be intimate and frank. Nevertheless, even when talking to himself, the speaker is not entirely free of the punishment which has been accorded his behavior by others. The Judaeo-Christian "conscience," like the Freudian superego, represents an inner controlling mechanism concerned with the automatic self-punishment conditioned by the punishments

[11] Brill, A. A. (Tr.) *Freud's Psychopathology of Everyday Life* (Pelican Books), p. 70.

meted out by society. The control exercised by the self as audience may be reduced if the speaker develops a sharper discrimination between this and other audiences. Such a discrimination is developed when extensive private speech remains free of external aversive consequences even though public speech remains subject to punishment.

The "confidant" is a nonpunishing audience—any sympathetic person to whom one may speak with less fear of punishment than to listeners at random. The psychotherapist usually establishes himself as a confidant in this sense. The effects of a nonpunishing audience upon the nonverbal and verbal behavior of the patient have been interpreted from this point of view elsewhere.[12] Free association ("free" of the punishment normally accorded illogical or excessive intraverbals) is encouraged by a permissive audience.

Children ordinarily punish verbal behavior less drastically than adults. Complete nonsense may be tolerated, as when two children become "silly." Playful verbal behavior in the adult is encouraged by the listener who is in the mood to laugh. Humorous books and articles are addressed to readers of this sort. A sort of license, close to poetic license, permits the emission of behavior which would otherwise be edited by the writer. The distortions of Ogden Nash and S. J. Perelman (see Chapter 11) exemplify one effect of the low level of editing in humorous writing. Fowler [13] lists several other types of effects under Mock Mistakes (for example, an incorrect textual response—*Eyetalian*—is emitted, though punishable under other circumstances), Popular Etymology (similarly faulty textual responses—*highstrikes* for *hysterics*), Mock Latin (mostly irrelevant intraverbal sequences borrowed from Latin—*hocus-pocus*), Incongruous Latin Trimmings (*Omnium Gatherum*), and many others.

The king's jester profited from a lenient amused audience. A king is usually, as we have noted in Chapter 7, a negative audience in whose presence almost all forms of verbal behavior are punished. The jester, however, was permitted to speak without punishment. As a characteristic effect of the nonpunishing audience, his behavior often became aggressive, obscene, or otherwise normally punishable. That he was not completely free of the threat of punishment is shown by his recourse to wit, where a remark is punishable only with respect to one of two or more controlling variables. In a rather legalistic sense, as we have seen, such a remark permits the speaker to

[12] *Science and Human Behavior*, Chapter 24.

[13] Fowler, H. W., *Modern English Usage*, p. 164.

escape punishment by denying the relevance of the variable with respect to which the response is offensive and pleading exclusive control from the harmless source.

The Literary Audience

The world of literature shows special reinforcing characteristics which encourage a low level of editing. Literary effects upon the reader do not in general depend upon the maintenance of a correspondence between the writer's behavior and a given state of affairs. The reader does not take practical action, is therefore not seriously misled, and makes no effort to hold the writer to a strict stimulus control. Several results need to be distinguished.

In the first place, literary behavior is marked by "license." It is rich in verbal magic, trivial controlling variables, and multiple effects. For this reason, as we have seen, it is an excellent source of examples of subtle behavioral effects. It is also rich in metaphor, not only in the colorful figures which account for much of the emotional and imaginal behavior of the reader, but those far-fetched generic or metaphorical extensions which are semi-intellectual in their effect but which would not be tolerated within the stricter canons of science. In scientific writing only a modest metaphorical extension is permitted. Coleridge's wild metaphor *The Birth of Time and Nature by the Polarization of the Chaos* extends to the problem of the creation of an ordered nature a familiar principle illustrated, perhaps, by the behavior of scattered iron filings brought near a magnet. As a creative idea it had a very low potential productivity. It was a literary rather than scientific thought. So was Stendhal's extension of the notion of crystallization to describe one stage of a developing love affair. But there is possibly nothing different in kind between the literary and scientific metaphor. The distinction is in how far the metaphor has been "fetched," the scientific verbal community having learned, as we shall see, that far-fetched metaphors are seldom productive of other useful verbal behavior or of effective action.

Literature is also the sphere of the symbol. A symbolic response is metaphorical; but where the metaphor is often useful because a nonmetaphorical response is lacking, the symbolic response emerges because a nonsymbolic response is subject to punishment. The symbol represents the selection of a response from a thematic group in which other responses are weakened by "negative sources of strength." When an object is described with a symbolic term, alternative tacts, extended or otherwise, are usually found to be commonly punished, either for their form alone or when emitted in connection with a particular stimulus. The emergence of the symbolic form follows from the dynamics of multiple causation and need not represent any special process of composition or editing. What the literary environment has to offer is a tolerance for symbol similar to the tolerance for far-fetched "intellectual" metaphors. As a world in which highly metaphorical language is permitted, it is also a world in which the individual may talk about states of affairs with respect to which most of his verbal repertoire is unavailable because of punishment.

In addition to responses of trivial strength or far-fetched metaphors and symbols, the literary environment tolerates verbal behavior organized around powerful themes—behavior which is otherwise withheld, not necessarily because of earlier punishment, but simply because the occasion for the behavior would otherwise be lacking.

The development of literary communities as tolerant nonpunishing audiences may be traced in the growth of literary art forms. From time to time new literary devices are discovered which make it possible for the writer to avoid editing his behavior. With the discovery of the stream-of-consciousness novel, for example, patterns of behavior which would ordinarily be rejected on grounds of grammar, logic, elegance, or order could be emitted freely (as in free association). The novel written in the form of a series of letters was an earlier discovery having a similar effect, letters being relatively unedited and unstructured.

The history of literature also reveals the discovery of special forms of writing, such as fable, allegory, or satire, which avoid censure or other forms of punishment by resorting to multiple variables. The political tract written in the form of a child's story perhaps deceives no one who is not also deceived by aggressive wit, but it permits the writer to engage in verbal behavior which he would otherwise need to withhold. Freudian symbolism has been exploited by many writers with the same effect.

A literary discovery which permitted the emission of unpunished verbal behavior was the novel of character. By telling a story about a character, the author is often able to engage in extensive behavior which on his own part would lead to possibly severe punishment. If the autobiographical nature of character writing is too clear, of course, punishment is not wholly evaded. The mechanism is useful with respect to variables which are not "revealing." The author engaged in the composition of a novel is freer to behave in many ways, most of them verbal, than in everyday life. There is perhaps always an element of accident when a writer hits upon a character which serves his purposes most efficiently. The *reader* may also use the character novel for similar purposes, and also usually as the result of a happy accident. As we have seen, "conversation" is prized in a novel because it most directly corresponds with the supplemented behavior of both writer and reader. In the modern novel the writer can display several "personalities" in the sense of groups of responses organized in terms of emotions, motivational states, or environmental histories. Platonic dialogue permits the writer to subdivide various "lines of thought" and to deliver himself of each under an appropriate name.

The effect of the literary environment in permitting the emission of behavior showing strong personal themes has led to the "analyses" of hundreds of literary works, mostly within the framework of psychoanalysis. Efforts have been made to show that the great themes of literature are the great themes of life, that a writer's character explains his work, that a literary work throws light on the writer's character. We have no reason to discuss these themes or "archetypal patterns" [14] in detail here.

The effect of the literary environment in furthering the emission of behavior without editing has a parallel in the behavior of the reader. A text is a world in which one behaves with a minimum of effort, not only because of the promptings and probings discussed in Chapter 10 or because the "right" book for a given reader strengthens just that behavior which is strong, but because the behavior can usually be emitted without editing. One can read without guilt much which one could not say for other reasons. The book itself and the act of reading constitute a tolerant situation in which verbal behavior is freely emitted.

Differences in verbal effusiveness are not all, of course, to be attributed to differences in the extent of editing peculiar to a culture or to a personal history. Madame de Staël's heroine Corinne differs enormously from a contemporary counterpart in the extent of overt verbal behavior. Before leaving her beloved Rome, possibly forever, Corinne spends a whole night driving from one part of the city to

[14] Bodkin, Maud, *Archetypal Patterns in Poetry* (London, 1934).

another proclaiming elaborate farewells to each. A woman of the same education and background today would probably avoid all such "scenes," perhaps even occupying herself with trivial matters to avoid all verbalization at the moment of parting. But it is not correct to say that the modern Corinne possesses all the behavior of her earlier prototype in latent form, and that the difference is entirely one of editing. Madame de Staël's Corinne was extensively reinforced for verbal behavior, not only for her conversation in the salon but for improvisations—literary compositions composed extempore often upon an arbitrarily assigned subject. It is therefore not merely a difference in the momentary extent of editing or even in the history of editing, but rather in the extent to which the two environments differentially reinforce behavior of a given form.

The Notion of "Release"

It is often said that both humorous and literary audiences "release" verbal behavior from the effects of editing or repressing which are ultimately attributable to punishment. Verbal behavior may be strong (because of a history of powerful reinforcement, for example, or from extreme deprivation) even though it has been punished, but it is not emitted. Metaphorically we say that it is displaced, concealed, suppressed, or repressed. It is only a modest extension of the metaphor to say that a response which is emitted in spite of such a history—for example, a verbal response which emerges unedited—has "escaped from or evaded censorship" or has been "released." A further extension describes the behavior before release as "pent or dammed up." The repressed material may or may not reach the point of a breakthrough, but in any case it is troublesome. "Break, my heart, for I must hold my tongue." The goal of psychotherapy is often regarded as releasing repressed and trouble-making behavior—somewhat on the analogy of removing a tumor, draining an infected wound, or administering a cathartic.

A bosom friend may serve in place of a psychiatrist. As Daniel Defoe put it in *Moll Flanders,*

> A secret of moment should always have a confidant, a bosom friend, to whom we may communicate the joy of it, or the grief of it, be it which it will, or it will be a double weight upon the spirits.

Only in this way can we avoid the objectionable consequences of repressed behavior.

> Men of the greatest and best qualities in other ways . . . have not been able to bear the weight of a secret joy or of a secret sorrow, but have been obliged to disclose it even for the mere giving vent to themselves . . . and such people, had they struggled longer with the oppression, would certainly have told it in their sleep.

Defoe suggests a technique of preventing the occurrence of punished behavior by emitting it under nonpunishing circumstances. He describes a thief who had to have himself locked up so that no one would hear him disclose his activities as he talked in his sleep—a technique of self-control comparable to clapping the hand over the mouth. But "if he had told all the particulars . . . to any comrade, any brother thief, or to his employers . . . then all was well with him, and he slept as quietly as other people."

The metaphor of repression and release is unfortunate because it misrepresents several processes in the act of fusing them into one. The principal relevant facts may be listed as follows:

(1) Incipient stages of behavior which has been punished generate aversive stimuli, and possibly the concomitant emotional effect called anxiety, and the speaker escapes from these and avoids punishment by "doing something else"—including stubbornly doing nothing. The displaced behavior is nevertheless still strong, for it will emerge in the presence of a nonpunishing audience—for example, in talking to a psychotherapist or in writing a diary or story—or will enter into the multiple determination of behavior—as in strengthening responses to the textual stimuli of a book, to the echoic stimuli of a play, or to one component of a pun or other instance of "double meaning." We need not assume, however, that the displacement has increased the strength of the response.

(2) Behavior which is emitted often changes the conditions responsible for its strength (Chapter 8). Unemitted behavior cannot, of course, do this. Since conditions which make verbal behavior strong are frequently aversive, a person possessing strong verbal behavior may "do something about it." For example, if strong behavior is unemitted because there is no audience, the speaker may act to get an audience, perhaps by simply manding one. If the behavior is unemitted because of editing, he may "look for" a form of response which will not be punished but will nevertheless alter the situation to reduce the strength of both forms. If no behavior is emitted because none is appropriate to the situation, a response may be "looked for," as one "looks for" a forgotten name. But this does not mean that

the eventual emission is due to any special mental or behavioral process not included among those to be analyzed in the rest of Part V.

(3) Because of punishment, incipient stages of behavior often produce conditioned aversive stimuli which evoke emotional reactions, mainly anxiety. The punishment of strong behavior may result in repeated automatic aversive stimuli which maintain a chronic anxiety. There are two important possible consequences: (a) the responses reinforced by a partial reduction in such stimulation may be aversive to the individual or to others—for example, they may exhaust his strength or "annoy" others; (b) the chronic emotional reaction may lead to "psychosomatic" symptoms. In either case the man is said to be ill. A reversal of the effect of punishment in therapy may reduce the troublesome avoidance or escape behavior of (a) or the pathological condition of (b).

(4) Sometimes the change is accompanied by a sudden display of strong verbal behavior. Hundreds of pages of automatic writing may be followed by psychological "relief." The patient seems to be "emptied out," to have "got something off his chest." On the analogy of catharsis the emptying process is held to be responsible for a "cure." Various neuroses, not to say psychoses, have been said to be alleviated by an exhausting logorrhea. But it does not follow that if "talking it out" is followed by relief, an inability to talk it out has caused the trouble. As in all therapy aimed at getting a patient to talk about his troubles, the causal relation is not clear. Whenever verbal behavior leads to satiation, or changes any of the variables responsible for its earlier strength, it can perhaps be said to have produced an improved condition. But if the slow therapeutic establishment of a nonpunishing audience has reduced the automatically punishing effect of incipient behavior (and with it the stimuli possibly responsible for chronic anxiety), then the emergence of protracted and vigorous verbal behavior may be the *effect* of the "cure" rather than the *cause*. The notion of catharsis, strengthened by the medical analogy, obscures this possibility. All speakers tend to emit strong verbal behavior. As Samuel Butler suggested, the poet writes a poem as a hen lays an egg; both may feel better afterwards.

The notion of "escape" has another dangerous metaphorical implication. It is often easier to mand a state of affairs than to create it oneself. Those who can afford to employ others to work for them frequently do. In the magical mand the verbal response is often the *only* available behavior. But the fact that verbal behavior, if available and in greater relative strength, is prepotent over nonverbal behavior is not aptly described as escape. When the starving man talks about food, or the lover pretends to converse with his beloved, or the enraged weakling fantasies an episode in which he tells off his enemy, verbal responses are emitted because no other behavior under the same powerful motivational control is available. But this is simple prepotency rather than the result of a special process of sublimation or a search for a way out of a practical difficulty. It is possible that Dostoevsky in writing a book about a hated father and his sons created the opportunity to emit many responses which were strong in him with respect to his own father, just as it is possible that the reader of his book may be deeply moved because he finds in these passages the opportunity to emit similar behavior which would be censured under other circumstances. But although such behavior escapes punishment, it is emitted simply as the strongest behavior available. It is not invented as a mode of escape.

Punishment which does not lead to escape may generate revolt or stubborn resistance.[15] Verbal behavior may show a Bohemian refusal to conform or the complete break with punishing agencies seen in the psychotic. The verbal behavior of Bohemian and psychotic alike is likely to be preoccupied with punishable material; it is obscene, say, or blasphemous. "Normal" verbal behavior may have the primary effect of shocking the listener or otherwise courting punishment on a smaller scale if the punishment which generally leads to editing and rejection has miscarried.

[15] *Science and Human Behavior,* Chapter 24.

Chapter 17

. . . .

Self-Strengthening of Verbal Behavior

IN THE PROCESSES of composition and editing the speaker arranges, qualifies, withholds, or releases verbal behavior which already exists in some strength in his repertoire. Much of the behavior emitted upon any occasion "just grows"—it springs from the current changing environment and from other verbal behavior in progress. We have now to consider certain specific activities which have the effect of strengthening responses in the speaker's behavior and hence of increasing the supply of behavior to be composed and edited. For the moment we shall confine ourselves to the procedures the speaker employs to increase the availability of behavior which already exists in some strength. The techniques involve most of the variables so far discussed. A person controls his own behavior, verbal or otherwise, as he controls the behavior of others.[1]

There are occasions upon which we say that the speaker "needs a verbal response." The circumstances may be incomplete, as when variables which strengthen behavior without respect to form need supplementary sources of strength. Current contingencies would be satisfied by practically any response, provided it were verbal, but no response is in sufficient strength. Thus, in finding something to say to fill an embarrassing pause, we cast about for a stimulus—the weather is usually available—and respond to it. "Casting about" is the sort of activity at issue here.

Other important occasions for "casting about" do more than strengthen verbal behavior without respect to form. A response is demanded which will have more specific properties. There are, so to speak, advance specifications which the response must fulfill, though they are not sufficient to determine its form. When someone points

[1] *Science and Human Behavior,* Chapter 15.

to an object and says *What is that?*, an appropriate response may be entirely lacking. The speaker has "never known the name of the object," and if he is to answer, he must take steps to acquire new verbal behavior. Possibly, however, the appropriate response has been acquired but is too weak to be emitted—for example, the speaker has simply "forgotten the name." The "specification" of the response he seeks is that it be appropriately reinforced as the name of the object. The speaker will be able to judge whether a response, once emitted, fulfills the specification because the behavior of the listener is more readily available than that of the speaker; although he cannot emit an appropriate response, he can as listener reinforce it as "right."

The procedures employed in finding a response are also useful when the response can be emitted but not with sufficient strength to justify a strong autoclitic—when the speaker "knows the name" but is "not sure it is right." In this case, relevant techniques will increase the strength until the response can be emitted with such an autoclitic as *I know*.

A tact may be weak for other reasons. Perhaps it has not been forgotten but simply inadequately learned. In ordering a meal in a relatively unfamiliar foreign language, for example, it may be necessary to resort to special ways of strengthening behavior, as in consulting the textual stimulus of a dictionary. A tact may also be weak because the stimulus is inadequate: the speaker might know the response if he had more information about the stimulus. In a very important case, as in commenting upon a very confused state of affairs, the stimulus is so complex that no appropriate tact is strong.

Intraverbal responses are commonly weak because of inadequate conditioning, forgetting, or obscure stimuli. The speaker may need to engage in supplementary activities to find equivalent terms in another language, to recite a poem, or to recall mathematical tables. Echoic and textual responses are seldom "forgotten," but they may be weak for other reasons. Some of the techniques employed in "catching what someone has said," or in "deciphering a barely legible text," or in responding to a remote verbal stimulus function directly to strengthen weak responses. As an example of the latter we may have been told to buy something at a store but are "unable to recall what it is." Within certain temporal limits, the required behavior may be echoic but weak because the stimulus is remote. A familiar case is the self-echoic behavior of recalling what you were on the point of saying. The relevant procedures may, of course, involve the manipulation of the variables which originally evoked the response in covert form; but they may also be used to strengthen a remote self-echoic response. (It is sometimes difficult, especially in such pathological conditions as Korsakoff's syndrome, to repeat or recall what one has actually said overtly.) A parallel textual case is recalling what one has recently read. The writer is faced with many problems of this sort as he catches an idea on the wing or teases out half-formed verbal behavior.

The same techniques are relevant even when the speaker will not recognize the response as "right" once it has been found. The fit with the specifications must be externally tested. When a response has been emitted, it is accepted by the speaker or others only in relation to other variables. In finding a rhyme, for example, the specification is that the response will rhyme while satisfying other thematic variables involved in a verse. Alliterative and stress patterns supply similar specifications. Sometimes what the speaker "looks for" is an alternative response which will be less awkward, less difficult, or less punishing in some other sense. The stutterer withholds a difficult pattern and must find a replacement. One withholds a response because it will be offensive to the present audience and must search for an inoffensive alternative. A poet withholds the literal term and must search for the metaphorical.

Frequently the specifications have to do with composition. The fragmentary responses which are available must be made into an acceptable sentence, or the witty word must be placed in a syntactic frame. The practiced writer or wit may have a stock of such frames, while the unpracticed may fall back upon the lame formula: *One might say something about. . . .*

TECHNIQUES

Manipulating Stimuli

When a speaker is unable to name an object correctly or describe it adequately, he may find it useful simply to improve his contact with it. He may get a better view, under better conditions. He may magnify the stimulus, possibly with appropriate optical instruments, and he may look at it many times or study it for a period of time. In this way he creates a favorable opportunity for appropriate responses already in his repertoire, metaphorical or otherwise. The shopper who is unable to respond appropriately because he has forgotten what he came to buy may find it helpful simply to observe the objects on the shelves and counters. Similar procedures are available for weak intraverbal responses. We look more closely at the verbal stimulus, read a passage repeatedly, at different speeds, aloud, and so on.

Self-prompts. Verbal stimuli are commonly used as formal prompts. A shopper may search for an appropriate verbal stimulus by going down a list of reminders of things to buy. A memorandum is a verbal stimulus constructed for such future use.

Explicit formal self-prompts are produced by mnemonic devices. A poem acquired as intraverbal behavior may supply formal prompts for a list of responses of lower strength. The medical student can better recall the cranial nerves in their correct order if he has learned a jingle which begins *On old Olympus' piney top. . . .* A rhyming dictionary supplies fragmentary formal prompts to the versifier: the appropriate rhyme emerges as the result of formal strength from the dictionary and thematic strength from the poem. We use a self-echoic prompt to strengthen textual behavior when, in looking for a name in a telephone directory, we keep repeating the name as we run down the list. This may have the collateral effect of preventing textual responses to other names which might cause confusion, but it is primarily effective in making it more likely that we will read the appropriate name, possibly "out of the corner of our eye."

Thematic self-prompts are familiar to everyone. We facilitate the recall of a word by repeating synonyms or near-synonyms, hoping that an intraverbal relation will supply needed strength. We may try to recall a forgotten name by responding to relevant nonverbal stimuli: *Oh, what IS his name? I met him at so-and-so's; he is studying mycology.* We repeat the line of verse which precedes a forgotten line in order to increase feeble intraverbal tendencies through summation. We solve verbal problems by repeatedly going over relevant material. We reread what we have written to supply a running start for what is to follow and reconstruct the "idea" which has escaped us by going over the verbal or other material originally responsible for it.

Self-probes. A nonverbal probe commonly used by the speaker to encourage his own verbal behavior is a crystal ball or other source of vague visual stimuli. Fortune-tellers use such devices for their effect upon the observer. The fortune-teller is more readily accepted as a "seer" if he is looking at something—perhaps only what he sees with his eyes closed—because this suggests some *external* variable rather than variables of the sort controlling pure fiction. But the fortune-teller may find the ball useful in reducing the labor of verbal invention. Auditory probes serving a similar function for oracles and prophets include ritualistic chants and incantations, which function in the manner of the verbal summator.

Verbal self-probes are exemplified by the patterns taken by tea leaves and fortune-telling cards, by astronomical and numerological data, and by various signs and omens. When a pattern corresponds roughly to verbal responses already in some strength, it functions as a probe, and a particular fortune is "read." When the emperor Augustus was an old man, lightning melted the letter *C* from *CAESAR* on a statue of him. The omen was read in essentially this form: *He will live only 100* (*C*) *days and will be deified* (*AESAR* = *God* in Etruscan).

Standard verbal stimuli may be permuted and combined in random or systematic fashion. Some professional writers create new plots and characters by permuting and combining terms describing personal characteristics, relationships, and episodes, often with the help of mechanical devices. A list of ten occupations (for example, *butcher, insurance salesman, writer*), ten traits (*optimistic, stubborn, excitable*), and ten major preoccupations (*money, babies, sports*) will yield one thousand different "characters," for example, "an excitable butcher interested in babies." Personal relationships and episodic material may be generated in the same way. The results are incomplete (that is, merely "suggestive") but they are used as probes to bring out other behavior in the writer's repertoire. Something of the sort also occurs in writing less mechanical fiction. Thus, an overheard fragmentary conversation may set off the development of a full-fledged character. We judge the product "good"—that is, we admire or otherwise reinforce the writer—in inverse proportion to the contribution of the probe. A wholly mechanical production is not "credited" to anyone.

Certain practices of rearrangement for the sake of probing verbal behavior have been identified in classical rhetoric. Although rhetorical figures and tropes are usually considered for their effects upon the listener, many are recipes for the production of behavior in the speaker. New material may be generated if the parts of a sentence are repeated in reverse order:

> We thought her dying when she slept,
> And sleeping when she died.

If the reversed order serves as a useful probe in evoking behavior which is strong for other reasons (if it "makes sense"), the effect may be to lead the writer to make other explicit reversals. A sentence is written, the elements are reversed, and if the result conceivably "says something" it is released; otherwise, it is rejected. The practice not only supplies additional verbal material, the multiple contribution of the second part suggests wit or style. Edgar Allan Poe's M. Dupin put it cynically: "The mass of the people regard as profound only him who suggests pungent contradictions of the general idea." [2] Oscar Wilde was addicted to the practice:

> The amount of women in London who flirt with their own husbands is perfectly scandalous. It looks so bad. It is simply washing one's clean linen in public.[3]

Among the devices which encourage the production of verbal behavior by manipulating stimuli we should list the removing of distractions. If verbal behavior is weak or lacking because one "cannot hear one's self think," the remedy is to escape into silence. The writer who seeks solitude is encouraging his own verbal behavior by eliminating incompatible stimuli.

Changing the audience as a variable. The speaker or writer may strengthen his verbal behavior by finding an audience appropriate to a given repertoire or subject matter. (This is not to be confused with finding an audience in the presence of which behavior already in strength may be *overtly* emitted.) Thus, a speaker who has been unduly "inhibited" by being punished for blasphemous, obscene, or illogical responses may find a confidant or other audience with respect to which he frankly engages in such behavior. If punishing consequences are not forthcoming under these circumstances, the conditioned aversive stimulation will undergo extinction. This is, as we have seen, the point of one procedure of the psychoanalyst.

The writer is particularly likely to suffer from a lack of clarity in the audience as a controlling variable, but he can often compensate for this by finding a reader or listener who immediately reinforces him. An effective audience not only selectively reinforces particular kinds of behavior, it raises the strength of behavior in general. Sometimes this seems to be the only recourse of the writer suffering from the "abulia" of extinction. A writer who finds it difficult to "put his thoughts on paper" may be able to emit the behavior in the presence

[2] Poe, E. A., *The Mystery of Marie Roget, and Other Tales.*

[3] Wilde, Oscar, *The Importance of Being Earnest,* cf. J. Marouzeau, "Dire 'non,'" *Mélanges de Linguistique Offerts à Charles Bally* (Genève, 1939).

of a favorable audience. This is exemplified by the unusual way in which a manuscript of the logician Wittgenstein was generated. Four or five select pupils

> met with Wittgenstein twice a week—sometimes oftener—for discussions of from two to three hours length. The first part of the meeting was devoted to questions asked by the students; following this Wittgenstein dictated, keeping close to the subject matter of the preceding questions, and endeavoring, as far as possible, to connect each dictation with the previous one. Some one of the students then typewrote the dictations and submitted them to Wittgenstein for correction. The dictations were mimeographed, for a limited circulation.[4]

In this way verbal behavior which was evidently too weak to be emitted with respect to the ultimate readers of a book was nevertheless evoked and put into permanent form.

Other conditions of a favorable audience may be manipulated by the speaker or writer. The relation to a listener or reader may be emphasized by external trappings. The punctilious dress which was so helpful to Buffon is not far from cap and gown or clerical garb. A "role" or other favorable "condition of editing" is physically constructed. When a writer searches for forms of writing which are suitable to him—trying his hand at children's stories, satire, stream-of-consciousness writing, and so on, he is trying particular types of audience in the broadest sense of that term.

Trollope, as we have seen, constructed an audience-like environment appropriate to the emission and reinforcement of a particular kind of verbal behavior. He had only to enter the environment to strengthen the behavior. Audience-like variables of less clear physical dimensions are not so compelling. The writer must usually "warm up"; he must write something to serve as a discriminative stimulus associated with the reinforcement of other verbal behavior. The first part of a paragraph, chapter, or book is often the most difficult; but once a substantial part has been written, it is available as an audience-like variable to strengthen similar behavior. This is only a more general case of the shift to a special repertoire in which one "works into" a particular language, jargon, or style.

All audience variables increase their control with the passage of time. Trollope's principle of *nulla dies sine linea* does not come into its full effect at once. A novelist "drops into" the role of a character

[4] From a privately circulated manuscript.

with increasing readiness as the writing progresses. The change resembles the increasing ease with which the hypnotic subject falls into a trance. In Gertrude Stein's experiments on automatic writing, she found it easier and easier to respond verbally under the experimental conditions she had set up.

It is sometimes valuable to eliminate audience variables, as we eliminate distracting stimuli. The greater frequency and strength of covert behavior is directly due to consequences attributable to a special audience. Just as there are speakers who require an optimal audience for their best verbal achievements, so there are those who are productive verbally only when writing in solitude, and for themselves. Solitude is not only freedom from distraction, it is a condition in which the self is an important audience.

Changing the Level of Editing

A speaker, or more often a writer, may encourage his own verbal behavior by "dropping into" a special condition of editing. Self-induced hypnotic trances are possibly the extreme case. A commoner example is "getting into the mood." Neither is well understood. Relevant variables must be constructed; and often a sample of behavior appropriate to the condition suffices. When two children try to work themselves into the "silly" mood which they have enjoyed on another day, their efforts usually consist of repeating silly behavior, verbal or otherwise. Something of the same sort may happen when an adult falls into the mood required to be witty or amusing—to give full sway to multiple sources of strength, to provoke unedited, distorted, or ungrammatical expressions, and so on. A kind of expression, read partly as French and partly as English, has enjoyed a vogue as "fractured French." For example, *femme de ménage* may be translated *woman of my own age*. It is difficult for anyone under the control of sharply defined audience variables to produce such material, and one who speaks only French or English cannot, of course, produce any. Most successful is the speaker whose textual behavior in response to printed French is not under sharp audience control. Such a person does not always "fracture" the language, but asked to supply new examples he may "drop into" the necessary state. Part of this is the construction of a mixed-audience control. The steps may include reviewing earlier examples, reading French as English, and so on. But equally necessary is some relaxation of the conditions of self-editing.

Mechanical Production of "Verbal Behavior"

A product resembling a record of verbal behavior can be created by the random or systematic manipulation of letters or words. It can be read or otherwise reacted to as a text whenever it approaches a standard pattern. It is not a very efficient way to produce "verbal behavior." It may be that a monkey striking the keys of a typewriter in random order would, if immortal, eventually produce all the works in the British Museum, but the result would nevertheless be worthless if there were not also a reader, also with infinite time at his disposal, who would select the parts of the product which satisfied specifications. When mechanical rearrangements are used as prompts or probes, as in generating thematic material for stories, the eventual product is full-fledged verbal behavior, but if the only process of "composition" is rearrangement, the behavior requires no analysis. A scrambled sentence is a limited universe of movable responses, but the behavior of rearranging words until a complete sequence "makes sense" is similar to solving pictorial jig-saw puzzles and need not be analyzed as verbal. Many of the techniques of cryptanalysis also lie outside the present field, although the decoded message is verbal.

Distorted "verbal behavior" (for humorous purposes, for example) may be produced by disturbing the normal arrangements of responses or printed letters or words as records of responses. Spoonerisms and pig-latin can be produced by a gross mechanical rearrangement of initial consonants or, often with great skill, in the act of emitting verbal behavior.

"Verbal behavior" can also be generated by mechanically rearranging variables. In a familiar game, words printed on counters are drawn to fill blanks in a text, and the result may be entertaining for children at an appropriate stage of development although, as we have just seen, the act of filling the blanks is not verbal. The blanks could be filled by randomly naming objects found in some sort of array—that is, by selecting at random from a set of variables controlling verbal responses. New "verbal behavior" may be generated by manipulating such variables. Children sometimes compose ludicrous "verbal behavior" by forcibly shifting variables. A child may break off the intraverbal *Jack and Jill went up the* and look about for the stimulus for an unrelated tact such as *bicycle*. Comedians generate strings of nonsequiturs or crude flights of ideas by an equally mechanical rearrangement of controlling variables.

Changing Motivational and Emotional Variables

Levels of deprivation and satiation are occasionally manipulated by the speaker in order to strengthen his own verbal behavior. He may use any of the controlling relations of Chapter 8. Ascetic regimens have been recommended for their effects on verbal productivity, among them various diets (especially vegetarianism), sexual deprivation, and the social deprivation resulting from personal isolation or hermitism. A man may also generate aversive conditions from which he can escape only by engaging in verbal behavior, as by accepting an invitation to speak or an advance royalty. The behavior generated is appropriate to the contingencies of avoidance or escape: he writes whatever is necessary to avoid the repayment of the royalty or the disapproval contingent on a poorly prepared lecture. Somewhat less specific is the aversive self-stimulation of shame or guilt, from which the speaker escapes only by responding verbally. The speaker may force his own verbal behavior by plunging into a conversation although he has nothing to say and thus submitting himself to the threat of punishment contingent upon an incomplete remark. Such aversive stimulation will not, of itself, produce verbal behavior of useful form, but the effect may summate with relevant variables.

Emotional variables are also manipulated. A man may increase the probability that he will answer a letter by rereading it and thus generating an appropriate emotional disposition—to console the writer, say, or attack him. He may review the outrageous behavior of the opposition to further the composition of a political address. He may go for a walk in the rain, listen to music, or read emotional literature to get into the "mood" appropriate to a particular type of composition. Threatened with stage fright, he may screw his courage to the sticking place by giving himself a pep talk.

The use of drugs in controlling one's own verbal behavior has, of course, a long history, as the references in Chapter 8 suggest. Physiological conditions manipulated for the same reason include the self-induced illnesses of the hangover and indigestion, and extreme physical exhaustion. Good health and vigorous exercise have been advocated as favoring other kinds of verbal behavior. The appropriate practice in each case is determined by the nature of the behavior to be produced and by other variables in the history of the speaker.

INCUBATION

So-called unconscious thought-processes have received considerable attention, particularly since Poincaré emphasized sudden insight in mathematical thinking. Poincaré argued that the occasional illumination was a "manifest sign of long-unconscious prior work." [5] The view is obviously related to doctrines of an inner creator in the explanation of verbal behavior. Since we do not require an explanatory concept of this sort in the case of "conscious" verbal behavior, we have no reason to argue for similar inner thought-processes in the unconscious case. The verbal behavior of a mathematician, as of anyone else, is presumably a function of variables in the external environment and in other parts of his own behavior. The accounts of insightful illuminations always note prior conscious work, largely of the sort to be described in the following chapter. The fact that this work did not lead immediately to the insightful "idea" does not mean that more work was necessary. A re-sorting of variables could be enough. Weak verbal responses characteristically have long latencies. Although we cannot prove that unconscious verbal behavior does not go on during a period of incubation, there is at the moment no reason to argue that it does.

What is important in these observations is the relevance of a period of incubation. Certain practical devices for the encouragement of verbal behavior consist of arranging such periods. A skilled thinker knows when to rest to permit variables to fall into a possibly more favorable arrangement. He may arrive at more adequate verbal behavior in the face of complex circumstances by "sleeping on it." More immediately, he may encourage the emission of verbal behavior by briefly doing something else or, as we say, by thinking of something else. Such behavior is acquired as the skilled lookout acquires the use of his peripheral vision in watching for something under low illumination.

Sometimes a competing variable, of the sort which disappears during incubation, may be dealt with directly. A prepotent response sometimes obviously interferes with appropriate verbal behavior. In attempting to recall a name, for example, the speaker may repeatedly emit the wrong name and may comment: *I keep thinking of so-and-so, but obviously that is not right.* Withholding interfering responses

[5] Poincaré, H., *Mathematical Creation,* translated by G. Bruce Halstead in *The Foundations of Science* (New York, 1913).

is a sort of special editing, sometimes described as "keeping one's mind a blank." (The instruction "not to think of anything" is often part of hypnotic suggestions.) Possibly the speaker learns to "keep his mind a blank" by acquiring "not-responding" as a specific operant. The behavior described as "thinking of something else" is often more easily identified. It is recommended in Souriau's dictum: *"Pour inventer, il faut penser à côté."*

PRODUCTION AND EDITING

The techniques which the speaker uses to encourage his own verbal behavior are usually intimately interwoven with processes of editing. The greater part of what is produced through the manipulation of variables will probably be withheld or revoked, because it does not conform to specifications. Although one may learn to speak in clichés by constructing an "audience" appropriate to this special language, as in writing a part in a play for a character who speaks in clichés, it is usually necessary to emit many responses appropriate to a given situation and to withhold all which are not sufficiently shopworn. Conversely, to write without clichés it may be necessary to withhold or revoke many responses before a fresh one appears. Similarly, to write in the role of a demanding character, it may be necessary to withhold or revoke all softened forms of mands. To be less demanding, on the other hand, it may be necessary to withhold or revoke straight mands. One may need to scan a number of intraverbal responses to find an appropriate pun, as one may need to scan a number of responses to find one which attains a special effect upon a given reader. The speaker or writer proceeds by alternate production and editing, and all acceptable behavior is then subject to the "composition" of Chapter 14.

A convincing account of the writer's encouragement of his own verbal behavior is given by Jules Romains in the sixth volume of his *Men of Good Will.*[6] An aging poet, Strigelius, has not been greatly reinforced for his behavior as a poet and has found the poetic springs drying up. He resolves to try a relatively mechanical process of composition. He selects pairs of words at random from a dictionary until he hits upon a pair (*lesson* and *cenotaph*) which serve as a verbal

[6] Romains, Jules, *Men of Good Will,* Vol. 6, *The Depths and the Heights.* The English translation of the chapter by Gerard Hopkins is in essence a new text written to illustrate the same point, the original chapter being impossible to translate because of the lack of corresponding intraverbals in French and English.

probe to suggest the theme *The Lesson of the Cenotaph.* He then resorts to processes of free association, of "holding the mind a blank," of catching evanescent phrases on the wing, of prompting himself either formally with stress patterns (*te ta te ta te ta*) and rhyming syllables or thematically by enumerating groups of intraverbals. Eventually he arrives at a creditable ten-line poem. It is composed of fragments which must have been parts of Strigelius' verbal repertoire, except for the two selected words which set the behavior in motion, but the ultimate pattern of the poem is created by alternate processes of production and editing.

BUILDING NEW VERBAL RESPONSES

The foregoing techniques are powerless if a set of specifications cannot be filled by any behavior in the repertoire of a speaker or writer regardless of strength. New responses may be needed. An assignment to write a story about a given subject will not suffice if behavior with respect to that subject is lacking. The writer must then set about acquiring appropriate behavior. He may build a battery of new tacts by extending his experience. Thus, a reporter "looks into conditions" in a given field, an investigator "gets the facts," an explorer discovers a new country or a new people, and a scientist conducts an experiment. All these activities bring new verbal responses into being. The writer may also acquire new intraverbal behavior by reading a book or studying a text. Reading "for" knowledge or information is usually reading undertaken for the sake of the new verbal behavior which results.

Appropriate verbal responses to stimuli which are no longer present are acquired in a special way. One may respond *book* to an actual book lying on a table when someone asks *What is on the table?*, but the response is slightly less likely to be made to the question *What was on the table a moment ago?* when the book has been removed and concealed. We say that we did not "notice the book." A more technical analysis is possible. In the first case the question can evoke an observing response, sharpening the effect of the book as a stimulus. This is not possible in the second case. If, however, the second question is often repeated, and especially if other variables are powerful, one may engage in explicit observing behavior before questions are asked. One begins to "notice objects one may be asked about." Thus, the student who must report what he sees on a journey behaves in a different way from the casual traveler. Intraverbal behavior to departed stimuli is furthered by a similar "close observance." The student "studies" a text, and his behavior in doing so differs from simple reading in the extent to which intraverbal behavior is set up.

The explicit reinforcing of "observing" behavior has only recently been studied experimentally, and mostly on lower organisms.[7] Enough has been learned, however, to justify certain distinctions. Any behavior is reinforced if it clarifies or otherwise intensifies the effect of a stimulus which serves an important discriminative function. Turning on a light to read by, adjusting the focus of a television picture, and wiping the dust off an old book-cover in the attic are examples of observing behavior which involves the manipulation of external objects. Looking toward an object, focusing upon it, and moving the head to reduce glare have similar effects but involve only the observer's body. The subtle activity of attending, which has the same effect, is more difficult to observe.

The contingencies of reinforcement of verbal behavior often extend over long periods of time. Thus, an envoy is sent to observe events in a foreign country and to report upon his return. Such contingencies may be successful in developing a remote stimulus control, presumably through the automatic reinforcement of observing behavior. The envoy will visit places where important things happen, will sit close to someone to hear what he has to say, and so on. In this way he generates or facilitates verbal behavior by manipulating stimuli.

But distant stimuli are nevertheless weak variables, and contingencies which involve them usually reinforce "bridging" behavior. The distant stimulus may be represented in a form which survives until a response can be made. Pictures and maps permit an eventual tact to an immediate stimulus which satisfies the contingencies involving the remote stimulus. Verbal responses may be recorded on the spot in the form of notes or logs; the ultimate contingencies are then satisfied by textual behavior (when the notes or logs are read) or by long-distance tacts supplemented by textual prompts (when events are described with the aid of notes).

The gap can be bridged in other ways. By memorizing a series of tacts on the spot, the speaker may later describe the scene with the intraverbal behavior he thus sets up. The bridging is accomplished

7 See, however, Holland, J. G. *Science, 125* (1957), 348-350.

by some property of the ultimate situation which sets off a verbal response evoking the intraverbal sequence. Brief spans of time are frequently bridged by setting up self-echoic chains, as in carrying a telephone number from the directory to the phone by repeating it until it has been dialled.

Chapter 18

Logical and Scientific Verbal Behavior

THE LITERARY COMMUNITY of Chapter 16 arose with the discovery and invention of contingencies which gave verbal behavior a broader scope by emphasizing its nonpractical consequences. The behavior of the writer is not checked against the immediate environment, and the special consequences discussed in Chapter 6 and the multiplication of variables discussed in Part III may therefore hold sway. But most verbal behavior has to do with effective action. When a speaker accurately reports, identifies, or describes a given state of affairs, he increases the likelihood that the listener will act successfully with respect to it, and when the listener looks to the speaker for an extension of his own sensory capacities, or for contact with distant events, or for an accurate characterization of a puzzling situation, the speaker's behavior is most useful to him if the environmental control has not been disturbed by other variables. This is the distinction between fact and fancy, truth and fiction, *Wahrheit* and *Dichtung*. Similarly, when a speaker intraverbally reconstructs directions, rules of conduct, and "laws of thought," he increases the likelihood of successful practical, ethical, and intellectual behavior, respectively, and his success in doing so depends upon the "purity" of the controlling relations.

In the history of logic and science we can trace the development of a verbal community especially concerned with verbal behavior which contributes to successful action. The behavior maintained by that community differs from the devices employed to maintain it, as effective discourse, for example, differs from rules for effective discourse. The latter—the canons, laws, and prescriptions of scientific methodology which help in defining terms, in composing sentences, in testing sentences for internal consistency, in determining truth-value, and so on—arose relatively late in the history of logical and scientific verbal behavior. We may turn first to the characteristics of that behavior itself. The practices of the community may then be explained in terms of their special achievements.

SHARPENING STIMULUS CONTROL

Nonverbal Stimuli

The scientific community encourages the precise stimulus control under which an object or property of an object is identified or characterized in such a way that practical action will be most effective. It conditions responses under favorable circumstances, where relevant and irrelevant properties of stimuli can usually be manipulated. To dispose of irrelevant controlling relations, it sets up new forms of response as arbitrary replacements for the lay vocabulary—not only the special vocabulary of science but graphs, models, tables, and other ways of "representing the properties of nature." These are verbal within the terms of our definition: representing an equation on Cartesian co-ordinates, constructing a three-dimensional model of a complex molecule, and setting a pointer on a dial are all verbal responses supplying scientific "readers" with "texts" which often correspond with their relevant stimuli in one or more dimensional systems. (Pointing to a graph, model, or scale or "reading it" for another listener, are also verbal responses, comparable to pointing to a word on a list or reading a text.)

The scientific and logical community sharpens the discriminative control of verbal responses with classificatory schemes. The scientist calls a rat a rodent not only because he has acquired a scientific name for a particular kind of animal but because his verbal behavior is controlled by a generic property which the scientific community has pointed up by establishing a classificatory operant.

Generic extensions are tolerated in scientific practice, but metaphorical, metonymical, and solecistic extensions are usually extinguished or punished. Metaphorical extension may occur, but either the controlling property is quickly emphasized by additional contingencies which convert the response into an abstraction or the metaphor is robbed of its metaphorical nature through the advent of additional stimulus control. Thus, the molecular theory of gas probably began as a metaphor in the sense that the pressure on the wall of a container was described with terms appropriate to the pelting of a wall with pebbles. Eventually other kinds of evidence removed or greatly reduced the metaphorical nature of the terms.

In ruling out the effects of other consequences of verbal behavior the contingencies established by the scientific community work to prevent exaggeration or understatement, misrepresentation, lying, and fiction. Audience variables are clarified by specifying a "universe of discourse" as a subdivision of the repertoire to be employed, from which terms appropriate to other audiences are specifically excluded. Scientific verbal behavior is most effective when it is free of multiple sources of strength; and humor, wit, style, the devices of poetry, and fragmentary recombinations and distortions of form all go unreinforced, if they are not actually punished, by the scientific community.

The nature of the stimulus control is described to the listener with appropriate autoclitics. Scientific and logical writing contains many descriptions of the speaker's behavior (*I observe, I conclude*), frequent characterizations or qualifications (*It is true, . . . probable, . . . possible that . . .*), and quantifying autoclitics descriptive of the range of application of a response (*some, any, all, no,* etc.). Much of this is involved in the nature of scientific assertion. Additional autoclitics of predication tell the reader how to relate the separate parts of the verbal stimuli which they accompany.

The contingencies of reinforcement which create a special scientific repertoire and sharpen its stimulus control provide for a kind of behavior which serves the listener as (1) an optimally effective *discriminative stimulus* in evoking any behavior he may already possess with respect to a situation and (2) a fruitful source of *instruction* in altering his behavior with respect to new situations.

Verbal Stimuli

The logical and scientific community also sharpens and restricts verbal behavior in response to *verbal* stimuli. Assuring the accuracy of echoic and textual behavior is an obvious example; it is important to know what was actually said, in either vocal or written form. In general, however, practices are designed to clarify the relation between a verbal response made to a verbal stimulus and the *nonverbal* circumstances responsible for it. The community is concerned with getting back to the original state of affairs and with avoiding any distortion due to the intervening verbal linkage. For example, if a speaker emits a tact which in the practices of the community is controlled by either of two very different stimuli (for example, if he says *light,* which may be a response to an object of little weight or to visible radiation), and if a second speaker responds to this echoically (or textually if the first response was written), his listener may take action with respect to the wrong state of affairs. The original speaker would have been in a position to supply helpful autoclitics—for example, by emitting a synonym normally under the control of only one stimulus or by qualifying his remark with *I mean "light" in the sense of "not heavy"*—but he is not in contact with the listener to whom the distinction is important and may be unaffected by the contingencies which generate autoclitics. The speaker who reports the behavior is restrained by the logical and scientific community to find appropriate qualifiers. In other words, in responding echoically or textually to the verbal behavior of another speaker the logician or scientist is under special pressure to "make sure of the meaning." This pressure is exerted by reinforcing contingencies which generate more than mere echoic or textual behavior.

(When both speaker and listener exist within a single skin, one may still respond "erroneously" to the other's verbal behavior. Extreme examples are supplied by aphasics, whose "thought processes go astray" when a trivial intraverbal response brings a "change of meaning" in midstream, but the effect is not uncommon in the normal speaker, especially when the behavior is written and the action as reader delayed so that the speaker "forgets what he meant to say.")

The logical and scientific community eliminates intraverbal responses which interfere with a "logical train of thought." Sells described some of these in his study of the "atmosphere effect." [1] The community guards against confusing or misleading collateral responses to verbal stimuli in several ways. A special scientific vocabulary (used within a given "universe of discourse") is relatively free of responses under other sorts of stimulus control—that is, of superfluous intraverbal relations. The symbols which appear so often in logical and scientific behavior (often as replacements for terms in the lay vocabulary) are especially important in eliminating unwanted echoic, textual, and intraverbal responses.

Logicians and scientists have, of course, extensive repertoires of intraverbal behavior, but these are composed of items which have been found to have satisfactory practical results. The acquisition of definitions, memorized facts, tables of constants, and so on, is a substantial part of the training of a scientist, as is learning the proper use

[1] Sells, S. B. *Arch. Psychol., N. Y.,* 29 (1936), No. 200.

of written or printed definitions, facts, tables, or other verbal stimuli which have been especially composed so that useful textual responses may be emitted on appropriate occasions.

Rules of logical and mathematical thinking, Laws of Thought, forms of syllogisms, and so on, have a related use. The distinction between the logical structure of a sentence and the particular terms which happen to occur in it is the distinction between autoclitic responses (particularly the grammatical frames of Chapter 14) and simple verbal operants. In engaging in verbal behavior which is logical and scientific the speaker slowly acquires skeletal intraverbal sequences which combine with responses appropriate to a given occasion. Just as the poet who has written many iambic pentameters finds it easy to "think" in that meter, so the logician who has emitted many responses having a given logical structure will find it easy to compose others on the same pattern. He is helped by the fact that fragmentary or skeletal operants combine with other responses in multiple causation and also by the fact that responses which do not have a customary pattern are speedily rejected as awkward and strange.

The practices which restrict responses to verbal stimuli are supported by suitable autoclitics with which the speaker represents the nature of the control of his behavior. The role of verbal stimuli is made clear by referring to "authorities," both for statements of fact (*Harvey's discovery of the circulation of the blood made it clear that . . .*) and laws (*From Newton's second law, it follows . . .*) and by citing previously listed axioms or definitions (*. . . which is true by definition*).

CONSTRUCTING NEW VERBAL BEHAVIOR

The logical and scientific verbal community has slowly accumulated a set of techniques for the construction of effective verbal behavior. The speaker moves from one set of responses to a possibly more useful set.[2] He may eventually emit, for example, what appears to be a tact or intraverbal response for which immediate appropriate stimuli are lacking but which nevertheless leads to effective action. The practices which bring this about seem to have been empirical discoveries. They are not always successful, but the growth of the

[2] The "statement composition" with which logic is said to be concerned is not to be confused with the "composition" of Chapter 14. What is meant is the present process of construction.

logical and scientific verbal community has greatly extended the likelihood of success.

A familiar example of constructing a verbal response is counting. When a speaker says *four* in response to four men seated about a table, his response may be as directly controlled by a property of the situation as *men* or *sitting*. But if he says *four* after checking a dozen rooms, some of which contain men, his response is not a simple tact. It is the result of a special use of the intraverbal linkage, *one, two, three, four,* where (because he has "learned to count") he has emitted one response in the sequence whenever he has seen a man and now reports the last response so made. Such a response as *one hundred* is always constructed—either in this way, if it is controlled by counting one hundred objects, or by other operations. Mathematics is largely concerned with verbal behavior constructed by counting or by derivative processes.

Manipulating Responses

Although the notion of a word as something "used" by the speaker has had unfortunate results, records or traces of verbal responses can, of course, be treated as independent objects. Useful verbal behavior can be constructed by the mechanical manipulation and arrangement of such objects. Even when responses are not in written form, behavior is evidently "manipulated" in the same sense. In order to restrict oneself to terms falling within a limited universe of discourse or to employ only a particular set of axioms, for example, the logician or scientist commonly sets down a list of responses in written form. His subsequent verbal behavior is reinforced by himself or others only if the responses he emits can also be emitted as textual responses to the stimuli in such a list. A list of rules, in the sense of permissible activities in constructing new responses, may also be employed. Rules of evidence in a court of law restrict the verbal behavior of witnesses; the rules of chess restrict the movements of the pieces; logical rules have a comparable effect on the logician. Constructing such a list, consulting it, restraining oneself from emitting a response which is not represented on it, and so on, are extremely complex behaviors and must be laboriously conditioned by the verbal community. The behavior and the special problems it raises are similar to those discussed under Editing in Chapter 15.

The productive manipulation of verbal responses is illustrated by the substitution of terms. If words are written on slips of paper, and if mutually replaceable slips are so marked, then the act of substitution consists simply of removing one slip and replacing it with an allowable substitute. Crossing out a set of marks on a sheet of paper and writing down another set is a commoner example. Even when the act is more difficult to observe, it presumably occurs for the same reasons and with the same consequences. Other examples of the manipulation of verbal responses are writing an expression "in an equivalent logical structure," transposing, clearing fractions, and entering values in an equation.

Many problems in semantics and deductive logic are concerned with rules for the substitution of terms. This is obvious in discussions of synonymy, but many other kinds of responses—quantifying autoclitics, for example—may also simply specify substitutability. In *The three blind mice all ran after the farmer's wife* the response *all* may be a tact comparable to the young child's ready *All gone*. But *All mice are mammals* cannot be a tact, since no one has ever observed "all mice." Emphasizing the autoclitic function by translating *Always if you can say "mouse," you can say "mammal"* does not solve the problem, since no one has observed all instances of saying *mouse*. The response is, instead, constructed from the definitions of *mouse* and *mammal* and from a unilateral rule for substitution derived from these.

The product of the manipulation of terms is usually a textual stimulus (a new equation, for example, or a new form of an expression) which may then lead to other behavior. Sometimes the new expression "solves a problem," sometimes it corresponds with an earlier statement of an hypothesis or theory (this result may be indicated with the autoclitic *Q.E.D.*), and sometimes the constructed behavior simply leads to effective, possibly nonverbal, action. It is part of the empirical discovery of the logical and scientific verbal community that behavior arrived at in this fashion may be reacted to as if it were a tact or intraverbal response, or some larger sample of the same nature. The behavior of reacting to it in such a way must also be conditioned by the community.

Logical verbal behavior was explicitly conditioned in some experiments of Moore and Anderson,[3] in which naive subjects were trained to solve problems in the calculus of propositions. A subject was given certain premises, certain transformation rules, and a conclusion to be reached. His behavior at any stage consisted simply of specifying

[3] Moore, O. K. and Anderson, S. B. *J. Psychol.*, *38* (1954), 151-160.

a rule—calling out its number, say, or pointing to it in written form. The result of the application of the rule was immediately supplied, and he then specified another rule. (He himself could have arrived at the result of each application through the use of other rules.) It was found possible to create skillful manipulators of the calculus of propositions even when the relevance of the procedure to practical behavior remained obscure—that is, when the subject did not "know the meaning" of his operations. A child may learn a chess opening in the same way.

The construction of new verbal material is usually described by appropriate autoclitics. These include literal comments like *substituting* or *transposing* as well as explicit mands upon the listener to engage in a particular action (*Let x equal the number of bricks one man can lay in one day*). Certain relational and quantifying autoclitics, many of which are familiar to the layman but are used more strictly in logical and scientific discourse, are often indicated. Autoclitics which point out the constructed nature of the responses they accompany are *Therefore* and *It follows that. . . .*

Confirmation

When new verbal behavior has been constructed, it must often be "confirmed." The process is not limited to constructed sentences. We confirm any verbal response when we generate additional variables to increase its probability. Thus, our guess that something seen at a distance is a telescope is confirmed by moving closer until the weak response (*I think*) *it's a telescope* may be replaced by the strong (*I know*) *it's a telescope.* Similarly, our guess that a rather unfamiliar object is a *kind* of telescope is confirmed if we find that it can be used as such. In using it successfully, we provide additional stimulation for the unextended tact *telescope.*

Frequently we confirm a response by finding variables which control a similar form of response in some other type of operant. Thus, we confirm our guess that an animal at the zoo is a lemur by reading the sign on the cage; in doing so we add a textual response to a weak tact. (We no doubt also profit from added "instruction"; we no longer "guess" even when not looking at the sign.) If, instead, we ask an attendant, the supplementary response is echoic. When we confirm our recollection of a fact by "looking it up" in the encyclopedia, we add a textual response; when we confirm it by asking an authority, we add an echoic response. Confirmation of new verbal responses constructed with the procedures of logical and scientific verbal behavior is important when the emerging response has never been possessed as a tact or as an intraverbal. The importance of confirmation grows with the length of the series of steps taken in the act of construction, since a generated response is emitted more and more hesitantly as the possibility of error grows.

It is useful to maintain the distinction between the confirmation of a tact and of an intraverbal. If we have put something in one of two boxes labeled *A* and *B* and as the result of looking in *B* we say *It is not in B,* we can also construct the response *It is in A.* This has the form of a complex tact, such as might be emitted after looking in *A,* but it is reached by construction. We may use an autoclitic to refer to the process (*I therefore CONCLUDE it is in A,* or *It MUST BE in A*) or to indicate some surviving weakness (*It is PROBABLY in A*). We confirm the constructed response by generating the stimulus for a comparable tact—that is, by looking in *A*. We confirm responses to *verbal* stimuli when we complete a cross-word puzzle. Our guess of the synonym for a key word given in the puzzle (an intraverbal response) is confirmed by showing that it fits the specifications of (i.e., permits us to make a textual response to) the letters in the same spaces contributed by the crossing words. On the other hand the fragmentary verbal stimuli generated by the crossing words may serve as a formal prompt for a tentative response which is then confirmed by an intraverbal response to the synonym given.

The constructed responses of logical and scientific verbal behavior are also confirmed either as tacts or intraverbals. A series of verbal manipulations respecting the orbits of the known planets may lead to a statement of the position and size of a hypothetical planet. With the aid of a telescope a response of similar form may be made as a tact. Subsequently the astronomer may emit such a sentence as *There is a planet of such and such a size at such and such a place* as a response with at least two sources of strength: the observational data with respect to which the response is a tact and the calculations which construct a comparable response. When, however, confirmation by finding the stimulus for a tact is not possible, additional constructions may supply additional strength. A single proposition is "proved" when the response is constructed in another way, as a theory is bolstered by several lines of verbal evidence, but in neither case is a comparable tact found. The theory of evolution cannot be confirmed by a set of tacts to the actual events taking place in the remote past, but a single set of verbal responses which appear to be tacts to such events is made more plausible—is strengthened—by several types of construction based upon verbal responses in geology, paleontology, genetics, and so on. Only a current event of the same nature (for example, the appearance or production of a new species under the proper circumstances) would generate a tact of the same form and convert the theory into a fact in that sense.

In proving a theory deductively the positions of specification and search are reversed. The logical and scientific manipulation is now an example of constructing previously specified behavior. In stating an hypothesis or theory we set down a complete specification of verbal behavior to be constructed. Hypotheses and theories do not, of course, arise spontaneously; they are often extended tacts or weak intraverbals. Verbal behavior is required which will have the same form but will be controlled by more substantial, if possibly more remote, circumstances. Thus, if we begin with a compound tact (for example, a description of the orbit of a planet), our task is to reach comparable verbal behavior by manipulating available responses concerned with other orbits and planets according to a set of rules. If we are successful, we confirm the usefulness of the responses and the rules we have used, among which may be axioms, postulates, hypotheses, and theories.

An example will serve to summarize the process of confirmation. Suppose someone says *That book contains four hundred pages.* The listener can act on this response with maximal confidence if it is an actual tact—if the speaker has looked at the last page in the book and found it numbered 400 (his response is more than textual because the "reading" of the number on the last page is the occasion upon which the response is reinforced by the community) or if he has counted the pages and found himself saying *four hundred* at the last page. The extent to which the listener judges the response as true, valid, or correct is governed by the extent to which comparable responses by the same speaker have proved useful in the past. In actual fact, however, the response may be of another sort. It is the vague tact called a guess if the speaker has merely noticed the thickness of the book or hefted it in his hand. It is an echoic response if he is simply repeating what he has just heard. It is a textual response if he is merely reading it. It may be a possibly defective intraverbal if he has heard or read it sometime ago or if he has memorized the numbers of pages in a long list of books, including this one. It may be a response constructed from the responses: *The book contains ten chapters* and *The average length of a chapter is 40 pages.* Conceivably the response could be an induction if many previous books by the same author have all contained precisely 400 pages (the speaker's response is then also a vague tact or guess where the controlling stimulus is mainly the author's name rather than, say, the thickness of the book).

In each case the speaker or listener may confirm the response by accumulating variables which raise its probability to a maximum. A step in this direction is taken if the response is made for any two of the reasons just given. But what is usually meant by confirmation is the generation of the response as a tact (to the page number appearing on the last page) or as a response constructed by counting. To such responses the listener reacts with maximal (but, of course, by no means necessarily complete) confidence.

"Scientific Research"

Empirical science is only in part concerned with the construction and confirmation of verbal behavior. In broader terms, it is a set of practices which are productive of useful behavior. A large part of this is verbal and a part of this, in turn, constructed. Instrumentation, for example, is a characteristic feature of scientific method which extends our responses to nature by enormously amplifying and clarifying events which can serve as stimuli (as when we look at something through a telescope or microscope), by converting some forms of energy into others to which we are able to react (as when we "listen" to a Geiger counter), and in many other ways. Much of what we do in response to the stimuli so generated or modified is verbal.

Other experimental methods bring responses under a stricter stimulus control by manipulating states of affairs so that relevant properties are emphasized. If some property of a stimulus has been responsible for the metaphorical extension we call a theory, experimental practices may permit us to isolate that property (perhaps as the common member of several stimuli) and hence to replace the metaphor with an abstract response. Other methods are concerned with testing the range of broadly generalized responses or laws.

Evaluation

An important part of scientific practice is the evaluation of the probability that a verbal response is "right" or "true"—that it may be acted upon successfully. (Logic is concerned with this in its analysis of the internal, and eventually tautological, relationships among autoclitic frames.) Constructed responses are not always fully confirmed, extended tacts are controlled by deviant stimuli, responses to poorly defined or poorly sampled classes of events suffer corresponding disadvantages, generalized reinforcement minimizes but never wholly destroys the effect of the momentary condition of the speaker, and so on. These shortcomings, and their significance for the listener, are reflected in everyday life when we emit such responses only in moderate strength and qualify them with appropriate autoclitics. Traditional logic has clarified the force of quantifying autoclitics, and scientific practice adds a sort of numerical quantification. As a result, scientific writing is heavily larded with expressions such as *plus or minus 2 per cent* or *at the 5-per-cent level of confidence* which, like all autoclitics, increase the probability that the listener will react with appropriate caution or conviction.

Scientific Methodology

Logical and scientific verbal behavior differs from the verbal behavior of the layman (and particularly from literary behavior) because of the emphasis on practical consequences. These are not always matters of mundane technology. The test of scientific prediction is often, as the word implies, *verbal* confirmation. But the behavior of both logician and scientist leads at last to effective nonverbal action, and it is here that we must find the ultimate reinforcing contingencies which maintain the logical and scientific verbal community. We can now only speculate on how the advantages of certain kinds of verbal behavior in furthering the prediction and control of nature must first have made themselves felt. A verbal community would come to suppress exaggerated or dishonest behavior and to reinforce responses under more accurate stimulus control, as it would reinforce the correct repetition and recitation of rules of conduct (ethical or otherwise), the correct recollection of facts, and so on, because of substantial practical consequences. Its interests in this respect, however, must have conflicted with, say, its taste for verbal entertainment. It is a distinction among the kinds of advantages gained by the community which permits us to distinguish between literary and logical and scientific subdivisions. These subcommunities are not, of course, necessarily composed of different members. At times a community shapes and maintains the entertaining behavior of poets and story-tellers;

at other times, and usually with respect to other speakers, it shapes and maintains verbal behavior which yields practical results.

Logical and scientific verbal behavior, as well as the practices of the community which shape and maintain it, have been analyzed in *logical and scientific methodology*. Once a special community concerned with practical consequences has arisen, it becomes a proper object of study. What are the defining properties of scientific and logical verbal behavior? When is such behavior effective or valid? How do the practices of the community generate and maintain it? How do these practices work? Can scientific and logical verbal behavior be improved, and if so, what practices would bring about improvement?

Three steps appear to lead to this sort of methodological inquiry: (1) some kinds of verbal behavior, including appropriate relational and quantifying autoclitics, prove to have important practical consequences for both speaker and listener, (2) the community discovers and adopts explicit practices which encourage such behavior, being reinforced for this by even more extensive practical consequences, and (3) the practices of the community are then studied and improved, presumably also because of increasingly successful consequences. As an example in logic (1) some intraverbal responses are found useful by the average listener, (2) the community then encourages such behavior by constraining speakers to observe laws of thought, employ acceptable syllogistic formulae, and so on, and (3) the laws of thought, syllogisms, and other logical rules and formulae are then analyzed for internal consistency and validity and with an eye to possible improvement. A parallel sequence in science might be as follows: (1) relatively abstract responses specifying particular properties of stimuli prove useful, (2) the scientific community arranges contingencies of reinforcement which constrain speakers to respond to isolated properties, and (3) the rules and canons of scientific thinking which govern classification and abstraction are studied to explain the effectiveness of (1) and (2) and possibly to suggest improved behavior and practices. The analytical disciplines at Stage 3 may be said to be concerned with the ultimate "validity" of logical and scientific discourse in the sense of specifying the defining consequences of logical and scientific behavior.

The techniques of logical and scientific methodology must, of course, be adapted to the phenomena of verbal behavior. At the moment the full implications of the subject matter are usually missed. Logic has avoided many of the confusing problems of "meaning" by emphasizing formal analyses. Autoclitic frames need to be studied and practices need to be devised which maximize the tautological validity or truth to be inferred from relationships among such frames. But all such analyses, together with their products, are verbal behavior and subject to some such analysis as the present. That is also true of studies of the relation between verbal behavior and extraverbal events, either in linguistic or logical semantics or in the statistical or probabilistic considerations of scientific methodology. The verbal processes of logical and scientific thought deserve and require a more precise analysis than they have yet received. One of the ultimate accomplishments of a science of verbal behavior may be an empirical logic, or a descriptive and analytical scientific epistemology, the terms and practices of which will be adapted to human behavior as a subject matter.

Chapter 19

. . . .

Thinking

THE PLACE OF verbal behavior in group co-ordination is often discussed in speculating about the origin of language. As soon as men began to work together in hunting, fishing, building shelters, or making war, situations must have arisen in which rudimentary verbal responses would be of use.[1] In a co-operative fishing enterprise, for example, one man might be in a position to see the fish while another could pull the net. Any response which the former might make to the fish would improve the timing of the latter, possibly with advantages for both. Comparable co-ordinating functions are easily discovered in the behavior of a well-developed verbal community.

Plausible advantages are not, as such, an explanation of the origin and maintenance of verbal behavior, but they point to the reinforcing contingencies which are. Verbal behavior extends both the sensory powers of the listener, who can now respond to the behavior of others rather than directly to things and events, and the power of action of the speaker, who can now speak rather than do. If, as a result of a division of labor, the wise-but-weak can control the uninformed-but-strong, their combined accomplishments may exceed anything possible for either alone. Co-operative enterprises are not always for the benefit of all parties, but the interlocking contingencies necessary to sustain verbal behavior prevail even in the extremely unsymmetrical relation of master and slave.

Verbal behavior must have become much more valuable, both to the group as a whole and severally to its members, when responses began to be transmitted from one man to another. "Word-of-mouth" transmission became possible with the development of echoic and

[1] See Malinowski's appendix to *The Meaning of Meaning* of Ogden, C. K. and Richards, I. A.

intraverbal behavior, while the invention of writing and the subsequent development of textual behavior permitted an even more effective mode. The "speaker" who leaves an enduring record of his behavior can affect "listeners" in distant places and times, and these in turn profit from the special points of vantage of the remote "speaker." The achievement of the transmission of verbal behavior is seen today in codes of law, books of wisdom, formularies, and religious writings, which amplify almost without limit the effects of the behavior which originally produced them, and in histories, biographies, diaries, and experimental reports, which give the reader an almost unlimited contact with the environments of other men.

Emergence of Other Functions

A useful division of labor is not the only achievement of verbal behavior. Other functions must soon have emerged from the mands and tacts (and the corresponding nonverbal and verbal responses of the listener) which were first effective in facilitating group co-ordination. The special effects discussed in Chapter 6 would soon have become possible, with results which we see epitomized in literature when a particular work arouses the reader emotionally or entertains him in various ways. These collateral reactions of listeners must soon have altered the behavior of speakers. Moreover, as soon as the listener also became an accomplished speaker, verbal behavior could arouse *verbal* reactions in him—delighting him with humorous or stylistic effects in multiple causation, prompting and probing his behavior in persuasion or thoughtful stimulation, and so on.

These additional uses of verbal behavior do not result from an extension of sensory or motor power. They may or may not have a bearing on group co-ordination. They are most interesting when a group is not involved—when, in short, a man talks to himself. Once a speaker also becomes a listener, the stage is set for a drama in which one man plays several roles. The initial advantages for group coordination are missing, but there are compensating gains. This has been recognized traditionally when the behavior of a speaker with respect to himself as listener, particularly when his behavior is not observable by others, is set aside as a special human achievement called "thinking."

An account of verbal behavior is not complete until its relation to the rest of the behavior of the organism has been made clear. This can be done conveniently by discussing the problem of thinking.

Covert Verbal Behavior

If someone who is sitting quite still is asked *What are you doing?*, he may reply *Nothing, I'm just thinking.* In the terminology of the layman (and of many specialists) thinking is often simply opposed to doing. But as a living organism a man is behaving in some sense while "doing nothing," even though his behavior may not be easily observed by others or possibly even by himself. We do not discuss these activities effectively because they are almost always accessible only to the "thinker" and useful verbal responses to them cannot easily be developed. Some progress has been made in improving public observation through the instrumental amplification of small-scale behavior, but the problem of explaining the normal occurrence of such behavior remains.

In a sense verbal behavior which cannot be observed by others is not properly part of our field. It is tempting to avoid the problems it raises by confining ourselves to observable events, letting anyone extend the analysis to his own covert behavior who wishes to do so. But there would then be certain embarrassing gaps in our account. In intraverbal chaining, for example, necessary links are sometimes missing from the observable data. When someone solves a problem in "mental arithmetic," the initial statement of the problem and the final overt answer can often be related only by inferring covert events. We also have to account for verbal behavior which is under the control of covert speech—which reports it (Chapter 5) or qualifies it with autoclitics (Chapter 12). Covert behavior has also had to be considered in discussing grammar (Chapter 13), sentence composition (Chapter 14), editing (Chapter 15), and other topics of Part V. Some discussion of its dimensions is therefore required.

Covert behavior often seems to be like overt except that it occurs on a smaller scale. If we recite the alphabet while speaking and whispering alternate letters, it is easy to observe the voicing which makes the difference: *A-b-C-d-E-f-G-h.* . . . If we whisper every other letter while saying the rest silently, we observe what appears to be a comparable difference between overt and covert forms: *a*-( )-*c*-( )-*e*-( ) -*g*-( ). . . . But the silent response may recede to very subtle dimensions. The muscular involvement demonstrated by mechanical or electrical amplification can often be detected by trying to "think" such a response as *bubble, bubble* while holding the mouth as wide open as possible. But this can often be done, especially after a little practice, and there are other difficulties in assuming that covert behavior is always executed by the muscular apparatus responsible for the overt form. Experienced public speakers, especially those who say the same thing many times, appear to "think" one verbal response while saying another aloud, and one sometimes appears to read aloud mechanically while carrying on, say, a "fantasied" conversation. Small-scale muscular activity is also not very plausible in representing incipient verbal behavior. *I was going to say . . .* may be followed by a response which has not been previously emitted, even subaudibly. A rapid speaker may compose a sentence to provide for a response which has yet to be executed, and it is difficult to explain this by assuming rapid silent rehearsal. We break off an unhappy remark before damage is done and, though we may complete it subaudibly, evidently before it has actually occurred.

We do not need to make guesses about the muscular or neural substratum of verbal events. We account for the probability or strength of a suppressed or manipulated response as we account for the probability of any behavior. In an instance of editing, for example, we observe that behavior which is ordinarily followed by a given response is suddenly interrupted. The fact that it is "ordinarily" so followed is a behavioral fact concerning past occurrences of the response under given circumstances. Physiological processes mediate the probability of covert and overt responses alike, as they undoubtedly mediate all the relations disclosed in a functional analysis of behavior, but we can talk about both forms of response "when they are not being emitted" without identifying physiological mediators. The data which give rise to the notion of covert speech can be dealt with as such with the degree of rigor prevailing elsewhere in a science of verbal behavior at the present time.

Other questions, however, remain to be answered. Why should a response become covert at all? Operant behavior almost always begins in a form which affects the external environment, for it would not otherwise be reinforced. (Exceptions are certain responses which are automatically reinforced by the organism itself.) Why does it not remain overt?

Behavior becomes covert when, in the first place, its strength drops below the value needed for overt emission. It may be weak because the controlling variables are deficient. When we say *I thought that was Jones* (*but I see it is not*), we actually emit the response *Jones;* but we are describing a previous covert instance which was weak because the stimulus was inadequate. If the response *Jones* had been weak because it was poorly conditioned or partially forgotten, the report might have taken the form *I thought his name was Jones.*

Covert behavior may be strong, however, as shown by the fact that it will appear at the overt level under other circumstances. The covert response is simply the easiest or, for any reason, the likeliest at the moment. The energy level of nonverbal behavior usually declines so long as the reinforcing contingencies are maintained. When Thorndike reinforced a cat for licking its paw, the movement grew slighter and slighter until it could scarcely be detected.[2] The reinforcing contingencies could not be maintained beyond that point. (We might say that the cat could not be reinforced for "thinking" about licking its paw.) But a considerable reinforcement survives in covert *verbal* behavior when the speaker is his own listener. One important consequence of our definition is that, when talking to oneself, it is unnecessary to speak aloud and easier not to. A response which is subaudible for reasons of convenience will become audible if an advantage is to be gained. We speak aloud to ourselves upon occasion—for example, when the audible response improves intraverbal chaining. In the solution of a difficult problem, mathematical or otherwise, we resort to overt responses, vocal or written. For the same reason such covert behavior as counting money or adding figures is likely to become overt in the presence of distracting stimuli.

Covert speech is not, however, wholly or perhaps even primarily a labor-saving practice. As we have seen, verbal behavior is frequently punished. Audible behavior in the child is reinforced and tolerated up to a point; then it becomes annoying, and the child is punished for speaking. Comparable aversive consequences continue into the adult years. Punishment is not always in the nature of reproof, for speech which is overheard may have other kinds of undesirable effects, such as giving away a secret. The privacy of covert behavior has a practical value. So long as a verbal response is emitted primarily for its effect upon the speaker himself, it is best confined to that audience. (The content of autistic verbal behavior is often significant to the therapist just because it is relatively free of the control exercised by a punishing audience.)

That avoidance of punishment is a more likely explanation than convenience is shown by the fact that covert behavior returns to the

2 Thorndike, E. L., *Animal Intelligence* (New York, 1898).

overt level when a punishing audience is no longer in control though convenience has not been altered. Many people who live alone gradually come to talk to themselves aloud. In the presence of other people the return to the overt level may take time, for the nonpunishing character of an audience cannot be established in a moment. It is usually hard to induce people to "think aloud"—that is, to emit in the presence of an external audience behavior which is primarily controlled by the speaker himself. The extent of the special control exerted by the private audience is seen in the fact that overt behavior in the absence of an external listener frequently generates anxiety or other emotional effects. Many people are embarrassed when using a dictating machine for the first time, or when rehearsing a speech aloud in an empty room. A full release of previously covert behavior at the audible level may come very slowly. The noncensuring audience provided by the psychoanalyst is not immediately effective, though overt speech of otherwise punishable form may eventually appear.

There are, then, important variables which determine whether a response will be overt or covert. But they do not greatly affect its other properties. They do not suggest that there is any important distinction between the two levels or forms. Nothing is gained, therefore, by identifying thinking with subaudible talking. This was done in certain early behavioristic analyses, apparently in an effort to find replacements for the so-called mental processes. The traditional view that an idea occurs first and that the speaker then expresses it in words had to be discarded. The actual precursors of speech are, as we have seen, the independent variables of which it is a function, but these are for the most part outside the organism and hence not very plausible replacements for ideas as inner causes. It was tempting to suppose that the speaker "thought about what he was going to say" in the simple sense of saying it first to himself. But the covert response, if it occurs, is in no sense the cause of the overt. The full force of the expression of ideas cannot be carried by a mere sequence of covert and overt responses.

Other "mental processes" rejected in a behavioristic analysis are not easily replaced by covert verbal behavior, but their traditional prestige no doubt contributed to the need to find inner replacements. Some of these are exemplified when a speaker acquires or retains a response (the mental processes of "learning" and "memory"), responds differently to different stimuli ("discrimination"), reacts with one response-form rather than another ("differentiation"), responds in a given way to a new stimulus bearing some resemblance to the old ("generalization," "metaphor," or "analogical thinking"), responds under the control of a single property or a special set of properties of a stimulus ("abstraction"), arrives at a constructed response through a controlled intraverbal chain ("reasoning"), and so on. These are not *behaviors,* covert or overt. They are controlling relations or the changes in probability which result from changes in such relations.

The theory that thinking was merely subaudible speech had at least the favorable effect of identifying thinking with behaving. But speech is only a special case of behavior and subaudible speech a further subdivision. The range of verbal behavior is roughly suggested, in descending order of energy, by shouting, loud talking, quiet talking, whispering, muttering "under one's breath," subaudible speech with detectable muscular action, subaudible speech of unclear dimensions, and perhaps even the "unconscious thinking" sometimes inferred in instances of problem solving. There is no point at which it is profitable to draw a line distinguishing thinking from acting on this continuum. So far as we know, the events at the covert end have no special properties, observe no special laws, and can be credited with no special achievements.

THE SPEAKER AS HIS OWN LISTENER

A better case can be made for identifying thinking with behaving which automatically affects the behaver and is reinforcing because it does so. This can be either covert or overt. We can explain the tendency to identify thinking with covert behavior by pointing out that the reinforcing effects of covert behavior *must* arise from self-stimulation. But self-stimulation is possible, and indeed more effective, at the overt level.

When a man talks to himself, aloud or silently, he is an excellent listener in the sense of Chapter 10. He speaks the same language or languages and has had the same verbal and nonverbal experience as his listener. He is subject to the same deprivations and aversive stimulations, and these vary from day to day or from moment to moment in the same way. As listener he is ready for his own behavior as speaker at just the right time and is optimally prepared to "understand" what he has said. Very little time is lost in transmission and the behavior may acquire subtle dimensions. It is not surprising, then, that verbal self-stimulation has been regarded as possessing special properties and has even been identified with thinking.

Simple Soliloquy

The speaker's own verbal behavior automatically supplies stimuli for echoic, textual, or intraverbal behavior, and these in turn generate stimuli for further responses. The result is the "soliloquy"—as exemplified in its dramatic use and in some stream-of-consciousness writing. It is not essentially productive thinking. Unexpected twists may turn up, but subsequent soliloquizing is modified only slightly, if at all, as a result. Dashiell [3] has analyzed Hamlet's *To be or not to be* in this spirit. An intraverbal connection between *die* and *sleep* leads to another between *sleep* and *dream,* and *dream* then strengthens an incipient response which is broken off with *Aye, there's the rub.* Regardless of the respectability of the connections, such a "train of thought" is a mere intraverbal or self-echoic linkage and scarcely to be distinguished from a "flight of ideas."

Thinking is more productive when verbal responses lead to specific consequences *and are reinforced because they do so.* Autistic behavior is a step in this direction. The verbal fantasy, whether overt or covert, is automatically reinforcing to the speaker as listener. Just as the musician plays or composes what he is reinforced by hearing, or as the artist paints what reinforces him visually, so the speaker engaged in verbal fantasy says what he is reinforced by hearing or writes what he is reinforced by reading. This is the realm of the verbal daydream and of much poetry, fiction, and other forms of literature. The writer composes verbal stimuli which arouse (in himself and, incidentally, in others) emotional or other kinds of responses, or serve as prompts or probes to permit him to behave verbally when he would otherwise remain silent for lack of energy or wit or because of punishing circumstances. The writer constitutes within himself an adequate community for the sustained production of literary behavior, and he may continue to write for a long time with no further contribution from the external community. The practices of the inner community often drift toward disturbing idiosyncrasies, however, as the work of such a poet as Emily Dickinson suggests.

[3] Dashiell, J. F., *Fundamentals of Objective Psychology* (Boston, 1928).

Verbal Behavior Having Practical Effects Upon The Speaker As Listener

Aside from autistic or artistic behavior, verbal responses may be automatically reinforced by practical consequences. These may follow even when the speaker is his own listener. Although he cannot extend his own sensory or motor powers, many of the substantial mediating contingencies which generate and maintain verbal behavior continue in force.

A self-mand is not as useless as it may at first appear. A man may enjoin himself to get out of bed on a cold morning, to stop when he has made a mistake, or to be sure to remember an errand. These are not wholly magical mands. The verbal response comes first because it has less aversive consequences than the behavior manded. *Get up!*, for example, is easier to execute than getting out of bed and less likely to be followed by a cold shock. It may be strong by induction from instances in which we have induced other people to get up, and it may be effective if it increases the likelihood of our getting out of bed by induction from behavior with respect to other speakers. It might be supposed that self-mands supported only by induction would eventually suffer extinction as the two audiences are more sharply discriminated, but there are continuing sources of reinforcement. Let us suppose that a man is learning to hunt under circumstances in which it is advantageous to stand quite still (in order to let the quarry approach) in spite of a strong inclination to reduce the distance more quickly by advancing. An instructor generates the correct behavior by saying *Stand still!*, and the would-be hunter may achieve the same effect by manding his own behavior. He may have acquired the verbal response at an earlier date—perhaps from a book —or it may have been more readily learned on the spot as a briefer and more sharply defined response than "standing still." In any case the hunter who can tell himself *Stand still!* is probably at an advantage in controlling himself effectively in the field. The result may continue to reinforce verbal behavior in the form of self-mands.

The possibility that the speaker may respond to his own *verbal* stimuli in echoing himself or reading notes he has written has already been pointed out. He may also respond to his own intraverbal stimuli, as in opening a combination lock by following the directions he gives himself by reciting the combination as an intraverbal chain.

A man may usefully "speak to himself" or "write to himself" in the form of tacts. Thus, from some momentary point of vantage he may compose a text which he then responds to as a reader at a later date. Daybooks, diaries, memoranda, and similar devices bridge the temporal gap between behavior and controlling variables. The ultimate behavior may be verbal or nonverbal. The self-tact has an immediate effect in helping the speaker identify or clarify the situation to which it is a response. A confusing international situation falls into a standard pattern with the official declaration *This is war.* One's behavior with respect to a vaguely familiar person changes when his name can at last be recalled. Faced with an unfamiliar object in a hardware store, one can marshal appropriate behavior (and dismiss a possibly aversive state of puzzlement) if one can say, even tentatively, *It's a can-opener.* Categorizing responses are especially effective in this way. The zoologist hitting upon the proper classification of an unfamiliar insect, the young mother identifying the behavior of her child as an example of a pattern described by a psychologist, or the business man deciding that a chart shows that the time has come to buy a particular stock, all show substantial changes in behavior as a result of categorizing responses. *Nomina si nescis, perit et cognitio rerum.*

The automatic clarification produced by the tact is no doubt supported by self-instruction. The speaker's future behavior will be different, although the response is not necessarily emitted again. In thinking out a difficult problem, we may reaffirm certain key relationships or re-identify relevant facts, especially when these tend to be forgotten or obscured by other matters, even though the categorizing effect has already been felt. Thus, in solving a detective-story crime we may find ourselves insisting that a character is guilty in spite of a small but conclusive bit of evidence to the contrary. As we drift again and again toward the wrong conclusion, we may re-instruct ourselves: *No! No! It CAN'T be Billingsly. Billingsly was in the conservatory talking to the gardener.* We are not telling ourselves anything we did not know, but we are altering the *extent* to which we know it, and we make it less likely that we shall emit other responses placing Billingsly at the scene of the crime.

Although the speaker may find his own responses useful when they have the form of tacts, the special consequences which destroy the purity of the relation (Chapter 6) are likely to be operative. Since automatic reinforcement need not respect the contingencies which prevail in the external verbal environment, controlling relations can be "stretched" at will, beginning perhaps with a slight exaggeration but leading eventually to fiction and lying. The verbal behavior of people who live alone and talk mostly to themselves often seems "queer" to the occasional external listener. The speaker, as his own audience, has come to control a special subdivision of his verbal repertoire, distorted by special effects. The public contingencies may need replenishment, although some automatic correction will occur if the intrusion of irrelevant consequences destroys eventual practical advantages.

The special characteristics of verbal behavior having multiple sources of strength prevail when the speaker is his own listener and provide other reasons for talking to oneself. Indeed, they may be especially marked because of the optimal correspondence in verbal strength between the speaker and listener in the same skin. The autoclitics and the grammatical and syntactical ordering of verbal behavior in composition are imposed upon verbal behavior primarily for their effects upon the speaker himself, and the principal activity in editing may be specifically attributed to such effects, particularly when they result from earlier punishment. The special conditions under which editing is at a minimum and verbal behavior therefore "released" may be ultimately reinforcing to the speaker and lead him to arrange or induce such conditions.

Another source of automatic reinforcement is seen in "problem solving," where the speaker generates stimuli to *supplement* other behavior already in his repertoire. He prompts and probes his own behavior, as in recalling a half-forgotten name or teasing out an effective classifying response. He may do this because he has been reinforced for similar behavior by other listeners, but automatic practical consequences may supply the necessary contingencies. Scientific behavior "pays off" even when the scientist is talking to himself. Thus, it is often automatically reinforcing to calculate the odds at poker rather than to play according to accidental reinforcements. It is often automatically reinforcing to count a number of objects rather than estimate them. It is automatically reinforcing to use a watch (a special kind of text) rather than trust to one's own "sense of time." It is automatically reinforcing to use special mnemonics or algorithms in the construction of new verbal behavior rather than trust to the miscellaneous intraverbals of the moment.

Verbal self-supplementation plays an important role in decision making. A man escapes from an aversive indecision by tossing a coin. Having set up the substitutability of *Go!* for *Heads* and *Stay!* for

Tails, he constructs one or the other of these texts (by tossing the coin), reads it, makes the appropriate substitution, and responds to the resulting mand.

The Freudian dynamisms describe activities which are automatically reinforcing, usually because they permit one to avoid or escape from aversive consequences due to previous punishment. Many are verbal, and some almost necessarily so. "Rationalizing" is an example. Men are generally punished for hurting others but are permitted to hurt in special cases—for example, in punishing undesirable behavior or bringing bad news which cannot be concealed. The community distinguishes between two classes of rather similar behavior, punishing only one of them. As a result, when an emotional situation disposes a man to hurt someone, a member of the unpunished class of injurious responses is most likely to emerge. That is to say, men are more likely to punish or carry bad news to those whom they do not like. When the two classes of behavior are not easily distinguished, as is often the case, a man is less likely to be punished by the external community or to suffer the conditioned aversive stimulation of "guilt" if he can characterize his behavior as belonging in the unpunished class: *I spanked him "for his own good."*

Another sort of rationalization consists of characterizing an event as positively reinforcing when it is more likely to be aversive. We may suffer less from an unfortunate event by calling it a blessing in disguise. Boswell reports that Dr. Johnson was aware of the process:

> Sir, all the arguments which are brought to represent poverty as no evil, show it to be evidently a great evil. You never find people laboring to convince you that you may live very happily upon a plentiful fortune.

As these examples suggest, verbal behavior which is reinforced because it alters subsequent behavior in the speaker is often of ethical significance. The troublesome expressions *ought* and *should* can be interpreted as describing contingencies of reinforcement. When we say *The young man ought to have said "No"*, we assert that there were consequences of saying *No,* not further identified, which were reinforcing. Perhaps *No* would have saved him from aversive labor or injury. In the ethical case, where saying *No* is the "right" thing to do, the response might have prevented group censure or brought praise. When, then, a man tells himself *I ought to say "No,"* he is asserting that *No* would have certain reinforcing consequences (not further specified). His response differs from the self-mand *Say "No"* in the source of its power. The mand exploits an old paradigm of controlling relations which may ultimately lose its effectiveness, but the response containing *ought* identifies or clarifies a more lasting reinforcing contingency and may successfully increase its effect on the speaker. The vicar of society within the individual, the Freudian superego or the Judaeo-Christian conscience, is essentially verbal. It is the "still small *voice*."

A "resolution" is a sort of mand upon oneself which masquerades as a tact. *I am not going to smoke for the next three months* is not a response to a future event. Its value in self-control lies in the fact that it can be made now when appropriate contingencies, possibly involving aversive events, are powerful, whereas "not smoking for three months" requires three months for its execution, during which time the underlying deprivation or aversive stimulation may change. The resolution creates a set of conditions under which smoking is particularly punished (as "breaking a promise") either by the speaker himself or by others. The effect is greater if the resolution is publicly announced or, better, conspicuously posted during the period in which it is in force.

The following example of sustained self-stimulating verbal behavior exemplifies many of these points. It is a direct transcription of the responses a nine-year-old girl made to herself while practicing the piano. The behavior was overt, but of the sort which would have receded to the covert level with a little more punishment. The transcription begins after several minutes at the piano. A mistake is made. *No, wait!* (Plays correctly and reaches end of piece.) *Hah!* (Plays a few bars of a new piece.) *Let's see. Is that right? I'll do it once more.* (Finishes the piece.) *Ah, now I can study on something else.* (Looks at new piece.) *That's written in the key of G.* (Plays and sings words at same time. Finishes and looks at clock.) *That takes one minute. One minute to play that whole song.* (Starts another piece, and makes mistake.) *All right, now I'll start the whole thing over.* (Makes another mistake.) *I'll have to start all over again.* (Difficult piece. Emits a few *Gosh's.* Works on difficult passage. Presses finger on correct key.) *Oh, my finger, it hurts so much! But I'm going to MAKE it work!* (Forces finger against key again. Looks at finger.) *Hah! Makes beautiful designs on it.* (Notices clock.) *Wowee! I've taken some of my other things' time.* (Looks at another piece.) *Aw, I can't do that!*

(Notices clock.) *Just a minute.* (Takes up clock.) *I'm putting it back five minutes. There! Got a lot more time to practice.* (Plays, notices clock again.) *Hey! Don't! Don't do that. You're going too fast.* (Adjusts clock.) *Better. Five minutes.* (Plays and makes mistake.) *Aw!* (Looks at clock.) *Come ON!* (Adjusts clock. Calls out to father in next room.) *Daddy, I'm making this clock go slowly—I don't have time to practice. I turned it around an hour. I've got so much time to practice.*

In this example of "thinking aloud" mands like *No, wait, Just a minute,* and *Is that right?* accompany behavior of stopping and looking, which they may have some effect in strengthening. The resolutions *I'll do it once more* and *I'll have to start all over again* precede the behavior which they appear to describe. They may or may not strengthen it, but they clarify each act as an instance of "starting all over because of a mistake." The tact *That's written in the key of G* is probably helpful in strengthening appropriate nonverbal behavior. *My finger, it hurts so much* can scarcely be useful in the same way and seems to be a mere comment—emitted because of the special strength of the stimulus. The juxtaposition of *I'm putting it back five minutes* and *Got a lot more time to practice* may strengthen further behavior toward the clock. A similar pair of responses occur later, and turning the clock back an hour may be the result of the clarification of the connection between moving the clock and having more time to practice. The magical mand addressed to the clock *Don't do that! You're going too fast!* may also contribute to the behavior of turning the clock back. There is very little intraverbal chaining in the sample because it is intimately connected with concurrent nonverbal behavior. The chaining is from verbal to nonverbal and back again. The example is closer to productive verbal thinking for this reason.

There are good reasons, then, why a speaker also conditioned by the verbal community as a listener should turn his verbal behavior upon himself. The result is close to "thinking" in many traditional senses of the term. Such behavior can, of course, be subtle and swift, especially because the speaker is optimally prepared for his own speech as listener. But all the important properties of the behavior are to be found in verbal systems composed of separate speakers and listeners. A necessary connection between verbal thinking and self-stimulation might be said to arise from the fact that, in the strictest sense of our definition, any behavior which is reinforced because it modifies subsequent behavior in the same individual is necessarily verbal regardless of its dimensions. The reinforcement is "mediated by an organism," if not strictly another organism, and responses which do not have the usual dimensions of vocal, written, or gestured behavior may acquire some of the characteristics of verbal behavior. The refinement of the definition given in Chapter 8, however, permits us to maintain such a distinction as that between visual and verbal fantasy, for example, by excluding the former from the verbal category. In any case, although self-stimulating behavior may be in some sense necessarily verbal, verbal behavior need not be self-stimulating. When Plato asks, then, "Is not thought the same as speech with this exception: thought is the unuttered conversation of the soul with herself?", we must decline to allow the exception.

Thought as Verbal Behavior

Are we to be content with the rest of Plato's phrase: "thought is the same as speech"? Disregarding the distinction between overt and covert and the possibility that verbal behavior may be especially effective upon the speaker himself, are we to conclude that thinking is simply verbal behavior? Admittedly, this has been an appealing notion. "He gave man speech, and speech created thought, which is the measure of the Universe." [4] Some version of the doctrine has been actively propounded by behaviorists as a solution to the psychological problem of knowledge, and by logical positivists for their own epistemological purposes. Much earlier, in *The Diversions of Purley,*[5] John Horne Tooke attacked British empiricism in the same spirit:

> Perhaps it was for mankind a lucky mistake, for it was a mistake, which Mr. Locke made, when he called his book "An Essay on Human Understanding," for some part of the inestimable benefit of that book has, merely on account of its title, reached to many thousands more than, I fear, it would have done, had he called it (what it is merely) a *Grammatical* Essay, or a Treatise on *Words,* or on *Language.* . . .
>
> . . . . I only desire you to read the Essay over again with attention, and see whether all that its immortal author has justly concluded will not hold equally true and clear, if you substitute the composition [association], &c. of terms, wherever he has supposed a composition [association], &c. of ideas.[6]

[4] Shelley, Percy Bysshe, *Prometheus Unbound.*

[5] Tooke, John Horne, *The Diversions of Purley* (London, 1857).

[6] Compare also the following passage (written, as is most of the book, in the form of a dialogue):

"B—What difference then do you imagine it would have made in Mr. Locke's Essay,

Tooke and others who have advocated this solution have been preoccupied with a kind of human behavior which, because it is verbal, possesses certain properties relevant to the problem of thinking. It is tempting to suppose that other peculiarly verbal properties will solve the problem as a whole. But this is evidently not the case. The results of thinking are often quite surprising and apparently impossible to explain. We can sympathize with the urge to find an explanation at the earliest possible moment and with the belief that the process will be found to have a touch of the mysterious or even miraculous. Covert behavior is an appealing modern substitute for thought processes because of its difficult dimensions, and verbal behavior which is self-stimulating is also a promising candidate because of the fact that it *can* be private and that after a long period of working alone the thinker may emit astonishingly effective behavior. (It has always been easy for "thinkers" to claim special powers.)

Verbal behavior, quite apart from its covert or overt form or from the identity of the listener upon whom it is effective, also has some of the magic we expect to find in a thought process. It is relatively free of environmental conditions and temporal restrictions. Faced with a piece of music at the piano, we can react nonverbally to its being in the key of G (for example, by playing it correctly) but we cannot do this all at once. The verbal response *That's in the key of G* is quick and clear-cut, and it achieves an immediate result by clarifying the situation and heightening the probable effectiveness of the nonverbal behavior to follow. A unitary response to something which takes place over a period of time or in more than one place is almost necessarily verbal, and it seems to transcend great obstacles in achieving this result. When we solve a practical problem verbally, we construct a guide to a nonverbal solution; but before we have made use of it, we have found the *whole* solution at once in verbal form. Responses which are concerned with number illustrate the same point. If there is an act which is equivalent to, or identical with, "thinking of one hundred," it is the verbal response *one hundred.*

---

if he had sooner been aware of the inseparable connexion between words and knowledge; or, in the language of Sir Hugh, in Shakespear, that 'the lips is *parcel* of the *mind?*'

H—Much. And amongst many other things, I think he would not have talked of the *composition* of *ideas;* but would have seen that it was merely a contrivance of Language: and that the only composition was in *terms;* and consequently that it was as improper to speak of a *complex idea,* as it would be to call a constellation a complex star: And that they are not ideas, but merely *terms,* which are general and *abstract. . . .*"

Whether it is constructed by counting a hundred objects or in some other way (when it is under the control of other variables), it seems to transcend the awkward numerosity of one hundred things.

A verbal response makes it possible to "think about" *one* property of nature at a time. Since there is no practical response appropriate to all instances of red, the abstract tact *red* is an evidently unique verbal accomplishment. The response *fox* is abstract in this sense, in spite of the fact that it refers to an object which is usually called concrete, and our reaction to the fact that one has said *fox* may be nothing more than our own verbal response *fox,* particularly if we possess no useful practical behavior with respect to foxes. A piece of music may lead us to say *I think that's Mozart,* and there is little more to be done to the music of Mozart *as such.* Locke [7] himself was aware of this function of terms. "In mixed moods," he says, "it is the name that ties the combination together and makes it a species." Thus, without the term *triumphus* we might have had descriptions of what "passed in that solemnity: but yet, I think, that which holds those different parts together, in the unity of one complex idea, is that very word annexed to it; without which the several parts of that would no more be thought to make one thing, than any other show. . . ." For Locke, however, the term merely supported the idea for which it stood.

These are important and distinctive functions of verbal behavior, but they are nevertheless not relevant to a definition of thinking. Nor are certain other accidental reasons why this solution has been so often reached. Those who have looked at themselves thinking have frequently seen *verbal* behavior. Led by prevailing philosophies to search for inner thought processes, they have naturally been impressed by the convenience of execution of covert verbal behavior—as contrasted, say, with nonverbal parallels such as turning a cartwheel or driving a car "silently," where the coordination of movement normally involves the physical environment. Verbal behavior is also easy to see because it is relatively easy to describe. We can report *I said to myself "That's ridiculous"* much more readily than we can describe covert nonverbal behavior evoked under the same circumstances. A verbal conclusion "comes to one," or "is reached," in a relatively conspicuous way.

But not all covert behavior is verbal. Most people can turn some sort of elliptical cartwheel privately, and we discover that we are driving from the back seat when, in an emergency, we break into

[7] Locke, John, *Essay on Human Understanding.*

overt behavior and press our feet against the floor to stop the car. The layman's use of *I think* covers nonverbal behavior. *I think I shall be going* can be translated *I find myself going, I seem to be going,* or *I am on the point of going.* It would be awkward to interpret this by saying that the behavior of going gives rise to the verbal response *I am going* and that this is qualified by the response *I think.* Covert nonverbal behavior is described, as it is in the less committal *It occurs to me to go.* Nonverbal "ideas" and "thoughts" are common in descriptions of problem solving. In *The thought* (*or idea*) *occurred to me to try the door* the speaker is reporting the appearance of a nonverbal act.

Thought as Behavior

The simplest and most satisfactory view is that thought is simply *behavior*—verbal or nonverbal, covert or overt. It is not some mysterious process responsible for behavior but the very behavior itself in all the complexity of its controlling relations, with respect to both man the behaver and the environment in which he lives. The concepts and methods which have emerged from the analysis of behavior, verbal or otherwise, are most appropriate to the study of what has traditionally been called the human mind.

The field of human behavior can be conveniently subdivided with respect to the problems it presents and the corresponding terms and methods to be used. A useful distinction may be made between reflexes, conditioned or otherwise, and the operant behavior generated and maintained by the contingencies of reinforcement in a given environment. Tradition and expedience seem to agree in confining the analysis of human thought to operant behavior. So conceived, thought is not a mystical cause or precursor of action, or an inaccessible ritual, but action itself, subject to analysis with the concepts and techniques of the natural sciences, and ultimately to be accounted for in terms of controlling variables.

The emphasis upon controlling variables is important. A practical consequence is that such a scientific account implies a technology. There is no reason why methods of thinking and of the teaching of thinking cannot be analyzed and made more effective. But there is a more immediate theoretical issue. Nothing is gained by regarding thought as behavior in the sense of a mere *form* of action. We cannot move very far in the study of behavior apart from the circumstances under which it occurs. Bertrand Russell has tried to improve upon a merely formal analysis, but he has never been fully successful because the methods available to the logician are not appropriate to the study of behavior. Consider, for example, the following passage from *An Inquiry into Meaning and Truth:* [8]

> Thought, in so far as it is communicable, cannot have any greater complexity than is possessed by the various possible kinds of series to be made out of twenty-six kinds of shapes. Shakespeare's mind may have been very wonderful, but our evidence of its merits is wholly derived from black shapes on a white ground.

Russell might have gone a step further and reduced all of Shakespeare's "mind" to a series of dots and dashes, since the plays and poems could be sent or received in that form by a skilled telegraphist. It is true that evidence of the "merits of Shakespeare's mind" is derived from black shapes on a white ground, but it does not follow that thought, communicable or not, has no greater "complexity." Shakespeare's thought was his behavior *with respect to his extremely complex environment.* We do not, of course, have an adequate record of it in that sense. We have almost no independent information about the environment and cannot infer much about it from the works themselves. In discussing Shakespeare's thought, then, we merely guess at a plausible set of circumstances or deal with our own behavior in responding to the works. This is not very satisfactory, but we cannot improve the situation by identifying thought with mere form of behavior.[9]

An emphasis upon form obscures the significance of behavior in relation to controlling variables. It is obvious that two forms of response constitute very different "thoughts" if they are emitted under different circumstances. Moreover, some apparent instances of verbal behavior, satisfying all the formal criteria, may not be "thoughts" at all. Thus, accidental arrangements of anagrams or sentences constructed by the random manipulation of printed words are not records of verbal behavior, although they may be read as texts. It may serve some purpose in logic to say that "For any sentence, however long, we can construct a longer sentence by adding 'and the moon is round,'" but the resulting sentences could be accounted for in relation to trivial variables which do not warrant our calling them verbal. A

[8] Russell, Bertrand, *An Inqury into Meaning and Truth* (New York, 1940), p. 413.

[9] Molière carried the formalistic argument one step nearer the ridiculous. All that is most beautiful in literature, one of his characters argues, is to be found in the dictionaries. "It is only the words which are transposed."

similar neglect of the controlling relation is seen in Russell's remark "It is difficult to describe a statement without making it." Emitting a response having the form of a statement as an echoic response or hypostatical tact is not to be confused with emitting the same form of response under the kinds of circumstances which permit us to call it a statement.

This concern with form has left the study of the content of thought in an unsatisfactory state, but the "facts," "propositions," and other "referents of statements" find an adequate representation among our controlling variables. The functional relations between behavior and the environment are usually complex and very often confusing, but we are not in doubt as to their dimensions or the techniques with which they may be studied. We can disregard the troublesome dissection of human thought into the familiar pattern of (1) a *man* possessing (2) *knowledge* of (3) a *world.* Men are part of the world, and they interact with other parts of it, including other men. As their behavior changes, they may interact more effectively, gaining control and power. Their "knowledge" is their behavior with respect to themselves and the rest of the world and can be studied as such.

The "effects of language on thought" must, of course, be restated. If it is "impossible to express a given idea" in a given language because a necessary term is lacking, we have only to say that the contingencies arranged by a given verbal community fail to respect a possible variable. If it is difficult "to express the same idea in two languages," we have merely to say that the reinforcing practices of two verbal communities differ. Any sort of behavior may be confusing and ineffective. The subtle contingencies of reinforcement arranged by a verbal community easily miscarry: a tact may be extended beyond warrant, an important autoclitic may be omitted, incompatible responses may result from faulty constructions. From the point of view of the listener, verbal behavior may fall far short of the nonverbal circumstances under which it arose; the thing itself may seem very different from the description of the thing. There is *indescribable* beauty in the sense in which there are colors which cannot be named in a given language. There are *ineffable* thoughts in the sense that contingencies in a nonverbal environment generate behavior which has no parallel among verbal responses. All behavior, verbal or otherwise, is subject to Kantian a priori's in the sense that man as a behaving system has inescapable characteristics and limitations.

When we study human thought, we study behavior. In the broadest possible sense, the thought of Julius Caesar was simply the sum total of his responses to the complex world in which he lived. We can study only those of which we have records. For obvious reasons, it is primarily his verbal behavior which has survived in recorded form, but from this and other records we know something about his nonverbal behavior. When we say that he "thought Brutus could be trusted," we do not necessarily mean that he ever said as much. He behaved, verbally and otherwise, as if Brutus could be trusted. The rest of his behavior, his plans and achievements, are also part of his thought in this sense.

It is a salutary consequence of this point of view to accept the fact that the thoughts of great men are inaccessible to us today. When we study great works, we study the effect *upon us* of surviving records of the behavior of men. It is *our* behavior with respect to such records which we observe; we study *our* thought, not theirs. Fortunately, the contemporary thinker can be subjected to a different kind of analysis. So far as a science of behavior is concerned, Man Thinking is simply Man Behaving.

There is nothing exclusively or essentially verbal in the material analyzed in this book. It is all part of a broader field—of the behavior of a most complex creature in contact with a world of endless variety. For practical purposes a special field has been set apart in terms of characteristics imparted to it by special controlling variables. It is in terms of these variables—of the contingencies arranged by the verbal community—that verbal behavior can be defined and analyzed.

Two Personal Epilogues

THE AUTHOR'S *William James Lectures* at Harvard University in 1947 closed with material in essentially the following form.

I. THE VALIDITY OF THE AUTHOR'S VERBAL BEHAVIOR

When me they fly, I am the wings—EMERSON.

It is sometimes argued that if a scientific account of human behavior is sound, the scientist must be as mechanistically determined as the people he studies, and hence his verbal behavior cannot be "valid," "certain," or "true." Russell [1] puts a similar point this way:

> When the behaviorist observes the doings of animals, and decides whether these show knowledge or error, he is not thinking of himself as an animal, but as an at least hypothetically inerrant recorder of what actually happens. He "knows" that animals are deceived by mirrors, and believes himself to "know" that *he* is not being similarly deceived. By omitting the fact that *he*—an organism like any other—is observing, he gives a false air of objectivity to the results of his observation. . . . When he thinks he is recording observations about the outer world, [he] is really recording observations about what is happening in him.

In one sense, this is a fair shot. The hardiest determinist will recognize a tendency to believe that what he is saying is, for the moment at least, reserved from the field of determined action. But the student of behavior is not the only one to face this dilemma. Behaving about behaving raises the same difficulty as knowing about knowing. Russell pictures the behaviorist deciding whether the doings of animals

[1] *Inquiry into Meaning and Truth,* p. 14.

show knowledge or error instead of, as is more likely, measuring predispositions to act with respect to a given set of circumstances, and he describes the behaviorist as "reporting his observations about the outer world," although observation is suspiciously like "idea," or at least "image," and would probably be avoided in favor of an expression like "reaction to the outer world." But the crux of the problem survives in translation. The present study offers a case in point. If what I have said is reasonably correct, considering the present state of knowledge in the science of human behavior, what interpretation is to be placed on my behavior in writing this book? I have been behaving verbally and, unless my analysis is deficient at some point, my behavior must have followed the processes already set forth and no others. What does this mean with respect to the certainty or truth of what I have said?

This is no time to abandon our program. Let us see just what I *have* been doing. To begin with, I exposed myself to a great deal of material in the field of verbal behavior. This was the result of a growing interest in the field, which followed from other circumstances too remote to affect the present issue. Hundreds of the books and articles which I read were not a direct exposure to the subject matter of verbal behavior itself, but they generated verbal tendencies with respect to it which show an enormous variety and a fabulous inconsistency. I have also read books, not for what they said *about* verbal behavior, but as records of verbal behavior. I have done my share of comma-counting. I have listened to people speaking and jotted down slips, curious phrases, or interesting intraverbal sequences, and I have watched subjects in the laboratory responding to the faint patterns of the verbal summator, filling out word-association blanks, and so on.

The notes which I made of all this were my first reactions—both to verbal behavior itself and to verbal behavior about verbal behavior. In the course of time I arranged and rearranged this material many times, using several sorts of mechanical filing systems and an elaborate decimal notation, so that similarities and differences might be detected and respected. I discarded many classifications and saved a few which seemed to work. In this way I arrived at what seemed to be useful and productive properties of verbal behavior—properties which proved to be worth talking about.

My explorations in this direction were helped by work in the field of nonverbal behavior. Originally it appeared that an entirely separate formulation would be required, but, as time went on, and as concurrent work in the field of general behavior proved more successful, it was possible to approach a common formulation. I believe that the present book realizes an effective synthesis which represents the place of verbal behavior in the larger field of human behavior as a whole. Gradually I settled upon a minimal repertoire which singled out those aspects of verbal behavior which appeared to be useful as dependent variables, and identified and classified various kinds of circumstances in the present and past environments of the speaker which seemed to be relevant independent variables. So far as possible, I have tried to conform to the special reinforcing contingencies of the scientific community in the representation and analysis of these relationships.

On the other side of the medal, what effect may I presume to have had on the reader? I have not tried to induce autonomic behavior and shall not be disappointed if the reader has not salivated or wept or blushed at anything I have said. I have not tried to arouse immediate overt action and am quite content that he will not have shouted *Down with Aristotle!* or have tried to burn a library. The effects which I have hoped to achieve fall in other categories of the behavior of the listener.

I have not described much new material. The reader has not, I am afraid, learned many new facts, and I could easily have limited myself to material with which all intelligent people could be assumed to be familiar. It has not been my purpose to present the facts of verbal behavior as such, and that is why I have not been greatly concerned with experimental or statistical proof. Some "instruction" in the sense of Chapter 14 has, I hope, taken place in the form of definitions. I have invented a few new terms—"mand," "tact," "autoclitic," and so on—which are perhaps now part of the reader's vocabulary, though in what strength I would not undertake to say. I have repeatedly used established terms which are perhaps more familiar to the reader now than when he began the book. I have, as it were, put the reader through a set of exercises for the express purpose of strengthening a particular verbal repertoire. Stating the matter in the most selfish light, I have been trying to get the reader to behave verbally as I behave. What teacher, writer, or friend does not? And, like all teachers, writers, and friends, I shall cherish whatever I subsequently discover of any "influence" I may have had. If I have strengthened the reader's verbal behavior with spurious devices of ornamentation and persuasion, then he will do well to resist, but I plead not guilty. If I had been solely interested in building a verbal repertoire, I should have behaved in a very different way.

But a repertoire is not enough. The responses which I have tried to get the reader to make function by singling out events or aspects of verbal behavior which should make his subsequent behavior more expedient. I have emphasized certain facts and ignored others. The justification for this has been that the facts emphasized seemed to belong together and that in talking about them to the exclusion of other facts, greater progress is made toward a unified account. Perhaps I have wanted the reader to pay attention to this field and to talk about it in a special way mainly because I myself have done so with pleasure and profit. I have assumed a common interest in the field of verbal behavior. It is my belief that something like the present analysis reduces the total vocabulary needed for a scientific account. It eliminates far more terms than it creates, and the terms created are derived from a few prior technical terms common to the whole field of human behavior. As one who has applied the analysis to fields not covered in these lectures, I believe I can say that it works. It has reached the stage where it does more work for me than I for it. It swallows new material avidly yet gracefully, and good digestion seems to wait on appetite. Hundreds of puzzling questions and obscure propositions about verbal behavior may be dismissed, while the new questions and propositions which arise to take their place are susceptible to experimental check as part of a more unified pattern.

In many ways, then, this seems to me to be a better way of talking about verbal behavior, and that is why I have tried to get the reader to talk about it in this way too. But have I told him the truth? Who can say? A science of verbal behavior probably makes no provision for truth or certainty (but we cannot even be certain of the truth of that).

II. NO BLACK SCORPION

In 1934, while dining at the Harvard Society of Fellows, I found myself seated next to Professor Alfred North Whitehead. We dropped into a discussion of behaviorism, which was then still very much an "ism," and of which I was a zealous devotee. Here was an opportunity which I could not overlook to strike a blow for the cause, and I began to set forth the principal arguments of behaviorism with enthusiasm. Professor Whitehead was equally in earnest—not in defending his own position, but in trying to understand what I was saying and (I suppose) to discover how I could possibly bring myself to say it. Eventually we took the following stand. He agreed that science might be successful in accounting for human behavior provided one made an exception of *verbal* behavior. Here, he insisted, something else must be at work. He brought the discussion to a close with a friendly challenge: "Let me see you," he said, "account for my behavior as I sit here saying 'No black scorpion is falling upon this table.' " The next morning I drew up the outline of the present study.

Perhaps it is time to consider Professor Whitehead's challenge. Can we indeed account for the fact that he said, "No black scorpion is falling upon this table"? As a particular instance of verbal behavior, emitted under a set of circumstances now long since largely forgotten, we cannot. It is as unfair to ask a science of behavior to do this as to ask the science of physics to account for the changes in temperature which were taking place in the room at the same time. Suppose a thermographic record had been made from which we could now reconstruct those changes, at least as accurately as I have reconstructed Professor Whitehead's verbal behavior. What could now be done with it? It provides a rough account of a series of changes in a dependent variable, but it supplies little or no information about the independent variables of which those changes were a function. The physicist is helpless because he does not have the whole story. He may, of course, *suggest* that a sudden drop in temperature might have occurred because someone had left the door ajar, or that a window was opened at about that time, or that the heat was turned off. But it is obvious to the physicist and to everyone else that these are merely guesses.

Unfortunately we have been led to expect something else in verbal behavior. Linguists make extensive use of recorded speech with little or no information of the conditions under which it was recorded. The logician analyzes sentences as "form" alone. The critic interprets literary works written centuries ago although few, if any, facts about the writer survive. Almost anyone will tell you what a passage "means." This is possible only because the linguist, logician, and critic can observe, in addition to the recorded behavior, its effect upon themselves as listeners or readers. These data are offered in lieu of the missing variables. As thermographs which have often reacted in much the same way, we are much more ready to say what must have caused a particular deflection. But if it were easy to check the validity of such inferences—to find out, for example, what a passage actually "meant" to the speaker or writer—the practice might long since have disappeared from the behavior of responsible people.

A few relevant facts about the conditions under which Professor Whitehead made his remark are available. So far as I know there was no black scorpion falling on the table. The response was emitted to make a point—taken, as it were, out of the blue. This was, in fact, the point of the example: why did Professor Whitehead not say "autumn leaf" or "snowflake" rather than "black scorpion?" The response was meant to be a poser just because it was *not* obviously controlled by a present stimulus. But this is, of course, the kind of material the Freudians relish, for it is under just such circumstances that other variables get their chance. The form of the response may have been weakly determined, but it was not necessarily free. Perhaps there was a stimulus which evoked the response *black scorpion falling upon this table,* which in turn led to the autoclitic *No.* The stimulus may not have been much, but in a determined system it must have been something. Just as the physicist may suggest various explanations of the drop in temperature in order to show that it could be explained in lawful terms, so it is not entirely beside the point to make a guess here. I suggest, then, that *black scorpion* was a metaphorical response to the topic under discussion. The black scorpion was behaviorism.

Science seems to be inevitably iconoclastic. It usurps the place of the explanatory fictions which men have invented as prescientific devices to account for nature. For reasons which are not entirely unfamiliar to psychologists, the explanatory fictions are usually more flattering than the scientific accounts which take their place. As science advances, it strips men of fancied achievements. The Copernican system elbowed man out of the center of things, and astronomy has never ceased to reduce his proportionate share of the universe. Darwinism dealt the fancied pre-eminence of man another blow by suggesting a greater continuity with other animals than man himself had wished to recognize. And while the science of chemistry was on the one hand crowding the supposedly unique accomplishments of living systems into a tighter and tighter corner, the sciences of anthropology and comparative religion were shaking man's confidence in his mode of communication with the supernatural. It was inevitable that psychology should enter these lists. The Freudian emphasis upon the role of the irrational was offensive; but although Freud was a determinist certain controlling forces remained within man himself, no matter how unworthy they may have seemed. The crowning blow to the apparent sovereignty of man came with the shift of attention to external determiners of action. The social sciences and psychology reached this stage at about the same time. Whenever some feature of the environment—past or present—is shown to have an effect upon human conduct, the fancied contribution of the individual himself is reduced. The program of a radical behaviorism left no originating control inside the skin.

Those who knew Professor Whitehead will realize that he would do his best to understand such a view and to interpret it in the most generous way. He would probably have been happy to discover that the matter was entirely terminological and that my position was identical with some earlier one which either had been disproved or had been shown to leave an opening for human responsibility and creativeness. It is possible, then, that as I described my position—doubtless in the most shocking terms I could command—he was telling himself that the part which he had played in encouraging me as a young scholar was not entirely misguided, that I was probably not typical of all young men in psychology and the social sciences, that there *must* be a brighter side—in other words, that on this pleasant and stimulating table no black scorpion had fallen.

If that was the explanation—and it is, of course, only a most improbable guess—then the statement was appropriate enough. There was no cause for alarm. The history of science is the history of the growth of man's place in nature. Men have extended their capacities to react to nature discriminatively by inventing microscopes, telescopes, and thousands of amplifiers, indicators, and tests. They have extended their power to alter and control the physical world with machines and instruments of many sorts. A large part of this achievement has been verbal. The discoveries and achievements of individual men have been preserved and improved and transmitted to others. The growth of science is positively accelerated, and we have reached a breathless rate of advance.

There is no reason why scientific methods cannot now be applied to the study of man himself—to practical problems of society and, above all, to the behavior of the individual. We must not turn back because the prospect suddenly becomes frightening. The truth may be strange, and it may threaten cherished beliefs, but as the history of science shows, the sooner a truth is faced, the better. No scientific advance has ever actually damaged man's position in the world. It has merely characterized it in a different way. Indeed, each achievement has in a sense *increased* the role which men play in the scheme of things. If we eventually give a plausible account of human behavior as part of a lawfully determined system, man's power will increase even more rapidly. Men will never become originating centers of control, because their behavior will itself be controlled, but their role as mediators may be extended without limit. The technological applications of such a scientific achievement cannot now be fathomed. It is difficult to foresee the verbal adjustments which will have to be made. "Personal freedom" and "responsibility" will make way for other bywords which, as is the nature of bywords, will probably prove satisfying enough.

I have found it necessary from time to time to attack traditional concepts which assign spontaneous control to the special inner self called the speaker. Only in this way could I make room for the alternative explanation of action which it is the business of a science of verbal behavior to construct. But whatever the reader may think of the success of this venture, I hope he will agree that the analysis has shown respect for human achievement and that it is compatible with a sense of dignity—in short, that no black scorpion *has* fallen upon this table.

Appendix

. . . .

The Verbal Community

THE "LANGUAGES" studied by the linguist are the reinforcing practices of verbal communities. When we say that *also* means *in addition* or *besides* "in English," we are not referring to the verbal behavior of any one speaker of English or the average performance of many speakers, but to the conditions under which a response is characteristically reinforced by a verbal community. (The lexical definition simply mentions other responses reinforced under the same circumstances; it does not describe the circumstances.) In studying the practices of the community rather than the behavior of the speaker, the linguist has not been concerned with verbal behavior in the present sense.

A functional analysis of the verbal community is not part of this book, but a few standard problems call for comment. One of them is the old question of the origin of language. Early man was probably not very different from his modern descendants with respect to behavioral processes. If brought into a current verbal community, he would probably develop elaborate verbal behavior. What was lacking was not any special capacity for speech but certain environmental circumstances. The origin of language is the origin of such circumstances. How could a verbal environment have arisen out of nonverbal sources? Other classical problems have their parallels. How is a verbal community perpetuated, and why and how does it change? How do new forms of response and new controlling relations evolve, so that a language becomes more complex, more sensitive, more embracing, and more effective?

How the first verbal environment arose will probably always remain a matter for speculation. Theoretically it should be possible to rear a group of human infants in social isolation to discover whether verbal behavior would develop, and if so what it would be like, but there are obvious ethical problems. An experiment appears to have been tried by Frederick the Great in which children were reared in isolation with the object of discovering whether they would naturally speak Hebrew. The experiment failed when all the subjects died. Occasionally, through accidental circumstances, two or more children have grown up in partial isolation from established verbal communities and have developed fairly extensive idiosyncratic verbal systems, but the isolation has never been complete enough to prove that a verbal environment will arise spontaneously in the absence of prior verbal behavior.

Animal Cries

A superficial resemblance between verbal behavior and the instinctive signal systems of animals (many of them vocal) has been the source of much confusion. The imitative vocal behavior of parrots, cat-birds, and so on, which duplicates the *forms* of human speech, has added to the confusion. It is true that vocal and other responses of animals constitute "systems of communication." The lost lamb bleats and in so doing "tells its mother where it is." The grazing animal "cries out in alarm" and "warns the rest of the flock of approaching danger." Mating calls bring male and female together. The mother drives predators away from her young with growls or cries of anger. Animal gestures have their place in this system of communication and have recently received special attention from the ethologists.[1] The language of bees has been analyzed by Von Frisch.[2]

Such responses appear to be elicited (or "released") by characteristic situations as part of the behavioral equipment of a given species. To say that they are instinctive is merely to say that each form of behavior is observed in most members of a given species, when there has been no opportunity for individual learning. In such cases we must fall back on an evolutionary explanation. Like other activities of the organism, such as digestion, respiration, or reproduction, some behavior with respect to the environment is acquired through natural selection because of its consequences in preserving the species.

There is a parallel between natural selection and operant conditioning. The selection of an instinctive response by its effect in

[1] Tinbergen, N., *The Study of Instinct* (London, 1951).

[2] Von Frisch, K., *Bees, Their Vision, Chemical Senses, and Language,* (Ithaca, N.Y., 1950).

promoting the survival of a species resembles, except for enormous differences in time scales, the selection of a response through reinforcement. The similarity is seen in the apparent purposiveness of both forms. Innate and acquired responses both appear to be emitted "in order to achieve effects"—in order to promote the welfare of the species or the individual. (In both cases it can be shown, of course, that only *prior* instances of such consequences are needed to explain the behavior.) When the instinctive response gains its advantage by affecting the behavior of another organism (when, for example, it is a cry), the parallel with verbal behavior is marked. The mother bird cries out in alarm "in order to" warn her young of approaching danger, as the human mother calls to her child in the street in order to save him from an approaching car. The young bird reacts to its mother's cry "in order to" escape danger, as the child responds to his mother's warning to avoid being hurt. But the interlocking systems in the two cases must be explained in quite different ways. The mother bird cries out not "in order to warn her young" but because the young of earlier members of the species who have cried out have survived to perpetuate the behavior. The young bird does not run for cover upon hearing the cry "in order to escape danger" but because earlier birds who have run under these circumstances have lived to bear their own young, possibly showing the same behavior. The behaviors of the human mother and child, on the other hand, are acquired during their life-times through the processes discussed in Part II. De Laguna [3] has ingeniously traced parallels between the two systems, identifying the circumstances under which a cry (or other vocal or nonvocal response) may be classed as a command, a proclamation, a declaration, and so on. As in the present analysis, the distinctions depend upon the situations of "speaker" and "listener" and upon the consequences for both. But the analogy remains an analogy.

It is unlikely, moreover, that verbal behavior in the present sense arose from instinctive cries. Well-defined emotional and other innate responses comprise reflex systems which are difficult, if not impossible, to modify by operant reinforcement. Vocal behavior below the human level is especially refractory. Although it is easy to condition a cat to assume various postures, move its limbs, and manipulate features of the environment through operant reinforcement, it appears to be impossible to get it to miaow or to purr exclusively

[3] De Laguna, Grace A. *Speech: Its Function and Development* (New Haven, 1927).

through the same process. Apparent exceptions prove upon examination to be samples of a different process. The cat at the door, miaowing "to be let out," may actually be miaowing because it is *not* being let out. The miaow is an emotional response in a frustrating situation. It occurs at approximately the same time and with the same frequency as such an operant as scratching the door, but the two forms of behavior are under different forms of environmental control. Such refractory material does not seem propitious as a precursor of verbal behavior in the present sense. Whether innate *nonverbal* responses can be conditioned in the operant pattern is difficult to say, because the same musculature can be brought under operant control. The experimenter may succeed merely in producing an operant which imitates the innate response. (Since innate responses are commonly associated with emotional situations, the parallel with verbal behavior has been most compelling in explaining emotional "expression." Indeed, the doctrine of expression is sometimes reserved for verbal or nonverbal behavior under the control of emotional variables. Expressive theories of the origin of language build on this pattern.)

This is not to say that lower organisms are incapable of verbal behavior in the present sense. All the controlling relations analyzed in Part II can be demonstrated in nonhuman behavior, as can some of the more complex relations of later parts of the analysis. With sufficient exposure to relevant variables vocal verbal behavior could conceivably be set up. But the verbal behavior acquired by the individual under the reinforcing practices of a verbal community does not appear to be a modification of vocalizations acquired by the species because of specific consequences having survival value. The relatively undifferentiated babbling of the human infant from which vocal verbal behavior develops is undoubtedly an evolutionary product, but it is not the sort of behavior which is evoked (or "released") in specific forms on specific occasions. The same may be said of nonverbal behavior. In general, operant behavior emerges from undifferentiated, previously unorganized, and undirected movements.

We can account for the origin of a verbal response in the form of a mand if any behavior associated with a state of deprivation is an important stimulus for a "listener" who is disposed to reinforce the "speaker" with respect to that state of deprivation. Consider, for example, a nursing mother and her baby. It is possible that there is an innate response of the human female to innate cries of the hungry human infant, similar to the systems of communication in other species, but we do not need to assume that this is the case. If a hungry infant behaves in some distinctive fashion—let us say, by crying or squirming in response to painful stimulation of the stomach—and if a mother is inclined to nurse her child, perhaps to escape from the aversive stimulation of a full breast, then the baby's cry (correlated, as it is, with a tendency to suck) will eventually control the mother's behavior of putting the baby to her breast. Once the mother has acquired this discrimination, her behavior of nursing her baby is contingent upon the baby's cry, and this may be reinforcing. Where the baby first cried as a reflex response to painful stimulation, it may now cry as an operant. It is probably not the reflex response which is reinforced but behavior resembling it. The form of the response is free to undergo a change provided the mother maintains the reinforcement. Eventually the response may not closely resemble the reflex pattern.

Such a response is reinforced with food, and its strength is a function of deprivation. The controlling relation which survives is characteristic of a full-fledged mand. Since we assumed a predisposition on the part of the mother to reinforce, it is the species of mand called a request. But eventually the mother may no longer be predisposed to reinforce with food, and the baby must compensate by creating an aversive condition from which the mother can escape only by supplying appropriate reinforcement. The baby's cry becomes "annoying," and the mother reinforces because the baby then stops crying. The response is no longer a request but a command.

A nonverbal environment may produce another kind of mand concerned with the "attention of the listener." Let us say that *A* is pouring drinks for a group, but has overlooked *B*. Any conspicuous movement by *B*, particularly if this produces a noise, will get the attention of *A* who may then reinforce *B* with a drink. Once this has happened, the behavior becomes verbal, similar to explicit mands of the form *Look here!* Verbal communities commonly reinforce mands which cannot have departed very far from the original nonverbal forms. Knocking at the door of a house is a conventional verbal response, which is easily traced to nonverbal origins, for it must have been originally close to the behavior of a dog scratching at the door "to be let in." It acquires a special style (the number, speed, and intensity of the knocks approach a standard) under appropriate reinforcement by the verbal environment. Rapping on an empty glass or table at a restaurant is comparable, as is the vocal *Har-rumph!*

Any behavior which has an effect upon another person as a mechanical object (pulling, pushing, striking, blocking, and so on) may acquire a behavioral effect if incipient stages of the behavior serve as stimuli. The contingent reinforcement is usually avoidance of, or escape from, the later stages of the behavior. For example, *A* stops the approach of *B* by holding out his arm and placing the palm of his hand against *B's* chest. At this stage the behavior of *A* would be roughly the same if *B* were an inanimate object (if *B* were swinging toward *A,* for example, at the end of a long rope). But if being stopped by *A* is aversive to *B,* or if *A* stops *B* only when likely to treat *B* aversively, *B* eventually responds to *A's* outstretched arm to avoid actual contact. When this change has occurred in *B, A's* response is reinforced not by its mechanical effect on *B* but by *B's* behavior. It becomes a "gesture" and is classified as verbal. Every listener and speaker need not pass through similar changes, for the gesture is eventually set up by the community. The traffic policeman's gestured "stop" is as culturally determined as a red light or the vocal response *Stop!*

Such gestures may gain current strength from similar nonverbal contingencies. The "speaker" may be readier to respond in a given way and achieve a more consistent effect upon the listener because of related mechanical effects. Even the railroad semaphore in its "stop" position probably borrows strength from the resemblance to an actual barring of the way. Familiar gestures having roughly the same effects as *Go away!, Come here!* (gestured with either the whole arm or the index finger), *Pass by!, Sit down!* (as to an audience), and *Stand up!* are subject to similar interpretations. These are all mands which specify behavior resembling the mechanical effect of the nonverbal responses from which they are derived. (Putting a finger on one's *own* lips shows something like the metaphorical extension of putting a finger on the lips of someone else. The latter may occur if the parties are close together.)

If, for purely physical reasons, *A* cups his hand behind his ear in order to hear *B* more clearly this becomes for *B* a stimulus in the presence of which louder behavior (vocal or nonvocal) is differentially reinforced. If *B* increases the intensity *because A cups his hand,* cupping the hand becomes a "gesture" and may be classed as verbal.

If *B* can avoid punishment at the hands of *A* by engaging in a particular form of activity, *A* may shape *B's* behavior by delivering of withholding aversive stimulation. For example, if *A* drives *B* away from a supply of food by beating him, *A's* raised fist eventually causes *B* to withdraw in order to *avoid* blows rather than to wait to *escape* from them. When this has happened, *A* may *gesture* rather than strike. If *A* sometimes allows *B* to eat, *B* eventually responds to *A's* fist as a stimulus upon which punishment for approach is contingent. *A* may eventually use a raised fist for finer shaping of behavior. For example, *B* may be kept active if *A* responds as soon as *B* stops. The contingencies are the same as in keeping a horse moving by *cracking* a whip. In addition to starting or stopping, *B's* behavior may also be *guided* in direction or intensity level.

If *B* is predisposed to reinforce *A, A* may shape *B's* behavior with any reaction indicating its reinforcing effect upon him. For example, conspicuous ingestive behavior on the part of *A* may reinforce *B* for cooking or serving a special kind of food. *A's* behavior in licking his chops may become a gesture equivalent to *Give me some more of that* as his vocal *m-m* may become the equivalent of the *Yum-yum* shaped by a particular verbal community. The unconditioned behavior of an audience which has been reinforced by an entertainer reinforces the entertainer in turn. Part of the reinforcing effect is the contrast between the intense quiet of the enthralled audience and the noisy release as the entertainer stops. If the audience can induce the entertainer to continue by heightening this contrast, the noise may become a gesture. Clapping, stamping, whistling, and other forms of applause are verbal responses equivalent to *Again!, Encore!,* or *Bis!* Eventually such a response may be used to shape up the behavior of a speaker—as in parliamentary debate.

Most of the mands we can account for without assuming a prior verbal environment are gestures. Paget [4] has tried to derive vocal parallels by pointing to the fact that movements of the tongue are likely to accompany movements of the hand. A child, engrossed in some manual skill may be observed to chew his tongue or move it about his lips. Paget has suggested that movements of the tongue accompanying manual gestures could modify breathing sounds or primitive vocalizations to supply vocal responses. But even such a process makes little progress in accounting for the diversity of vocal responses which specify kinds of reinforcement.

In explaining verbal behavior in the form of the tact, we must look

[4] Paget, R. A., *Human Speech* (New York, 1930).

for different sources of nonverbal materials, for the behavior of the "speaker" must be related to *stimulating circumstances* rather than to aversive stimulation or deprivation.

The behavior of a hunting dog may be said to "signal" the presence of game to the human hunter, as the barking of a watch dog "signals" the approach of an intruder. In so far as these are relatively invariable and unconditioned, the hunter and the householder respond to them as to any stimulus associated with a given event—say, the noise produced by the game or the intruder. It is only when the dog is trained as a "speaker" that new phenomena arise. As soon as the hunting dog is *reinforced* for pointing, or the watch-dog for barking, the topography of the behavior may come to depend upon the contingencies of reinforcement rather than upon unconditioned reflex systems. In these examples the behavior is never greatly changed, but in others the form is eventually determined by the community—that is, it becomes conventional. It has often been pointed out that the frequency of initial *m*'s in words for *mother* may have some relation to the frequency of that sound as an unconditioned response in situations in which mothers frequently figure, where the rest of each word is presumably shaped by the particular community. The shortage of unconditioned vocal responses appropriate to specific situations is an obvious limitation in explaining an extensive repertoire in this way.

Another common explanation appeals to onomatopoeia. The old "bow-wow" theory of the origin of language emphasized formal similarities between stimulus and response which survive in onomatopoetic or "model-building" repertoires. We can "warn someone of the approach of a dog" by imitating its bark, as the tourist draws a picture of the article he wants to buy but cannot name, or as the Indian guide announces good fishing by moving his hand sinuously. The vocal, pictorial, or gestured response is effective because it is physically similar to "the situation described." But the "use of such signs" by either "speaker" or "listener" is not thereby accounted for. If we assume, however, that certain listeners-to-be run away when they hear a dog bark and that this is reinforcing to certain speakers-to-be, we have only to wait—a few thousand years if necessary—for someone to emit a vocal response similar enough to the bark of a dog to be reinforced by its effect on a listener. The result is at best an impure tact, scarcely to be distinguished from a mand. All onomatopoetic responses suffer from the fact that their distinguishing formal properties affect the listener in a way which is closely tied to a particular situation. But listeners may react to dogs in many ways and for many reasons, and some sort of generalized reinforcement could conceivably follow.

The origins of most forms of response will probably always remain obscure, but if we can explain the beginnings of even the most rudimentary verbal environment, the well-established processes of linguistic change will explain the multiplication of verbal forms and the creation of new controlling relationships. Fortunately changes in reinforcing contingencies can be traced historically and observed in current communities. On the side of form of response, we do not need to suppose that changes follow any particular pattern (such as that of Grimm's Law); indeed, to explain the creation of large numbers of forms, the more accidental changes there are the better. On the side of "meaning" modern historical linguistics has identified many sources of variation. Some are concerned with accidents or faults in transmission. Others arise from the structure of the verbal community. New controlling relations arise when a literal response is taken metaphorically or when a metaphorical response through subsequent restricted reinforcement becomes abstract. As an example of the latter process, if we assume that the standard response *orange* has been brought under the stimulus control of oranges, then we can imagine a first occasion upon which some other object of the same color evokes the response. If it is effective upon the listener, as it may be without special conditioning, it may be reinforced with respect to color alone. If this is sufficiently useful to the community, the relatively abstract color-term *orange* emerges.

More subtle abstractions seem to emerge in the same way. The *fall* of a coin or die leads at last to the concept of *chance* when the defining properties are free of instances in which something falls. The method of John Horne Tooke is relevant again here. A *Sequel to the Diversions of Purley* by John Barclay (London, 1826) examines the origins of terms concerning spirit and mind in an early anticipation of twentieth-century behaviorism, tracing them back etymologically to more robust concepts in human behavior.

It has often been pointed out, particularly in explaining the origin of myths, that this process works in reverse—that a metaphorical response may be taken literally. The metaphorical report that a man became *beastly* when drunk gives rise to the story of a man transformed into an animal upon drinking a magic potion. In the elaboration of such stories, new variables gain control of old responses.

The study of the verbal behavior of speaker and listener, as well as of the practices of the verbal environment which generates such behavior, may not contribute directly to historical or descriptive linguistics, but it is enough for our present purposes to be able to say that a verbal environment could have arisen from nonverbal sources and, in its transmission from generation to generation, would have been subject to influences which might account for the multiplication of forms and controlling relations and the increasing effectiveness of verbal behavior as a whole.

INDEX

THE CENTURY PSYCHOLOGY SERIES

Richard M. Elliott, *Editor*

Kenneth MacCorquodale, *Assistant Editor*

Social Psychology, by Charles Bird
Learning More by Effective Study, by Charles and Dorothy Bird
Psychological Counseling, by Edward S. Bordin
A History of Experimental Psychology, 2d ed., by Edwin G. Boring
Sensation and Perception in the History of Experimental Psychology, by Edwin G. Boring
Readings in Modern Methods of Counseling, edited by Arthur H. Brayfield
A Casebook of Counseling, by Robert Callis, Paul C. Polmantier, and Edward C. Roeber
Beauty and Human Nature, by Albert R. Chandler
Readings in the History of Psychology, edited by Wayne Dennis
Modern Learning Theory, by William K. Estes, Sigmund Koch, Kenneth MacCorquodale, Paul E. Meehl, Conrad G. Mueller, Jr., William N. Schoenfeld, and William S. Verplanck
Schedules of Reinforcement, by C. B. Ferster and B. F. Skinner
Social Relations and Morale in Small Groups, by Eric F. Gardner and George G. Thompson
Great Experiments in Psychology, 3d ed., by Henry E. Garrett
Developmental Psychology, 2d ed., by Florence L. Goodenough
Exceptional Children, by Florence L. Goodenough
Physiological Psychology, by Starke R. Hathaway
Seven Psychologies, by Edna Heidbreder
Theories of Learning, 2d ed., by Ernest R. Hilgard
Conditioning and Learning, by Ernest R. Hilgard and Donald G. Marquis
Hypnosis and Suggestibility, by Clark L. Hull
Principles of Behavior, by Clark L. Hull
Development in Adolescence, by Harold E. Jones
The Definition of Psychology, by Fred S. Keller
Principles of Psychology, by Fred S. Keller and William N. Schoenfeld
Psychological Studies of Human Development, by Raymond G. Kuhlen and George G. Thompson
The Cultural Background of Personality, by Ralph Linton
Vocational Counseling with the Physically Handicapped, by Lloyd H. Lofquist
Studies in Motivation, edited by David C. McClelland

The Achievement Motive, by David C. McClelland, John W. Atkinson, Russell A. Clark, and Edgar L. Lowell

Principles of Applied Psychology, by A. T. Poffenberger

The Behavior of Organisms: An Experimental Analysis, by B. F. Skinner

Verbal Behavior, by B. F. Skinner

Diagnosing Personality and Conduct, by Percival M. Symonds

Dynamic Psychology, by Percival M. Symonds

The Dynamics of Human Adjustment, by Percival M. Symonds

The Ego and the Self, by Percival M. Symonds

The Psychology of Parent-Child Relationships, by Percival M. Symonds

Selected Writings from a Connectionist's Psychology, by Edward L. Thorndike

Introduction to Methods in Experimental Psychology, 2d ed., by Miles A. Tinker

The Psychology of Human Differences, 3d ed., by Leona E. Tyler

The Work of the Counselor, by Leona E. Tyler

Experimental Psychology: An Introduction, by Benton J. Underwood

Psychological Research, by Benton J. Underwood

Elementary Statistics, by Benton J. Underwood, Carl P. Duncan, Janet A. Taylor, and John W. Cotton. Also accompanying Workbook by the same authors.

Persons and Personality, by Sister Annette Walters and Sister Kevin O'Hara